FEDERAL JOBS FOR COLLEGE GRADUATES

Robert Goldenkoff & Dana Morgan

Prentice Hall
New York • London • Toronto • Sydney • Tokyo • Singapore

Prentice Hall General Reference
15 Columbus Circle
New York, NY 10023

An Arco Book

Prentice Hall and colophons are
registered trademarks of Simon & Schuster, Inc.

Manufactured in the United States of America

1 2 3 4 5 6 7 8 9 10

Library of Congress Cataloging-in-Publication Data

Goldenkoff, Robert,
Federal jobs for college graduates / by Robert Goldenkoff & Dana Morgan
p. cm.
"An Arco book."
ISBN 0-13-963752-4
1. Civil service positions—United States. 2. College graduates—Employment—United States. I. Morgan, Dana. II. Title.
JK716.G63 1991 91-21052
CIP

Contents

Introduction

Welcome to the most complete, up-to-date and thorough federal career directory ever published! Whether you are a career explorer just beginning your journey or an experienced federal job seeker, this resource provides the information you need to help you narrow down your interests, your career choices, and your job search tactics. It is different from any other federal career resource because it not only lists agencies and the positions they offer, but it describes each agency's positions in detail. What follows is a brief guide to the format of this book, to help you use it to its fullest potential.

Part One

1. So You Want a Federal Career?

The book begins with a brief look at federal employment, breaking it down into no-nonsense facts: is it for you, or isn't it? This section is designed to help those who are just beginning to consider federal employment to understand the differences between public and private sector employment.

2. Searching Out and Landing a Federal Job

This section offers a step-by-step approach to the federal career search and job hunt, including tips on reaching the right people, making your application stand out from the crowd, and understanding the system.

3. Federal Hiring Procedures

This chapter gives a technical overview of the federal hiring process. It explains the role of the Office of Personnel Management (OPM), the new ACWA exam, the SF-171 application form, and the general federal application procedures.

4. Salaries and Benefits

Because federal salaries and benefits are generally consistent across all agencies, and because they are unique to the public sector, a chapter is devoted to explaining the federal salary and benefit opportunities. This focuses most heavily upon the entry level general schedule positions.

5. Student and Special Needs Employment Programs

This chapter focuses on the National Student Employment Programs, such as the federal co-op, internship, Stay-in-School, and Junior Fellowship programs. It gives a broad look at what the jobs are, where they are, the salaries, the work schedules, and where to look for more information. Also covered in this chapter are the veteran's hiring programs, and programs for hiring disabled persons.

6. Positions in Demand

Some federal position titles are likely to be found at almost every government agency (e.g. Computer Scientist, Management Analyst, Economist). Since the duties of these positions are similar at all agencies, their descriptions are not repeated under each agency entry, but are given separately in this chapter. These positions account for a large percentage of federal entry level jobs.

PART TWO

Agency Profiles

The Agency Profiles section, making up the bulk of the book, gives a concise look at *all* of the agencies in the federal government. Each agency entry is divided into the following headings:

1. **Nature of Work** Each agency has been assigned to one or several "mission" categories, giving it a one- or two-word statement that describes its overall purpose.
2. **Number of Employees** This simply gives a current look at the number of employees in that agency nationwide so that a reader can easily gauge the size of the agency.
3. **Headquarters** Gives the location of the headquarters office. Some have several headquarters offices for different regions of the country.
4. **Regional Locations** Listed here are the main regional office or area office locations. Some agencies have few or none. Others have several main area offices as well as suboffices, or an office in every state. This provides the reader a quick glance at possible job sites; complete addresses are given in the Application Procedures section of the agency entry.
5. **Typical Majors of New Hires** This is a guide to those academic majors that are most often sought after for the most prevalent entry level positions in that agency. It is by no means a list of the ONLY qualified majors for those positions.
6. **Mission** Provides a brief synopsis of the agency's purpose and goals.

7. **Job Descriptions** The Job Descriptions section gives a concise look at the job function and typical duties of the most common entry level positions in that agency. As opposed to most other career directories, these descriptions are specific to each agency, so that the description for a Dietitian in one agency might look quite different from the description for a Dietitian in another agency.

   The positions described typically begin at the GS-5, 7, and 9 salary levels (see page 31 for 1991 salary chart); if no salary is indicated in the job description then it falls within this range. In some agencies, only upper level positions (GS-11 and above) are filled on a regular basis; in that case, those positions are listed in this category. The positions described are those most often recruited for by the agencies, but the list is not intended to be all-inclusive. Other positions, available less often, may exist at the entry level. Note that the very typical federal positions, those that can be found in almost every government agency, are not listed separately in each agency profile, but can be found in the "Common Government Positions" chapter in full detail.

8. **Major Activities and Divisions** Provides a breakdown of the agency organization according to its major activities, goals, or program areas.

9. **Alternative Employment Programs** Describes any programs geared toward hiring students, such as the co-op, intern, or summer programs for students. Some student hiring programs are government-wide, so that the salary, qualifications, and hiring procedures are standard from one agency to another. These National Student Programs are mentioned under the agency profile, and are described in detail in chapter 5.

10. **Remarks** Provides miscellaneous information regarding agency locations, incentive programs, special hiring procedures, scholarships, or any unusual facts that are pertinent to a prospective employee.

11. **Application Procedures** Explains the basic steps needed to apply to that agency, and gives the current mailing addresses and phone numbers so that questions on vacancies or hiring procedures will be directed to the appropriate office. Many indicate that applicants should direct their inquiries to the region which handles their area of interest, in which case regional addresses and telephone numbers are provided as space permits.

CAREER SEARCH INDEX

This unique cross-reference system personalizes the job search process by allowing the career-seeker to narrow down all 200 federal agencies according to work location, college majors hired, and agency mission. It identifies which agencies fit the individual's career interests and allows him to narrow his search to only those agencies that meet his needs.

Part One

Federal Career Opportunities

CHAPTER 1

So You Want a Federal Career

From astronaut to zoologist, the federal government is the nation's largest employer. One look at the scope of its work will tell you why: The government's responsibilities range from highways to human rights; from pollution control to arms control; from the ocean floor to outer space. In short, federal employees ensure the safety, health, and quality of life of all Americans.

Surveys indicate that the majority of federal employees enjoy their jobs; and, while many workers transfer from agency to agency, comparatively few leave the government altogether. However, the question remains, is federal employment for you?

THE ADVANTAGES AND DISADVANTAGES OF A FEDERAL CAREER

The federal government is extremely large, with over 200 departments, agencies, and bureaus. Consequently, the experience of any one employee will vary from agency to agency, and job to job. However, federal employment does offer the following rewards:

1. **Challenging Work**: Federal employees often work at the cutting edge of science, technology, and public policy. The Commerce Department's National Institute of Standards and Technology, for example, performs some of the world's most advanced research in computer-automated manufacturing, semiconductor processing, and mechanical behavior. Similar state-of-the-art work is conducted (and in some cases may *only* be conducted) at federal labs across the country. Knowledge gained from such pursuits is applied to curing diseases such as cancer and AIDS; creating heartier crops; designing trans-atmospheric spaceplanes; and finding new sources of energy.

   And if you don't have a technical degree, there's plenty of challenging work for you as well. Specialists in law enforcement, education, housing, and economics are formulating, implementing, and evaluating public policies designed to alleviate crime and drug abuse, illiteracy, homelessness, and poverty.

2. **Location**: Working for the federal government means your choice of worksites is virtually unlimited. Contrary to popular belief, most federal jobs are *not* located in Washington, DC. In fact, 85% of all federal civilian jobs are located *outside* of the nation's capital. What this means for prospective employees is that federal employment can be found in the largest cities, the smallest towns, and around the world. The Interior Department's National Park Service provides a good example. From New York City's Gateway National Recreation Area, to Alaska's Noatak National Preserve, Park Service employees can be found in the most and least densely populated areas of the nation.

3. **Responsibility**: Federal employees tend to get considerable responsibility early in their careers. Promotions usually come quickly, and new employees may find themselves managing programs after just three years on the job. But you may not even have to wait that long. In many instances, you're given considerable responsibility from the first day on the job. New attorneys at the Justice Department, for example, may immediately find themselves arguing motions in court, taking and defending expert depositions, and cross-examining witnesses.

4. **Job Mobility and Diverse Career Paths**: Finding your niche in the federal government can be fairly easy. Its size gives you upward mobility to advance within a particular field, and lateral mobility to explore different occupations. Many federal employees transfer between regional and headquarters offices, or to different agencies altogether. Others leave federal service for a few years, broaden their experience in the private sector, and then return to government.

5. **Flexible Hours**: Many federal agencies offer flexible work schedules. While you must work 80 hours in a two-week pay period to be considered a full-time employee, how you allocate those hours is up to you. For example, some federal employees work 10-hour days four days a week.

6. **Public Service**: When working for the federal government, you're not just catering to your personal interests—you're serving the greater good of the nation. Many federal employees derive satisfaction by knowing that a group of people or a particular program is better off because of their work. In the years ahead, the country will face some extraordinary challenges: Poverty, global pollution, racism, nuclear proliferation . . . the list goes on and on. Your time and talent will help ensure successful outcomes. The hours may be long, and the tasks enormous, but one thing is clear: You can make a difference!

Like all careers, federal employment is not without its disadvantages. Here are some of them:

1. **Cumbersome Bureaucracies**: Paperwork and rules abound in the federal government. Though together they help ensure accountability to the public, you may find yourself filling out lots of forms and adhering to restrictive policies

and regulations. Consequently, getting things accomplished can take longer than expected.

2. **Uncompetitive Pay**: Federal entry-level pay is often lower than in the private sector. This is particularly true for scientific and engineering occupations. While some hard to fill occupations receive special pay rates, on average, federal salaries at all levels are about 25 percent lower than those offered by private firms for comparable jobs. However, recent legislation should help alleviate this in the future.

3. **Feeling Lost in the System**: The vast size of federal agencies means that you may find yourself feeling lost in a large hierarchy. While you may be friendly with the people in your immediate work group, the people in the office next door may be complete strangers. Additionally, you must create your own career paths. This means you'll have to network with colleagues to learn about opportunities within your agency, and find your own mentors to provide you with career guidance.

4. **Poor Physical Environment**: Many federal offices are worn, cramped, and privacy, especially at the lower levels, can be a scarce commodity. Moreover, support equipment such as personal computers, copiers, and facsimile machines are sometimes in short supply. In some cases, these conditions are balanced by on-site fitness, health, and day-care facilities.

Now that you know some of the advantages and disadvantages of federal employment, a few more facts and figures should help you decide if a federal career is for you.

ORGANIZATION OF THE FEDERAL GOVERNMENT

The first three articles of the Constitution divide the federal government into three branches—the legislative, executive, and judiciary. This division results in the separation of powers that ensures our democratic system of government. Simply put, the legislative branch makes the laws, the executive branch implements them, and the judiciary enforces them.

With over three million employees, the executive is the largest branch of the federal government. This is followed by the legislative branch (37,500 employees), and the judiciary (22,000 employees).

Federal employment is certainly not for everyone. However, if you have the skills, motivation, and commitment federal jobs require, you'll find a rewarding career with your Uncle Sam.

CHAPTER 2

Searching Out and Landing a Federal Job

With this book you have all the information you could ever want about the federal government right at your fingertips. Still confused, though, about where to begin? How do you go about putting this information to use to get the federal job you want? We'll start from the beginning and look at what you can do to search out, learn about, and apply for the federal career position that's right for you. Let's take it step by step.

STEP 1: GET FOCUSED!

What do you want to do with your life? Where do you want to be in five years, ten, or even twenty? Where do you want to live? What kind of lifestyle do you want to have? All of these questions certainly need to be answered BEFORE you start pursuing a career focus and even before you decide on an education. Dig down deep inside and work on getting to know yourself. What makes you happy, satisfied, proud? What are your strengths, your weaknesses? Getting to know what makes you YOU will help you get focused. If you start a career search without a direction, you'll simply wander aimlessly and get nowhere. FOCUS. Take the blurriness of your mind and make it clear.

Ask yourself these questions before going any further:

How important a factor is salary in my career search?
Where would I like to live as I work in my career?
Do I want a fast-paced or slow-paced office?
Do I want to travel? If so, how far and how often?
Do I enjoy contact with people on an ongoing basis?
Do I want to be in an office or outdoor setting?
Do I want to work regular 9 to 5 hours?
Do I prefer working in a large or small office setting?
What are the skills and talents I hope to use in my job?

Remember, you're not answering these questions for a lifetime—just for today. Goal setting is an ongoing process which involves change. If your goals today are no different than they were ten years ago, they are probably stale and untried. So dare to focus in on what you want from a career, and spare yourself the discouragement and frustration of a meandering career search. Most people find it extremely difficult to sort out their needs and interests, and appreciate some tools to help them get started. If you would like to do a bit more exploring in this area, there are plenty of tests you can take, books you can read, and programs to follow that help you narrow down career interests. A few are listed below.

Books

What Color is Your Parachute? by Richard Nelson Bolles (Ten Speed Press, Box 7123, Berkeley, CA 94707). Probably the best book to begin with if you are unsure about career direction. In fact, this is a terrific resource for anyone who is exploring a new career path or job change.

What Can I Do With A Major In? How To Choose and Use Your College Major by Laurence R. Malnig with Anita Malnig (Abbott Press, Box 433, Ridgefield, NJ 07567). This resource lists current occupations of graduates who majored in various academic disciplines. It gives brief descriptions of the different academic majors and suggests some occupations that the major might lead to. Typical hiring institutions are also listed for each occupation, including government agencies.

Guide For Occupational Exploration edited by Thomas F. Harrington and Arthur J. O'Shea, U.S. Employment and Training Administration. Helps a job seeker relate his interests, skills, and aptitudes to the requirements of the occupations in the job market.

Occupational Outlook Handbook. U.S. Department of Labor, Bureau of Labor Statistics. Gives descriptions of occupations and the typical training needed for each. Don't let the statistics on future openings or typical earnings scare you, though. One should never make a career decision based on salary information or occupational trends. These things change too drastically from year to year and according to geographic area.

Tests

Probably the best test a career seeker can take is the *Self-Directed Search* by John L. Holland (Psychological Assessment Resources, Inc., Box 998, Odessa, FL 33556). It offers an excellent technique for self-exploration and provides a way to link personal skills and preferences to occupational categories. The Self-Directed Search, when completed, provides the test-taker with an Occupational Code of three letters, indicating his personality and skills characteristics. This three-letter code, (the RIASEC code), can then be matched to occupations which tend to be filled by people with those same personality characteristics.

There are hundreds of other resources career searchers can use to narrow down their interests. The best place to begin a search is at the local community library, school library, or career resource center in your school or office. Simply seek and you shall find.

STEP 2: FIND OUT ABOUT IT!

Now that you've clarified your goals a little bit, you're ready to do some investigation into federal career possibilities. Do you think you might be satisfied and fulfilled in a position with Uncle Sam as your boss? The variety of federal career opportunities makes this a difficult question. Federal employees can be anything from nuclear scientists to veterinarians to home economists. The choices are wide-ranging.

Nonetheless, many people underestimate what federal service has to offer them. Somehow, over the years our government has gotten (and maybe earned) the reputation of being one great endless maze of drab grey offices full of anemic, uninspired employees plodding away hour after hour, day after day, with little rubber stamps and mounds of useless papers ten feet high in front of them.

Federal service may have resembled this bleak picture once, but no longer. Government employment has gone through a radical change over the last twenty or so years. Today, there are opportunities in the government abounding with possibilities for travel, art, music, languages, foreign relations, scientific exploration, recreation, technology, and just about anything else you can think of. It is not all pencil pushing, red tape, and bureaucracy as the old stereotypes would have you believe. There are positions that demand keen wit, a sense of danger, subtle humor, political aptitude, razor-sharp marketing skills, and big-business acumen.

There is, of course, a not-so-glamorous side to federal employment as well. Not every position at every agency is fun, stimulating, and full of potential. But neither is that true about the private sector. To be fair, the federal government is huge. With over three million employees, it is by far the largest employer in the United States. It has a Herculean mission—to keep the entire country stable and contented economically, socially, medically, technologically. And so, it does have its share of bureaucracy, of red tape, of outdated methods, of arcane rules and regulations. And most agencies, even the small ones, reflect that in some way. So be realistic in your expectations and explore your needs. Is a large organizational structure what you're looking for? Think about what that would mean to you and whether you'd be happy.

How To Start

There's no better place to start an investigation into federal employment than right here with this book. It enables you to find out what federal agencies there are, what kinds of people they hire, and how to apply for a job. How can you use this resource to your best advantage? Do you want to work for an agency that is devoted to scientific research? Aiding the poor or disabled? Working with foreign countries? Jot down those agencies that appeal to you, then look them up under the agency profiles section. Do you find them attractive? Do you like the size, the positions offered, the locations?

Maybe you have a specific part of the country in mind in which you'd like to work. Want to stay out west where your family is? Always dreamed of moving to New York City? Plan to live by the ocean somewhere? Refer to the locations chart. Jot down those agencies that fit your location intentions. Do they seem like agencies you'd like to work for? Do they hire people with backgrounds like yours?

Or, you may just want to discover what you can do with a major like yours in the federal government. Who hires landscape architects, or chemical engineers, or psychology majors? Refer to the college majors chart to find the answers. This will tell you which agencies hire the most of which college majors.

Time For Action

Okay, so you've narrowed down a few agencies and positions that appeal to you. It's a good idea at this point to learn more about them—maybe gather some brochures and job announcements from the agencies themselves. That means it's time to switch from the research mode to the action mode.

Ready? Take a look at the agency profile you have in mind and refer to the application procedures section of the profile. You'll see that almost every agency lists a telephone number for their personnel or recruiting office. So that makes it easy—simply pick up the phone and call. Tell a personnel person your circumstances and that you are interested in a certain position and see what he or she says. One word of caution, however. Because you are dealing with a large bureaucratic system, you may run into some trouble gathering information that is outside the standard operating procedure for that office. Most agencies have a procedure set up for dealing with job seekers, and anything outside of that system might not be very welcome. Let me try to address a few problems you might have on the phone:

THE SCREENER: Screeners are the people who were put on earth to make sure you don't get to talk to the person you wanted to talk to. Your conversation may go something like:

> YOU: Hello. I'd like to find out more information about the basket weaver positions you have at your agency.
>
> SCREENER: What do you want to know?
>
> YOU: Well, I just wanted to find out more details about the qualifications and when you might anticipate any openings.
>
> SCREENER: Well, we don't have any positions open for basket weavers right now. Try back next year. *click*.

You know you're doomed when you can't get past the receptionist. If the *Screener* sounds pretty adamant about keeping you from getting the information you want, tell him or her you'll be glad to call back another time and *ask for the name of a personnel staffing specialist or recruiter*. Next time you call, (which can be in a matter of minutes if you're feeling assertive) ask for that person directly and avoid the *Screener* completely.

THE GOVERNMENTEASER: This is the person whose sole intention it is to confuse everyone he speaks to by using esoteric acronyms for everything that's acronym-able. Your conversation might go something like:

YOU: Hi. Thanks for speaking with me. I just wanted to find out a bit more information about the sheep shearer positions you have there.

GOVERNMENTEASER: Well, we're all out of 0-57's on that right now, but OPM says the 623's or the ACWA are okay for that. Have you tried ADMANA yet?

In this case, go for the questions. It's okay to admit you lost him back at the first acronym. In the government, people use acronyms so often that they simply forget they're speaking in code to everyone else. You might also be smart to have a pen and piece of paper handy when you make the call, and quickly write down the words that you don't understand so you can ask questions about them later.

THE BUCK-PASSER: This is the person who has perfected the art of getting out of work by suggesting someone else (anyone else) to help you who is "much more qualified." This person will invariably say something like:

YOU: Hi. I'd like to ask you just a couple of quick questions about the soapmaker position at your agency.

BUCKPASSER: That's really not my area. Why don't you try the public affairs office?

YOU: But isn't there someone there in personnel who might know about the position?

BUCKPASSER: No. I'd try public affairs. They can help you. *click*.

Okay, first make sure you got that person's name. It's always nice to have a name to throw around in future conversations, such as, "John Buckpasser suggested I talk to you about the soapmaker positions you have." This will make the next person less likely to pass you on to yet another and another and so on. It's also slightly flattering to the next person that John Buckpasser considered him qualified to help you, unless Mr. Buckpasser is known around the office as the loafer he is, in which case the person he suggested you to will probably be annoyed with him (and you've managed to exact a bit of revenge!).

If you're sure the department to which he referred you to is not going to be able to help you, nip it in the bud right away and call back to the original office and start over again. Tell the person who answers the phone: "Look, I just called to get information about the soapmaker position and the person you gave me to, Mr. Buckpasser, was unable to help. Is there anyone else in personnel you might let me talk to?" If at this point the person you're talking to starts acting like a *Screener*, ask, "What is the name of the person in charge of the co-op program?" At least this way you'll have collected another name in the personnel department, and you never know, maybe they hire co-op soapmakers and the co-op director can actually give you the information you want. At the least, he might be able to suggest yet another party who can answer your questions.

THE PERPETUAL HOLDER: These are perhaps the most frustrating people of all. These are the folks who, for whatever reason, put you in the never-never land of hold until the cows come home or until you hang up. I got the impression as I was doing my research that, because my questions were a bit unconventional and admittedly confusing, some people would actually just get rid of me by putting me on hold with no intention of ever coming back! Especially when you're calling long distance, this is really annoying. In dealing with suspected *Perpetual Holders*, I suggest assertiveness.

YOU: Hi. I'm calling to get a bit of information about the hog caller positions you have.

PERPETUAL HOLDER: Hold on. *click*.

At this point, you have no idea whether she's gone to find someone to help you, is answering another call, or what the devil she's doing. Five minutes go by.

PERPETUAL HOLDER: Can I help you?

YOU: Yes, I was calling about the hog caller positions. Is there someone I can talk to?

PERPETUAL HOLDER: Hold On. *click*.

Five more minutes pass. Now you're getting steamed.

PERPETUAL HOLDER: Can I help you?

YOU: Look, I was calling about the hog caller positions and you've had me on hold for ten minutes. Is there someone there who can help me or not?

PERPETUAL HOLDER: The person you'd need to speak with just left for lunch five minutes ago. Can you call back in two hours?

Like I said before, assertiveness! Tell whoever answers the phone right away that you are on long distance, and if she is polite enough to ask you if you'll hold (and wait for a response) tell her you'd prefer not to hold too long since it's costing you money. If she keeps putting you on perpetual hold, give up on your first request, and start over with her. For example:

YOU: Hi. I'm calling to get some information on the apple picker positions you have.

PERPETUAL HOLDER: Hold on. *click*.

What she may be doing here is trying desperately to figure out who she can get to help you. There may be no one person assigned to the apple picker jobs. She tries several personnel staffing specialists, who all tell her she should try someone else. In desperation, she comes back to you.

PERPETUAL HOLDER: Can I help you?

YOU: Yes, I think you were trying to find me someone to talk to about the apple picker positions. Is someone available to talk to?

PERPETUAL HOLDER: Well, uh . . . that person is out of the office right now. Can I take a message?

YOU: What would the name of that person be?

PERPETUAL HOLDER: Name? Uh . . . well, Mr. Durkin might be able to answer your questions . . . or Mrs. Lowe . . .

YOU: Is either of them in today?

PERPETUAL HOLDER: Well, Mr. Durkin is out of the country until early next month. Mrs. Lowe is in a meeting today, but should be back in the office on Monday. Should I have her call you?

YOU: Well, you could leave a message for her, yes, please. Also, is your co-op director in?

What you did here is directed the conversation the way *you* wanted it to go. And you kept her from getting flustered enough to resort to the perpetual hold tactic to get rid of you. By the way, in leaving a message, since your name is not likely to be one that anyone will recognize on their message sheet, you'll probably be put in the bottom of the stack and may never be called back. You may want to leave a message, but you should probably call back yourself.

And here I suggested asking for the co-op director again. The reason for this is not that I think co-op directors are blessed with an inordinate amount of wisdom or good will, but simply because it focuses the receptionist on one person. There are usually several staffing specialists in a personnel department, but only one co-op director. And since almost every agency hires co-op people, almost every agency has someone who fits this title. It simply narrows down your request to something and someone that the receptionist can understand.

When You Finally Get to Talk to the Right Person

Ahhh! You've reached a helpful, informed person and are ready to gather some facts. If the person seems receptive, you may want to request a personal "information interview", an information-gathering meeting where you find out about the agency and it's positions without applying for a specific opening. These are a wonderful way to meet someone within the agency face-to-face, and to have a contact for when that special job opening does occur. It's also a good idea to have researched the agency a bit before you make your phone call, so that you don't waste the person's time with questions that could be easily answered somewhere else. Below is a list of questions you may want to ask, whether on the phone or in person:

1. Could you explain to me the typical duties of the *Carrot Peeler* position?
2. How many people with that job title are employed by your agency?
3. Do these people typically work in headquarters or at a field office?
4. At what grade level does the typical new hire begin?
5. What level of education and experience do you usually look for to fill this position?
6. About how many new hires do you have annually for this position?
7. Do you recruit on college campuses?
8. Do you use an "open announcement" for this position, or do you fill openings as they occur?
9. Does your agency bring on interns or co-op students for this position?
10. Do you have any literature on this position or on your agency in general that you could send me?
11. Do you anticipate any openings in the near future?
12. Is there a special application I would need to fill out, or would an SF–171 suffice?

Once you've spoken to the right person on the phone, make sure not to hang up without a promise from them to send you an application package, detailed recruitment literature, or a vacancy announcement which explains the duties and qualifications of the position you had in mind. You might also receive an SF–171, which is the federal government's version of an application form. Instructions on the best way to fill it out are given in Chapter 3.

When the information arrives, you might notice that nowhere in the application package does it mention a resume. *Most government agencies do not have a system of responding to resumes and prefer not to receive them.* Because of the volume of hiring that most agencies do, they work better with a standard form like the SF–171 for all positions regardless of grade level or background. Therefore, make sure you've filled it out very carefully and have made plenty of copies to stash in a file for future use. Agencies will accept a neat copy instead of an original as long as it has an original signature and date. In federal job hunting, the SF–171 basically replaces the resume.

You might also notice, especially if you receive a vacancy announcement, that the qualifications for the position in which you are interested are very detailed and rigid, including so many semester hours of such-and-such a class, and a GPA of such-and-such. As opposed to most positions in the private sector, which are fairly flexible as far as qualifications, these details should be taken seriously. There are very few things that are left up to interpretation in federal entry-level hiring. About the only matter left up to the discretion of the individual who screens the incoming applications is whether past experience "directly relates" to the position you are applying for. If you don't meet the exact qualifications, you will probably be screened out somewhere along the line.

You should also be aware of the fact that in most federal agencies, the personnel department has nothing to do with the final decision as to who is hired and who is not. Most agencies are set up so that the personnel department writes the vacancy announcements and sees that they are distributed to the appropriate places, and then receives the incoming applications. The personnel person typically then sorts the applications according to "Qualified" or "Unqualified" status, and passes on the qualified candidates either to OPM for ranking, or directly to the hiring department to review.

Your status typically will be ascertained according to whether you meet the following criteria, depending upon the job requirements:

1. Did your application arrive by the stated deadline?
2. Are you a U.S. citizen?
3. Is your application COMPLETE, with original signature and date?
4. Do you meet the educational requirements? Do you qualify for Superior Academic Achievement?
5. Is your past work experience related to this position?
6. Do you qualify for preference hiring (*e.g.*, veteran, American Indian, etc.)?

Community experience and awards may also be considered, as well as letters of reference.

Be aware that federal hiring processes tend to take quite a long time, and it is essential to start early. Don't expect to be called in for interviews within mere weeks of taking the ACWA or putting your name on a register. People have been known to lanquish for years on a register without ever landing a single bite. There are ways to circumvent the system, however. Read on:

Getting Your Foot in the Door

Despite the rigidity of the system, there are ways to make your application stand out a bit from the rest. It's not as easy to do in a federal job hunt as in the private sector, but it's possible. Here are a few things to try:

1. *Networking*. Yup, making connections with people in important places still stands out as number one even in the federal job hunt. In some agencies, especially the independent ones, you might even be able to forego most of the red-tape rigmarole if you've met the right people, they like you, and they want to hire you. It's how my brother landed several interviews that he probably never would have gotten if his application had been just one in a stack of 1,000. This is what he did:

Brandt wanted a job with the General Services Administration. His background was good—a recent college graduate with superior academic achievement and a couple years of related work experience. But he knew there were probably hundreds of others with equal or better qualifications. Somehow he had to make them *see* him so he could prove how good a candidate he was. So, instead of mailing in his application, he drove downtown and walked it in personally. He greeted the receptionist in a friendly manner and chatted with her a bit. He asked if there was anyone he might talk to about the position. He *got the name of the person doing the hiring*. He didn't, however, get to speak with that person at that time. On the way out, riding down the elevator, he struck up a conversation with a man riding with him. Through that conversation, he discovered that the man had a position identical to the one for which my brother was applying. So he asked the man if he might do an information interview with him, to give him a better sense of the job. Five minutes later, my brother was sitting in the man's office chatting about the job, the agency, common interests. When Brandt got home, he wrote a note to the receptionist thanking her for her help, and an assertive thank-you note to the man who granted him the information interview. Later in the week, he phoned back to the receptionist and asked to speak with the man doing the hiring. This time he was able to speak with the man directly, and was granted a job interview the following week.

I'm convinced that if Brandt had simply mailed in his application in the first place, he would never have gotten a chance to prove himself in person.

I know that striking up conversations with strangers can be difficult. There is nothing to lose by it and *everything* to gain. So shake off your nervousness, smile, and walk in with confidence.

Another example I remember from my days as a college relations specialist is the tenacity of a girl I'll call Evelyn. In my agency, we had a yearly vacancy announcement for about fifty positions, in response to which we would typically receive over 1,000 applications. The odds for anyone getting a position were about 1 in 20. Evelyn must have known the odds were against her because somehow she managed to penetrate the system with her presence. For about three weeks, Evelyn was everywhere. She even managed to have a sit-down interview with *me*, and I had nothing whatsoever to do with the hiring for those positions. She was just like a politician, in there shaking hands with whoever had a hand free to shake. Sure enough, a month later, I ran into her in the hall. It was her first day on the job.

The moral of the story: the best way to land a job is, and always will be, to know someone in the organization. And if you don't know someone when you start out, GET to know someone. It's the one way you can be assured that your application will stand out from the rest. Always ask for names, always write thank you notes, and always have plenty of SF–171's handy.

2. *Emphasize that good* GPA! The federal government is truly one place where a superior academic record pays off. The many benefits of a GPA above 3.5 (on a 4.0 scale) or being in the top 10% of your college graduating class are as follows:

1. It enables you to avoid taking the ACWA test altogether. (Kind of like being able to skip the final exam if you've done well in class all year).
2. A high GPA allows federal agencies with vacancies to hire you directly on the basis of your GPA or scholastic record. This way you can apply directly to the agency you are interested in and avoid the OPM middle man.
3. An academic record outstanding enough to qualify you for Superior Academic Achievement puts you at the next higher grade level as you start your job. If you would have entered the position at the GS-5 level, for example, you will now start at the GS-7 level. If money isn't a great motivator to get good grades, I don't know what is!

3. *Keep abreast of the recruiting happenings at your college campus and at the agency itself.* There's nothing more frustrating than discovering on Friday that the agency you've been dying to interview with was recruiting at your campus on Thursday. Federal agencies do a lot of recruiting these days, many at campuses all across the country. If you can't get up-to-date recruiting information from your campus placement office, call the agency directly and ask if they plan to visit your campus for recruitment interviews.

4. *Keep an eye out for career fairs.* Most campuses hold annual career fairs. This provides an excellent opportunity to talk informally with representatives of many different federal agencies. Often, too, they are aware of current or upcoming job openings in their agencies for which you might want to submit your SF–171. One important point: Many agencies will conduct employment interviews at career fairs and can hire on the spot. Make sure to get the names of the people you talk with at the career fair so that you can write them a thank-you note and follow up with them if you have an interview or submit an application. Also, as always, be sure to have those 171's handy!

5. *Send an application directly to the hiring official as well as to the personnel office.* As I said before, the personnel department can screen you out, but they can't do anything to promote your application. Only the hiring official can make the decision to bring you on board, so it can't hurt to put your application on his (or her) desk yourself by mailing it to him (or better still, walking it in to him) directly.

6. *If you are a veteran, American Indian, or a disabled person, make sure the agency knows it.* Preference is often given to veterans, disabled veterans, and American Indians in the hiring process. This is usually in the form of extra points awarded after the application has been rated. Some agencies hire veterans or American Indians almost exclusively. Others make special accommodations for persons with disabilities. Don't overlook these sections on your application if you qualify.

7. *Be very careful that the application you send in is timely and complete.* If you do not answer a critical question on your SF–171, if you fail to sign it with an *original*

signature and date, or if it arrives after the closing date, your application will be screened out *immediately*. No second chances. Period.

STEP 3: LANDING THAT JOB

So now you've not only figured out which agencies might be interested in a person with your background, and which positions in the federal government would be jobs you'd enjoy, but you've actually located some openings that you want to apply for. Now what?

FIRST: Figure out if you need to take the ACWA test. The list in Chapter 3 will tell you which positions require the ACWA exam and which category you fall into. Most federal jobs are in the competitive service, which means that the Office of Personnel Management intervenes in the hiring process, and that applicants are required to establish eligibility by taking the ACWA test for that position. Remember—if your GPA is above 3.5, you are exempt from taking the ACWA test, and agencies have the authority to hire you on the spot. For more information on the ACWA exam, call 1-202-606-2700. Be prepared to be put on hold before you get to talk with anyone.

SECOND: Tailor your SF–171 to fit the exact qualifications of the job opening you want. This does not mean you have to fill out a brand new 171 from top to bottom. Just rewrite the experience portion of the form to fit the specifics of the position. Study the job announcement carefully. Think about all areas of your background—job related experience, school experiences, community action or volunteer programs you've been involved in, awards you've received—and consider how they might apply to the qualifications stated in the vacancy announcement. Also check the "Selected Placement Factors" and "Quality Ranking Factors" sections of the vacancy announcement. Personnel officers will use a score sheet to evaluate and rank your application according to how well you can convince them that you have what it takes to perform the job duties. Here's a brief look at the journey your federal application takes:

1. If the position you are applying for is one that requires you to take the ACWA, your application and test results will be screened and rated by OPM. OPM then puts the names of all eligible applicants, in order of ACWA test score, on a "list of eligibles" so that an agency, when it wants to fill a vacancy, must call OPM and request a list of qualified people. OPM will send the agency the top three names on the list, but will never overlap names among agencies. Thus, if the Environmental Protection Agency and the U.S. Forest Service were both requesting candidates for Soil Conservationist positions at the same time, they would each receive a *different* set of three names.

2. If you are able to apply to the agency directly and circumvent the OPM system, your application typically goes directly to the agency personnel office. The personnel screening committee will consider your application either "qualified" or "unqualified" according to the number of points it receives in

the review process. Some applications will be screened out immediately, especially if they arrived after the closing date, or if the applicant is not a U.S. citizen. Points are given according to the "Selected Placement Factors" and the "Quality Ranking Factors" sections of the vacancy announcement. Your background must match the qualifications listed under "Selected Placement Factors" in order to continue being considered. The qualifications listed under "Quality Ranking Factors" are good to have, but you generally won't be ruled out for lacking them. If you filled out a Knowledges, Skills, and Abilities (KSA) supplement, you will probably be assigned points directly from this portion of your application as well. The KSA supplement offers you a chance to rate *yourself* rather than having personnel rate you. *Do not be humble* in filling out these sections, then. The process of assigning points is very objective. If you underestimate your ability on the KSA supplement, the personnel office will not assign you extra points for humility. They will merely give you fewer points for ability, which may very well cause you to be prematurely screened out of the process. A job resume and a job interview are no place to be humble! If your application amasses enough points, it will be passed on to the hiring official for further review. If the hiring official is impressed, you may be called in for an interview.

THIRD: Even if you have to go through OPM before you can get hired, be sure to submit an application and copy of your transcript to the agency directly. Don't sit back and wait for OPM to do it. Imagine how many tests and how many applications OPM sees daily. It is extremely unlikely that yours is going to be marked with a big bright star and sent to several agencies for review. In reality, it'll probably arrive at OPM and then sit there for a long while. Your tactic to circumvent this system is to *contact the agency directly*. I can't emphasize this enough. Agencies have the ability to specify an applicant's name when it requests eligibles from OPM's ACWA roster. If the "name requested" applicant is on the list of eligibles, OPM will forward the applicant's name to that agency, thereby granting them permission to hire that applicant. In other words, don't sit back and hope OPM sends your name to the agency you want to work for—do it yourself! As I said before—there's nothing better than networking to land the job you desire.

WAYS TO FIND OUT ABOUT CURRENT FEDERAL OPENINGS

Once you begin the process of searching for a federal job, it's amazing to learn how much information is out there and easily accessible. Although I don't think there is any better method than picking up the telephone and talking to the agency itself, here are a few other tried and true methods:

Federal Job Information Centers (FJIC)

The Office of Personnel Management has set up several accessible locations that allow federal job seekers to browse through vacancy announcements and job listings available in the geographic area. There are 45 job information and testing offices at locations across the United States and in Puerto Rico and Guam (see Appendix for complete addresses and phone numbers). FJIC Offices provide general information on federal employment, information on how to apply for specific types of jobs, and can provide you with the SF–171 and other forms.

Message Directory

This self-service telephone system allow you to access the current job openings which are listed with OPM. Call 1-202-606-2700. Press 406 for recruiting bulletin positions. Other positions are also explained by pressing 401-410.

Career America College Hotline

You can find out about selected current openings in the federal government by calling 1-900-990-9200. Prepare to pay 40 cents per minute for automated information.

Federal Career Opportunities

This is a publication put out by the Federal Research Service, Inc., PO Box 1059 Vienna, VA 22180-1059. It is a biweekly publication which lists currently available federal jobs, nationwide and overseas, at Grades 5 through SES. It is organized by agency and gives the complete application mailing address for each position. It is available at most newsstands (especially in the Washington-Virginia-Maryland metropolitan area), or is available by subscription by calling (703) 281-0200.

Federal Jobs Digest

A biweekly publication put out by Breakthrough Publications for Federal Jobs Digest 325 Pennsylvania Avenue, S.E., Washington, DC 20003. Rates: $29 6 issues, $54 12 issues, $110 25 issues, Call 1-800-824-5000. It can be found in most community libraries. Although it's not as all-encompassing in its current job section as the Federal Career Opportunities, it offers more insight into recent happenings in the federal employment market.

Federal Times Newspaper

Available from Federal Times, 475 School Street, S.W., Washington, DC 20003. This is a weekly publication intended primarily for current government employees. It contains news and editorials concerning federal employment, and emphasizes defense and postal jobs, and those in the SES.

CHAPTER 3

Federal Hiring Procedures

About 80 percent of all federal jobs are filled competitively, where applicants' qualifications are determined either by a written exam or by an assessment of their education and work experience. Together, these jobs comprise the Competitive Service. Most of the remaining positions make up what is known as the Excepted Service. These jobs are filled through a set of hiring rules that are usually unique to a particular agency.

COMPETITIVE SERVICE

Occupations in this category are filled by a variety of methods depending on the type of job and your undergraduate grade point average. In general, they can be divided into five broad categories: Administrative (nonclerical); Accounting/Auditor; Scientific/Technical; Medical; and Public Safety. Application procedures for each category are described below.

Administrative Occupations

Administrative occupations are filled by the Office of Personnel Management (OPM) through a program known as Administrative Careers With America (ACWA). It applies to over 115 different occupations at the GS-5 and GS-7 levels typically filled by college graduates. Each of these occupations falls under one of six groupings:

Group I:	Health, Safety, and Environmental
Group II:	Writing and Public Information
Group III:	Business, Finance, and Management
Group IV:	Personnel, Administration, and Computer
Group V:	Benefits Review, Tax, and Legal
Group VI:	Law Enforcement and Investigation

The greatest number of future employment opportunities are expected in Groups I, IV, V, and VI.

You can qualify for these positions by achieving superior college grades (the Outstanding Scholar Program), or by passing a written OPM exam.

A seventh category of jobs does not require a written test but does require the completion of specific college course work. These occupations, known as Group VII, include:

> Archeology, archival work, community planning, economics, educational programming, foreign affairs, general anthropology, general education and training, geography, history, international relations, manpower research and analysis, museum management (curator), psychology, social science, and sociology.

Since hiring for these 16 nontest positions is limited, applications will only be accepted after a local OPM Area Office announces that vacancies are available.

Basic Qualifications

To be eligible for any of the ACWA positions, you must meet the following requirements within 9 months of applying.

1. Grade GS-5 Positions:
   a. Four years of education leading to a bachelor's degree; or
   b. three years of responsible experience; or
   c. an equivalent combination of education and experience (this is described more fully in #3 below).

2. Grade GS-7 Positions:
   a. A bachelor's degree and *one* of the following Superior Academic Achievement provisions
      - A grade point average (GPA) of 3.0 or higher for all completed undergraduate courses, or those completed in the last 2 years of undergraduate study;
      - a GPA of 3.5 or higher for all courses in your major field of study, or those courses in your major completed in the last 2 years of undergraduate study;
      - rank in the upper one-third of your class in the college, university, or major subdivision;
      - membership in a national scholastic honor society (other than freshman honor societies) recognized by the Association of College Honor Societies; or
   b. One full year of graduate education, law school, or a graduate degree; or
   c. One year of work experience in a field related to the position. The experience must be equivalent to the GS-5 level or higher in the federal service; or
   d. An equivalent combination of education and experience (this is described more fully in #3 below).

3. Combining Education and Experience:

   You may combine education and experience to meet the basic qualifications. One academic year of full-time study (30 semester hours or 45 quarter hours) is equivalent to 9 months of responsible experience. A bachelor's degree is equivalent to 3 years of responsible experience.

   To be considered as qualifying experience for these positions, your experience must include all of the following: Analyzing problems and presenting solutions; planning and organizing work; and written and verbal communication.

   Successful completion of college study in non-accredited institutions will be accepted to the extent that a) the courses are accepted for advanced credit at an accredited institution; or b) the institution is one whose transcript is given full credit by a state university; or c) the courses have been evaluated and approved by a state department of education; or d) the coursework has been evaluated by an organization recognized for accreditation by the Council on Postsecondary Accreditation.

As noted above, you can qualify for the ACWA positions in one of two ways: The Outstanding Scholar Program (OSP), or a job-related OPM exam.

If you have a grade point average of 3.5 or above on a 4.0 scale for all *undergraduate* coursework; or, if you have graduated in the upper 10 percent of your undergraduate class, you automatically qualify for the Outstanding Scholar Program and can apply directly to any agency. A 3.44 is rounded down to 3.4; a 3.45 is rounded up to 3.5.

If you are not eligible for the OSP, you can qualify by taking a written exam consisting of two parts: job-related questions that measure your ability to do the work for which you are applying; and a test known as the Individual Achievement Record (IAR), which assesses how well you have used the opportunities you have had in school, work, or outside activities. A separate exam is required for each occupational *grouping* in which you are interested; and, you must receive a score of 70 or above to be eligible for further consideration. Although each test currently takes 4 1/2 hours, OPM is developing a new version that will take 1 hour and fifteen minutes. OPM exects to begin using the shorter version in October, 1991. (For sample exam questions see Arco's ACWA: *Administrative Careers With America* by Eve P. Steinberg.)

How to Apply for the Written Test

The first step in taking the ACWA exam is to obtain an application packet from a college or university placement office; state employment office; or Federal Job Information Center (phone numbers and locations are listed in the Appendix). If you are unable to obtain an application through these sources, you can call OPM's Career America College Hotline by dialing 1-900-990-9200. The service is available 24 hours a day and each call will cost you 40 cents a minute. When calling the Hotline, you will be offered a list of career-related topics from which to choose. One option allows you to leave your name and address so that OPM can send you ACWA application materials.

The exams are offered at local OPM offices, certain college campuses, and federal agencies, and special sites designated by OPM. In areas such as Washington DC where there are large numbers of applicants, OPM gives the exam on a walk-in basis.

After the Exam—Then What?

Once you have completed the exam, it is scored by OPM, and within four weeks you should receive a notice of results. The names of all applicants receiving a score of 70 or above are then placed on lists called registers. When agencies have a vacancy, they contact OPM which provides them with applicants in the order of their scores.

The length of time it will take to get an offer depends on your exam score; the demand for new employees; and how quickly an agency makes an offer once it has a list of names. If an agency does not offer you a job; or, if you decline an agency's job offer, your name will be returned to the register.

If you have already passed an ACWA exam, you may not retake the exam for that occupational category until 12 months has elapsed. If you do not pass, however, you may retake it immediately.

Bilingual/Bicultural Program

If you pass the exam and are proficient in Spanish or are knowledgeable of Hispanic culture, you may be hired directly by agencies for positions which require such ability. Once you have received your exam score you may then apply directly to the agencies you're interested in.

Accounting/Auditor Occupations

Applicants for accounting/auditor positions at the GS-5 to GS-9 levels must have at least 24 semester hours in accounting. If you have a GPA of 3.5 or above in accounting, you can apply directly to any agency. If not, you should apply through OPM by contacting the Federal Job Information Center (FJIC) that serves the location where you seek employment (see Appendix). Application materials may also be obtained by calling OPM's College Hotline at 1-900-990-9200. You should also apply through OPM if you have a grade point average greater than 3.5 and would like to be considered for employment by more than one agency.

Scientific/Technical Occupations

Agricultural Sciences: Applications are handled directly by the agency. Contact the personnel office where you want to work.

For Agricultural Management Specialist positions, apply to the Farmers Home Administration: Room 6090 S., 14th and Independence Ave., S.W., 20024 Washington, DC. Or call (202) 245-5561.

For Agricultural Engineer, Range Conservation, Soil Conservation, and Soil Science careers, apply to the Soil Conservation Service: P.O. Box 37636, Washington, DC 20013 or call (202) 447-4543.

Biological Sciences (GS-5 and GS-7): The occupations most frequently filled are General Biologist, Microbiologist, Wildlife Biologist, and Fisheries Biologist. These positions generally require degrees in biology and coursework in the specialty. One application may be used for consideration in any or all of these occupations. It may be obtained through the FJIC that serves the location where you want to work (see Appendix), or by calling OPM's College Hotline at 1-900-990-9200.

Botanists, Zoologists, Pharmacologists, and several other biological specialties are needed less frequently by agencies. As a result, specific vacancies are announced by OPM as the need arises. Contact the FJIC (see Appendix) that serves the location where you seek employment to see if applications are being accepted for that area.

Engineer: Employment opportunities in this field are excellent. Moreover, starting salaries are 30 percent higher than regular federal pay rates. You may apply to any agency by submitting a resume and college transcripts. You may also apply through OPM for consideration by multiple agencies. Applications may be obtained by contacting any FJIC (see Appendix) or by calling OPM's College Hotline at 1-900-990-9200.

Forester: This position is filled infrequently by agencies. Consequently, specific vacancies are announced by OPM as the need arises. Contact the FJIC (see Appendix) that serves the location where you seek employment to see if applications are being accepted for that area.

Food Inspector: Applications for this position are handled directly by the agency. Contact the personnel office where you want to work.

Mathematics: This field includes occupations such as Mathematician, Mathematical Statistician, Statistician, Actuary, Computer Scientist, and Operations Research Analyst. Agencies will consider you for all of these occupations if you apply through OPM. Application packages may be obtained by contacting any FJIC (see Appendix) or by calling OPM's College Hotline at 1-900-990-9200.

NASA hires mathematicians for a variety of aerospace jobs. If you are interested in such a position, you should apply to any NASA facility.

Physical Sciences: Chemists, physicists, geologists, astronomers, and related occupations should apply through OPM to be considered by all agencies hiring these positions. Application packages may be obtained by contacting any FJIC (see Appendix) or by calling OPM's College Hotline at 1-900-990-9200.

If you're interested in positions at NASA, contact the installation where you want to work.

Meteorologists should apply through the Commerce Department by dialing 1-800-537-4101.

Medical Occupations

Medical and Dental Technician: Applications for this position are handled directly by the agency. Contact the personnel office where you want to work.

Medical Technologist: Applications for this position are handled directly by the agency. Contact the personnel office where you want to work.

Nurse: Applications for this position are handled directly by the agency. Contact the personnel office where you want to work.

Physician and Physician's Assistant: Applications for these positions are handled directly by the agency. Contact the personnel office where you want to work.

Veterinary Medical Officer: Applications for this position are handled directly by the agency. Contact the personnel office where you want to work.

Public Safety Occupations

Correctional Officer: Applications for this position are handled directly by the Justice Department's Bureau of Prisons. Contact the Bureau of Prisons personnel office where you want to work.

EXCEPTED SERVICE POSITIONS

As a result of federal statute, presidential order, or OPM regulation, certain agencies and occupations fall under what is known as the Excepted Service. The agencies and occupations comprising the Excepted Service include:

- Agency for International Development
- Board of Governors of the Federal Reserve System
- Central Intelligence Agency
- Defense Intelligence Agency
- Federal Bureau of Investigation
- General Accounting Office
- National Security Agency
- Nuclear Regulatory Commission
- Postal Rate Commission
- State Department (Foreign Service positions)
- U.S. Postal Service
- Attorney
- Chaplain

Several agencies accept applications on an on going basis, while others accept applications only when vacancies arise. Therefore, it is best to obtain precise hiring procedures by contacting the specific agency's personnel office.

USING THE SF-171 TO GET THE JOB YOU WANT

The standard application form used to apply for many government positions is the SF-171. It is a written record containing facts about yourself, your education, and your past experience. Copies of the form may be obtained from the agency you're applying to, college placement offices, state employment agencies, and the FJIC that services your state. From time to time OPM revises the SF-171, so make sure you are using the most current form; otherwise, it may be rejected by the agency.

Perhaps you know someone who has completed an SF-171. If so, they may have told you it's a time-consuming process. However, if you have a current resume, then you already have much of the information you'll need. Also, several companies have produced software that allow you to complete your SF-171 using a personal computer. These include:

FEDFORM-171 Laser
Arumon Group
P.O. Box 25090 CFJ
Arlington, VA 22202
(703) 751-6549

Quick and Easy
Federal Research Service Inc.
P.O. Box 1059
Vienna, VA 22183-1059
(703) 281-0200

SF-171 Automated
Software Den
103 Loudon St., S.W.
Leesburg, VA 22075
(703) 771-3901

Just like private employers looking at your resume, agency officials will scan your SF-171 and determine your qualifications based on your experience, education, awards, and outside activities. Therefore, all the rules for preparing a results-oriented resume apply to your SF-171: Make sure it is neat, easy to read, and contains no misspellings or mistakes. Type it if you can. Use "action" verbs that describe your experience and accomplishments. Keep your experience descriptions concise, and list them in chronological order. Skillful embellishment is okay; *just make sure it's honest.*

The SF-171 One Section at a Time

1. General Information

This is the easiest section of the SF-171 to complete since it merely requires short answers or checking off boxes. The first question asks, "What kind of job are you applying for?" Leave this question blank for now. Fill it in only after you photocopy the form and are ready to submit a copy to an agency. This way, you won't have to retype the entire form every time you apply for a federal job. Complete the rest of this section as appropriate.

2. Availability

In response to, "When can you start work?", enter the earliest date you'll be available. If you're unsure, the phrase, "Two weeks notice" is generally acceptable.

When asked, "What is the lowest pay you will accept?", leave this blank until you actually submit the application since your circumstances may change. Also, enter either a salary *or* a grade level, but not both. Complete the rest of this section based on your preferences.

3. Military Service and Veteran Preference

Depending on your circumstance, either 5 or 10 points will be added to your rating based on your military experience. Therefore, complete this section carefully. If you are claiming the 10-point preference (the criteria are listed on the form) be sure to also attach a Standard Form 15, "Application for 10-Point Veteran Preference," which is available from any FJIC (see Appendix).

4. Work Experience

In this section, you want to demonstrate that your prior experience has prepared you for the position you're applying for; therefore, the first thing to ask yourself is, "What does the job require?" The answer can be found in several sources. First, there's the vacancy announcement which describes the experience and skills the job requires, generally in the order of importance. Pay close attention to the section that identifies the knowledge, skills, and abilities you'll need. A second source is the position description, which provides a more complete description of duties and responsibilities. A third source is the government's classification manual called *Handbook X-118* which contains the experience needed at each grade level for every job in the federal government. Your local public or college library or OPM Job Information Center may have copies of the handbook. Another good source of information is someone already in the position. Ask a personnel officer for his or her phone number.

If you don't have much work experience, then include relevant outside activities in this section. In many cases, they can substitute for specialized experience in a particular area. For example, let's say the job you're applying for requires good planning skills. Does your present job require such skills? If not, think about outside or prior activities in which you've participated. Were you a member of a club or organization where you planned meetings and events? If so, include such activities in the experience section. Just remember to use your own words and *never* use a position description's language.

If you need additional space, some experts recommend *not* using the continuation sheet. They recommend splicing in additional lines and photocopying the "new" form. Others suggest pasting the top section (containing boxes for the name and address of your former employer, dates employed, salary range, etc.) to the top of a blank sheet of paper and photocopying that to create a new form.

5. Education

In addition to college classes, this section also asks applicants to record any training and development they've completed. Be sure to list *everything* that shows you are prepared for this next job. This includes, aside from your degree(s), conferences, seminars, adult education classes, on-the-job training, special projects, and rotational assignments in which you have participated. List the objectives of the various training activities and the knowledge you acquired. Your goal is to show a selecting official how you've made yourself into a more capable employee.

6. Special Skills, Accomplishments, and Awards

These three items reveal your initiative and resourcefulness. Therefore, don't limit yourself strictly to work situations. Include skills, accomplishments, and awards obtained through outside activities as well.

7. References

The thing to remember when completing this part is not to list relatives or supervisors you included in the "Experience" section. References should know your skills and abilities to do the job for which you're applying. If you don't have much work experience, then use former professors, classmates, or people under whom you did volunteer work. If you do have significant work experience, you can use current or past co-workers. Just make sure to tell them that you are using them as references so they are prepared if contacted by an agency.

8. Background Information

Fill out this section as appropriate.

9. Signature, Certification, and Release of Information

Leave this section blank for now. Agencies will only accept original signatures so sign and date the copies when you apply for each job.

Well, now you're done. All you have to do is photocopy the form, and fill in the sections you've left blank as you apply for each vacancy. Good luck!

CHAPTER 4

Salaries and Benefits

FEDERAL SALARIES

Most white collar federal employees are paid according to a system known as the General Schedule or GS. It consists of a series of levels or grades ranging from GS-1 at the bottom to GS-18 at the top.

Typically, new employees with bachelor's degrees start at the GS-5 or GS-7 levels, which in 1991 paid $16,973 and $21,023 respectively. If you have a master's degree and little to no professional experience, you can start as high as a GS-9, which paid $25,717 in 1991. (Note: A table of 1991 salaries is included at the end of this chapter.)

While these salaries may be lower than what many private firms offer, there are several things to keep in mind. First, initial promotions come fairly quickly. With satisfactory performance, it takes about a year to go from a GS-5 to a GS-7, and another year to be promoted from a GS-7 to a GS-9. One to two years are usually required to progress from a GS-9 to a GS-11 (Grades 6, 8, and 10 are used for clerical employees). Moreover, pay increases are possible without promotions. This is because each grade level is divided into 10 steps. Movement between steps is determined by years of service.

Second, Congress recently passed legislation that attempts to make federal salaries comparable to those of private firms by linking employees' pay to local labor markets. Moreover, beginning in 1994, workers living in cities with high costs of living will receive additional pay.

Third, accounting, engineering, computer science, medical, and several other hard-to-fill occupations receive special pay rates in certain parts of the country. In some cases (such as engineering), this can be as much as 30 percent higher than standard federal salaries.

The fourth thing to consider is that several agencies (The Federal Reserve, General Accounting Office, Federal Deposit Insurance Corporation, National Institute of Standards and Technology, among others), have their own pay scales for certain occupations.

The federal government also grants its employees cost of living adjustments each year. While these vary from year to year, recent adjustments have averaged about 3 percent.

VACATION, SICK LEAVE AND HOLIDAY BENEFITS

Vacation days are earned according to the length of time you've been with the federal government. You earn 13 days a year for the first three years, 20 days a year for the next 12 years, and 26 days a year after 15 years. A maximum of 30 days may be accumulated and carried forward from year to year.

Thirteen days of sick leave are earned each year with no limitation on the total accumulation.

Federal employees also receive paid time off for ten national holidays.

HEALTH BENEFITS AND INSURANCE PLANS

Federal employees are offered a variety of subsidized health plans that are administered by private insurers. Workers can thus select the plan that best suits them. Low-cost group term life insurance is also available.

RETIREMENT BENEFITS

The government's pension program is known as the Federal Employees Retirement System (FERS). Under FERS, agencies match employees' contributions up to 5 percent of their base pay. Additionally, employees' contributions are tax deferrable. Lastly, if you leave the government before you retire, your retirement account may be transferred to an Individual Retirement Account or other eligible retirement plan.

WORK SCHEDULES

At the discretion of agency management, several schedule options are offered. These include full-time, part-time, flexible, and compressed schedules. Flexible work schedules, commonly called flexitime, allow workers to vary their arrival and departure times. Compressed schedules allow employees to complete the basic work requirement of 80 hours in a two-week pay period in less than 10 working days. The government is also considering home-based employment options as well.

OTHER EMPLOYEE BENEFITS

The federal government has an Incentive Awards Program that allows agencies to pay up to $25,000 in cash to an employee whose suggestion or invention reduces costs or improves government operations. Agencies may also award employees cash for one-time special achievements. Individual agencies also offer a number of benefits such as on-site day care, credit unions, employee organizations, and fitness facilities.

1991 Federal Salary Schedule

Step	1	2	3	4	5	6	7	8	9	10
GS-1	$11,015	$11,383	$11,749	$12,114	$12,482	$12,697	$13,058	$13,422	$13,439	$13,776
2	12,385	12,679	13,090	13,439	13,590	13,990	14,390	14,790	15,190	15,590
3	13,515	13,966	14,417	14,868	15,319	15,770	16,221	16,672	17,123	17,574
4	15,171	15,677	16,183	16,689	17,195	17,701	18,207	18,713	19,219	19,725
5	16,973	17,539	18,105	18,671	19,237	19,803	20,369	20,935	21,501	22,067
6	18,919	19,550	20,181	20,812	21,443	22,074	22,705	23,336	23,967	24,598
7	21,023	21,724	22,425	23,126	23,827	24,528	25,229	25,930	26,631	27,332
8	23,284	24,060	24,836	25,612	26,388	27,164	27,940	28,716	29,492	30,268
9	25,717	26,574	27,431	28,288	29,145	30,002	30,859	31,716	32,573	33,430
10	28,322	29,266	30,210	31,154	32,098	33,042	33,986	34,930	35,874	36,818
11	31,116	32,153	33,190	34,227	35,264	36,301	37,338	38,375	39,412	40,449
12	37,294	38,537	39,780	41,023	42,266	43,509	44,752	45,995	47,238	48,481
13	44,348	45,826	47,304	48,782	50,260	51,738	53,216	54,694	56,172	57,650
14	52,406	54,153	55,900	57,647	59,394	61,141	62,888	64,635	66,382	68,129
15	61,643	63,698	65,753	67,808	69,863	71,918	73,973	76,028	78,083	80,138
16	72,298	74,708	77,118	79,528	81,396	82,697	85,060	87,424	89,787	
17	83,032	85,800	88,568	91,336	94,104					
18	97,317									

CHAPTER 5

Student and Special Needs Employment Programs

Most federal agencies use some form of student employment program to attract students into the public sector. Some agencies have programs that are specific to their particular organization, while others use student employment programs that are government-wide and have procedures and regulations that are standard throughout the public sector.

You may want to refer to the Alternative Employment Programs section of an individual agency in the *Agency Profiles* portion of this book to see if a particular agency participates in one of these national programs. The Alternative Employment Programs section will also list any student programs that are unique to that particular agency, and will indicate how to receive more information on those programs.

The following is a list of the major National Student Employment programs in the federal government:

COOPERATIVE EDUCATION PROGRAM

The federal government is currently the largest employer of co-op students in this country, with 18,000 federal co-op employees across the United States. More than 57 federal agencies participate in the program at nearly 1500 worksites.

What are the Jobs?

There are over 200 federal co-op occupations from which to choose. Students at all academic levels work in professional positions that are related to their school studies and extend the learning experience out of the classroom and into the workplace.

Where are the Jobs?

Co-op students can work across the country in all types of work settings—offices, laboratories, parks, and hospitals. More than a quarter of all federal agencies hire co-op students, with the largest employers including the Department of the Air Force, the Department of Agriculture, the Department of the Army, the Department of Commerce, the Department of Labor, the Central Intelligence Agency, the Environmental Protection Agency, the General Services Administration, the Department of Health and Human Services, the Department of the Interior, the National Aeronautics and Space Administration, the National Security Agency, the Department of the Navy, the Department of Transportation, the Department of the Treasury, and the Department of Veterans Affairs.

What is the Salary?

Co-op students receive a salary which depends upon the education and work experiences of the individual student. For students in undergraduate level programs, appointments are made in the GS-1 and GS-5 salary range, with some students entering at the GS-7 level if they meet the standards for superior academic achievement. Students in a master's degree program may be appointed at grades up to and including GS-9. Doctoral and professional degree candidates may be appointed at grades up to and including the GS-11 level. Most agencies have pay systems that provide increases as co-op students advance in responsibility and experience.

Are Benefits Included?

All co-op students automatically receive federal benefits such as paid vacations, holidays, and sick leave; major medical, dental, and life insurance; retirement/investment plans. Some co-op students may also receive training and tuition assistance; payment for transportation between school and work site; and membership in an employee credit union.

What is the Work Schedule?

The Federal Cooperative Education program allows the student, the school, and the federal agency to choose what work schedule is best for all concerned. Schedules may alternate full-time work experiences with full semesters or quarters of study in the classroom. Or, part-time periods of work and school may be interwoven. Agencies, schools, and students have the flexibility to design a schedule that works best for them.

Who is Eligible for These Positions?

Students who meet the Federal Cooperative Education program requirements are those who are pursuing a professional, graduate, baccalaureate, or associate degree, undergraduate certificate or diploma, or high school diploma and are in good academic standing at the school. A student must also be enrolled in the school's cooperative education program and be recommended for a co-op assignment by that school. U.S. citizenship is also required.

How Can I Learn More?

Contact your school's cooperative education department to find out more information on the Federal Co-op program. You may also contact the personnel office at the federal agency(ies) in which you are interested, and ask for the Cooperative Education Program Manager.

FEDERAL JUNIOR FELLOWSHIP PROGRAM

What are the Jobs?

The Federal Junior Fellowship Program puts students into federal positions that relate to their intended academic field of study on a part-time basis. Thus, it gives students the opportunity to learn about a career through direct work experience, as well as earning money for college studies.

Where are the Jobs?

Positions are available across the United States.

What is the Salary?

The initial rate of pay is based on education and work experience, typically falling in the GS-3 to -4 range. Increases and awards are possible for motivated Junior Fellows.

Are Benefits Included?

Junior Fellows receive health and life insurance, paid vacations, holidays, and sick leave, retirement/investment plans, and tuition assistance.

What is the Work Schedule?

Junior Fellows may work part-time while attending college and full-time during summer and vacation periods while in college. The first work experience usually begins immediately following high school graduation.

Who is Eligible for These Positions?

Those high school seniors who will be pursuing a baccalaureate degree in college and who meet financial-need criteria are eligible. Disabled students qualify without financial need. Students must be nominated for the program by their high schools, and final selection by the federal agencies is based on academic achievement, financial need, intended college major, extracurricular activities, and career goals.

How Can I Learn More?

Federal agencies notify high schools directly for nominations typically in the late spring. Interested high school students should ask their guidance counselors for more information about the application process.

STAY-IN-SCHOOL PROGRAM

The Stay-in-School Program was designed to allow students with strong financial need to continue their education. Approximately 20,000 students participate in the program each year.

What are the Jobs?

Stay-in-School positions are typically clerical or technical in nature.

Where are the Jobs?

The Stay-in-School program offers positions throughout the federal government across the United States.

What is the Salary?

Students are paid at regular government salary rates or the federal minimum wage, depending upon the duties of the position. A promotion and reward system does exist for outstanding performance.

Are Benefits Included?

Stay-in-Schoolers can earn paid vacation days, holidays, and sick leave.

What is the Work Schedule?

Stay-in-School students typically work part-time when school is in session, and full-time during vacation periods. Some students may also work on an "as needed" intermittent schedule.

Who is Eligible for These Positions?

Students are eligible for employment if they are at least 16 years of age and enrolled or accepted for enrollment as a full-time student in any high school, vocational school, or baccalaureate program. A satisfactory academic record must be maintained. Students must meet financial-need criteria to qualify, except students with a disability, who are eligible regardless of financial need.

How Can I Learn More?

Contact your school's placement, career, or guidance office for more information. Agencies recruit candidates directly from schools or through local offices of the State Employment or Job Service.

PRESIDENTIAL MANAGEMENT INTERN PROGRAM

The Presidential Management Intern Program is designed to be a starting point for individuals who wish to pursue a management career in the federal service. Through a variety of rotational assignments, seminars, discussion groups, and other activities, it provides a unique training experience which prepares the interns for future positions as managers.

What are the Jobs?

Presidential Management Intern positions provide a special means of entry into the federal service for graduate degree recipients. The positions focus upon developing in the interns management skills and a thorough knowledge of many facets of an agency. Career development opportunities may take the form of rotations among offices in a federal agency or between headquarters and field offices. Positions often cover a variety of functional areas. Management skills are emphasized.

Where are the Jobs?

Most PMIP positions are located in the Washington, DC area. Those outside of Washington are typically located at military and scientific installations near major metropolitan areas.

What is the Salary?

Most interns start at Grade 9, Step 1.

Are Benefits Included?

Interns receive federal benefits, including health and life insurance, retirement, annual leave, and paid sick leave.

What is the Work Schedule?

Presidential Management Interns receive two-year excepted service appointments. PMI's work the same type of schedule as a regular full-time employee at that agency. However, because of rotational assignments and special PMI activities, an intern's daily schedule tends to be somewhat more flexible.

Who is Eligible for These Positions?

Students who complete or expect to complete an advanced degree focusing on the analysis or management of public policies and programs from an accredited U.S. college or university during the current academic year are eligible to be nominated for the program. Nominations should be made by the college or university official who has an appropriate knowledge of the nominee's abilities and achievements. Nominations should come from the school dean, academic program director, or chairperson. Nominations from individual professors, advisors, or placement counselors are not accepted. Presidential Management Internships cannot be used to fulfill a degree requirement. All degree requirements must be met at the time of appointment to an internship.

To be considered eligible, the course of study pursued at the graduate level must demonstrate a commitment to a career in the analysis and management of public policies and programs. A variety of academic disciplines are eligible.

How Can I Learn More?

Application materials are made available to graduate schools in the early fall. Application packages include complete information on the PMI program, as well as further eligibility requirements. Completed applications must be postmarked no later than December 1st, and addressed to:

Office of Personnel Management
Attn: PMIP Review Committee
1900 E Street N.W., Room 6336
Washington, DC 20415

You may also wish to direct inquiries to one of the Office of Personnel Management offices listed in the *Agency Profiles* portion of this book.

SUMMER EMPLOYMENT/SUMMER AID PROGRAMS

The Summer Employment/Summer Aid Programs create training and work opportunities for students during summer months from May 13 to September 30.

What are the Jobs?

The summer programs offer various positions from office support, trade and labor occupations, to professional positions.

Where are the Jobs?

Summer employment positions are available at federal agencies across the United States.

What is the Salary?

Students are paid at regular government salary rates, which depend upon the employment position and experience or academic qualifications that the student possesses.

Are Benefits Included?

Benefits are not provided for students in the summer programs.

What is the Work Schedule?

Students work only during the summer months. Typically, students are employed full-time during this period.

Who is Eligible for These Positions?

Applicants for most summer positions must be at least 16 years old and must show financial need (except those who qualify as disabled students).

How Can I Learn More?

Job opportunities are advertised in the "Summer Jobs" Announcement No. 414, which is available each December from Office of Personnel Management Area Offices throughout the country (see Appendix for complete addresses and telephone numbers). Deadlines for applying for summer jobs vary from agency to agency. Contact an agency directly for more specific information.

STUDENT VOLUNTEER SERVICES

What are the Jobs?

A variety of positions exist throughout the federal government, depending upon the needs of the hiring agency.

Where are the Jobs?

Positions exist in many federal agencies throughout the United States.

What is the Salary?

Volunteer Services are uncompensated.

Are Benefits Provided?

Federal fringe benefits are not provided.

What is the Work Schedule?

Agencies vary on the work schedule that volunteer students follow. Often the schedule depends upon the needs of the student, the agency, and the school that the student attends.

Who is Eligible for These Positions?

Students enrolled at least part-time in high school, trade school, or college can participate in the Student Volunteer program if the school agrees. Some colleges and universities have included volunteer service internships in their public administration curricula, so that students can earn college credit by being a Student Volunteer.

How Can I Learn More?

Contact federal agencies directly to learn more about the specifics of the Student Volunteer Services program in their organization, or visit the placement office at your school.

OTHER SPECIAL EMPLOYMENT PROGRAMS

Vietnam Era and Disabled Veterans Programs

1. Veterans Readjustment Appointment (VRA) Authority

In order to qualify for the VRA, one must be a veteran of the Vietnam era and have a discharge other than dishonorable. More than 180 days must have been served, any part of which must be during the period of August 5, 1964, through May 7, 1975. The requirement for more than 180 days active duty service does not apply to disabled Vietnam era veterans. One must have no more than 14 years of education (2 years beyond the high school level). The 14-year educational restriction is waived, however, for compensably disabled veterans and veterans discharged because of service-connected disabilities.

2. Direct Hire of Severely Disabled Veterans

In order to qualify for Direct Hire, one must be a disabled veteran with a compensably service-connected disability of 30 percent or more. One must have the disability rating by the VA dated within the preceding year. The veteran must also meet the minimum requirements for the position, and must serve under any appropriate temporary authority not limited to 60 days or less.

3. Veterans Preference Credit

Preference is given to veterans in competitive examinations such as the ACWA test, in appointments to positions, and in retention during reductions-in-force. Five additional points may be added to a passing score on exams for a nondisabled veteran, and 10 additional points may be added for a disabled veteran.

4. Disabled Veterans Affirmative Action Program (DVAAP)

DVAAP is a planned program in each federal agency. Its purpose is to encourage agencies to recruit and hire qualified disabled veterans for federal jobs, and to advance them in their careers.

For Further Information:

Veterans should contact the personnel office and/or the Veterans Employment Program Manager of any federal agency to learn more about positions and programs for veterans.

Job Opportunities for Persons With Disabilities

1. Special Appointing Authorities

To meet the needs of those who have severe physical impairments or mental disabilities, an agency may use a variety of special appointing authorities to bring the disabled person on board by avoiding typical competitive appointment procedures.

2. Special Accommodations on the Job

The federal government provides reasonable accommodations in the duties of a job or in the worksite to make it easier for a disabled person to perform the duties of a position. This includes providing interpreters for persons with hearing impairments, readers for persons with visual impairments, alteration of work schedules to match the needs of the person, and special equipment or furniture as needed.

For More Information:

Persons with disabilities should contact the personnel office or Selective Placement Program Manager of the federal agency of interest. Selective Placement Managers work with supervisors and managers to match the skills and qualifications of disabled persons to available job openings.

Affirmative Employment Programs

The federal government has established special recruitment programs to attract qualified women, Hispanics, Blacks, American Indians, Alaska Natives, Asians, and Pacific Islanders into the federal service.

Hispanic Employment Program

Most federal agencies have Hispanic Employment Program Managers. Hispanic applicants may want to contact these managers for assistance in applying.

Federal Women's Program

The Federal Women's Program was designed to promote the employment of women into federal service. It focuses on attracting women into key positions, especially in nontraditional occupations. Contact the federal agency directly for more information.

Other Sources to Check

OPM is currently working on some computer programs to be used on college campuses which allow students to explore special hiring programs. Ask your placement office if they have:

1. STEP-Updated every semester, this program allows the student to access information on specific co-op positions within the different agencies.

2. A database for minorities, yet unnamed, is being created to allow students at HBCU (historically black colleges/universities) schools to explore opportunities for minority candidates.

CHAPTER 6

Positions in Demand

The following positions can be found in virtually every federal agency in the U.S. government, and thus are not listed separately under each agency profile in this book.

If the position you desire is described in this chapter, you can assume with confidence that the list of government agencies that have career opportunities you'd be interested in is very long and very broad indeed.

OCCUPATIONAL GROUPINGS

The federal government assigns related positions to common occupational groupings. Each occupational group contains several position titles, each with an assigned series number. There are 450 federal occupations that have been grouped into the following 23 groups:

GS-000	MISCELLANEOUS OCCUPATIONS GROUP
GS-100	SOCIAL SCIENCE, PSYCHOLOGY, AND WELFARE GROUP
GS-200	PERSONNEL MANAGEMENT AND INDUSTRIAL RELATIONS GROUP
GS-300	GENERAL ADMINISTRATIVE, CLERICAL, AND OFFICE SERVICES GROUP
GS-400	BIOLOGICAL SCIENCES GROUP
GS-500	ACCOUNTING AND BUDGET GROUP
GS-600	MEDICAL, HOSPITAL, DENTAL, AND PUBLIC HEALTH GROUP
GS-700	VETERINARY MEDICAL SCIENCE GROUP
GS-800	ENGINEERING AND ARCHITECTURE GROUP
GS-900	LEGAL AND KINDRED GROUP
GS-1000	INFORMATION AND ARTS GROUP
GS-1100	BUSINESS AND INDUSTRY GROUP
GS-1200	COPYRIGHT, PATENT, AND TRADEMARK GROUP
GS-1300	PHYSICAL SCIENCES GROUP
GS-1400	LIBRARY AND ARCHIVES GROUP
GS-1500	MATHEMATICS AND STATISTICS GROUP

GS-1600	EQUIPMENT, FACILITIES, AND SERVICE GROUP
GS-1700	EDUCATION GROUP
GS-1800	INVESTIGATION GROUP
GS-1900	QUALITY ASSURANCE, INSPECTION, AND GRADING GROUP
GS-2000	SUPPLY GROUP
GS-2100	TRANSPORTATION GROUP
GS-2300	POSTAL OPERATIONS GROUP

These groupings encompass all of the typical federal occupations. Additional details on federal occupational groupings and series codes can be found in the Office of Personnel Management's X-118 occupational series handbook. The X-118 gives job descriptions and exact qualifications and requirements for each of the 450 federal occupations. This resource can be found at some public libraries.

GENERAL POSITION DESCRIPTIONS

The following list contains those professional positions that tend to be common throughout the government, and are found at over half the federal agencies. Unless indicated otherwise, all of those listed below begin at the GS-5 level for recent graduates of bachelor degree programs with no work experience in the appropriate field. Since the job descriptions vary only slightly from agency to agency, one general position description is given here.

Social Science Analyst (G-101)

Social Science Analysts perform work in one or any combination of the behavioral or social sciences. This position requires a background of knowledge and skills gained from professional training in behavioral or social science.

There are over 2500 federal positions in the social science series. Over 100 government organizations hire Social Science Analysts and related social science workers.

Economist (G-110)

Economists do professional work or provide professional consultation involving research into economic phenomena. They analyze economic data, and prepare special or continuing reports on economic activities.

There are over 5300 federal positions in the economist series. Over 140 government organizations hire Economists.

Personnel Staffing Specialist (G-212)

Other Titles in This Series: Personnel Management Specialist (G-201); Position Classification Specialist (G-221); Personnel Officer (G-201)

Personnel staffing specialists perform work involving the recruitment, examination, selection, or placement of employees to fill staff positions in government organizations.

There are over 3800 federal Personnel Staffing Specialist positions. Nearly 200 government organizations hire Staffing Specialists.

Computer Specialist (G-334)

Computer Specialists perform work necessary to design or implement systems for solving problems or accomplishing work by the use of computers. Specializations within the computer specialist series include:

Computer Systems Analysts: Analyze problems or processes and design computerized systems for accomplishing work.

Computer Programmers: Translate system designs into the plans of instructions and logic by which computers can produce desired actions or products. Knowledge of a particular programming language is an important consideration in recruitment for these positions.

Computer Programmer Analysts: Perform work which is a combination of Computer Systems Analysts and Computer Programmer duties.

Computer Systems Programmers: Concerned with systems software. This typically involves maintenance and modification of assemblers, compilers, debugging routines, and similar internal computer programs necessary for the processing of other programs.

Computer Equipment Analysts: Concerned with the selection or utilization of computer equipment. These positions do not involve design or repair of equipment; concern is with the relative merit of equipment items and the arrangement of the items into equipment systems appropriate to an organization's needs.

There are over 27,500 federal Computer Specialist positions. More than 250 agencies hire Computer Specialists.

Related to the Computer Specialist position, but much less common in the federal government, is the Computer Scientist position described below:

Computer Scientist (G-1550)

Computer Scientists perform professional research or development work to evolve new concepts, methods, and techniques to store, manipulate, transform, and present information by means of digital computer systems. The work involves either the development of new fields of computer science research or responses to problems arising from use of digital computers within the federal service.

There are nearly 400 federal Computer Scientist positions. Approximately 50 government organizations hire Computer Scientists.

Management Analyst (G-343)

Management Analysts provide advice and service to management in such areas as planning, policy development, work methods and procedures, manpower utilization, organizational structures, information management, or similar areas with the objective of improving managerial effectiveness. The paramount qualifications required are a high order of analytical ability and a knowledge of the principles of management.

There are nearly 12,000 federal Management Analyst positions. More than 250 government organizations hire Management Analysts.

Program Analyst (G-345)

Program analysts evaluate the actual or potential effectiveness of current or projected operating programs in achieving their objectives. This includes such duties as analyzing the objectives of operating programs, identifying problem areas, trends, and areas of imbalance, and evaluating alternative actions in terms of effect on the program.

There are over 11,500 federal Program Analyst positions. More than 250 government organizations hire Program Analysts.

Logistics Management Specialist (G-346)

Logistics Management Specialists typically perform staff work in planning and coordinating logistical support activities to provide the money, manpower, material, facilities, and services needed to support a specific mission at the time and place they are needed. The Logistics Management Specialist identifies the activities involved and integrates the efforts of each activity into a comprehensive logistical plan.

There are over 3,500 federal Logistics Management Specialist positions and related occupations. More than 100 government organizations hire Logistics Management Specialists.

Accountant (G-510)/ Auditor (G-511)

Accountants and auditors perform professional work in any of several capacities depending upon the accounting system involved, the organizations and operating programs served, and the financial data sought.

Accountants: Classify and evaluate financial data; record transactions in financial records; develop and install new accounting systems, and prepare financial statements.

Auditors: Evaluate accounts for the purpose of certifying that various financial statements accurately represent the financial position of the activity audited in terms of assets, liabilities, net worth, and income and expenses.

There are nearly 25,000 federal Accountant/Auditor positions. More than 250 government organizations hire Accountants and/or Auditors.

Budget Analyst (G-560)

Other Titles in This Series: Budget Officer (G-11-15), Budget Examiner (G-5-15)

Positions in this series perform work in the phases or systems of budget administration currently in use in the federal service. Budget Analysts evaluate the relative costs and benefits of alternate courses of budget and program action, check the propriety of obligations and expenditures, establish standard rates and charges to customers, or develop budgetary policy.

There are over 9,000 federal Budget Analyst positions. More than 250 government organizations hire Budget Analysts.

Public Information Specialist (G-1081)

Employees in the Public Information Series disseminate information about the activities of the federal government through the newspapers, radio, television, periodicals, and other information media, or through employee periodicals. They evaluate the public information potential of written materials, illustrations, photographs, exhibits, and radio, television, and motion picture materials, and furnish advice to management concerning the information needs of the public.

There are nearly 3,000 federal Public Information Series positions. Over 200 government organizations hire Public Information Specialists or related positions.

Writer-Editor (G-1082)

Other Titles in This Series: Writer (G-5-15), Editor (G-5-15)

Employees in this series write or edit articles, news releases, pamphlets, reports, brochures, speeches, scripts, or other similar items. Writer-Editors acquire (through library research, background interview, and reading) information about the subject involved. They then select the pertinent information and write or edit the final drafts or manuscripts.

There are nearly 2,000 federal Writer-Editor positions. More than 200 government organizations hire Writer-Editors.

Contract Specialist, Procurement Analyst (G-1102)

Other Titles in This Series: Contract Negotiator, Contract Administrator, Contract Termination Specialist, Contract Price/Cost Analyst, Supervisory Contract Specialist (G-9-15)

Positions in this series perform work involving the procurement of supplies, services, construction, or research using formal advertising or negotiation methods. They evaluate contract price/cost proposals by applying a knowledge of the legislation, regulations, and methods used in contracting, and of business and industry practices.

Contract Specialists: Plan and conduct the contracting process from the initial description of the requirements through contract delivery.

Procurement Analysts: Plan and evaluate procurement programs, and review contractual actions for conformance with regulatory requirements and procurement practices.

There are over 19,000 federal Contract/Procurement positions. Nearly 250 government organizations hire Contract Specialists and related positions.

Training Specialist, Training Instructor (G-1712)

Other Titles in This Series: Training Administrator

Training Specialists and Instructors perform work involved in a program of instructional training in an occupation or other subject. They may be instructors in specific subject areas, may develop or review special subject-matter course materials, training aids, and manuals for training programs, or may administer training programs. The duties of some positions will include demonstration in the use of equipment, techniques, and principles of the subject being taught.

There are over 6,000 federal positions in the training series. Over 120 government organizations hire Training Specialists and related positions.

PART TWO

Agency Profiles

Introduction to Agency Profiles

This portion of the book contains a brief profile of every federal agency that employs 200 people or more. It offers a look at how the agency is set up, who they hire, and how to find out more information about them. A few things to keep in mind as you browse through:

Positions Begin at GS-5-7-9 Unless Otherwise Stated

The positions that are described in each profile tend to be entry level, falling in the GS-5,7, and 9 salary ranges. These positions earn between $16,973 and $25,717 upon entering federal service, and increase on a step system each year (see chapter 5 for details on federal salaries). If there is no indication of GS-level under a specific job description, then the reader can assume that the position is entry level.

Common Positions Are Listed Elsewhere

The very typical federal positions, those that can be found in almost every government agency, are not included in this section, but can be found in the *Positions in Demand* chapter in full detail.

Only Entry Level Positions Are Listed

The positions covered in this section focus on those that are entry-level professional level. Wage grade positions, and those that start below the GS-5 level, such as technician and clerical jobs, are generally not included.

Executive Agencies

The Department of Agriculture

The Department of Agriculture, created in May of 1862, works to improve and stabilize farm income and to develop agricultural markets in foreign countries. Its agencies provide grading and inspection services for various commodities, maintain statistics on the agricultural economy, develop environmental protection programs, and administer food assistance programs.

These services ensure that the animal and plant resources of the United States are free of disease and pests, that an adequate supply of food and fiber exists for the nation's population, and that agricultural commodities are properly marketed, both in this country and abroad.

The Department of Agriculture is also dedicated to solving problems in plant and animal protection through applied research and education programs. It conducts research into agricultural technologies, crop and animal quality and productivity, human nutrition, and conservation, and links these to the needs of the people.

The eighteen agencies within the Department of Agriculture are listed below:

Agricultural Marketing Service
Agricultural Research Service
Agricultural Stabilization and Conservation Service
Animal and Plant Health Inspection Service
Economic Research Service
Extension Service
Farmers Home Administration
Federal Crop Insurance Corporation
Federal Grain Inspection Service
Food and Nutrition Service
Food Safety and Inspection Service
Foreign Agricultural Service
Forest Service
National Agricultural Library
National Agricultural Statistics Service
Office of International Cooperation and Development
Rural Electrification Administration
Soil Conservation Service

AGRICULTURAL MARKETING SERVICE (AMS)

Nature of Work: Agriculture, consumer protection, marketing, scientific research, trade, wages/prices/rates
Number of Employees: 6,783
Headquarters: Washington, DC
Regional Locations: None
Typical Majors of New Hires: Agriculture, agronomy, business, marketing

Mission

AMS promotes the orderly and efficient marketing of agricultural products from the farm gate to the consumer's table. In carrying out its mission, AMS is responsible for providing market news, commodity standards, and grading and inspection services for various agricultural commodities, including cotton, tobacco, dairy products, fruits and vegetables, livestock, meat, poultry, and egg products.

Job Descriptions

AGRICULTURAL COMMODITY GRADER: Examines and evaluates agricultural products to determine their official U.S. grade and to evaluate their quality in accordance with official standards. Inspects or monitors the conditions under which the product is processed, stored, or transported to determine the effect of these conditions on product quality.

AGRICULTURAL MARKETING SPECIALIST: Incorporates a knowledge of the commodity exchanges and markets, agricultural statutory provisions, and agribusiness operations to analyze, manage, and regulate the marketing of agricultural commodities.

MARKET NEWS REPORTER: Gathers, analyzes, and disseminates current information on available supplies, demand, prices, marketing trends, and other facts relating to the marketing of agricultural products.

Major Activities and Divisions

Information: AMS provides information on supplies, demand, prices, location, and quality to producers, processors, and distributors.

Regulation: AMS develops grade standards for agricultural commodities, and establishes marketing agreements.

Research: AMS conducts studies of the facilities and methods used in the physical distribution of food and farm products.

Alternative Employment Programs

AMS maintains a limited co-op program, typically for students with majors related to agriculture. The Stay-in-School Program for clerical positions also exists.

Remarks

None.

Application Procedures

Direct inquiries to AMS headquarters:

Agricultural Marketing Service
Department of Agriculture
P.O. Box 96456
Washington, DC 20250

(202) 447-3967

AGRICULTURAL RESEARCH SERVICE (ARS)

Nature of Work: Agriculture, scientific research
Number of Employees: 7,183
Headquarters: Washington, DC
Regional Locations: Albany, CA; Athens, GA; Beltsville, MD; College Station, TX; Ft. Collins, CO; Peoria, IL; Philadelphia, PA; Stoneville, MS
Typical Majors of New Hires: Agriculture, agronomy, biology, biological sciences (animal science, entomology, genetics, physiology, plant science), chemistry, engineering, physical sciences, soil science, veterinary medicine

Mission

ARS is responsible for planning and conducting research that provides new knowledge and technologies to ensure an adequate supply of food and fiber for the nation's population. The agency's objectives include research and development in the area of natural resources, crop and animal quality and productivity, commodity conversion and delivery, and human health.

Job Descriptions

AGRONOMIST: Performs research on breeding, production, and culture of aquatic, field, and horticultural crops. Studies relationships of plants and soil, weed control, and plant adaptation.

ANIMAL SCIENTIST: Studies the classification, structure, ecology, parasitological phenomena, and the evolutional history of livestock animals. Performs research in the areas of animal quality and productivity.

CHEMIST: Performs research in the areas of analytical chemistry, biochemistry, and organic chemistry. Investigates agricultural commodities in terms of composition, molecular structure, and chemical properties. Examines the effects of chemical applications and chemical transformations.

ENTOMOLOGIST: Investigates plant-eating insects for the control of weeds and evaluates insect-resistant plant varieties. Studies chemical and nonchemical methods of insect control in the control of pest populations. Classifies and examines the geographical distribution of insects and mites, and investigates the role of insects as vectors of diseases affecting crops, animals, and humans.

ENGINEER (AGRICULTURAL, CHEMICAL, CIVIL, ELECTRICAL, HYDRAULIC, INDUSTRIAL, MECHANICAL): Depending upon the area of specialization, ARS engineers can focus on a certain agricultural research area: soil and water conservation; the design of specialized equipment and facilities; the design of farmsteads; the development of farm machinery; the use of electricity in agriculture; or agricultural marketing procedures.

GENETICIST: Performs research in inheritance and interaction of genetic characters, their environment, and basic physiological principles. Develops breeding methods and selection procedures.

MICROBIOLOGIST: Studies the characteristics and life processes of microorganisms and their relationships to plant and animal lifeforms. Conducts research into such fields as immunology, medical parasitology, physiology, genetics, and cytology. Develops scientific microbiological methods in the investigation and use of microorganisms in agriculture.

PHYSIOLOGIST: Performs research on the physiological processes of plants, including photosynthesis, mineral element nutrition, absorption, and the effects of chemicals, light, and moisture.

PLANT PATHOLOGIST: Performs research on plant diseases caused by parasitic or nonparasitic microorganisms and viruses. Studies the life cycles of disease-producing organisms and host-parasite relationships, and explores methods for disease prevention and control. Examines the effects of diseases on the culture, harvest, transportation, and storage of plants.

PLANT PHYSIOLOGIST: Performs research on physiological processes in plants, including photosynthesis, respiration, mineral element nutrition, water relations, and absorption. Studies the effects of light, temperature, moisture, and chemicals on the growth, ripening, and quality of plants.

SOIL SCIENTIST: Studies the relationship between plants and soil. Examines effects of various soil mixtures and mineral components on maturity, ripening, and quality of plants and plant processes.

VETERINARY MEDICAL OFFICER: Conducts research into the breeding, feeding, and hygienic management of livestock and poultry. Studies diseases which affect livestock, such as tuberculosis, cattle-tick, and scabies, and examines methods of prevention or eradication of such diseases.

Programs and Divisions

Research in Soil and Water Conservation: Investigates such things as erosion control, water control, drainage, irrigation, canals, dams, and the protection of streambanks.

Pilot Plant Facilities Design: Involved in the design of pilot plant assemblies and specialized equipment for the effective use of agricultural commodities.

Farm Structures Design: Gathers data relating to the design, construction, and use of farm buildings and farmsteads.

Research in Production and Harvesting Equipment and Methods: Develops farm machines for tilling, planting, fertilizing, and pest control.

Use of Electricity and Radiant Energy in Agricultural Operations: Researches the use of electricity on the farm, and the effects of electromagnetic radiation on growth.

Research in Transportation and Marketing Equipment and Procedures: Develops techniques, operating procedures, and equipment for conditioning, drying, handling, storing, and preparing agricultural products for market.

Alternative Employment Programs

ARS maintains an active co-op program. Positions typically filled are Biological Aid/Technician and Physical Science Aid/Technician. ARS typically hires fewer than ten co-ops per year, usually at the GS-3 or GS-9 levels, depending upon education and experience. Contact your school placement office for more information. ARS also conducts an extensive volunteer program for students, and offers the Stay-In-School, Federal Junior Fellowship, and Summer Aid programs.

Remarks

Research activities are carried out at 121 domestic locations, including Puerto Rico, the Virgin Islands, and in 8 foreign countries.

Application Procedures

Direct inquiries to the area office in which you would like to work:

BELTSVILLE AREA
Bldg. 005
Beltsville Ag. Research Center-West
Beltsville, MD 20705
(301) 344-2264 or (301) 344-1124 (vacancies)

MIDSOUTH AREA
P.O. Box 225
Stoneville, MS 38776
(601) 686-9406

NORTHERN PLAINS AREA
2625 Redwing Road
Ft. Collins, CO 80526
(303) 229-5531

NORTH ATLANTIC AREA
600 E. Mermaid Lane
Philadelphia, PA 19118

PACIFIC WEST AREA
800 Buchanan Street
Albany, CA 94710
(415) 559-5779

SOUTH ATLANTIC AREA
P.O. Box 5677
Athens, GA 30613

SOUTHERN PLAINS AREA
7607 East Mark Drive
Suite 230
College Station, TX 77840

JOB HOTLINE NUMBER: 301-344-2288

AGRICULTURAL STABILIZATION AND CONSERVATION SERVICE (ASCS)

Nature of Work: Agriculture, disaster assistance, emergency preparedness, environmental protection, forestry/wildlife, inventory/supply, marketing, trade
Number of Employees: 3,551
Headquarters: Washington, DC
Regional Locations: Kansas City, MO; Puerto Rico; Salt Lake City, UT. ASCS also has field offices in each state and in most counties.
Typical Majors of New Hires: Accounting, agriculture, agronomy, business, economics, marketing, mathematics, soil science, statistics, transportation

Mission

ASCS administers agricultural commodity, conservation, environmental protection, and emergency programs. The primary goals are establishing commodity price stability, orderly marketing, and resource conservation programs. Administration of the farm programs authorized by the Congress is handled through a system of State and County Committees throughout the 50 states.

Job Descriptions

AGRICULTURAL ECONOMIST (TRAINEE): Analyzes and interprets economic data relating to agricultural trends. Prepares special reports on economic facts and agricultural activities as they affect the market balance.

AGRICULTURAL MARKETING SPECIALIST (TRAINEE): Conducts research and makes recommendations concerning the marketing of one or more agricultural commodities, or marketing facilities and services. Works with various agricultural trade groups in the sale, exchange, purchase, and disposition of agricultural commodities.

AGRICULTURAL PROGRAM SPECIALIST (TRAINEE): Assists in formulating policy by making recommendations for consideration of State Committees on current and proposed service. Directs the grain storage programs of the Commodity Credit Corporation (CCC). Assists in program operations and conducts meetings with county and community committee members, farmers, grower's associations, warehousemen, and processors on various programs. Also conducts the State and County Office Manager training programs.

TRAFFIC MANAGEMENT SPECIALIST (TRAINEE): Plans and develops traffic management programs by formulating policies, evaluating programs and operations, and conducting special studies. Furnishes technical traffic management advisory services.

COUNTY EXECUTIVE DIRECTOR (TRAINEE): Works with the elected County Committee in managing the day-to-day operations of one of the 2,600 County Offices. County Executive Directors are not federal employees, but receive federal benefits. The trainee positions are filled at a level comparable to a GS-5. Service as a County Executive Director is a stepping stone to federal positions in field and Washington ASCS offices.

Major Activities and Divisions

Commodity Programs: ASCS administers the CCC's commodity stabilization programs.

Emergency Assistance: In the aftermath of a natural disaster, ASCS assists farmers with cost-sharing to carry out emergency conservation practices on damaged farmland.

Conservation Programs: ASCS conservation programs target such environmental concerns as soil erosion, water pollution, wetland protection, and timberstand improvement.

Commodity Purchases and Donations: ASCS employees are the administrative agents for CCC, which provides financing for farm programs, and for the purchase, storage, and disposal of commodities in federal stocks.

Alternative Employment Programs

ASCS hires co-op students at the undergraduate and graduate levels. Contact your school's placement or cooperative education office for more information.

Remarks

ASCS regional offices are distributed as follows:

State Offices: Each state ASCS office has an administrative staff and agricultural program specialists.

County Offices: The agency has a locally administered office in most counties headed by a County Committee and a County Executive Director.

Area Offices: There are two ASCS offices in Kansas City, each with a separate function. The Kansas City Commodity Office (KCCO) is responsible for acquiring, storing, and disposing of bulk and processed commodities. The Kansas City Management Office (KCMO) serves as the processing office for ASCS and CCC programs. There is also a Caribbean area office in Puerto Rico.

The Aerial Photography Field Office: Houses aerial photographs covering all of the nation's major cropland areas. The photos provide visual information for local planning groups and are widely sold to other agencies and to the public.

Application Procedures

Direct inquiries to either office:

USDA-ASCS-Personnel Division
Room 4971-So. Building
P.O. Box 2415
Washington, DC 20013
(202) 447-7614

Or:

USDA-ASCS-KCMO-Personnel Division
P.O. Box 419205
Kansas City, MO 64141-0205
(816) 926-6647

ANIMAL AND PLANT HEALTH INSPECTION SERVICE (APHIS)

Nature of Work: Agriculture, health/health care, import/export, forestry/wildlife
Number of Employees: 6,374
Headquarters: Washington, DC
Regional Locations: Employees work at ports of entry across the U.S. and in several foreign countries.
Typical Majors of New Hires: Biology, biological sciences (botany, microbiology), veterinary medicine (DVM), environmental sciences

Mission

APHIS protects the animal and plant resources of the nation from disease and pests to preserve the marketability of U.S. agricultural products in this country and abroad. In cooperation with state governments, APHIS administers federal laws and regulations pertaining to animal and plant health and quarantine, humane treatment of animals, and the control and eradication of pests and diseases.

Job Descriptions

MICROBIOLOGIST: Conducts scientific research into the characteristics and life processes of microorganisms and their relationships to other living forms. Studies the distribution of microorganisms in agricultural and animal commodities and products, their reaction to physical and chemical factors in the environment, their role as pathogenic and immunizing agents, and their isolation, cultivation, identification, and classification.

PLANT PROTECTION AND QUARANTINE OFFICER: Administers federal regulations that prohibit or restrict the entry of foreign pests and plants or products. Inspects and certifies domestic commodities for export, regulates the import and export of endangered plant species, ensures that imported seed is free of noxious weeds, and regulates genetically engineered organisms that present a plant pest risk. May work at any major port of entry in the U.S. or overseas.

VETERINARY MEDICAL OFFICER: Maintains inspection and quarantine service at designated ports of entry for imported animals and birds. Determines the existence or extent of outbreaks of disease and pests affecting livestock and poultry. Organizes control and eradication programs in cooperation with state officials, and cooperates with animal health officials in other countries in planning and conducting disease control efforts. Monitors the handling of livestock and poultry to assure humane treatment, and ensures that laws governing the transportation, sale, and handling of dogs, cats, circus, and zoo animals are obeyed.

WILDLIFE BIOLOGIST: Conducts professional scientific biological work in the conservation and management of wildlife. Applies biological facts and procedures necessary for the conservation and management of wildlife.

Major Activities and Divisions

Inspection Activities: APHIS conducts inspection and quarantine activities at U.S. ports of entry to prevent the introduction of exotic animal and plant diseases and pests.

Regulatory Activities: APHIS develops standards for veterinary biologics, and inspects establishments which handle animals intended for research or exhibition.

Wildlife Control: APHIS carries out cooperative operational programs to control wildlife damage.

Alternative Employment Programs

APHIS hires approximately 10 to 20 co-op students per year. Students typically begin at the GS-5 or -7 levels, and are often hired during their junior year in school. Co-ops typically fill Management Intern positions. APHIS also hires Stay-in-School students for clerical positions.

Remarks

None.

Application Procedures

For further information on positions in the U.S. contact:

Field Personnel Services
APHIS
Field Servicing Office
Butler Square West, 5th Floor
100 North 6th Street
Minneapolis, MN 55403
(612) 370-2493

For further information on positions abroad contact:

Resources Management Staff
APHIS
International Programs 6505
Belcrest Road
Rm. 668 Federal Building
Hyattsville, MD 20782
(301) 436-6490

THE ECONOMIC RESEARCH SERVICE (ERS)

Nature of Work: Agriculture, communications/media, economic policy, scholarly research
Number of Employees: 698
Headquarters: Washington, DC
Regional Locations: None
Typical Majors of New Hires: Agriculture, economics, geography, history, law, mathematics, political science, social work/sociology, statistics

Mission

The Economic Research Service generates economic and social information that agricultural decision makers use to measure and improve the performance of agriculture and rural America.

Job Descriptions

AGRICULTURAL ECONOMIST: Monitors and analyzes U.S. and world agricultural production and demand for agricultural commodities. Evaluates the economic performance of U.S. agricultural production and marketing, and estimates the effects of government policies on farmers, rural communities, and natural resources. There are 397 Agricultural Economists at ERS. Positions may be filled in any one of the four program divisions at ERS headquarters.

ECONOMIST: Conducts economic research into issues such as agricultural supply, demand, consumption patterns, international trade, and domestic policy. Conducts situation and outlook reporting activities and prepares interpretive reports.

GEOGRAPHER: Collects and analyzes information regarding geographical issues such as land ownership, use, and value. Monitors the nation's land and resource base and analyzes the interrelationships between land resources, economic returns, and the competition for agricultural land.

HISTORIAN: Performs historical research on agricultural, economic, and policy issues. Collects historical facts on such things as the effects of government programs on farmers and the economic performance of U.S. agricultural production. Analyzes current agricultural and rural issues for the view of the U.S. and world economies, and provides a historical view on the forces shaping those economies.

MATHEMATICIAN: Performs research using basic mathematical principles and methods. Develops mathematical techniques in the solution of agricultural economic, marketing, and production problems and issues.

SOCIOLOGIST: Performs research and scientific study into the culture, structure, and functioning of agricultural communities. Assesses rural areas in terms of demographics and agricultural production. Monitors trends in rural populations, employment, income, and farm-ownership.

STATISTICIAN: Gathers and interprets quantified information. Prepares situation and outlook reports on agricultural issues including supply, demand, trade, and production.

Major Activities and Divisions

The Commodity Economics Division (CED) carries out a program of analysis designed to improve understanding of U.S. and world markets for agricultural products.

The Agriculture and Trade Analysis Division (ATAD) provides research information on agricultural trade and development relationships between foreign countries and the U.S.

The Resources and Technology Division (RTD) provides economic analyses of agricultural resource and technology issues at both national and regional levels.

The Agriculture and Rural Economy Division (ARED) conducts a program of research to increase understanding of national and regional trends in agriculture and rural areas.

Alternative Employment Programs

ERS hires both co-op students and interns. Students must have a major in economics, statistics, or a related field.

Remarks

ERS publishes several magazines and periodicals, including *Farmline, Rural Development Perspectives,* and *National Food Review.*

Application Procedures

Most recruiting for agricultural economists is done through an open continuous vacancy announcement. Applicants for agricultural economist jobs in the agency may apply by submitting an SF–171. Applicants for other positions may respond to individual position announcements. Direct inquiries to:

USDA/EMS/PD/REAP Branch
Examining Unit
Room 1447 South Building
14th Street and Independence Avenue, S.W.
Washington, DC 20250

(202) 447-7638

EXTENSION SERVICE (ES)

Nature of Work: Agriculture, education, scientific research, volunteers
Number of Employees: 211
Headquarters: Washington, DC
Regional Locations: Federal employees work in the DC headquarters only. Cooperative Extension Service employees (state or county employees) work across the country in conjunction with ES.
Typical Majors of New Hires: Agriculture, agronomy, biological sciences (animal science, horticulture), education, home economics

Mission

The Extension Service is the educational agency of the Department of Agriculture and the federal partner in the Cooperative Extension System, integrating federal, state, and county governments. All three partners share in financing, planning, and conducting ES's educational programs, which link research, science, and technology to the needs of people.

Job Descriptions

AGRICULTURAL EXTENSION SPECIALIST: This is a very broad title encompassing all of the ES program area employees who may specialize in a certain area of agriculture or home economics such as horticulture, animal science, or agronomy. Agricultural Extension Specialists in Washington are responsible for disseminating information on research, trends, marketing, and other agricultural or home economics issues through the nationwide educational network. They also provide national-level policy formulation, program leadership, and evaluation systems in support of the Cooperative Extension System.

Major Activities and Divisions

There are currently four educational program areas at ES. They are agriculture, natural resources management, home economics, and the 4-H program. Together these cover such national issues as competitiveness and profitability of American agriculture; water quality; revitalizing rural America; management of natural resources; family and economic well-being; improving nutrition, diet, and health; and building human capital.

Alternative Employment Programs

The Extension Service maintains an internship program in its Washington office.

Remarks

The Cooperative Extension Services at the land-grant universities have professional staff located at the state, county, and area level. They work in cooperation with the Extension Service in Washington to assess clientele needs and develop educational programs to assist farmers, families, individuals, and communities in cultivating problem-solving and decision-making skills. They apply new communications technologies, including computers, video, satellites, and teleconferencing in producing and delivering educational programs.

Application Procedures

Direct inquiries to:

Personnel and Management Services Division
Cooperative Management Staff, USDA
Room 3547, South Building
Washington, DC 20250

(202) 447-3029

FARMER'S HOME ADMINISTRATION (FmHA)

Nature of Work: Agriculture, disaster assistance, regional development
Number of Employees: 11,000
Headquarters: Washington, DC
Regional Locations: There is an FmHA office in almost every state (46 offices)
Typical Majors of New Hires: Accounting, agriculture, business, finance/banking

Mission

FmHA is the federal government's chief credit agency for agriculture and rural development. It provides financial and other assistance to family farmers who are unable to obtain credit from regular commercial lenders. FmHA also administers nonfarm programs which are designed to benefit rural areas by offering a temporary source of supervised credit and technical support for improving housing conditions, community facilities, and other business endeavors.

Job Descriptions

AGRICULTURAL MANAGEMENT SPECIALIST: Acts on debt settlement matters, and assists or provides credit counseling for borrowers. This position requires a working knowledge of farm business organization, agricultural credit, rural housing, and farm management practices. Position can grow into a County Supervisor post.

LOAN SPECIALIST: Provides supervised credit to family farmers, rural residents, and small communities. Reviews applications and assesses borrower eligibility and soundness of loan proposals.

Major Activities and Divisions

FmHA's credit delivery system is carried out through a network of local offices which serve every rural county or parish in the 50 states. The network includes 46 state offices, 260 district offices, and about 1,930 county offices.

Alternative Employment Programs

FmHA maintains a paid co-op program for students, typically beginning at the GS-4 level. Co-op positions are usually Agricultural Management Specialist (Student Trainee), and Computer Specialist (Student Trainee) positions. Contact the personnel office for more information. FmHA also conducts a Stay-in-School program for clerical support positions.

Remarks

None.

Application Procedures

Direct inquiries to the headquarters office in Washington:

U.S. Department of Agriculture
Farmers Home Administration
14th Street and Independence Avenue, S.W.
Personnel
Washington, DC 20250

(202) 245-5569

FEDERAL CROP INSURANCE CORPORATION (FCIC)

Nature of Work: Agriculture, disaster assistance, insurance
Number of Employees: 933
Headquarters: Washington, DC
Regional Locations: Billings, MT; Bismarck, ND; College Station, TX; Columbia, SC; Des Moines, IA; Harrisburg, PA; Indianapolis, IN; Jackson, MS; Lincoln, NE; Manhattan, KS; Nashville, TN; Oklahoma City, OK; Raleigh, NC; Sacramento, CA; Spokane, WA; Springfield, IL; St. Paul, MN; Topeka, KS; Valdosta, GA
Typical Majors of New Hires: Accounting, agriculture, business, marketing, statistics

Mission

The Federal Crop Insurance Corporation is responsible for developing and administering crop insurance programs in a way that provides as many producers as possible the opportunity to protect their crop investments against losses due to natural disasters.

Job Descriptions

AREA CLAIMS SPECIALIST: Establishes and maintains a program for claims processing and quality assurance. Assigns work to Loss Adjustment Contractors. No degree is required, but an applicant should have experience with or knowledge of crops, farming practices, agricultural marketing trends, and natural crop hazards.

COMPLIANCE INVESTIGATOR: Conducts independent, on-site compliance reviews. Evaluates general FCIC program activities and the operations of private insurance companies under contract with or reinsured by FCIC. Performs reviews to ensure compliance with policies, procedures, and guidelines. No degree is needed, but requirements for the position include knowledge of investigative techniques and agricultural practices of the farming industry.

CROP INSURANCE SPECIALIST: Plans and directs the operation of contract service programs. Develops and recommends FCIC policies and practices related to sales and contract servicing. Requires a broad knowledge of crops, farming practices, crop hazards, and crop insurance policies.

CROP INSURANCE UNDERWRITER: Assists in establishing county actuarial structures by analyzing soil capabilities and limitations, farming practices, production, and climatological data. Assigns premium rates and crop coverages in a specified region according to regulations. Requires a bachelor's degree in agriculture or experience which demonstrates a knowledge of agricultural principles such as herbicide and insecticide requirements, planting dates, drainage, and soils.

LOSS ADJUSTMENT CONTRACTOR: Visits farms to inspect damaged or destroyed crops. Appraises potential crop production, measures acreage, and explains contractual responsibilities to insureds. Determines time and cause of loss, and measures farm-stored production. Promotes the crop insurance program and maintains positive relationships with insureds. NOTE: Loss Adjustment Contractor positions are NOT available through the Federal Employment program. Because they work closely with FCIC, however, you may inquire with FCIC personnel for further information.

STATISTICIAN: Develops coverages and premium rates using various statistical methods. Requires a bachelor's degree.

Major Activities and Divisions

The FCIC offers insurance through two basic delivery systems: sales and service agencies (Master Marketers), and private insurance companies which it reinsures. Master Marketers provide management, supervision of at least 25 agents, and contract servicing. Reinsured companies offer crop insurance under their own brand names and provide marketing, distribution, servicing, and loss adjustment functions. The FCIC carries out all other activities, such as loss adjustment and claims functions on policies sold by Master Marketers, training for agents and loss adjusters, marketing services, and quality control.

Alternative Employment Programs

FCIC participates in a paid co-op program for students with appropriate majors.

Remarks

None.

Application Procedures

Contact one of the two FCIC personnel offices. They may direct you to the appropriate regional office.

U.S. Dept. of Agriculture
Federal Crop Insurance Corp.
South Agriculture Building
14th Street and Independence
Avenue, S.W.
Washington, DC 20250
(202) 382-9801

U.S. Dept. of Agriculture
Federal Crop Insurance Corp.
9435 Holmes Rd.
Kansas City, MO 64131
(816) 926-7007

FEDERAL GRAIN INSPECTION SERVICE (FGIS)

Nature of Work: Agriculture, import/export
Number of Employees: 700
Headquarters: Washington, DC
Regional Locations: FGIS has an office in almost every state
Typical Majors of New Hires: Agriculture, business, economics

Mission

The Federal Grain Inspection Service establishes official U.S. standards for grading grain, and sees that these standards are uniformly applied. It provides for an official inspection system for grain, and regulates the weighing of grain shipped in interstate or foreign commerce.

Job Descriptions

AGRICULTURAL COMMODITY GRADER: Examines and evaluates products to determine their official U.S. grade and/or their acceptability in terms of quality or condition. Inspects or monitors the conditions under which the product is stored, processed, or transported.

AGRICULTURAL MARKETING SPECIALIST: Conducts research and analysis into the marketing of one or more agricultural commodities or products. Incorporates a knowledge of marketing practices, the commodity exchanges and markets, agricultural trade, and statutory provisions to establish agricultural marketing programs.

SCALES AND WEIGHING SPECIALIST: Provides official weighing services at export port locations and at inland locations for domestic grain. Provides oversight, guidance, and assistance to nonfederal agencies performing official weighing activities. These positions are typically not filled at the entry level.

Major Activities and Divisions

The FGIS is involved in four primary activities: The inspection of grain at inland and port locations, the official weighing of grain at inland and port locations, establishing and maintaining official standards for grain and other commodities, and the investigation of reported violations of the U.S. Grain Standards Act.

Alternative Employment Programs

The Federal Grain Inspection Service hires approximately 1-10 co-op students per year. They typically begin at the GS-4 level, and fill the position of Physical Science Technician. Contact your school placement office for more information. FGIS also hires Stay-in-School students to fill clerical positions.

Remarks

None.

Application Procedures

All hiring for FGIS is done through the APHIS Field Servicing Office in Minneapolis. Address inquiries to:

USDA, APHIS, FSO
100 N. 6th Street
5th Floor
Butler Square
Minneapolis, MN 55403

(612) 370-2013

FOOD AND NUTRITION SERVICE (FNS)

Nature of Work: Low-income people, food/nutrition, education, health/health care
Number of Employees: 1,954
Headquarters: Alexandria, VA
Regional Locations: Atlanta, GA; Burlington, MA; Chicago, IL; Dallas, TX; Denver, CO; Robbinsville, NJ; San Francisco, CA
Typical Majors of New Hires: Business, food sciences (nutrition), home economics, public administration, public health

Mission

The Food and Nutrition Service administers USDA's numerous food assistance programs, which are designed to provide access to a more nutritious diet for persons with low incomes and to encourage better eating patterns among the nation's children.

Job Descriptions

FOOD PROGRAM SPECIALIST: (Comprise half of the employees of the FNS) Develops, evaluates, and promotes programs concerned with providing food to low-income households, schools, and nonprofit institutions through food assistance programs. Examines state and local operating programs, drafts regulations and instructions that put program legislation into effect, and develops national models to improve program effectiveness.

INVESTIGATOR: Conducts confidential reviews of firms and individuals suspected of committing Food Stamp Program violations. Travels extensively to visit sites and conduct interviews.

PUBLIC HEALTH NUTRITIONIST: Provides technical expertise in the areas of food and nutrition. Develops nutrition education materials, and administers national nutrition education programs.

Major Activities and Divisions

FNS oversees several food assistance programs operated in cooperation with state and local governments.

The Food Stamp Program provides food coupons to needy persons to increase their food purchasing power.

The Special Nutrition Programs are designed to improve the nutrition of children, especially those from low-income families.

The Food Distribution Program makes food available to eligible recipients through school programs and on Indian reservations.

The Special Supplemental Food Program for Women, Infants, and Children (WIC) provides specified nutritious food supplements to pregnant and nursing women up to 6 months postpartum, and to children up to 5 years of age.

The Commodity Supplemental Food Program provides supplemental foods to infants and children and to pregnant or breastfeeding women with low incomes and who reside in approved project areas.

The Nutrition Education and Training Program grants funds to the States for the dissemination of nutrition information.

Alternative Employment Programs

FNS is initiating a nation-wide co-op program for college students with appropriate majors. It currently offers a summer intern program, targeting college sophomores and filling about 20–25 positions nationwide. The closing date for the summer intern application is usually in mid-March. FNS also participates in the PMI and Stay-in-School programs.

Remarks

None.

Application Procedures

Direct inquiries to the regional office in which you would like to work:

Headquarters Address:

USDA Food and Nutrition Service
Personnel Division
Operations Branch, Room 620
3101 Park Center Drive
Alexandria, VA 22302
(703) 756-3348

Regional Offices:

Food and Nutrition Service

Mid-Atlantic Regional Office
1 Vahlsing Center
Robbinsville, NJ 08691
(609) 259-5025

Southeast Regional Office
77 Forsyth Street, S.W.
Atlanta, GA 30303
(404) 730-2565

Southwest Regional Office
1100 Commerce Street
Dallas, TX 75242
(214) 767-0222

Western Regional Office
550 Kearney Street
San Francisco, CA 94108
(415) 705-1310

Northeast Regional Office
10 Causeway Street
Boston, MA 02222-1062
(617) 565-6370

Midwest Regional Office
50 East Washington Street
Chicago, IL 60602
(312) 353-6664

Mountain Plains Reg. Office
1244 Speer Boulevard
Denver, CO 80204
(303) 844-0300

FOOD SAFETY AND INSPECTION SERVICE (FSIS)

Nature of Work: Consumer protection, food/nutrition, health/health care
Number of Employees: 10,078
Headquarters: Washington, DC
Regional Locations: Alameda, CA; Atlanta, GA (Inspection Office and lab); Dallas, TX; Des Moines, IA; Minneapolis, MN (Servicing Personnel Office), Philadelphia, PA; St. Louis, MO (lab); San Francisco, CA (lab)
Typical Majors of New Hires: Food science, veterinary medicine (DVM)

Mission

FSIS is responsible for assuring that federal health standards are met in the processing of meat products. It also conducts research projects to devise ways of improving meat products in terms of nutritional value, cholesterol levels, and other health-related aspects.

Job Descriptions

FOOD INSPECTOR: Inspects the slaughter and processing of food animals in meat or poultry plants, and/or inspects processed meat and poultry products.

FOOD TECHNOLOGIST: Monitors compliance with regulations concerning proper formulation and labeling of processed products, authorized levels of food additives, sanitation, and packaging. Technologists are assigned to meat packing plants in various cities throughout the U.S. Technologist positions offer rotational or stationary work options. These positions are technical rather than professional in nature and do not require a college degree.

VETERINARIAN: (Requires a DVM from an accredited veterinary school) Performs antemortem and postmortem inspection of food animals. Acts as resident pathologist, parasitologist, and epidemiologist at one or several packing plants. Identifies and removes from the food processing cycle those carcasses which are unfit for human consumption. Also ensures that plants and facilities meet federal standards of cleanliness, and that processed foods are truthfully labeled according to federal law.

Major Activities and Divisions

The FSIS is divided into 5 regional offices, 3 laboratories, and 26 small area offices. The bulk of FSIS employees are stationed in meat packing plants throughout the country.

Alternative Employment Programs

The FSIS has hired DVM students as co-op employees in the past. Currently, no co-op program exists. It does offer a Stay-in-School program for clerical employees.

Remarks

None.

Application Procedures

All hiring for FSIS field positions is done through the Minneapolis national personnel office. An SF–171 and an FSIS supplemental application should be sent to the address below regardless of the location in which you desire to work.

Direct inquiries in writing to:

USDA, FSIS, POB, Special
Examining Unit
Butler Square West, 4th Floor
100 North 6th Street
Minneapolis, MN 55403

(612) 370-2013

Headquarters Address:

US Department of Agriculture
Food Safety and Inspection Service
14th Street and Independence
Avenue, S.W.
Room 3161 South
Washington, DC 20250

FOREIGN AGRICULTURAL SERVICE (FAS)

Nature of Work: Agriculture, import/export, international affairs, marketing, trade
Number of Employees: 894
Headquarters: Washington, DC
Regional Locations: 74 American embassy and consulate locations around the world
Typical Majors of New Hires: Agriculture, economics, marketing

Mission

The Foreign Agricultural Service helps American farmers and traders take maximum advantage of increased opportunities to sell U.S. agricultural commodities abroad and helps increase U.S. farm income. The agency operates an information and market development program that serves U.S. agricultural communities and government decision makers.

Job Descriptions

AGRICULTURAL ECONOMIST: Analyzes and advises on the agricultural economy, developments, and trends in the U.S. and foreign countries. Conducts economic analyses in connection with the development of foreign markets for U.S. agricultural commodities.

AGRICULTURAL MARKETING SPECIALIST: Evaluates production and consumption trends and food and fiber requirements of foreign countries. Researches and designs international market development programs. Conducts competition studies and examines international marketing trends.

INTERNATIONAL ECONOMIST: Analyzes the trade policies and practices of foreign countries to ensure conformance with international treaty negotiations. Maintains an ongoing effort to reduce foreign trade barriers and practices that discourage the export of U.S. farm products. Conducts overseas travel for export promotion programs. Participates in international trade negotiations, and administers agricultural import quotas and regulations.

Major Activities and Divisions

FAS maintains a worldwide agricultural intelligence and reporting system through its attaché service. It also has a continuing marketing development program, and, through the Office of the General Sales Manager, manages agricultural functions under the Public Law 480 Program.

Alternative Employment Programs

FAS hires college students for both its co-op and summer intern programs. Typical majors are economics, marketing, computer science, and international business. Typical titles are Economist Assistant and Marketing Assistant. Contact the student coordinator at 447-4372 for more information.

Remarks

FAS does not place entry level personnel directly into overseas positions. Agricultural Economists and Marketing Specialists enter into the Professional Development Program, which prepares candidates for tours in the worldwide Agricultural Attaché Service after 1–3 years in Washington. The Agricultural Attaché monitors foreign agricultural markets and reports to Washington on matters of trade, analysis of supply and demand, market opportunities, and export programs.

Application Procedures

Direct inquiries to:

Recruitment Officer
Foreign Agricultural Service, USDA
FAS Personnel, Room 5627, South Building
Washington, DC 20250

(202) 382-1587

U.S. FOREST SERVICE

Nature of Work: Environmental protection, forestry/wildlife, recreation
Number of Employees: 29,211
Headquarters: Washington, DC
Regional Locations: Albuquerque, NM; Asheville, NC; Atlanta, GA; Berkeley, CA; Broomall, PA; Fort Collins, CO; Juneau, AK; Lakewood, CO; Madison, WI; Milwaukee, WI; Missoula, MT; New Orleans, LA; Ogden, UT; Portland, OR; San Francisco, CA (List includes regional offices and experiment stations)
Typical Majors of New Hires: Archaeology, biology, biological sciences (entomology, fisheries, wildlife biology, zoology), botany, earth sciences (hydrology), education (outdoor education), engineering, environmental sciences, forestry, geology, soil science

Mission

The Forest Service is responsible for managing the nation's almost 200 million acres of National Forest land, which contain vast reserves of timber and water resources and are home to many species of wildlife. Farmers and ranchers use its pastures for grazing their livestock, and industry buys its timber to produce wood products. The Forest Service also develops human resources through such programs as the Job Corps and the Youth Conservation Corps.

Job Descriptions

ARCHAEOLOGIST: Performs research or other professional or scientific work in archaeology, including the study of historic and prehistoric cultures. Conducts field studies, laboratory analyses, and library research. Prepares reports for publication, and advises on historic preservation issues.

ENGINEER (CIVIL, MECHANICAL, AGRICULTURAL, ELECTRICAL): Engineers provide technical expertise in forest resource management. Civil engineers work in systems planning design and construction for roads, bridges, buildings, waste treatment systems, and other facilities. Mechanical and agricultural engineers develop, test, and select mechanical equipment for use in tree planting, brush cutting, fire control, chemical spreading, timber harvesting, and other forest management projects. Electrical engineers analyze and make recommendations on the effects of power-line and water-power usage on national forests. They also design and select remote telephone systems, and microwave and electrical transmission systems.

ENTOMOLOGIST: Examines the geographical distribution of insects and investigates chemical and nonchemical methods of insect control. Studies the role of insects as carriers of diseases affecting plants and wildlife.

FISHERY BIOLOGIST: Conducts studies in the development, conservation, and management of fishery resources. Develops spawning beds for fish, stabilizes stream channels, and develops fishing lakes. Consults and cooperates with state fish agencies in the maintenance and improvement of fish habitats and the conservation of endangered aquatic species.

FORESTER: Develops, conserves, and manages the natural resources of forests, including timber, soil, land, water, wildlife, and fish habitats. Protects resources against fire, insects, disease, floods, and erosion. Interprets and implements legislation on the management of forest land.

GEOLOGIST: Determines geologic history, rock types, rock structure, the classification of land forms, and groundwater conditions. Applies data from geologic mapping, aerial photography, and seismic and electrical resistivity geophysical methods to solve problems concerning soil stability, landslides, road construction, and bridge sites. Conducts broad geologic surveys for planning road nets, timber harvesting, watershed studies, and soil inventories.

HYDROLOGIST: Determines and analyzes watershed conditions in terms of management potential and possible hazards. Recommends and designs flood control, watershed, and soil conservation practices. Examines the effects of recreation use, minerals management, grazing, timber harvest, waste disposal, and road construction on the water resources.

LANDSCAPE ARCHITECT: Assists in the planning and design of outdoor recreation facilities. Conducts land-use planning and feasibility studies, and makes recommendations on such projects as timber harvesting, transportation systems, fire control facilities design, and watershed improvements. Usually works as part of an interdisciplinary team made up of scientists and other professionals.

PLANT PATHOLOGIST: Performs scientific research into the cause, nature, prevalence, and severity of parasitic, nonparasitic, and virus diseases attacking plants. Investigates the relation of such diseases to the propagation, planting, location, cultivation, and transportation of plants and plant products.

RANGE CONSERVATIONIST: Analyzes the range resource on one or more of approximately 11,000 National Forest grazing allotments. Adjusts the number of game and livestock animals to the forage supply, and determines the proper grazing seasons and how much grazing the forage plants and soil can withstand. Determines the modification or replacement of low-value brush, and plans the construction of trails, range seeding, water developments, and fencing.

SOIL SCIENTIST: Conducts soil inventories on forest lands to determine the distribution of areas having similar characteristics. Maps soil area boundaries on aerial photographs, and determines the significance of basic differences in soil capability to forest management projects.

TEACHER: Works to develop skills of resource professionals, educators, and citizens' groups in environmental education. Informs the public on how it can use National Forest System lands, resources, and facilities. Works with environmental education and public participation programs.

WILDLIFE BIOLOGIST: Cooperates with state wildlife agencies and with the U.S. Fish and Wildlife Service in ensuring that state fish and game laws are effective and operative. Coordinates forest resource activities, such as timber harvest and minerals management, with the habitat needs of wildlife. Protects and improves habitat for both game and nongame species.

Major Activities and Divisions

Recreation: The Forest Service maintains 99,468 miles of trails, more than 6,000 picnic and campgrounds, 320 swimming sites, 1,106 boating sites, and 307 winter sports sites. More than 25,000 cultural, historical, and archaeological sites have been identified in the National Forest System.

Timber: Of the 191 million acres of National Forests, 86.5 million acres are classified as commercial forests, land that is available for timber harvest. The Forest Service annually sells about 11 billion board feet of timber. The agency reforests an average of 400,000 acres per year.

Water: The Forest Service's watershed management programs work to assure adequate yields of high quality water and continuing soil productivity.

Forage: The Forest Service manages more than 14 percent of the nation's 1.2 billion acres of forest range. The rangeland is managed to conserve the land and its vegetation while providing food for both domestic livestock and wildlife.

Wildlife and Fish Habitat: The Forest Service manages fish and wildlife habitat on the National Forests and National Grasslands in cooperation with the fish and game departments of the states.

Minerals and Energy: Responsibility for regulating and managing mineral activities on National Forest System lands is shared by the Forest Service and the Department of the Interior. The Forest Service administers mining claims on public domain lands.

Fire Management: The Forest Service has one of the world's largest wildland firefighting forces, and provides fire protection for National Forest System lands.

Forest Pest Management: Forest insect and disease prevention is carried out by the Forest Service on National Forest Lands and it provides technical and financial assistance to support these activities on other forested lands.

Research: Research is conducted at eight Forest and Range Experiment Stations and the Forest Products Laboratory, plus 75 research labs throughout the U.S., Puerto Rico, and the Pacific Trust Territories. The principal areas of Forest Service research are land and resource protection, resource management, and wood utilization.

Human Resource Programs: The agency administers programs that provide work, training, and education to minorities, the economically depressed, the elderly, the handicapped, and youth. Examples are the Youth Conservation Corps, the Forest Service Volunteers program, the Touch America Project, and the Senior Community Service Employment Program.

Alternative Employment Programs

The Forest Service maintains both a co-op and internship program for college students. It also offers a Stay-in-School program, and hires a small number of PMI's annually.

Remarks

None.

Application Procedures

Direct inquiries to the appropriate regional office:

Headquarters:

USDA, Forest Service
Staffing Branch
RPE Room 913
P.O. Box 9060
Washington, DC 20090-6090
(703) 235-3440 (personnel)
(703) 235-2730 (vacancies)

Southwestern Region
U.S. Forest Service
Federal Building
517 Gold Avenue, S.W.
Albuquerque, NM 87102
(505) 842-3292

Southern Region
U.S. Forest Service
1720 Peachtree Road, N.W.
Atlanta, GA 30367
(404) 347-2384

Alaska Region
U.S. Forest Service
Federal Office Building
P.O. Box 1628
Juneau, Alaska 99802
(907) 586-8863

Rocky Mountain Region
U.S. Forest Service
11177 West 8th Avenue
Box 25127
Lakewood, CO 80225
(203) 236-9431

Eastern Region
U.S. Forest Service
310 West Wisconsin Avenue
Milwaukee, WI 53203
(414) 297-3693

Northern Region
U.S. Forest Service
Federal Building
P.O. Box 7669
Missoula, MT 59807
(406) 329-3511

Intermountain Region
U.S. Forest Service
Federal Building
324 25th Street
Ogden, UT 84401
(801) 625-5352

Pacific Northwest Region
U.S. Forest Service
319 S.W. Pine Street
P.O. Box 3623
Portland, OR 97208
(503) 326-2971

Pacific Southwest Region
U.S. Forest Service
630 Sansome Street
San Francisco, CA 94111
(415) 705-2870

NATIONAL AGRICULTURAL LIBRARY (NAL)

Nature of Work: Agriculture, libraries
Number of Employees: 232
Headquarters: Beltsville, MD
Regional Locations: Washington, DC (DC Reference Center)
Typical Majors of New Hires: Agriculture, library science

Mission

NAL houses the world's largest collection of printed materials on agriculture and related sciences. It collects technical information on agriculture and related subjects from all over the world and makes it available to scientists, educators, and farmers in printed form and by using computer databases. The NAL is the coordinator for a national network of state land-grant and field libraries.

Job Descriptions

LIBRARIAN: Collects, organizes, and retrieves recorded knowledge for a wide cross-section of users, including USDA scientists and the general public. Uses advanced information technologies, such as AGRICOLA (an agricultural database system), and CD-ROM (a compact disc system). Coordinates projects with land-grant university libraries, Agricultural Research Service field office libraries, and others to share information among all the libraries and their users. Selects and acquires materials, and works in library management and systems planning. Often requires a specialized knowledge of the agriculture field, or coursework in an agricultural discipline.

TECHNICAL INFORMATION SPECIALIST: Analyzes and transmits the intellectual content of scientific or technological information. Acquires and indexes the subject content of documents, and prepares abstracts or extracts. May develop subject heading lists, lists of descriptors, or thesauri. Accepts questions from library users, performs searches using the AGRICOLA database, the compact disc system (CD-ROM), or laser optical disc. Develops new service relationships with the public and private sectors, and establishes dissemination networks. Requires substantial subject-matter knowledge in an agricultural discipline.

Major Activities and Divisions

The NAL is divided into twelve specialized information centers within the NAL system:

Agricultural Trade and Marketing
Alternative Farming Systems
Animal Welfare
Aquaculture
Biotechnology
Critical Agricultural Materials
Food and Nutrition
Food Irradiation
Family
Fiber and Textiles
Horticulture
Rural Development

Alternative Employment Programs

NAL participates in a formalized practicum program as well as a student intern program. Internship positions are unpaid, but positions are often funded through the participating universities.

Remarks

None.

Application Procedures

Direct inquiries to the main library location:

National Agricultural Library
10301 Baltimore Blvd.
Beltsville, MD 20705

(301) 344-4248

NATIONAL AGRICULTURAL STATISTICS SERVICE (NASS)

Nature of Work: Agriculture, statistics
Number of Employees: 1,051
Headquarters: Washington, DC
Regional Locations: There are 44 State Statistical Offices under NASS. Refer to address listing for locations.
Typical Majors of New Hires: Agronomy, business, mathematics, statistics

Mission

NASS prepares estimates and reports on production, supply, price, and other items necessary for the orderly operation of the U.S. agricultural economy. Information is gathered through a complex system of sample surveys of producers, processors, buyers, and others associated with agriculture. Data is collected by mail, telephone, personal interviews, and field visits. NASS also prepares periodic reports for free distribution to the news media and Congress.

Job Descriptions

AGRICULTURAL STATISTICIAN: Selects samples for survey purposes, develops crop and livestock estimates, and writes technical explanatory reports supporting estimates. Prepares and disseminates estimates to the news media.

MATHEMATICAL STATISTICIAN: Analyzes estimates and conducts statistical research to improve estimating procedures. Designs mathematical methods related to statistical processes. Develops crop and livestock estimates through information gathering techniques, and ensures statistical integrity of numerical data.

Programs and Divisions

The national office and the 44 state-federal offices prepare weekly, monthly, annual, and other periodic reports for free distribution to the news media, Congress, and survey respondents.

Alternative Employment Programs

NASS hires students with appropriate college majors as co-op students.

Remarks

Entry-level employees can begin their career at a field office or at headquarters in Washington. Statisticians typically travel extensively throughout the U.S.

Application Procedures

Contact the State Statistician for more information about a career with NASS (see addresses below), or direct inquiries to:

EMS Division of Personnel
U.S. Department of Agriculture
Washington, DC 20250
(202) 447-7657

Box 1071
Montgomery, AL 36192
(205) 832-7263

Box 799
Palmer, AK 99645
(907) 745-4272

201 E. Indianola
Suite 250
Phoenix, AZ 85012
(602) 241-2573

Box 1417
Little Rock, AR 72203
(501) 378-5145

Box 1258
Sacramento, CA 95806
(916) 551-1533

Box 17066
Denver, CO 80217
(303) 964-0250

1222 Woodward Street
Orlando, FL 32803
(305) 648-6013

Stephens Federal Building
Athens, GA 30613
(404) 546-2236

Box 22159
Honolulu, HI 96822
(808) 548-7155

Box 1699
Boise, ID 83701
(208) 334-1507

Box 19283
Springfield, IL 62794
(217) 492-4295

Purdue University
W. Lafayette, IN 47907
(317) 494-8371

210 Walnut Street
Des Moines, IA 50309
(515) 284-4340

444 S.E. Quincy Street
Topeka, KS 66683
(913) 295-2600

Box 1120
Louisville, KY 40201
(502) 582-5293

Box 5524
Alexandria, LA 71307
(318) 473-7971

50 H.S. Truman Parkway
Annapolis, MD 21401
(301) 841-5740

Box 20008
Lansing, MI 48901
(517) 377-1831

Box 7068
St. Paul, MN 55107
(612) 296-2230

Box 980
Jackson, MS 39205
(601) 965-4575

Box L
Columbia, MO 65205
(314) 875-5233

Box 4369
Helena, MT 59604
(406) 449-5303

Box 81069
Lincoln, NE 68501
(402) 471-5541

Box 8880
Reno, NV 89507
(702) 784-5584

Box 1444
Concord, NH 03301
(603) 224-9639

330 New Warren St.
Trenton, NJ 08625
(609) 292-6835

Box 1809
Las Cruces, NM 88004
(505) 523-8168

1 Winners Circle
Albany, NY 12235
(518) 457-5570

Box 27767
Raleigh, NC 27611
(919) 856-4394

Box 3166
Fargo, ND 58102
(701) 237-5771

608 New Federal Building
Columbus, OH 43215
(614) 469-5590

2800 N. Lincoln Boulevard
Ok. City, OK 73105
(405) 525-9226

1220 S.W. 3rd Avenue
Portland, OR 97204
(503) 221-2131

2301 N. Cameron Street
Harrisburg, PA 17110
(717) 787-3904

Box 1911
Columbia, SC 29202
(803) 765-5333

Box V
Sioux Falls, SD 57117
(605) 336-2980

Box 41505
Nashville, TN 37204
(615) 736-5136

Box 70
Austin, TX 78767
(512) 482-5581

Box 25007
Salt Lake City, UT
84125
(801) 524-5003

Box 1659
Richmond, VA 23213
(804) 786-3500

Box 609
Olympia, WA 98507
(206) 586-8919

State Dept. of Agriculture
Charleston, WV 25305
(304) 348-2217

Box 9160
Madison, WI 53715
(608) 264-5317

Box 1148
Cheyenne, WY 82003
(307) 772-2181

OFFICE OF INTERNATIONAL COOPERATION AND DEVELOPMENT (OICD)

Nature of Work: Agriculture, developing countries, international affairs, scientific research
Number of Employees: 204
Headquarters: Washington, DC
Regional Locations: None
Typical Majors of New Hires: Agriculture, business, economics, education

Mission

The programs of OICD focus on sharing knowledge of agriculture through development assistance and cooperation with other countries. These programs are designed to benefit both our foreign neighbors and American agricultural production.

Job Descriptions

INTERNATIONAL TRAINING SPECIALIST: Serves as a general development specialist in program design and implementation. Provides technical expertise to the Agency for International Development (AID) in the area of training. Supports field training advisors, and designs technical systems to improve the training abilities of OICD and AID.

Major Activities and Divisions

The Office's primary activities are providing technical assistance and training in agriculture to other countries, particularly the developing world; working with international food and agricultural organizations to solve world food problems; and sponsoring scientific exchanges and research that help farmers both in the U.S. and abroad.

Alternative Employment Programs

OICD sponsors student hiring programs in the form of Summer Paid Employment and Volunteer Intern programs.

Remarks

None.

Application Procedures

Direct inquiries to:

USDA/OICD
Personnel Office, Room 430
Washington, DC 20250-4300
(202) 653-9241

RURAL ELECTRIFICATION ADMINISTRATION (REA)

Nature of Work: Funds/Funding
Number of Employees: 538
Headquarters: Washington, DC
Regional Locations: None
Typical Majors of New Hires: Accounting, business, engineering (electrical, electronic), finance/banking

Mission

REA makes or guarantees loans to finance the provision of electric and telephone service to persons in rural areas. More than 26 million rural people in 46 states benefit from these services. REA also sponsors a guaranteed loan program which makes available funds from non-REA sources available to finance large-scale electric and telephone projects.

Job Descriptions

ELECTRICAL ENGINEER: Plans and designs systems for electric distribution and generation. Prepares construction standards, and conducts research into rural electric systems and needs.

ELECTRONIC ENGINEER: Provides technical assistance on construction and operation of rural telephone systems. Coordinates with private industry in the preparation of technical standards, construction practices, and equipment specifications.

FINANCIAL ANALYST: Coordinates and conducts studies of corporate financial and power supply arrangements of large utility systems. Reviews financial and managerial operations of electric and telephone systems.

LOAN SPECIALIST: Analyzes and evaluates credit risk factors and lending principles involved in loans that are granted, insured, or guaranteed by REA. Evaluates financial structures and practices of business organizations concerned with REA loans. Keeps abreast of pertinent statutory, regulatory, and administrative provisions.

Major Activities and Divisions

Electric Program: Assists rural electric utilities in obtaining financing for construction projects.

Telephone Program: REA makes loans to improve and extend telephone service in rural areas.

Alternative Employment Programs

REA offers a co-op program, hiring 1–10 students per year. Most co-ops work as computer specialists at the GS-4 level.

Remarks

Engineers enter into a six-month training program upon employment with REA. Although newly hired engineers are based in the Washington, DC headquarters, some travel with an REA field engineer is likely. Travel opportunities will exist throughout an engineer's term of employment at REA.

REA recruits on college and university campuses throughout the country.

Application Procedures

Direct inquiries to:

Director, Personnel Management Division
Rural Electrification Administration
U.S. Department of Agriculture
Washington, DC 20250-1500

(202) 382-1255

SOIL CONSERVATION SERVICE (SCS)

Nature of Work: Agriculture, environmental protection, forestry/wildlife, mining, recreation, regional development, waterways

Number of Employees: 15,892

Headquarters: Washington, DC

Regional Locations: There are over 3,000 field locations throughout the U.S.

Typical Majors of New Hires: Agriculture, agronomy, biological sciences (animal science, aquatic biology, plant science, wildlife biology), cartography, engineering, environmental sciences (natural resources management, range management), forestry, geology (hydrology), landscape architecture, recreation, soil science

Mission

The Soil Conservation Service has responsibility for developing and carrying out a national soil and water conservation program in cooperation with landowners and other land users. It assists in agricultural pollution control, environmental improvement, and rural community development.

Job Descriptions

ENGINEER: Job assignments for engineers vary, and may include work with water supply systems, concrete and earthen dams, and/or streambank erosion. SCS engineers can either specialize, or conduct work involving several fields. These include erosion control, water management, structural design, construction, hydraulics, soil mechanics, and environmental protection.

RANGE CONSERVATIONIST: Assists ranchers in managing their rangeland in an efficient and productive way, whether the land is used for supporting livestock, wildlife, or for recreational purposes. Helps plan grazing systems that increase production and prevent overgrazing. Suggests ways to control brush, and offers advice on water management and better ways to produce forage.

SOIL CONSERVATIONIST: Offers technical help and conservation planning to land users, such as family farmers, ranchers, land developers, and local government offices. Suggests ways to conserve the soil, build a farm pond, or cut down on water pollution. Assists teachers in starting outdoor laboratories for their students, and gives talks and slide programs to clubs and organizations.

SOIL SCIENTIST: Provides information on soils to farmers, commercial developers, and state and local planners. Maps and classifies soils, and identifies such problems as erosion and dampness. Writes soil descriptions, and identifies soil borders on aerial photographs. Spends time both in the field and in the office.

Major Activities and Divisions

Conservation Operations: SCS provides assistance to landowners and operators in carrying out soil and water conservation programs.

River Basin Surveys and Investigations: The Service, along with the Economic Research Service and Forest Service, studies the watersheds of rivers and other waterways.

Watershed Planning: The Service has responsibility for administering investigations and surveys of proposed small watershed projects in response to local requests.

Watershed and Flood Prevention Operations: SCS cooperates with local sponsors to reduce erosion, floodwater, and sediment damage.

Great Plains Conservation Program: SCS promotes conservation and agricultural stability in the Great Plains area.

Resource Conservation and Development Program: The Service assists in planning and developing land and water resources in multiple county areas.

Rural Abandoned Mine Program: The SCS assists land users in reclaiming abandoned or inadequately reclaimed coal-mined lands and water.

Alternative Employment Programs

The Soil Conservation Service maintains both a co-op program and a student trainee program for current college students, targeted to the college sophomore (GS-3) and junior (GS-4). Positions include Student Trainee level Soil Conservationists, Soil Scientists, Engineers, and Range Conservationists. A standard announcement (44S) reopens annually, and applications are typically accepted from September to December. SCS also hires volunteer and Stay-in-School students, but does not currently hire PMI's.

Remarks

Entry-level opportunities exist at headquarters, and in the many field locations.

Application Procedures

Direct inquiries to:

Special Examining Unit
Soil Conservation Service
P.O. Box 37636
Washington, DC 20013

(202) 447-5748
(202) 447-6365 (vacancies)

You may also contact the SCS offices in the localities in which you would like to work. SCS offices are listed in telephone directories under U.S. Government, Agriculture, Soil Conservation Service.

For information about jobs in Hawaii and the Pacific overseas areas, contact:

Office of Personnel Management
Honolulu Area Office
Prince Kuhio Federal Building Rm. 4316
300 Ala Moana Boulevard, P.O. Box 50028
Honolulu, Hawaii 96850
(808) 541-2603

AIR FORCE DEPARTMENT

Originally part of the Army, in 1947 the Air Force was organized as a separate department. Today, it is responsible for preserving the peace and security of the United States through air power.

The Air Force Systems Command and the Air Force Logistics Command generally have the largest need for entry-level employees, primarily those with scientific and technical backgrounds. Professional and administrative positions are generally filled through the Air Force Civilian Intern Program for Professional and Administrative Careers, which is a structured 2- or 3-year formal training program. Interns are given rotational assignments that give them a broad range of experiences within their particular specialty. Eligible interns with bachelor's degrees work for a year to get acclimated to the Air Force, and then go on to obtain a master's degree. The Air Force continues interns' salaries, and also pays for tuition and books.

AIR FORCE COMMUNICATIONS COMMAND—ENGINEERING INSTALLATION CENTER

Nature of Work: Aviation/space program, communications/media, defense/national security, military affairs
Number of Employees: 8,030
Headquarters: Tinker Air Force Base, OK
Regional Locations: Worldwide
Typical Majors of New Hires: Computer science, engineering

Mission

Provides base and point-to-point communications, flight facilities, air traffic control, and automated data processing services to the Air Force and other civil, national, and foreign government agencies.

Job Descriptions

CIVIL ENGINEER: Approves plans for construction projects such as antenna foundations, emergency electrical power and HVAC systems, and support facilities.

COMPUTER SCIENTIST: Designs local area networks, automated graphics systems, software, and other computer technologies.

ELECTRICAL ENGINEER: Provides technical expertise in such areas as electromagnetic compatibility for new and existing communication/electronics systems. Also conducts electromagnetic field analyses, spectrum surveys, and systems tests and acceptances.

ELECTRONICS ENGINEER: Designs intrusion detection systems, ground-to-air radio links, and display systems. Also develops UHF/VHF radio systems, antennas, transmitters, receivers, transceivers, multicouplers, encryption devices, HF radio systems, television and microwave systems.

SYSTEMS ENGINEER: Identifies a project's engineering requirements, develops master engineering schedules, and seeks solutions to funding shortages, priority shifts, and organizational and technological limitations.

Major Activities and Divisions

Standards Division: Manages the Communications Command's engineering installation standards program which consists of policies and procedures relating to all the systems the Command installs.

General Engineering Division: Provides advice on civil engineering matters and manages facility improvement plans.

Workload Support Division: Analyzes requests for technical assistance and specialized engineering services, and allocates engineering support.

Engineering Management Division: Oversees the work of the specific communications/electronics branches listed below.

The Communications Branch specializes in various global communications technologies including long haul HF radio systems, UHF and VHF radio links, and satellite terminals.

The Electronics Branch works on radar systems, communications, navigational aids, air traffic control, meteorology, intrusion detection, surveillance, and data display systems.

The Telephone Branch provides expertise in central office switching, satellite exchanges, audio and wideband cable distribution systems, and specialized intercom and telephone systems.

The Support Engineering Branch coordinates field tests and measurements support, and evaluates the hazards of electromagnetic radiation relating to personnel, fuel, and explosives.

The Systems Integration Branch manages large, complex projects requiring coordination between different engineering sections.

Alternative Employment Programs

The Engineering Installation Center maintains a summer employment program for students with more than 1 year of college, as well as a co-op program for engineering and computer science students.

Remarks

After 1 to 5 years of experience, employees may apply for overseas assignments which typically last 3 years.

Application Procedures

Direct inquiries to:

Recruitment Coordinator
Engineering Installation Center
Tinker Air Force Base, OK 73145-6343

(405) 339-3303

AIR FORCE LOGISTICS COMMAND—AIR LOGISTICS CENTERS

Nature of Work: Aviation/space program, military affairs, scientific research, weapons
Number of Employees: 72,954
Headquarters: Wright-Patterson Air Force Base, OH
Regional Locations: Hill Air Force Base, UT; Kelly Air Force Base, TX; McClellan Air Force Base, CA; Robins Air Force Base, GA; Tinker Air Force Base, OK
Typical Majors of New Hires: Chemistry, engineering

Mission

Provides worldwide logistical support to the Air Force ensuring that weapon systems are constantly ready. This is done by repairing and modifying missiles, engines, support equipment, and aircraft.

Job Descriptions

AEROSPACE ENGINEER: Designs airframes, powerplants, flight and environmental control systems.

CHEMIST: Synthesizes new industrial coatings to protect equipment in severe environments using gas chromatography, X-ray diffraction, and mass spectrometers.

CIVIL ENGINEER: Plans and designs roads, airfields, buildings, drainage systems, and water treatment plants.

ELECTRICAL ENGINEER: Designs, installs, and reconfigures generation and distribution systems, and oversees contractor work on such systems.

ELECTRONICS ENGINEER: Designs and services aircraft navigation and control systems, infra-red detection systems, radars, and laser bombing devices.

INDUSTRIAL ENGINEER: Recommends improved ways of integrating people, machines, materials, and computers. Designs repair facilities, hangars, and warehouses.

MATERIALS ENGINEER: Studies the behavior of materials under flight conditions and develops materials that resist fatigue and corrosion.

MECHANICAL ENGINEER: Oversees the development of heating and air conditioning systems, pneumatic and hydraulic systems for aircraft, and develops and modifies jet engines.

METALLURGIST: Develops special purpose alloys for aircraft, jet engines, missiles, and rocket nozzles.

Major Activities and Divisions

Each Air Logistics Center (ALC) repairs, modifies, and integrates specific weapons systems. For example, the Ogden ALC at Hill Air Force Base supports the F-16 and F-4 fighters, and the Minuteman III and Peacekeeper ballistic missiles. The Oklahoma City ALC maintains the B-1B bomber, C-135 transport/tanker, and engines used on various fighters. The Warner Robins ALC at Robins Air Force Base is responsible for the F-15 fighter, and C-141 and C-130 transport aircraft.

Alternative Employment Programs

Engineering majors may work as engineering technicians during the summer. Co-op positions are available to engineering students with 1 or more years of college.

Remarks

The ALCs are just one component of the Air Force Logistics Command but they hire the largest number of employees.

Application Procedures

Direct inquiries to the ALC where you would like to work.

Oklahoma City Air Logistics Center
2854 ABG/DPCSE(2)
Tinker Air Force Base, OK 73145

(405) 739-3807

Ogden Air Logistics Center
2849 ABS/DPCSE
Hill Air Force Base, UT 84056

(801) 777-3970

Sacramento Air Logistics Center
Chief Employment Unit/DPCSC
McClellan Air Force Base, CA 95652

(916) 643-2111

San Antonio Air Logistics Center
Kelly Air Force Base, TX 78241-5000

(512) 925-7396

Warner Robins Air Logistics Center
DPCSC(E)
Employment Office
Robins Air Force Base, GA 31098

(912) 926-5821
800-841-9193 (toll free)

AIR FORCE SYSTEMS COMMAND

Nature of Work: Aviation/space programs, military affairs, scientific research, weapons
Number of Employees: 28,769
Headquarters: Andrews AFB, MD
Regional Locations: Arnold AFB, TN; Bolling AFB, Washington, DC; Brooks, AFB, TX; Edwards AFB, CA; Eglin AFB, FL; Hanscom AFB, MA; Griffiss AFB, NY; Holloman AFB, NM; Kirtland AFB, NM; Los Angeles, CA; Norton AFB, CA; White Sands, NM; Wright-Patterson AFB, OH
Typical Majors of New Hires: Accounting, business, computer science, engineering, finance/banking, mathematics, meteorology, natural sciences, physical sciences

Mission

Advances aerospace technology through research, development, and testing of aircraft, missiles, satellites, weapons, and electronics.

Job Descriptions

AEROSPACE ENGINEER: Conducts aeronautical research involving fighters, bombers, transports, remotely piloted vehicles, missiles, and rockets.

BIOMEDICAL ENGINEER: Studies ergonomics, human systems, and biodynamics in order to improve such things as life-support systems, pressure suits, and flight suits.

CHEMICAL ENGINEER: Develops methods for handling, transporting, and disposing of toxic and hazardous chemicals.

CIVIL ENGINEER: Designs airfields, laboratories, buildings, housing, drainage systems, water treatment and distribution plants, and sewage treatment plants.

COMPUTER SCIENTIST: Develops language, logic, and instructions enabling computers to perform sophisticated aeronautical and meteorological research, as well as guide aircraft and rockets and conduct simulations.

CONTRACTING AND PROCUREMENT SPECIALIST: Negotiates and approves, and administers contracts.

ELECTRICAL ENGINEER: Designs, installs, and modifies electrical generating and distribution systems.

ELECTRONICS ENGINEER: Designs, tests, and integrates electronic systems and components including avionics, electronic warfare equipment, fire control systems, guidance and tracking systems, and communications and early-warning systems.

INDUSTRIAL ENGINEER: Uses systems engineering, human factors engineering, simulations, and mathematical modeling to develop standards and methods of management level activities.

MATERIALS ENGINEER: Tests and evaluates alloys for jet engines, aircraft structures, and rocket nozzles. Also develops new materials for preservation and packaging.

MATHEMATICIAN: Characterizes drag and lift coefficients and develops equations predicting the trajectories of aircraft and missiles.

MECHANICAL ENGINEER: Designs reciprocating, turbine, and rocket engines. Also develops aerodynamic structures and control mechanisms.

METEOROLOGIST: Makes local and global weather predictions and develops improved techniques for weather analysis and forecasting.

PHYSICIST: Studies aeronomy, radio and solar astronomy, geology, and gravity geodesy.

QUALITY ASSURANCE SPECIALIST: Monitors the work of defense contractors at their manufacturing plants ensuring they produce goods that meet accepted standards.

SAFETY ENGINEER: Identifies occupational hazards, assesses risks, and evaluates the adequacy of safety standards and compliance methods.

Major Activities and Divisions

Aeronautical Systems Division (Wright-Patterson AFB, OH): Manages the research, development, and acquisition of aircraft, missiles, engines, training systems, avionics, and electronic warfare systems.

Air Force Flight Test Center (Edwards AFB, CA): Conducts flight tests of new or modified aircraft and aerospace vehicles; operates the Air Force's Test Pilot School; and serves as the primary landing site for the space shuttle.

Arnold Engineering Development Center (Arnold AFB, TN): Performs aerodynamic tests of aircraft, missiles, and propulsion systems using wind-tunnels, jet and rocket engine test cells, and space environmental chambers.

Ballistic Systems Division (Norton AFB, CA): Oversees programs responsible for developing, modernizing, and integrating strategic missiles, launch facilities, and subcomponents.

Contract Management Division (Kirtland AFB, NM): Annually oversees tens of thousands of contracts worth over 100 billion dollars. This is accomplished through Plant Representative Offices located at the manufacturing plants of major Air Force contractors.

Electronic Systems Division (Hanscom AFB, MA): Directs the research, development, testing, acquisition, and integration of electronic systems such as command, control, communications, and intelligence equipment.

Foreign Technology Division (Wright-Patterson AFB, FL): Evaluates the aerospace systems of potential adversaries and develops intelligence data on their capabilities and deficiencies.

Human Systems Division (Brooks AFB, TX): Directs programs in such fields as aerospace research, human factors engineering, toxic hazards, aerospace medicine, and manpower and training programs.

Munitions Systems Division (Eglin AFB, FL): Directs the development, purchasing, testing, and integration of aerial weapon systems such as the Advanced Medium Range Air-to-Air Missile.

Office of Scientific Research (Bolling AFB, Washington, DC): Conducts research in the physical, geophysical, and life sciences as well as chemical, atmospheric, aerospace, electronic, material, mathematical, and information sciences.

Rome Air Development Center (Griffiss AFB, NY): Manages research and development programs involving electronic equipment such as solid state sciences, communications, electromagnetics, and electro-optical and radar surveillance technologies.

Space Systems Division (Los Angeles AFB, CA): Supervises the launch, tracking, and operation of communications, surveillance, early-warning, weather, and navigation satellites.

Wright Research and Development Center (Wright-Patterson AFB, OH): Conducts aeronautical research at 5 separate facilities. They are the 1) Aero Propulsion and Power Laboratory; 2) Avionics Laboratory; 3) Flight Dynamics Laboratory; 4) Materials Laboratory; and, 5) Electronic Technology Laboratory.

Alternative Employment Programs

The Systems Command maintains a co-op program for students enrolled in both master's and bachelor's degree programs. It also has a limited number of summer employment positions.

Remarks

The Systems Command has an Executive Development Program that trains employees at the GS-12 level to assume supervisory and managerial positions. It also offers opportunities for rotational assignments.

Application Procedures

Direct inquiries to:

Air Force Systems Command
Directorate of Civilian Personnel
HQ AFSC/MPKS
Andrews Air Force Base
Washington, DC 20334-5000
(301) 981-3793

ARMY DEPARTMENT

Established more than a year before the signing of the Declaration of Independence, the Army trains and equips active duty and reserve forces to maintain the security of the United States. Additionally, the Army conducts research in aerospace, weaponry, and medicine, and administers programs aimed at protecting the environment, improving waterway navigation, and reducing flooding.

ARMAMENT RESEARCH, DEVELOPMENT & ENGINEERING CENTER

Nature of Work: Military affairs, scientific research, weapons
Number of Employees: 6,050
Headquarters: Dover, NJ
Regional Locations: Aberdeen, MD; Watervliet, NY
Typical Majors of New Hires: Computer science, engineering, mathematics

Mission

Develops and improves nuclear and conventional weapons and ammunition through research, development, and testing.

Job Descriptions

CHEMICAL ENGINEER: Formulates energetic chemicals used in warheads and propulsion systems.

COMPUTER SCIENTIST: Develops graphics and computer-aided design systems for super- and mini-computer systems.

ELECTRONICS ENGINEER: Applies laser, radar, infrared, acoustic, and optics technology to surveillance, sensing, tracking and guidance systems.

MATERIALS ENGINEER: Produces new materials to enclose warheads, missiles, and artillery shells.

MATHEMATICIAN: Characterizes the flight characteristics and behavior of projectiles, and develops data to improve flight performance.

MECHANICAL ENGINEER: Conducts impact tests to predict and increase weapon system vulnerability and survivability.

METALLURGICAL ENGINEER: Fabricates special purpose alloys for armor, weapons, and warheads.

Major Activities and Divisions

Ballistic Research Laboratory (Aberdeen, MD): Studies communications, detection, tracking, surveillance, propulsion, guidance, and navigation.

Benet Weapons Laboratory (Watervliet, NY): Develops and improves upon large caliber weapons.

Fire Systems Laboratory (Dover, NJ): Develops small caliber arms and artillery as well as fire control systems.

Large Caliber Weapon Systems Laboratory (Dover, NJ): Designs artillery and shells for weapons larger than 40mm.

Alternative Employment Programs

Summer employment opportunities are available for students with 1 year of college or more. Co-op positions are available for engineering and computer science students.

Remarks

The Center maintains a "good neighbor" policy in the communities where its facilities are located through reciprocal fire protection agreements and involvement in community events.

Application Procedures

Direct inquiries to:

Armament Research, Development & Engineering Center
Professional Recruiter
Personnel Office
Building 151
Dover, NJ 07801-5001

(201) 724-2469

U.S. ARMY AUDIT AGENCY

Nature of Work: Accounting/auditing, military affairs
Number of Employees: 6,121
Headquarters: Alexandria, VA
Regional Locations: Atlanta, GA; Hanover, MD; Philadelphia, PA; San Antonio, TX; Sacramento, CA; St. Louis, MO; Frankfurt, Germany. These regional offices oversee operations at over 30 field offices.
Typical Majors of New Hires: Accounting

Mission

Evaluates the effectiveness and efficiency with which the Army's resources are controlled and managed.

Job Descriptions

AUDITOR: Examines financial and property records as well as research and development, procurement, logistics, readiness, training activities, and computer systems.

Major Activities and Divisions

All Army units are examined by the Army Audit Agency.

Alternative Employment Programs

Co-op positions are available depending on funding.

Remarks

After six months of employment, auditors attend a one-week training program at the Auditor Trainee School. This is followed up later in the auditor's career with training at the Intermediate Auditor and Senior Auditor Schools.

As each field office covers a large geographic area, auditors travel frequently. Assignments are available in Europe and the Far East after the first year of employment.

Application Procedures

Direct inquiries to:

U.S. Army Audit Agency
Attn: SAAG-PRM (PG)
3101 Park Center Drive
Alexandria, VA 22302-1596

(703) 756-2938

ARMY COMMUNICATIONS ELECTRONICS COMMAND (CECOM)

Nature of Work: Communications/media, military affairs, scientific research, weapons
Number of Employees: 8,175
Headquarters: Fort Monmouth, NJ
Regional Locations: Fort Belvoir, VA; Fort Huachuca, AZ; Fort Leavenworth, KS; Fort Sill, OK; Lakehurst, NJ; Warrenton, VA
Typical Majors of New Hires: Computer science, engineering

Mission

Oversees research, development, and testing of communications and electronics equipment for the Army.

Job Descriptions

COMPUTER SCIENTIST: Develops hardware and software for signals processing, fire support, and electronic warfare systems.

ELECTRONICS ENGINEER: Conducts research on electronic warfare systems; electro-optics; and command and control systems.

Major Activities and Divisions

Airborne Electronics Research Activity (Lakehurst, NJ): Oversees research in airborne sensors and communications.

Center for Night Vision & Electro-Optics (Fort Belvoir, VA): Performs research in such fields as infrared systems, image and signal processing, and lasers.

Center for Software Engineering (Fort Huachuca, AZ; Fort Leavenworth, KS; Fort Sill, OK): Develops software for communications, intelligence, electronic warfare, and fire support systems.

Signals Warfare Center (Warrenton, VA): Designs systems for signals intelligence and tactical electronic warfare.

Alternative Employment Programs

CECOM maintains a co-op program for computer science and engineering students. Summer employment opportunities are available for computer science and engineering students with one or more years of college.

Remarks

International assignments lasting 2 years are available to employees with 1 to 5 years of experience.

Application Procedures

Direct inquiries to:

Army Communications Electronics Command
Chief
Special Recruitment Section
Fort Monmouth, NJ 07703

(201) 532-5452

ARMY CORPS OF ENGINEERS

Nature of Work: Environmental protection, military affairs, waterways
Number of Employees: 42,101
Headquarters: Washington, DC
Regional Locations: Worldwide
Typical Majors of New Hires: Engineering

Mission

Provides military and civil engineering support for the Army and Air Force and protects and maintains the nation's navigable waters and wetlands.

Job Descriptions

CIVIL ENGINEER: Designs and builds military housing, dams, river channels, missile sites, space-launching facilities, pipelines, and air bases. Also involved with soil and water conservation, hydroelectric power, recreation, and related projects.

ELECTRICAL ENGINEER: Plans and supervises construction of major communications facilities.

ENVIRONMENTAL ENGINEER: Designs, operates, and maintains equipment and facilities used in reducing or preventing air, land, and water pollution.

MECHANICAL ENGINEER: Designs heating, ventilation and air conditioning systems, as well as energy production systems.

SAFETY ENGINEER: Develops and analyzes safety standards that reduce hazardous conditions at industrial and construction sites, recreational areas, and offices.

Major Activities and Divisions

Real Property Management: Acquires, operates, and ultimately re-sells real estate.

Investigation and Planning: Conducts engineering studies for flood control and protection, improved navigation systems, and other projects.

Engineering Design: Analyzes the operating requirements of various projects and designs facilities to meet those needs.

Recreation Management: Plans comprehensive water resource management programs that balance development requirements with environmental protection.

Alternative Employment Programs

The Army Corps of Engineers maintains a co-op and summer intern program.

Remarks

The Army Corps of Engineers is the world's largest construction organization and employs about 9,000 engineers.

Application Procedures

There are over 35 Army Corps of Engineers districts in the U.S., each of which hires applicants directly. Look in your local telephone directory under the "Government" section for the closest facility, or to obtain a complete listing, write to the Corps' headquarters:

Civilian Personnel Division
Army Corps of Engineers
Attn: CEPE-CS
Room 5105
Washington, DC 20314-1000

(202) 272-0720

ARMY LABORATORY COMMAND

Nature of Work: Military affairs, scientific research
Number of Employees: 4,122
Headquarters: Adelphi, MD
Regional Locations: Aberdeen, MD; Fort Monmouth, NJ; Natick, MA; Research Triangle Park, NC; Watertown, MA; White Sands, NM
Typical Majors of New Hires: Chemistry, computer science, engineering, mathematics, physics

Mission

Manages research and development in such diverse fields as atmospherics; command, control, and communications; electronics; and ballistics.

Job Descriptions

AEROSPACE ENGINEER: Studies ways of improving the aerodynamics of projectiles during launch and flight.

COMPUTER SCIENTIST: Develops hardware and software used for computer-aided design, simulations, and modeling.

ELECTRONICS ENGINEER: Investigates power sources such as batteries and electrolytes, and conducts research in such fields as microelectronics, microwave and signal processing devices, photo-electronics, solid state processes, and crystal oscillators and resonators.

MATHEMATICIAN: Develops equations used in ballistics research to determine, for example, the force and moment systems acting on a projectile.

MECHANICAL ENGINEER: Measures and predicts weapon system vulnerability and survivability by conducting and analyzing impact tests.

MATERIALS ENGINEER: Formulates new materials to protect soldiers and equipment from blast and heat damage associated with nuclear and conventional war.

PHYSICIST: Studies physical phenomena such as radiation, electromagnetic pulse, the electromagnetic spectrum, and atmospherics.

Major Activities and Divisions

Army Research Office (Research Triangle Park, NC): Manages Army research programs in such fields as electronics, chemical and biological sciences, physics, engineering, materials sciences, mathematical sciences, and geosciences.

Atmospheric Sciences Laboratory (White Sands, NM): Investigates atmospheric phenomena, and researches atmospheric technology and applications.

Ballistic Research Laboratory (Aberdeen, MD): Studies communications, detection, tracking, surveillance, propulsion, mobility, navigation, and energy conversion.

Communications Electronics (Fort Monmouth, NJ): Reduces the vulnerability of electronics, communications, and data links and studies the capabilities of foreign command, control, communications, and intelligence systems.

Electronic Technology and Devices Laboratory (Fort Monmouth, NJ): Performs research into electronic devices, power sources, microelectronics, and microwave and signal processing systems.

Harry Diamond Laboratories (Adelphi, MD): Operates three laboratories which study nuclear survivability and electromagnetic pulse; technology applications for electronic and mechanical systems; and target sensors and signal processing. A fourth lab provides technical support for environmental technology and simulation.

Human Engineering Laboratory (Aberdeen, MD): Incorporates into weapons systems and equipment human performance, behavior, anthropometric data, and biomedical factors.

Materials Technology Laboratory (Watertown, MA): Formulates new materials for ballistic missile defense and assesses the performance and reliability of emerging materials.

Vulnerability Assessment Laboratory (White Sands, NM): Evaluates the vulnerability of ground combat systems; air defense and space systems; command, control, communications, and intelligence systems; and electronic warfare devices.

Alternative Employment Programs

Summer intern and co-op programs are available for students enrolled in computer science, engineering, and physical science programs.

Remarks

The Laboratory Command is a major sub-unit of the Army's Materiel Command.

Application Procedures

Direct inquiries to the Command's headquarters, or, if applicable, the specific installation where you would like to work.

Army Laboratory Command
Personnel Management
Specialist
Attn: AMSLC-PE-SC
Adelphi, MD 20783-1145

(301) 394-3310

Army Laboratory Command
Electronic Technology and
Devices Laboratory
Civilian Personnel
Fort Monmouth, NJ 07703-5000

(201) 544-4205

Harry Diamond Laboratories
Personnel Staffing Specialist
SLCIS/CP/RP
2800 Powder Mill Road
Adelphi, MD

(301) 394-2816

ARMY MISSILE COMMAND

Nature of Work: Military affairs, scientific research, weapons
Number of Employees: 8,125
Headquarters: Redstone Arsenal, AL
Regional Locations: None
Typical Majors of New Hires: Engineering, physics

Mission

Designs and modifies the tactical missiles including surface-to-surface, antitank, and antiaircraft weapons.

Job Descriptions

AEROSPACE ENGINEER: Conducts research involving aerothermodynamics, aeroballistics, stability, stress vibration, aeroelasticity, and dynamic loading.

COMPUTER ENGINEER: Designs hardware and software used in missile guidance systems, modeling, and tests.

ELECTRONICS ENGINEER: Develops guidance, control, and sensing systems such as inertial systems, terminal homing devices, radar, and millimeter and microwave guidance systems.

MECHANICAL ENGINEER: Designs/tests missile propulsion and flight systems.

PHYSICIST: Conducts research into aerophysics; quantum physics; electromagnetic phenomena; and lasers and directed energy weapons.

Major Activities and Divisions

Flight and Fire Support Systems: Oversees research on such weapons systems as the Multiple Launch Rocket System, Hellfire air-to-surface missile, and TOW antitank weapon.

Air Defense Systems: Conducts research on antiaircraft missiles such as Stinger and Patriot.

Propulsion: Formulates more efficient and safer solid-fuel propellants.

Structures: Integrates warheads with rockets, and conducts research into composite materials.

Directed Energy Weapons: Investigates laser technology and unconventional beam technology for use as a weapon against armor and incoming missiles.

Systems Integration Office: Integrates air defense systems, close combat systems, and fire support systems.

Guidance and Control: Designs inertial systems, terminal homing systems, and other control equipment.

Advanced Sensors: Develops sensors for missile guidance systems.

Alternative Employment Programs

The Army Missile Command maintains a co-op and summer employment program for engineering and computer science students. Call (205) 876-8903 for more information. The agency also hires more than forty interns annually as scientists, engineers, analysts, contracting and procurement specialists, and administrators. Call (205) 876-8901 for information on internships. The Missle Command also participates in the Junior Fellowship Program.

Remarks

None.

Application Procedures

Direct inquiries to:

U.S. Army Missile Command
Chief, R&D Section
R&P Division
Civilian Personnel Office
Redstone Arsenal, AL 35898-5000

(205) 876-7572

ARMY TEST AND EVALUATION COMMAND (TEC)

Nature of Work: Military affairs, scientific research, weapons
Number of Employees: 8,450
Headquarters: Aberdeen, MD
Regional Locations: Dugway Proving Ground, UT; Fort Greely, AK; Fort Huachuca, AZ; Fort Rucker, AL; White Sands, NM; Yuma, AZ
Typical Majors of New Hires: Chemistry, engineering, mathematics, physics

Mission

Assesses most weapons and equipment used by soldiers, and determines which items should be included in the Army's inventory.

Job Descriptions

AEROSPACE ENGINEER: Studies and evaluates the flight characteristics of shaped charges and projectiles.

CHEMICAL ENGINEER: Develops items to protect soldiers from chemical warfare agents.

CHEMIST: Develops pollution control systems for chemical plants; prevents environmental contamination; and plans chemical analysis techniques.

ELECTRICAL/ELECTRONICS ENGINEER: Assesses the performance of electronic devices and their components. Specific projects include instrumentation, air defense systems, electrical weapons systems, and fire control systems.

MATHEMATICIAN: Applies computational research to the testing of ballistics and other combat systems.

MECHANICAL ENGINEER: Tests ordnance and equipment such as guns, ammunition, wheeled/tracked vehicles, earth-moving equipment, and generators.

PHYSICIST: Gathers data on the physics of armor penetration, fluid mechanics, molecular dynamics, gas flow permeability, and explosive blast effects.

Major Activities and Divisions

Army Cold Regions Test Center (Fort Greely, AK): Evaluates the performance of arms, ammunition, tanks, and combat and motor vehicles in extremely cold conditions.

Army Combat Systems Test Activity (Aberdeen, MD): Tests and evaluates artillery, automotive vehicles, electronics, general equipment, and infantry and aircraft weapons.

Army Tropic Test Site (Dugway Proving Ground, UT): Assesses the performance of Army vehicles, weapons, and support equipment in tropical conditions.

Army Aviation Development Test Activity (Fort Rucker, AL): Develops and tests combat support aircraft, attack helicopters, and weapons systems.

Army Electronic Proving Ground (Fort Huachuca, AZ): Develops and evaluates the performance of electronic instruments such as radar and navigation systems, and command, control, and communications equipment.

White Sands Missile Range (White Sands, NM): Assesses the Army's inventory of missiles and missile engines, and tests directed energy systems, foreign weapons, ground combat systems, and electronic warfare equipment.

Yuma Proving Ground (Yuma, AZ): Conducts tests of Army equipment and weapons under desert conditions.

Alternative Employment Programs

TEC maintains a summer employment program for students with more than 1 year of college, and a co-op program for engineering students.

Remarks

A security clearance may be required for certain TEC positions.

Application Procedures

Direct inquiries to:

Civilian Personnel Division
U.S. Army Test and Evaluation Command
AMSTE-PE-C
Room #312
Aberdeen Proving Ground, MD

(301) 278-4170

U.S. ARMY TRAINING AND DOCTRINE COMMAND (TRADOC)

Nature of Work: Education, military affairs
Number of Employees: 50,000
Headquarters: Fort Monroe, VA
Regional Locations: Nationwide
Typical Majors of New Hires: Accounting, business, computer science, education, engineering, international affairs, languages

Mission

Administers the Army school system, which trains Active Army and Army Reserve soldiers. There are 24 facilities in this school system, each responsible for a different specialty.

Job Descriptions

COMPUTER SPECIALIST: Provides automated data processing and programming services for TRADOC staff.

EDUCATION SERVICES OFFICER: Operates each installation's Army Education Center and is responsible for management, administration, counseling, and staff work.

EDUCATOR: Teaches the courses used to train Army personnel, develops curricula, and tests and evaluates students.

ENGINEER (ALL FIELDS): Designs and operates new equipment and processes. Engineers involved with construction provide engineering and management expertise for operating, maintaining, altering, and building plant facilities.

HOUSING MANAGEMENT SPECIALIST: Manages housing projects at TRADOC facilities, identifies housing requirements, monitors all contractual services, and facilitates repairs.

INFORMATION SECURITY SPECIALIST: Protects classified information, processes requests for disclosures of military information to foreign governments, and reviews accreditations of foreign visitors.

INTELLIGENCE ANALYST: Gathers intelligence data on foreign armies which is then incorporated into U.S. Army training doctrine.

MANPOWER MANAGEMENT SPECIALIST: Determines training needs at TRADOC installations by analyzing mission, workload, personnel, and equipment utilization.

MOTOR POOL MANAGER: Operates and maintains vehicles that support the local transportation needs of TRADOC facilities.

PERSONNEL SECURITY SPECIALIST: Administers programs that provide security clearances for TRADOC employees and contractors.

PHYSICAL SECURITY SPECIALIST: Inspects and evaluates security measures protecting TRADOC facilities and equipment, and determines security needs and recommends corrective measures.

PROCUREMENT OFFICER: Purchases all supplies, services, and construction necessary to operate TRADOC facilities.

SAFETY AND OCCUPATIONAL HEALTH MANAGER: Organizes and directs comprehensive loss prevention programs.

SAFETY SPECIALIST: Identifies hazards, assesses risks, and recommends solutions to workplace safety problems.

Major Activities and Divisions

TRADOC's work encompasses auditing, manpower and force management, housing, safety, supply, materiel maintenance, transportation, security, engineering, automated data processing, intelligence, procurement, public affairs, and training.

Alternative Employment Programs

TRADOC maintains co-op programs for many of its positions. Inquire with the civilian personnel office at the installation where you would like to work.

Remarks

Each TRADOC installation accepts employment applications directly. A complete list of facilities may be obtained from TRADOC headquarters at the address below.

Application Procedures

Direct inquiries to:

Civilian Intern and Student Program Coordinator
Army Training and Doctrine Command
Attn: ATPL-C
Fort Monroe, VA 23561-6000

(804) 727-3336

AVIATION SYSTEMS COMMAND (AVSCOM)

Nature of Work: Aviation/space programs, military affairs, scientific research, weapons
Number of Employees: 5,000
Headquarters: St. Louis, MO
Regional Locations: Edwards AFB, CA; Fort Monmouth, CA; Moffet Field, CA
Typical Majors of New Hires: Computer science, engineering, mathematics

Mission

Designs, tests, and improves combat, utility, and transport helicopters as well as avionics, armor, and propulsion systems. Determines the disposition of obsolete and excess aircraft.

Job Descriptions

MATERIAL MAINTENANCE MANAGER: Collects and analyzes information on equipment and advises those who design, test, produce, operate, repair, or dispose of such equipment.

PROFESSIONAL ENGINEER: AVSCOM's Engineering Career Intern program offers participants the option of selecting one of the following career fields to receive specialized technical/managerial training: Product/Production, Maintainability, Software, Quality and Reliability, Test and Evaluation, and Safety Engineering. Target positions include General Engineer, Safety Engineer, Electronics Engineer, Chemical Engineer, Electrical Engineer, and Industrial Engineer.

SUPPLY MANAGEMENT SPECIALIST: Manages inventory from initial planning, requirements analysis, through acquisition, distribution, and issuance.

TECHNICAL WRITER/EDITOR: Prepares papers, articles, or reports on technical matters using information obtained through interviews, research, and observing tests and experiments.

Major Activities and Divisions

Aviation Engineering Flight Activity (Edwards AFB, CA): Flight tests new and modified aircraft.

Aviation Research and Technology Activity (Moffett Field, CA): Conducts research on advanced flight systems, flight dynamics, structures, and propulsion.

Avionics Research and Development Activity (Fort Monmouth, NJ): Develops navigation, command, control, and communication systems for Army aircraft.

Alternative Employment Programs

AVSCOM maintains a co-op program for engineering and computer science students. Summer internships are available for students with one year of college or more.

Remarks

None.

Application Procedures

Direct inquiries to:

Aviation Systems Command
Department of the Army
Civilian Personnel Office
4300 Goodfellow Blvd.
St. Louis, MO 63120-1798

(314) 263-2093/2094

BELVOIR RESEARCH, DEVELOPMENT & ENGINEERING CENTER

Nature of Work: Military affairs, scientific research, weapons
Number of Employees: 850
Headquarters: Fort Belvoir, VA
Regional Locations: None
Typical Majors of New Hires: Chemistry, engineering, physics

Mission

Conducts research aimed at improving logistics, energy use, and the survivability of soldiers and weapon systems.

Job Descriptions

CHEMICAL ENGINEER: Investigates organic chemical coatings, fuels, and lubricants.

CHEMIST: Formulates coatings, lubricants, and fuels, and develops procedures used in transporting, storing, and disposal of chemical compounds.

ELECTRICAL ENGINEER: Develops surveillance, detection, security, and power generation systems.

MATERIALS SCIENTIST: Designs new materials and fabrication techniques for alloys, rubber, plastics, and ceramics.

MECHANICAL ENGINEER: Develops equipment to detect/neutralize mines and explosives and marine vessels for logistics, power generation, and assault.

PHYSICIST: Researches ways of protecting troops and equipment from radiation hazards and explosives.

Major Activities and Divisions

Belvoir's laboratories conduct research in such fields as combat engineering; marine and mechanical equipment; environmental control systems; and materials, fuels, and lubricants, and countermine systems.

Alternative Employment Programs

The Belvoir Research, Development & Engineering Center maintains summer internships which are available for students with one year of college or more.

Remarks

None.

Application Procedures

Direct inquiries to:

Belvoir Research, Development & Engineering Center
Scientist and Engineer Recruitment
Attn: STRBE-IL
Fort Belvoir, VA 22060-5606

(703) 664-1068

MEDICAL RESEARCH AND DEVELOPMENT COMMAND (MRDC)

Nature of Work: Health/health care, military affairs, scientific research
Number of Employees: 6,200
Headquarters: Fort Detrick, MD
Regional Locations: Aberdeen, MD; Fort Rucker, AL; Fort Sam Houston, TX; Natick, MA; San Francisco, CA; Washington, DC
Typical Majors of New Hires: Medical sciences, health sciences

Mission

Conducts research in infectious diseases, trauma, aeromedicine, and surgery.

Job Descriptions

BIOCHEMIST: Analyzes the chemicals and chemical processes occuring within organisms.

PATHOLOGIST: Studies and diagnoses the changes in diseased tissues.

PHARMACOLOGIST: Investigates the properties of drugs with respect to their ability to fight diseases.

PHYSICIAN: Conducts medical research in a wide variety of clinical fields.

VIROLOGIST: Studies the causes and prevention of diseases caused by viruses.

VETERINARIAN: Supervises biomedical research involving animals.

Major Activities and Divisions

Aeromedical Research Laboratory (Fort Rucker, AL): Studies the effects of altitude on aircrews.

Biomedical Research and Development Laboratory (Fort Detrick, MD): Performs basic and applied research in a variety of biomedical fields.

Institute of Dental Research (Washington, DC): Conducts pathological, physiological, chemical, and surgical research as they apply to dentistry.

Institute of Environmental Medicine (Natick, MA): Studies ergonomics, exercise physiology, nutrition, and the effects of altitude, heat, and cold.

Institute of Surgical Research (Fort Sam Houston, TX): Develops techniques aimed at improving surgical procedures and support services.

Letterman Army Institute of Research: Examines ocular hazards, military trauma, and blood.

Medical Research Institute of Chemical Defense (Aberdeen, MD): Develops and evaluates methods for the prevention, resuscitation, and treatment of chemical warfare injuries.

Medical Research Institute of Infectious Diseases (Fort Detrick, MD): Oversees research programs in disease assessment, pathology, pathophysiology, and virology.

Walter Reed Army Institute of Research (Washington, DC): Researches communicable diseases and immunology, biochemistry, experimental therapeutics, pathology, biometrics, neuropsychiatry, and veterinary medicine.

Alternative Employment Programs

Each installation maintains co-op and/or intern programs depending on the availability of funding.

Remarks

None.

Application Procedures

Direct inquiries to:

Department of the Army
Medical Research and Development Command
Civilian Personnel Officer
Fort Detrick, MD 21701

(301) 663-7613

MILITARY TRAFFIC MANAGEMENT COMMAND

Nature of Work: Military affairs, transportation
Number of Employees: 2,686
Headquarters: Falls Church, VA
Regional Locations: Worldwide
Typical Majors of New Hires: Business, engineering

Mission

Transports freight, personal property, and passengers for the military.

Job Descriptions

TRAFFIC MANAGEMENT SPECIALIST: Plans transportation systems consisting of distribution patterns, site locations, and special handling equipment. Also arranges the shipment, handling, and receiving of military equipment and household goods.

TRANSPORTATION SPECIALIST: Moves military personnel and supplies throughout the world. This is accomplished by scheduling transportation services, negotiating rates, and working with a variety of legal matters.

Major Activities and Divisions

The Military Traffic Management Command oversees the transport of supplies and household goods between industrial plants, depots, installations, and ocean and air terminals throughout the world.

Alternative Employment Programs

The Command maintains a limited co-op program for students depending on the availability of funding.

Remarks

None.

Application Procedures

Direct inquiries to the office closest to you:

Career Program Administrator
Military Traffic Management Command
Attn: MTPE-C
5611 Columbia Pike
Falls Church, VA 22041-5050

(703) 756-1797

Commander
MTMC Western Area
Attn: MTWA-PEC
Oakland Army Base
Oakland, CA 94626-5000

(415) 466-2132/33

Commander
MTMC Eastern Area
Attn: MTEA-PEC
Bayonne, NJ 07002-5302

(201) 823-6605

Commander
MTMC-Military Ocean Terminal, Sunny Point
Attn: MTEA-SU-CPO
Southport, NC 28461-5000

(919) 457-8342

NATICK RESEARCH, DEVELOPMENT AND ENGINEERING CENTER

Nature of Work: Food/nutrition, military affairs, scientific research
Number of Employees: 980
Headquarters: Natick, MA
Regional Locations: None
Typical Majors of New Hires: Chemistry, engineering, food science, health sciences, microbiology, operations, research, textile science

Mission

Determines how heat, cold, altitude, and fatigue affect troops, and develops rations, clothing, footwear, containers, airdrop equipment, tents, and other products to counter these effects.

Job Descriptions

CHEMIST: Synthesizes new compounds used in fabrics, footwear, and food to make them last longer in extreme conditions.

BIOLOGIST: Conducts research in such fields as bacteriology for developing and preserving rations.

FOOD TECHNOLOGIST: Develops military rations, tests new products, and examines foods for signs of toxicity, decomposition, and contamination.

PACKAGING SPECIALIST: Plans and develops packages used in protecting supplies, materials, and equipment between the time of purchase and use.

PHYSIOLOGIST: Studies the effects of heat, cold, high altitude, pressure, and climate on humans.

PSYCHOLOGIST: Examines the psychological dimensions of perception, fatigue, and learning, as well as the design of man-machine systems.

TEXTILE TECHNOLOGIST: Develops and modifies fabrics used in uniforms, tents, and other types of equipment. Explores the use of fibers for such products as parkas, flack vests, and fabrics that do not rot in the tropics.

Major Activities and Divisions

Advanced Systems Concept Directorate: Conducts long-range planning and determines soldiers' requirements.

Aero-Mechanical Engineering Directorate: Plans methods of airdropping supplies, personnel, and equipment in support of airborne assaults, special operations, and deep strikes.

Food Engineering Directorate: Develops new foods and packaging techniques that provide soldiers with nutritious meals.

Individual Protection Directorate: Designs life support systems, clothing, and materials used in protecting soldiers from climatic extremes.

Soldier Science Directorate: Conducts research in the behavioral and biological sciences to identify ways of making soldiers more effective.

Alternative Employment Programs

The Natick Research, Development & Engineering Center maintains a co-op program for students in engineering, physical science, computer science, and other disciplines. Summer internships are available for students with one year of college or more.

Remarks

Natick Research, Development & Engineering Center is a sub-unit of the Army's Materiel Command.

Application Procedures

Direct inquiries to:

U.S. Army Natick Research and Development Command
Attn: STRNC-BCR
Natick, MA 01760-5013

(508) 651-4371

TANK-AUTOMOTIVE COMMAND

Nature of Work: Military affairs, scientific research, transportation, weapons
Number of Employees: 6,050
Headquarters: Warren, MI
Regional Locations: None
Typical Majors of New Hires: Engineering

Mission

Designs, tests, and improves tanks and other armored vehicles, as well as transportation and construction equipment.

Job Descriptions

ELECTRONICS ENGINEER: Develops instruments such as sensors, communications systems, and laser range finders.

MATERIALS SCIENTIST: Formulates new materials used in compounding armor to reduce its vulnerability.

MECHANICAL ENGINEER: Designs turbine and piston engines, drive systems, and other vehicular components.

Major Activities and Divisions

Specific programs include light, medium, and heavy tactical vehicles; the M-1 tank, the Bradley fighting vehicle, and force modernization.

Alternative Employment Programs

The Tank-Automotive Command has a co-op program for engineering and computer science students, and internships for engineering students.

Remarks

None.

Application Procedures

Direct inquiries to:

U.S. Army Tank-Automotive Command
Personnel Staffing Specialist
AMSTA-PFR
6305 East 11 Mile Road
Warren, MI 48397-5000

(313) 574-6340

COMMERCE DEPARTMENT

Organized in 1913, the Commerce Department's responsibilities have grown over time to facilitate the nation's leadership in international trade. Today, the Department gathers and analyzes social and economic statistics used by government and business leaders; sponsors scientific and technological research; grants patents and registers trademarks; studies the earth's physical environment; promotes domestic economic development; and supports the growth of minority businesses.

BUREAU OF THE CENSUS

Nature of Work: Statistics
Number of Employees: 14,662
Headquarters: Suitland, MD
Regional Locations: Boston, MA; Charlotte, NC; Chicago, IL; Dallas, TX; Denver, CO; Detroit, MI; Kansas City, KS; Los Angeles, CA; New York City, NY; Philadelphia, PA; Seattle, WA
Typical Majors of New Hires: Computer science, economics, mathematics, statistics

Mission

Collects, tabulates, and publishes statistical data about the people and economy of the United States. These data are used to apportion legislative districts and allocate federal funds. Census reports are also used by state and local governments, business, industry, and nonprofit organizations.

Job Descriptions

APPLICATIONS PROGRAMMER: Designs programs that edit, correct, tabulate, and match data. Works with other specialists in designing and testing systems and programs.

MATHEMATICAL STATISTICIAN: Uses sampling and quality control modeling to improve methodologies and equipment. Also conducts ongoing reviews of statistical validity.

STATISTICIAN: Designs questionnaires, analyzes data, and develops systems for capturing and processing data. Survey statisticians in the Bureau's field offices recruit and train interviewers and supervise the various surveys.

SYSTEMS ANALYST: Designs and validates major processing systems and seeks solutions to unique processing problems.

Major Activities and Divisions

The Census Bureau collects data on population, housing, agriculture, state and local governments, industry, foreign trade, and transportation.

Alternative Employment Programs

The Census Bureau maintains a co-op program for certain occupations. Inquire with the personnel office.

Remarks

Foreign assignments in the fields of demographic, economic, and data processing are available for employees with 3 to 5 years of experience. These 2-year rotations support positions in the Bureau's foreign assistance programs.

Application Procedures

Direct inquiries to:

U.S. Bureau of the Census
Personnel Division
Room 3254, Building 3
Washington, DC 20233

(301) 763-7470
(301) 763-5537 (vacancies)

BUREAU OF ECONOMIC ANALYSIS (BEA)

Nature of Work: Business, economic policy, statistics
Number of Employees: 400
Headquarters: Washington, DC
Regional Locations: None
Typical Majors of New Hires: Accounting, computer science, economics, statistics

Mission

Provides policymakers and business leaders with information on the U.S. economy by preparing and interpreting data on economic indicators such as the gross national product.

Job Descriptions

ACCOUNTANT: Maintains the nation's economic accounts such as the national income and product accounts, U.S. balance of payments, and related foreign investment accounts.

COMPUTER SCIENTIST: Provides programming and systems analysis support.

ECONOMIST: Creates econometric models of the U.S. economy, and develops systems of leading, coincident, and lagging economic indicators.

STATISTICIAN: Compiles and analyzes data on the nation's economic accounts such as domestic production, distribution, and consumption of goods and services.

Major Activities and Divisions

The Bureau compiles statistics on various accounts which allow analysts to assess the health of the U.S. economy.

Alternative Employment Programs

BEA maintains a co-op program for certain occupations depending on funding availability.

Remarks

None.

Application Procedures

Direct inquiries to:

Office of Personnel Operations
Bureau of Economic Analysis
14th Street and Constitution Avenue, N.W., #H1069
Washington, DC 20230

(202) 377-5138

ECONOMIC DEVELOPMENT ADMINISTRATION (EDA)

Nature of Work: Economic policy, employment
Number of Employees: 355
Headquarters: Washington, DC
Regional Locations: Atlanta, GA; Austin, TX; Chicago, IL; Denver, CO; Philadelphia, PA; Seattle, WA. These regional offices oversee 43 sublocations.
Typical Majors of New Hires: Business, engineering (civil), economics, finance/banking

Mission

Provides loans, grants, and technical assistance to states, cities, Indian reservations, and private firms in order to increase employment and stimulate economic growth.

Job Descriptions

CIVIL ENGINEER: Develops industrial parks, access roads, water and sewer lines, harbors, airports, and other public facilities necessary for industrial and commercial growth.

ECONOMIST: Studies the economic feasibility of resource development to establish jobs; assists in planning and implementing economic development programs; determines the impact of existing and alternative programs.

FINANCIAL MANAGEMENT SPECIALIST: Coordinates budget, accounting, and managerial financial reporting; evaluates program accomplishments.

Major Activities and Divisions

Office of Grant Programs: Provides grants for public works and other projects that increase employment and stimulate growth.

Office of Loan Programs: Furnishes credit and debt management services to clients and liquidates property.

Alternative Employment Programs

EDA maintains several co-op positions depending on availability of funding.

Remarks

None.

Application Procedures

Direct inquiries to:

Office of Personnel Operations
Economic Development Administration
14th Street and Constitution Avenue, N.W.
H1069
Washington, DC 20230

INTERNATIONAL TRADE ADMINISTRATION (ITA)

Nature of Work: International affairs, trade
Number of Employees: 2,146
Headquarters: Washington, DC
Regional Locations: 48 district offices nationwide
Typical Majors of New Hires: Economics, international trade/affairs, law

Mission

Strengthens the nation's international trade and investment position by formulating foreign policy, monitoring international agreements, and developing markets for U.S. products.

Job Descriptions

ATTORNEY: Monitors behavior of foreign companies ensuring compliance with international agreements such as antidumping restrictions and tariffs.

ECONOMIST: Compiles extensive commercial and economic information on specific countries and regions. Forecasts international economic trends and reports on trade information and foreign investment.

FOREIGN COMMERCIAL SERVICE OFFICER: Promotes U.S. exports, resolves trade and investment disputes, and organizes trade promotion programs and events.

Major Activities and Divisions

International Economic Policy: Analyzes and implements international economic policies.

Import Administration: Develops and executes policies and programs concerning the administration of antidumping and countervailing duty law. Supervises programs dealing with foreign trade zones, quotas, and other statutory import programs.

Trade Development: Provides advice on international trade and investment policies; oversees programs promoting U.S. participation in foreign markets; and manages federal participation in international expositions held in the U.S.

Alternative Employment Programs

ITA typically hires 20-39 co-ops annually at the GS-4, 5, and 7 levels to work as International Trade Specialists. PMI and Stay-in-School positions are also available. Call (202) 377-3301 for more information.

Remarks

Foreign Commercial Service Officers, as members of the Foreign Service, must pass the Foreign Service Exam which consists of a written test and oral examination.

Application Procedures

For all occupations except Foreign Commercial Service Officer, direct inquiries to:

Personnel Officer
International Trade Administration
14th Street and Constitution Avenue, N.W.
H4211
Washington, DC 20230

(202) 377-3301

MINORITY BUSINESS DEVELOPMENT ADMINISTRATION (MBDA)

Nature of Work: Business, minorities/women
Number of Employees: 199
Headquarters: Washington, DC
Regional Locations: Atlanta, GA; Chicago, IL; Dallas, TX; New York, NY; San Francisco, CA; Washington, DC. There are also four district offices located in Boston, MA; Los Angeles, CA; Miami, FL; and Philadelphia, PA.
Typical Majors of New Hires: Business, economics, finance/banking, marketing, public administration

Mission

Strengthens the capabilities of minority businesses by providing technical and management expertise.

Job Descriptions

ECONOMIST: Participates in economic, fiscal, and budgetary planning, forecasting, and analysis.

FINANCIAL MANAGEMENT SPECIALIST: Examines the financial statements of minority-owned businesses and recommends ways of improving cash flow.

PROGRAM ANALYST: Determines whether a program is fulfilling its intended mission, and recommends improvements.

Major Activities and Divisions

Management and technical assistance is provided on request to minority firms through a network of business development centers funded by MBDA. The agency also helps funnel resources and business toward minority firms.

Alternative Employment Programs

MBDA maintains several co-op positions depending on availability of funding.

Remarks

None.

Application Procedures

Direct inquiries to:

Office of Personnel Operations
Minority Business Development Agency
14th Street and Constitution Avenue, N.W., H1069
Washington, DC 20230

(202) 377-5138

NATIONAL INSTITUTE OF STANDARDS AND TECHNOLOGY (NIST)

Nature of Work: Scientific research
Number of Employees: 3,223
Headquarters: Gaithersburg, MD
Regional Locations: Boulder, CO; Fort Collins, CO; Kauai, HI
Typical Majors of New Hires: Chemistry, computer science, engineering, mathematics, physical sciences

Mission

Provides basic physical measurement standards for science, industry, and government, and performs research that increases U.S. industrial productivity.

Job Descriptions

CHEMIST: Investigates the composition, structure, and properties of different materials.

COMPUTER SCIENTIST: Helps federal agencies solve specific computer application problems and develops standards for protecting sensitive information processed, stored, and transmitted by computer.

ELECTRICAL ENGINEER: Studies the applications of electrical energy, develops standards for electrical equipment, and devises or modifies electrical devices, materials, and procedures.

MATERIALS SCIENTIST: Characterizes the structure and properties of metals, polymers, ceramics, composites, and glasses, and assesses their performance under service conditions.

MECHANICAL ENGINEER: Evaluates the durability, quality, and strength of materials and products.

PHYSICIST: Develops accurate and uniform physical standards and measurement methods through research in fields such as atomic and molecular physics, radiation research, chemical kinetics, and thermodynamics.

Major Activities and Divisions

National Engineering Laboratory: Conducts research in statistical, computational, and mathematical modeling; electromagnetics, electronics, and semiconductors; metrology and engineering standards for computer-aided design, manufacture, and inspection; fire prevention and control; and the thermophysical properties of fluids and solids.

National Measurement Laboratory: Develops accurate and uniform physical and chemical standards, measurement methods, and reference data. Research areas include atomic and molecular physics, process and quality control, biotechnology, chemical kinetics, and thermodynamics.

Institute for Materials Science and Engineering: Develops standards, measurement methods, and data on metals, polymers, ceramics, composites, and glasses allowing their safe and efficient use under service conditions.

Institute for Computer Sciences and Technology: Works with federal agencies in developing standards for information processing and telecommunications systems.

Alternative Employment Programs

NIST maintains a co-op and summer employment program for all of its technical occupations.

Remarks

NIST has its own pay system that enables employees to receive higher salaries.

Application Procedures

Direct inquiries to the personnel office where you would like to work.

Personnel Officer
Administration Building, Room A-123
National Institute of Standards and Technology
Gaithersburg, MD 20899
(301) 975-3008
(703) 538-3344 (vacancies)

Personnel Officer
Mountain Administrative Support Center
U.S. Department of Commerce
325 Broadway
Boulder, CO 80303
(303) 497-6305

NATIONAL OCEANIC AND ATMOSPHERIC ADMINISTRATION (NOAA)

Nature of Work: Environmental protection, scientific research, waterways
Number of Employees: 12,000
Headquarters: Washington, DC
Regional Locations: Rockville, Silver Spring, and Suitland, MD; and nearly 20 locations nationwide
Typical Majors of New Hires: Biology, biological sciences, cartography, chemistry, computer science, earth sciences, mathematics, meteorology, oceanography, physics

Mission

Gathers scientific data on the oceans, atmosphere, space and sun which is then used to forecast the weather, manage ocean resources, produce nautical and aeronautical charts, and safeguard marine and estuarine sanctuaries.

Job Descriptions

CARTOGRAPHER: Constructs aeronautical and nautical charts. Also produces maps of earthquake zones, bathymetric charts, and other cartographic products.

COMPUTER SCIENTIST: Analyzes, archives, and disseminates environmental data.

ENGINEER: General, electrical, electronic, and mechanical engineers develop, test, and maintain instruments and equipment used in NOAA research.

FISHERY BIOLOGIST: Studies the problems of growth and reproduction of fish and shellfish.

HYDROLOGIST: Analyzes river flow, studies and forecasts floods, and issues flood warnings.

METEOROLOGIST: Analyzes weather data and prepares forecasts for the public, mariners, aviators, and farmers.

OCEANOGRAPHER: Studies the chemical composition of the water, as well as the contours, structure, and composition of the ocean floor.

Major Activities and Divisions

National Weather Service: Collects weather observations from surface and upper air stations, radars, ocean buoys, ships, satellites, and volunteers, and incorporates this information into atmospheric models.

National Ocean Service: Surveys and charts the nation's navigable coastal waterways, and maintains the National Geodetic Reference System which provides a precise geographic framework for all mapping and charting. Monitors the environmental health of the nation's coastline, and oversees a system of marine sanctuaries and estuarine research reserves.

National Environmental Satellite, Data, and Information Service: Operates the nation's earth observation satellites and global data centers that collect information on meteorology, land sciences, oceanography, solid-earth geophysics, and solar-terrestrial sciences.

Marine Fisheries Service: Manages coastal fishing, protects marine mammals and endangered species, and gathers information on the safety, quality, and nutritional value of seafood. Also maintains a nationwide system of fishery laboratories that performs diverse tasks such as resource assessment, experimental biology, pathobiology, fishery engineering, conservation engineering, and aquaculture research.

Office of Oceanic and Atmospheric Research: Performs environmental research at numerous laboratories, and supports university research examining national and global problems of the oceans and atmosphere.

NOAA *Corps:* Operates NOAA's fleet of research and survey ships and flies its aircraft.

Alternative Employment Programs

NOAA maintains a co-op and summer employment program for engineering and computer science positions.

Remarks

None.

Application Procedures

Direct inquiries to:

Personnel Division
National Oceanic and Atmospheric Administration
6010 Executive Boulevard
WSC #5 Room 706
Washington, DC 20852

(301) 427-2520

NATIONAL TECHNICAL INFORMATION SERVICE (NTIS)

Nature of Work: Communications/media, libraries
Number of Employees: 385
Headquarters: Springfield, VA
Regional Locations: None
Typical Majors of New Hires: Computer science, finance/banking, marketing
Entry-Level Job Titles: Technical Information Specialist

Mission

Catalogs and sells to the public U.S. government-sponsored research, development, and engineering reports, as well as foreign technical reports and other analyses produced by national and local government agencies.

Job Descriptions

TECHNICAL INFORMATION SPECIALIST: Analyzes the content of reports and prepares indices, bibliographies, and abstracts. Responds to requests for information from universities, industry, government agencies, and the general public.

Major Activities and Divisions

In addition to selling documents and microforms, NTIS summarizes current U.S. and foreign research reports in various publications. These include weekly newsletters, a biweekly journal, an annual index, and other formats. It also maintains an on-line bibliographic data base, and a microfiche service where continuing customers can automatically receive complete texts of documents relevant to their specific needs.

Alternative Employment Programs

Co-op opportunities may be available depending on funding. Contact the personnel office.

Remarks

NTIS is funded entirely by sales of its documents and microforms.

Application Procedures

Direct inquiries to:

Office of Personnel
National Technical Information Service
5285 Port Royal Road
Springfield, VA 22161

(703) 487-4680

NATIONAL TELECOMMUNICATIONS AND INFORMATION ADMINISTRATION (NTIA)

Nature of Work: Communications/media
Number of Employees: 295
Headquarters: Washington, DC
Regional Locations: Annapolis, MD; Boulder, CO
Typical Majors of New Hires: Communications, computer science, engineering (electronic), public administration

Mission

Develops policies designed to expand the telecommunications, information, and related industries and promotes the efficient use of telecommunications and information services.

Job Descriptions

ELECTRONICS ENGINEER: Offers technical assistance to minority groups involved in the telecommunications industry and studies ways of improving telephone systems and radio signal transmissions.

POLICY ANALYST: Studies and recommends specific policies promoting growth in the telecommunications industry. Also provides policy guidance for the federal government's use of the electromagnetic spectrum.

Major Activities and Divisions

NTIA encourages deregulation of the domestic telephone, radio and television industries, and acts to minimize U.S. and foreign government involvement in international telecommunications markets.

Alternative Employment Programs

NTIA maintains a co-op program depending on the availability of funding.

Remarks

None.

Application Procedures

Direct inquiries to the Personnel Officer in the location where you would like to work.

Office of Personnel Operations
National Telecommunications and
Information Administration
Washington, DC 20230

(202) 377-5138

Personnel Officer
Mountain Administrative Support
Center
Department of Commerce
325 Broadway
Boulder, CO 80303

(303) 497-6305

PATENT AND TRADEMARK OFFICE (PTO)

Nature of Work: Business, law/justice
Number of Employees: 4,070
Headquarters: Crystal City, VA
Regional Locations: None
Typical Majors of New Hires: Biology, biological sciences, chemistry, engineering, law, physics

Mission

Protects U.S. inventions, products, and corporate logos by issuing patents and trademarks, publishing patent and trademark information, maintaining public search files of domestic and foreign patents and trademarks, and providing copies of patents and trademarks to the public.

Job Descriptions

PATENT EXAMINER: Determines the patentability of an invention or discovery by assessing whether it will perform as claimed and whether any previous inventions exist that may be comparable to it.

Major Activities and Divisions

Examiners with backgrounds in biology, chemistry, microbiology, and related sciences judge the patentability of inventions relating to chemical or biotechnological products and processes.

Examiners with a physics background normally assess the patentability of inventions in such fields as semiconductor physics, radiant energy, atomic and nuclear physics, optics and lasers.

Examiners with engineering backgrounds judge the patentability of inventions in fields as diverse as photography, data processing, optics, aeronautics, surgery, heat generation, metallurgy, plastics, medicine, and phase separation.

Alternative Employment Programs

Co-op and internships may be available—inquire to the College Relations Manager.

Remarks

New employees receive four phases of training at the Patent Academy, which covers patent-examining practice and procedures, and the legal concepts required for these activities.

Application Procedures

Direct inquiries to:

Office of Personnel
Patent and Trademark Office
CPK-1, Suite 700
Washington, DC 20231

(703) 557-1244
1-800-368-3064 (for patent examiner job opportunities)
1-800-327-2909 (for attorney positions)
(703) 538-3360 (for job vacancy information)

U.S. AND FOREIGN COMMERCIAL SERVICE (US&FCS)

Nature of Work: Business, import/export, international affairs, marketing
Number of Employees: 1,300
Headquarters: Washington, DC
Regional Locations: 70 U.S cities, and 125 overseas posts in 68 countries
Typical Majors of New Hires: Business, international affairs, marketing

Mission

Facilitates U.S. exports by identifying agents and distributors for U.S. and foreign companies. Locates sources of financing for businesses, and conducts market research for U.S. firms.

Job Descriptions

FOREIGN SERVICE OFFICER (FSO): Introduces U.S. exporters to foreign businesses interested in representing their products. Assists in the resolution of trade and investment disputes, and organizes trade promotion programs.

Major Activities and Divisions

Commerce Department Foreign Service Officers (FSOs) work with State Department FSOs in the economic and political sections of U.S. embassies.

Alternative Employment Programs

None.

Remarks

Candidates must be available for worldwide assignment. All FSO candidates receive several weeks of orientation at the State Department's Foreign Service Institute in Washington, D.C.

US&FCS is particularly interested in candidates with knowledge of Arabic, Chinese, Japanese, or Russian.

Application Procedures

Direct inquiries to:

U.S. and Foreign Commercial Service
14th Street and Constitution Avenue, N.W.
H3813
Washington, DC 20044-0688

(202) 377-3133

Refer to the section on the Foreign Service for more information on application procedures.

U.S. TRAVEL AND TOURISM ADMINISTRATION (USTTA)

Nature of Work: Marketing, statistics
Number of Employees: 82
Headquarters: Washington, DC
Regional Locations: Amsterdam, Holland; Frankfurt, Germany; London, England; Mexico City, Mexico; Milan, Italy; Paris, France; Sydney, Australia; Tokyo, Japan; Toronto, Canada. An office servicing South American markets is located in Miami, FL.
Typical Majors of New Hires: Business, marketing, statistics

Mission

Advises the Secretary of Commerce on national tourism policy and encourages foreign travelers to visit the U.S. by conducting various educational and marketing programs.

Job Descriptions

MARKET ANALYST: Encourages overseas travel agents to select and market U.S. destinations to their clients. USTTA also assists international associations in selecting U.S. locations for future conferences.

STATISTICIAN: Collects and interprets travel and tourism data such as arrivals and departures. This information is used by national, state, and local governments to improve tourism in their particular jurisdictions.

Major Activities and Divisions

USTTA's goal is to use tourism for promoting the economic well-being of the U.S. and to ensure the compatibility of tourism and recreation with other national interests.

Alternative Employment Programs

None.

Remarks

None.

Application Procedures

Direct inquiries to:

Office of Personnel Operations
U.S. Travel and Tourism Administration
14th Street and Constitution Avenue, N.W.
H1069
Washington, DC 20230

(202) 377-5138

DEFENSE DEPARTMENT

With its headquarters in the Pentagon, the Defense Department is the largest federal agency, employing about a million civilian workers. They are located in all 50 states and around the world.

The largest units of the Defense Department are the Army, Navy, Air Force, and Marines which are organized as separate departments. The Defense Department also maintains a large number of support agencies.

DEFENSE COMMUNICATIONS AGENCY (DCA)

Nature of Work: Communications/media, defense/national security, military affairs
Number of Employees: 2,514
Headquarters: Arlington, VA
Regional Locations: Oahu, HI; Scott Air Force Base, IL; Reston, VA. Internationally, DCA has a major facility in Stuttgart, Germany, and smaller installations in Korea, Japan, Turkey, and the Philippines.
Typical Majors of New Hires: Computer science, engineering (electronic), mathematics, physics

Mission

Provides worldwide communications services to the military, State Department, and White House.

Job Descriptions

COMPUTER SCIENTIST: Designs software, networks, protocols, and information processing systems.

ELECTRONICS ENGINEER: Defines performance criteria and technical and procedural interface standards for command, control, communications, and information systems. Also develops joint architectures used in such systems.

MATHEMATICIAN: Develops theories and procedures for computerized damage assessment, modeling, and war gaming.

OPERATIONS RESEARCH ANALYST: Constructs mathematical models to develop cost-effective telecommunications systems. Methods include life-cycle costing and survivability analysis.

Major Activities and Divisions

DCA operates the Defense Communications System, a worldwide network for command, control, intelligence, weather, administration, logistics, and civil defense. DCA also plays a major role in developing and applying satellite communications for the Defense Department, the White House, NATO, and U.S. diplomats.

Alternative Employment Programs

DCA maintains a co-op and summer intern program for engineering and computer science students.

Remarks

A limited number of positions are available at DCA's offices in Germany and Hawaii for employees with 1 to 5 years of experience. Typical duty tours are 3 years.

Application Procedures

Direct inquiries to:

Special Programs Unit
Civilian Personnel Office
Defense Communications Agency
8th Street and South Courthouse Rd.
Building Two, Room 210
Arlington, VA 20305-2000

(703) 692-2783/84

DEFENSE CONTRACT AUDIT AGENCY (DCAA)

Nature of Work: Accounting/auditing, military affairs
Number of Employees: 7,078
Headquarters: Alexandria, VA
Regional Locations: Irving, TX; Los Angeles, CA; Marietta, GA; Philadelphia, PA; San Francisco, CA; Waltham, MA. These regional offices oversee operations at over 400 domestic and foreign audit sites.
Typical Majors of New Hires: Accounting

Mission

Audits Defense Department contractors, reviewing and reporting on costs incurred. It annually reviews over 10,000 businesses and issues about 60,000 audit reports.

Job Descriptions

AUDITOR: Evaluates management policies and decisions, financial records, and the internal controls of defense contractors.

Major Activities and Divisions

DCAA advises government procurement officials on analyzing and negotiating contractors' bids; renders opinions on contractors' financial capabilities; validates contractors' claimed costs; and engages in operational audits that assess the adequacy of internal control systems.

Alternative Employment Programs

Co-op positions may be available depending on funding. Contact the regional office where you would like to work.

Remarks

Entry-level auditors are trained at DCAA's Defense Contract Audit Institute in Memphis, TN. DCAA also encourages auditors to take the CPA exam, and helps them pass by sponsoring CPA review courses.

Application Procedures

Direct inquiries to the regional office where you would like to work.

Headquarters:
Nationwide Field Detachment
Defense Contract Audit Agency
Cameron Station, Attn: CAP,
Room 4A380
Alexandria, VA 22304-6178

(703) 274-7328
1-800-523-2986 (toll free)
1-800-223-0265 (toll free in Virginia)

Eastern Region:
Defense Contract Audit Agency
805 Walker Street
Suite 103
Marietta, GA 30060-2731

(404) 429-6533

Northeastern Region:
Defense Contract Audit Agency
424 Trapelo Road
Waltham, MA 02154-6397

(617) 647-8619

Central Region:
Defense Contract Audit Agency
5615 High Point Drive
Irving, TX 75038-2414

(214) 550-4871

Mid-Atlantic Region:
Defense Contract Audit Agency
Room 4400
600 Arch Street
Philadelphia, PA 19106-1604

(215) 597-7471

Western Region:
Defense Contract Audit Agency
450 Golden Gate Avenue
Box 36116
San Francisco, CA 94102-3563

(415) 556-4684

Southwestern Region:
Defense Contract Audit Agency
2500 Wilshire Boulevard
Suite 405
Los Angeles, CA 90057-4366

(213) 252-7659

DEFENSE INTELLIGENCE AGENCY (DIA)

Nature of Work: Defense/national security, intelligence, military affairs
Number of Employees: Classified
Headquarters: Washington, DC
Regional Locations: Worldwide
Typical Majors of New Hires: Computer science, economics, engineering, geography, international affairs, mathematics, political science

Mission

Gathers, analyzes, and disseminates intelligence information on the capabilities and intentions of foreign military forces.

Job Descriptions

INTELLIGENCE ANALYST: Interprets photographic, electronic, technical, and other types of information gathered from satellites, aerial reconnaissance, and ground observations, and develops data on foreign military forces.

Major Activities and Divisions

DIA furnishes military intelligence to the Secretary of Defense, the Joint Chiefs of Staff, and major components of the Defense Department. Intelligence is gathered through its own resources; through coordinating the intelligence units of other units of the Defense Department; or by cooperating with other intelligence agencies.

Alternative Employment Programs

DIA maintains a co-op program for engineering, computer science, and social science students.

Remarks

Because of intensive pre-employment screenings, interested candidates should apply to DIA at least six months prior to graduation.

Application Procedures

Direct inquiries to:

Civilian Staffing Operations Division
(RHR-2)
Recruitment Program
Department OP
Defense Intelligence Agency
Washington, DC 20340-3042

(202) 373-2628

DEFENSE INVESTIGATIVE SERVICE (DIS)

Nature of Work: Defense/national security, law enforcement
Number of Employees: 3,800
Headquarters: Washington, DC
Regional Locations: Alexandria, VA; Boston, MA; Cherry Hill, NJ; Chicago, IL; Irving, TX; Long Beach, CA; San Francisco, CA; Smyrna, GA; Field offices are located nationwide, as well as in Brussels, Belgium; Manheim, Germany; Seoul, South Korea; and Yokohama, Japan.
Typical Majors of New Hires: Criminal justice, liberal arts

Mission

Conducts background investigations of Defense Department employees and other federal workers requiring security clearances. Also oversees industrial security programs for Defense Department contractors.

Job Descriptions

INDUSTRIAL SECURITY SPECIALIST: Conducts security surveys and inspections of defense industrial contractor facilities possessing classified information/

material. Assists industrial contractors in developing security measures, and assesses facilities' vulnerability to terrorism and sabotage.

INVESTIGATOR: Confirms birth and citizenship; verifies education and employment claims; reviews local criminal justice and credit records; and interviews friends, neighbors, and relatives of federal personnel requiring security clearances.

Major Activities and Divisions

DIS is composed of eight regions, the personnel Investigations Center, and the Defense Industrial Security Clearance Office. Together they determine whether employees qualify for security clearances, and defense contractors comply with security regulations.

Alternative Employment Programs

DIS participates in a co-op program depending on the availability of funding.

Remarks

Occasional travel usually required for Investigators.

Application Procedures

Direct inquiries to:

Defense Investigative Service
Resources Directorate
Personnel Operations Division
Field Classification, Staffing, and Pay
Administrative Branch (V971)
1900 Half Street S.W.
Washington, DC 20324-1700

(202) 475-1084

DEFENSE LOGISTICS AGENCY (DLA)

Nature of Work: Inventory/supply, military affairs
Number of Employees: 52,718
Headquarters: Alexandria, VA
Regional Locations: Atlanta, GA; Boston, MA; Chicago, IL; Cleveland, OH; Dallas, TX; Los Angeles, CA; New York, NY; Philadelphia, PA; St. Louis, MO
Typical Majors of New Hires: Accounting, business, computer science, engineering

Mission

Purchases supplies and services for the military. This includes virtually all of its food, medicine, and clothing, as well as a large portion of its chemical, construction, electronics, and industrial supplies.

Job Descriptions

BUDGET ANALYST: Prepares, reviews, and justifies budget data, and makes recommendations to operating officials.

ENVIRONMENTAL PROTECTION SPECIALIST: Assists state and local governments develop and maintain adequate environmental protection programs.

INDUSTRIAL PROPERTY MANAGEMENT SPECIALIST: Approves contractors' property control systems and ensures they meet prescribed requirements.

INDUSTRIAL SPECIALIST: Assesses the ability of contractors to produce a particular item and monitors its production, ensuring that it meets technical specifications.

MANAGEMENT ANALYST: Advises management in such areas as policy development, work methods and procedures, manpower utilization, and organizational structure.

PROPERTY DISPOSAL SPECIALIST: Oversees the use, donation, merchandising, or disposal of excess or surplus property.

QUALITY ASSURANCE SPECIALIST: Ensures supplies comply with contractual performance standards.

SUPPLY MANAGEMENT SPECIALIST: Oversees the movement of freight and passengers from industrial plants and depots to installations, ocean/air terminals, and overseas locations.

Major Activities and Divisions

Defense Supply Centers: Six supply centers forecast demands, process recquisitions, award contracts, monitor inventory levels, and schedule production.

Defense Service Centers: Six service centers prepare item descriptions and conduct parts control, value engineering, and national stockpile management.

Defense Depots: Defense Depots store and care for assigned commodities.

Defense Contract: Each of the nine DCASRs furnish contract administration services such as quality control, data and financial management.

Alternative Employment Programs

The Defense Logistics Agency maintains a co-op and intern program for sophomores and juniors. About 20 of each are hired each year at the GS-3 and 4 levels, and work in a variety of occupations. PMI's are hired as well.

Remarks

None.

Application Procedures

Direct inquiries to:

Civilian Personnel Service Support Office
Defense Logistics Agency
DCPSO-S
P.O. Box 3990
Columbus, OH 43216-5000

1-800-458-7903 (toll free)

DEFENSE MAPPING AGENCY (DMA)

Nature of Work: Defense/national security, maritime activities, military affairs, scientific research
Number of Employees: 8,338
Headquarters: Washington, DC
Regional Locations: Fort Belvoir, VA; Fort Sam Houston, TX; McLean, VA; Reston, VA; St. Louis, MO. More than 50 sublocations worldwide.
Typical Majors of New Hires: Cartography, geography, geology

Mission

Provides mapping, charting, and geodetic products and services to the U.S. armed forces. DMA also produces nautical charts and marine navigational data for the merchant marine and private boaters.

Job Descriptions

AERONAUTICAL INFORMATION SPECIALIST: Gathers data necessary for producing precise aeronautical and space charts and flight information publications.

CARTOGRAPHER: Determines position, elevation, and shapes of geomorphic and topographic features and prepares charts for aerial navigation.

GEODESIST: Uses observations and measurements to determine the exact positions of points and areas on the earth's surface.

MARINE INFORMATION SPECIALIST: Conducts hydrographic surveys and determines the physical characteristics of bodies of water for navigation charts.

PHYSICAL SCIENTIST: Studies earth-related phenomena such as gravitational and magnetic fields used in navigation and map-making.

Major Activities and Divisions

Aerospace Center (St. Louis Air Force Station, MO): Provides mapping, charting, and geodesy services for aerospace missions.

Combat Support Center (Washington, DC): Distributes DMA products to military and civilian users.

Defense Mapping School (Fort Belvoir, VA): Trains members of the armed forces and other government employees in mapping, charting, and geodesy.

Hydrographic/Topographic Center (Washington, DC): Furnishes nautical and topographic products.

Telecommunications Services Center (Reston, VA): Operates DMA's telecommunications systems and maintains the long-haul equipment linking major production centers and field activities.

Reston Center (Reston, VA): Produces geodetic, mapping, and charting products.

Systems Center (McLean, VA): Enhances DMA's output using softcopy or computerized production techniques.

Alternative Employment Programs

DMA maintains a co-op program for students majoring in the physical sciences.

Remarks

DMA scientists work with the world's most advanced information processing equipment to handle digital, graphic, and textual data.

Application Procedures

Direct inquiries to the facility where you would like to work.

For jobs in the Washington, DC area:

Personnel Staffing Specialist
Defense Mapping Agency
Attn: PRSD
Washington, DC 20315-0030

(202) 653-0484
1-800-DMA-JOBS (toll free)

For jobs outside of Washington, DC:

Personnel Staffing Specialist
Aerospace Center
Attn: POR
Defense Mapping Agency
3200 South Second Street
Building 37
St. Louis, MO 63118

(314) 263-4460
1-800-777-6104 (toll free)

DEFENSE NUCLEAR AGENCY (DNA)

Nature of Work: Nuclear energy/issues, scientific research, weapons
Number of Employees: 840
Headquarters: Alexandria, VA
Regional Locations: Bethesda, MD; Kirtland Air Force Base, NM
Typical Majors of New Hires: Biology, chemistry, computer science, engineering, physics

Mission

Coordinates with the Department of Energy the development and testing of nuclear weapons; manages the U.S. nuclear stockpile; researches nuclear blast protection; and conducts safety inspections of theater nuclear forces.

Job Descriptions

BIOLOGIST: Investigates the biomedical effects of radiation from nuclear weapons.

COMPUTER SCIENTIST: Designs software used in computer simulations of nuclear blast effects.

MATERIALS SCIENTIST: Formulates new compounds for machines and structures to improve their ability to withstand nuclear blasts.

NUCLEAR ENGINEER: Develops safe methods for storing, transporting, and handling nuclear materials and weapons.

PHYSICIST: Participates in the development and testing of nuclear weapons and studies the effects of radiation.

STRUCTURAL ENGINEER: Conducts research into methods of hardening structures against nuclear radiation and blast.

Major Activities and Divisions

Armed Forces Radiobiology Research Institute (Bethesda, MD): Researches the biomedical effects of nuclear radiation on plants and animals and develops methods of protecting and treating them.

DNA *Field Command* (Kirtland Air Force Base, NM): Oversees field experiments including the construction of simulation facilities, and evaluating weapons tests.

Alternative Employment Programs

DNA maintains a summer employment program for biological science majors who have completed at least two years of college. DNA also has a co-op program for engineering and computer science students.

Remarks

DNA hires primarily those individuals with three to five years of experience.

Application Procedures

Direct inquiries to:

Defense Nuclear Agency
6801 Telegraph Road
Attn: MPCV (OPS)
Alexandria, VA 22310-3398

(202) 325-7095

NATIONAL SECURITY AGENCY (NSA)

Nature of Work: Defense/national security, intelligence, international affairs, scientific research
Number of Employees: 50,000
Headquarters: Fort Meade, MD
Regional Locations: Worldwide
Typical Majors of New Hires: Business, computer science, engineering, languages, mathematics, physical sciences

Mission

Intercepts and analyzes foreign telecommunications to protect U.S. national security. NSA also protects U.S. communications and computers from eavesdropping by foreign countries.

Job Descriptions

COMPUTER SCIENTIST: Supports NSA's data collection and analysis functions by designing database management, real-time programming, distributed processing, and other systems.

ELECTRICAL ENGINEER: Designs equipment used in collecting and analyzing foreign communications. Equipment may include antennas, computers, and devices that recognize telemetric patterns.

INTELLIGENCE ANALYST: Summarizes and interprets raw data and reports on the capabilities and intentions of foreign governments and military forces.

LINGUIST: Translates material into English, develops glossaries and handbooks, and participates in the development of computer-aided voice translation systems.

MATHEMATICIAN: Applies probability theory, statistics, algebra, matrix theory, stochastic processes, and other concepts to cryptography.

Major Activities and Divisions

Office of Signals Intelligence Operations: Intercepts, deciphers, and analyzes foreign telephone, telex, cable, radar, telemetry, and diplomatic traffic.

Office of Communications Security: Encrypts classified communications such as command and control, voice, data, teletype, and telemetry.

Office of Research and Engineering: Designs hardware such as ultrasensitive antennas and high-density magnetic tapes used in collecting intelligence data.

Office of Telecommunications and Computer Services: Designs and operates the computers that encrypt and decipher codes.

Alternative Employment Programs

NSA maintains a co-op and summer employment program for computer, electronics, and electrical engineering majors, as well as those students majoring in Slavic, Middle Eastern, and Asian languages. For more information, students should contact NSA Summer Employment Coordinator at the address below.

Remarks

Because of intensive pre-employment screenings, interested candidates should apply to NSA at least four months prior to graduation. New employees are trained at the National Cryptologic School, which is located at NSA's headquarters. The school offers technical, linguistic, and managerial courses.

Application Procedures

Direct inquiries to:

Office of Civilian Personnel
Recruitment Branch
National Security Agency
Attention: M322
Fort Meade, MD 20755-6000

(301) 859-6444
1-800-255-8415 (toll free)

THE DEPARTMENT OF EDUCATION

The Department of Education was established in 1979 to establish policy for, administer, and coordinate federal assistance to education. Its goal is to provide programs, services, and financial assistance to various forms of education, including vocational and technical education, special education, elementary and secondary education, and postsecondary education. The Department also administers federal financial assistance programs for students, such as the Basic Educational Opportunity Grants and the Guaranteed Student Loan Program.

Federal funds also partially support four educational institutions: the American Printing House for the Blind, Gallaudet University, Howard University, and the National Technical Institute for the Deaf.

DEPARTMENT OF EDUCATION

Nature of Work: Education, funds/funding
Number of Employees: 4,695
Headquarters: Washington, DC
Regional Locations: Atlanta, GA; Boston, MA; Chicago, IL; Dallas, TX; Denver, CO; Kansas City, KS; New York, NY; Philadelphia, PA; San Francisco, CA; Seattle, WA
Typical Majors of New Hires: Accounting, economics, education, law, public administration

Mission

The Department of Education establishes policy for, administers, monitors, and coordinates most federal assistance to education.

Job Descriptions

EDUCATION PROGRAM SPECIALIST: Maintains a working knowledge of the legislation and regulations relating to assigned educational programs. Provides technical assistance to state, local and other officials whose organizations are eligible for federal funds. Evaluates effectiveness of programs through review of technical and progress reports, on-site reviews, audit reports, and educational surveys. Makes recommendations for improvements in program policy and operations.

GRANT SPECIALIST: Develops plans, goals, and objectives for the accomplishment of assigned grants programs and activities. Conducts evaluations and identifies problems related to assigned programs. Exercises signatory authority to enter into or modify grants and cooperative agreements on behalf of the government.

INSTITUTIONAL REVIEW SPECIALIST: Conducts program reviews of post-secondary education institutions to determine whether institutions are complying with regulations and to provide assistance to improve administration of the program.

LENDER REVIEW SPECIALIST: Conducts program reviews of lenders and guarantee agencies to determine whether such institutions are in compliance with Federal statutory and regulatory provisions governing the administration of the Student Financial Assistance Programs, such as the Guaranteed Student Loan (GSL) Program and the Parent Loan to Undergraduate Student (PLUS) Programs. Prepares program review reports offering recommendations for improvement of the administration of the programs according to national policy. Follows up on the resolution of all discrepancies noted in the program review.

Major Activities and Divisions

Bilingual Education and Minority Languages Affairs: Ensures access to equal educational opportunity and improves the quality of programs for limited English proficiency and minority languages populations.

Civil Rights: Responsible for the administration and enforcement of civil rights laws related to education and the handicapped.

Education Research and Improvement: Involved in research, statistics, development, demonstration, and assessment.

Vocational and Adult Education: Administers programs of grants, contracts, and technical assistance for vocational and technical education, education professions development, community schools, and employment and training.

Special Education and Rehabilitative Services: Responsible for special education programs and services designed to meet the needs of and to develop the full potential of handicapped children.

Postsecondary Education: Coordinates programs for assistance to postsecondary educational institutions and students pursuing a postsecondary education.

Alternative Employment Programs

The Department of Education offers a co-op, Stay-in-School, and Summer Hire program for students of all ages.

Remarks

Approximately 8,000 postsecondary education institutions and $12 billion in SFA funds are subject to monitoring and compliance activities. This work is divided geographically among 10 regional offices and 3 regional divisions.

Application Procedures

Direct inquiries to:

Department of Education
Personnel Management Service
400 Maryland Avenue, S.W.
Washington, DC 20202

(202) 401-0559
TDD (202) 708-5936

THE DEPARTMENT OF ENERGY

The Department of Energy, established in 1977, is responsible for the nation's energy resources and the maintenance of balanced and efficient energy programs. The Department conducts technological research in the areas of defense, nuclear energy, energy conservation, and renewable energies. It is concerned with the international aspects of energy policy, and coordinates energy programs with foreign governments. And, the Department works to improve the energy efficiency of current structures and systems, such as transportation systems and existing buildings.

In its goal to provide a comprehensive national energy plan, the Department conducts programs to market federal power, conserve energy, regulate energy usage, and collect and analyze energy data. The Department maintains these programs through an extensive field structure that plays a large part in the implementation and management of departmental projects.

DEPARTMENT OF ENERGY (DOE)

Nature of Work: Defense and national security, disaster assistance, energy, hazardous materials, nuclear energy, scientific research

Number of Employees: 16,923

Headquarters: Washington, DC

Regional Locations: Albuquerque, NM; Chicago, IL; Las Vegas, NV; Oak Ridge, TN; Richland, WA; San Francisco, CA; Savannah River, GA; Idaho Falls, Idaho (Operations Offices)

Typical Majors of New Hires: Architecture, accounting, biological sciences, business, engineering, English (journalism), environmental sciences, finance/banking, earth sciences, physical sciences, social sciences

Mission

Through scientific research and the implementation of programs and projects, the Department of Energy works to move the U.S. from its current state of energy management to the energy environment of tomorrow. The DOE is responsible for foreseeing the future energy demands of the U.S., and for developing more efficient means of energy usage today.

Job Descriptions

ACCOUNTANT: Examines documents such as payrolls, invoices, and vouchers to ascertain that the transactions of companies subject to the jurisdiction of the DOE are properly supported. Typically a FERC position.

ARCHITECT: Designs, evaluates, performs research on, and advises on the construction or rehabilitation of buildings with consideration toward conservation of energy and the use of renewable resources such as solar or geothermal energy. Typically a Conservation and Renewable Energies position.

AUDITOR: Works individually or participates as a member of a field audit team engaged in examination and verification of the books, records, plant inventories, and other data supporting financial statements of licensees, electric utilities, and natural gas pipeline companies. Typically a FERC or ERA position.

BIOLOGIST: Assesses the effects of change or the introduction of new phenomena on biological ecosystems. Makes recommendations to conserve biological environments. Typically a Conservation and Renewable Energies position.

BOTANIST: Conducts botanical research, including plant taxonomy, morphology, ecology, and ethnobotany. Typically a Conservation and Renewable Energies position.

CHEMIST: Investigates and assesses the composition, molecular structure, and properties of nuclear, fossil, or other energy systems and substances. Examines the transformations which they undergo, and the amount of matter and energy included or generated in these transformations.

COMMUNITY PLANNER: Identifies community needs, resources, and energy problems, and assists citizens to make decisions that reflect energy conservation practices. Typically a Conservation and Renewable Energies position.

ECOLOGIST: Assembles and analyzes complex data on water quality, instream flows, and aquatic biology using limnological techniques. Makes recommendations regarding the effects of energy projects on ecological systems.

ECONOMIST: Prepares analyses on complex, long-term energy trends and the microeconomic and macroeconomic impacts of energy trends on regional and industrial sectors. Analyzes rate contracts and system operations of utilities. Prepares studies to determine the most economical sources of power. May specialize in industrial or mineral economics. Typically an FERC or EIA position.

ELECTRIC POWER INDUSTRY ANALYST: Conducts analyses into the electric power industry. Measures trends, assesses competition within the electric power industry, and analyzes the capital/financial structure of electric power companies. Typically an EIA position.

ENERGY CONSERVATION PROGRAM SPECIALIST: Develops programs and policies designed to broaden the use of renewable energies and to conserve nonrenewable resources.

ENGINEER (CHEMICAL): Researches, develops, evaluates, and improves processes, equipment, methods, or products relating to renewable resources and energy conservation practices, as well as other energy issues.

ENGINEER (CIVIL): Plans and designs structures and facilities that provide shelter, support transportation systems, and control natural resources. Surveys and maps the earth's physical features and phenomena. Applies a knowledge of hydraulics, mechanics, and solids (particularly soils), strength of materials, theory of structure, and surveying to the use of renewable resources and other energy issues.

ENGINEER (ELECTRICAL): Works with and conducts research related to electrical circuits, circuit elements, and associated phenomena concerned with electrical energy for purposes such as motive power, heating, illumination, chemical processes, or the production of localized electric or magnetic fields.

ENGINEER (MECHANICAL): Applies a knowledge of thermodynamics, mechanics, and other physical, mathematical, and engineering sciences to problems concerned with the production, transmission, measurement, and use of energy, especially health and mechanical power.

ENVIRONMENTAL PROTECTION SPECIALIST: Conducts studies and collects data on how the public use of land and water resources affects and is affected by the construction and operation of hydropower projects and natural gas pipelines. Works with such issues as air and water pollution and quality, endangered species protection, oil spill prevention and control, and hazardous waste management. Prepares testimony and exhibits for use at meetings and evidentiary hearings. Typically a FERC position.

ENVIRONMENTAL SAFETY SPECIALIST: Takes remedial action to treat or stabilize radioactive wastes at DOE surplus sites. Conducts technical analyses and provides advice concerning nonproliferation and radioactive waste decontamination. Typically a Nuclear Energy position.

FEDERAL FINANCING SPECIALIST: Administers federal financing programs related to the conservation of energy. Typically a Conservation and Renewable Energies position.

FISHERY BIOLOGIST: Examines the effects of hydropower projects and natural gas pipelines on the spawning of anadromous fish, fish passage, and other limnological phenomena.

INDUSTRIAL HYGIENIST: Collects and analyzes safety, health, and quality assurance data from field facilities. Provides advice concerning the industrial hygiene aspects peculiar to facilities, equipment, or experiments involving the use of nuclear reactors or sources of ionizing radiation.

INTELLIGENCE RESEARCH ANALYST: Performs analysis of intelligence regarding nuclear and general science issues provided by national level collection agencies.

METALLURGIST: Studies the properties and behavior of metals extracted from their ores as affected by the composition, treatment in manufacture, and conditions of use. Develops environmentally efficient methods of extraction and refinement.

NATURAL GAS INDUSTRY ANALYST: Conducts analyses into the natural gas industry. Measures trends, assesses competition with the natural gas industry, evaluates interfuel substitution, and analyzes the capital/financial structure of natural gas companies.

PHYSICAL SCIENTIST: Conducts research involving the physical sciences relating to conservation and energy, with no one area of specialization.

PHYSICIST: Conducts research and other scientific work in the applications of energy in the areas of mechanics, sound, optics, heat, electricity, magnetism, radiation, or atomic phenomena.

PUBLIC UTILITIES SPECIALIST: Analyzes rate contract and system operations of utility companies to determine whether service under contracts is subject to the FERC's jurisdiction. Evaluates data to determine the most economical sources of power generation. Typically a FERC position.

RADIOLOGICAL SCIENTIST: Conducts research on a wide range of radiological and fission energy projects, such as nuclear applications to the space program, nuclear reactor development, and decontamination strategies.

STATISTICIAN/MATHEMATICAL STATISTICIAN: Gathers information on energy trends, national energy resource levels, energy industry outlooks, energy production, and technology. Conducts mathematical analyses and applies statistical theories to interpret and quantify energy data.

WILDLIFE BIOLOGIST: Plans and conducts field investigations at existing and proposed hydropower projects or natural gas pipelines. Determines the nature and extent of probable impact of the projects on wildlife and surrounding terrestrial environments.

Major Activities and Divisions

International Affairs and Energy Emergencies: Coordinates cooperative international energy programs with foreign governments and international organizations such as the International Energy Agency and the International Atomic Energy Agency.

Conservation and Renewable Energies: Works to increase the production and utilization of renewable energies (solar, biomass, wind, geothermal, alcohol fuels, etc.) and to improve the energy efficiency of transportation, buildings, industrial systems, and related processes through support of long-term, high-risk research and development activities.

Office of Energy Research: Manages the basic energy sciences, high-energy physics, and fusion energy research programs. Funds research in mathematical and computation sciences critical to the development of supercomputers.

Defense Programs: Researches, develops, tests, manufactures, and retires all U.S. nuclear weapons. Produces all nuclear materials needed for the weapons program, and manages defense-related nuclear wastes.

Nuclear Energy: Conducts research and development programs relating to nuclear reactor development, nuclear fuel cycle, space nuclear applications, and uranium enrichment. Performs decontamination and decommissioning at DOE surplus radioactive waste sites.

Fossil Energy: Conducts research and development programs involving fossil fuels—coal, petroleum, and gas.

Energy Information Administration (EIA): Responsible for the collection, processing, and publication of data in the areas of energy resource reserves, energy production, demand, consumption, distribution, and technology.

Economic Regulatory Administration (ERA): Administers the DOE's regulatory programs other than those assigned to the Federal Energy Regulatory Commission.

Federal Energy Regulatory Commission (FERC): Ensures the nation's consumers adequate energy supplies at reasonable rates, while providing regulatory incentives for increased productivity, efficiency, and competition. Regulates certain aspects of the natural gas, electric utility, hydroelectric power, and oil pipeline industries.

Civilian Radioactive Waste Management: Manages programs for recommending, constructing, and operating repositories for disposal of high-level radioactive waste and spent nuclear fuel.

Alternative Employment Programs

The Department of Energy hires a limited number of high caliber individuals through its Management Intern Development Program (MIDP). The program is designed to provide interns with the managerial skills necessary to compete for future senior management positions in the Department. The position titles are Scientist Intern, Management Intern, or Engineering Intern, and all positions are available nationwide. Candidates must have a bachelor's degree in an appropriate field to qualify at the GS-7 level. Master's and PhD graduates are considered at the GS-9 and GS-11 levels. MIDP interns participate in special training activities and special assignments during the first 5 years of employment. For more information, contact the Internship Director at (202) 586-8495.

The DOE also hires approximately 10-20 co-op students annually, primarily to fill engineering positions. The co-op students usually begin work in the fall semester of their sophomore year. Contact the Headquarters' Program Coordinators at (202) 586-4494.

The DOE also participates in the PMI program (202) 586-8467, the Stay-in-School program, a Needy Youth program, and a volunteer student program.

Remarks

The DOE headquarters offers an on-site fitness center and a professionally staffed health unit.

Application Procedures

Applications for the Science, Engineering, or Management Intern positions are accepted during a limited time period, usually in January and February only. For an intern or other entry level position, direct inquiries to:

U.S. Department of Energy
Employee Development and
Training Division
AD-114.5/Room 4F-077
1000 Independence Avenue, S.W.
Washington, DC 20585
(202) 586-4494
(202) 586-4333 (vacancies)

DOE recruitment coordinators can be reached at the following locations:

Alaska Power
DOE
PO Box 020050
Juneau, AK 99802
(907)586-7405

Albuquerque Operations Office
DOE
PO Box 5400
Albuquerque, NM 87115
(505)845-4154

Bonneville Power Administration
DOE
PO Box 3621
Portland, OR 97208
(503)230-3056

Chicago Operations Office
DOE
9800 South Cass Avenue
Argonne, IL 60439
(708)972-2837

Dallas Support Office
DOE, Suite 400
1440 W. Mockingbird Lane
Dallas, TX 75247
(214)767-7134

Idaho Operations Office
DOE
785 DOE Place
Idaho Falls, ID 83402
(202)526-1565

Morgantown Energy Tech. Center
DOE
PO Box 880
Morgantown, WV 26507
(304)291-4739

Nevada Operations Office
DOE
PO Box 98518
Las Vegas, NV 89193-8518
(702)295-1736

Oak Ridge Operations Office
DOE
PO Box E
Oak Ridge, TN 37831
(615)576-9586

Pittsburgh Energy Tech Center
DOE
PO Box 10940
Pittsburgh, PA 15236
(412)892-6282

Pittsburgh Naval Reactor Office
DOE
PO Box 109
West Mifflin, PA 15122-0109
(412)476-7206

Richland Operations Office
DOE, A1-55
PO Box 550
Richland, WA 99352
(509)376-5923

San Francisco Operations Office
DOE
1333 Broadway
Oakland, CA 94612
(415)273-7936

Savannah Rivers Operations Office
DOE
PO Box A
Aiken, SC 29802
(803)725-3937

Schenectady Naval Reactor Office
DOE
PO Box 1069
Schenectady, NY 12301
(518)395-4204

Southeastern Power Administration
DOE
Samuel Elbert Building
Elberton, GA 30635
(404)283-9911

Southwestern Power Administration
DOE
PO Box 1619
Tulsa, OK 74101
(918)581-7432

Western Area Power Administration
DOE
PO Box 3402
Golden, CO 80401
ATTN: A1200
(303)231-7451

FEDERAL ENERGY REGULATORY COMMISSION (FERC)

Nature of Work: Energy, environmental protection
Number of Employees: 1,374
Headquarters: Washington, DC
Regional Locations: Atlanta, GA; Chicago, IL; New York, NY; Portland, OR; San Francisco, CA
Typical Majors of New Hires: Accounting, agriculture, biological sciences, business, chemistry, economics, engineering (civil), environmental sciences (natural resource management)

Mission

The Federal Energy Regulatory Commission's primary goal is to ensure the nation's consumers adequate energy supplies at just and reasonable rates, while providing regulatory incentives for increased productivity, efficiency, and competition.

Job Descriptions

ACCOUNTANT: Examines documents such as payrolls, invoices, and vouchers to ascertain that the transactions of companies subject to the jurisdiction of FERC are properly supported.

AUDITOR: Participates as a member of a field audit team engaged in examination and verification of the books, records, plant inventories, and other data supporting financial statements of licensees, electric utilities, and natural gas pipeline companies. Position requires extensive travel for extended periods (3-6 months).

CIVIL ENGINEER: Prepares engineering studies to determine the stability of various types of dams, powerhouses, and other project structures. Develops graphs, charts, tables, and statistical curves.

ECOLOGIST: Assembles and analyzes complex data on water quality, instream flows, and aquatic biology using limnological techniques. Makes recommendations regarding the effects of energy projects on ecological ecosystems.

ECONOMIST: Applies basic economic principles and skills to analyze rate contracts and system operations of utilities. Prepares economic studies to determine economical sources of power. May specialize in industrial or mineral economics.

ENVIRONMENTAL PROTECTION SPECIALIST: Conducts studies and collects data on how the public use of land and water resources affects and is affected by the construction and operation of hydropower projects and natural gas pipelines. Prepares testimony and exhibits for use at evidentiary hearings and public meetings.

FISHERY BIOLOGIST: Examines the effects of hydropower projects and natural gas pipelines on the spawning of anadromous fish, fish passage, and other limnological phenomena.

PUBLIC UTILITIES SPECIALIST: Analyzes rate contracts and system operations of utility companies to determine whether service under contracts is subject to the Commission's jurisdiction. Also involves analyzing data to determine the most economical sources of power generation.

WILDLIFE BIOLOGIST: Plans and conducts field investigations at existing and proposed hydropower projects or natural gas pipelines. Determines the nature and extent of probable impact of the projects on wildlife and surrounding terrestrial environments.

Major Activities and Divisions

The FERC has three major offices of regulation:

The Office of Electric Power Regulation: Responsible for overseeing wholesale electric power rates.

The Office of Hydropower Licensing: Responsible for licensing hydroelectric projects.

The Office of Pipeline and Producer Regulation: Oversees the natural gas and oil pipeline industries.

Alternative Employment Programs

The FERC maintains a co-op program for students pursuing an associate's degree, and for students enrolled in a baccalaureate or graduate program.

Remarks

None.

Application Procedures

Direct inquiries to:

The Federal Energy Regulatory Commission
Office of Human Resource Management and ADP Support
Room 418
810 First Street, N.E.
Washington, DC 20426

(202) 219-2800 (information)
(202) 219-2990 (personnel)

THE DEPARTMENT OF HEALTH AND HUMAN SERVICES (HHS)

The Department of Health and Human Services works to serve the people of the nation in matters of health, welfare, and income security plans. It promotes healthful lifestyles in the nation, represents the concerns of American Indians, provides for quality services to persons with disabilities, and promotes effective strategies to deal with the abuse of alcohol and drugs.

The Health and Human Services Department is also responsible for conducting research into human health issues, including the prevention and control of diseases, the labeling and safety of drug products, and the nutrition and quality of food and food additives.

The agencies of HHS include:

- The Family Support Administration
- The Health Care Financing Administration
- The Office of Human Development Services
- The Social Security Administration
- The Public Health Service
  - Alcohol, Drug Abuse, and Mental Health Administration
  - Food and Drug Administration
  - Health Resources Administration
  - Centers for Disease Control
  - National Institutes of Health
  - Indian Health Service

FAMILY SUPPORT ADMINISTRATION
Nature of Work: Aged/children, funds/funding, low income people **Number of Employees:** 1,027 **Headquarters:** Washington, DC **Regional Locations:** None **Typical Majors of New Hires:** Public administration, social sciences

Mission

The Family Support Administration manages and coordinates the nationwide administration of federal-states financial and other support programs designed to promote family stability, security, responsibility, and self-reliance.

Job Descriptions

PROGRAM ANALYST/SPECIALIST: Administers the Child Support Enforcement and Family Assistance Programs. Develops and evaluates program policies and guidelines, and assesses their effectiveness. Prepares reports concerning program outcomes, impact, and projections.

Major Activities and Divisions

The Office of Family Assistance: Administers the Aid to Families with Dependent Children Program, which helps needy families in which there are children.

The Office of Child Support Enforcement: Coordinates the Department's Child Support Enforcement programs and activities, which require states to enforce support obligations owed by absent parents to their children.

The Office of Community Services: Administers the Community Services block grant and discretionary grant programs. Also carries out the Low Income Home Energy Assistance Program, which provides assistance to low-income households in meeting the costs of home energy.

The Office of Refugee Resettlement: Administers the Refugee Assistance Program, which is designed to assimilate refugees and Cuban and Haitian entrants into American society.

Alternative Employment Programs

The Family Support Administration hires 20-30 people annually for its summer employment program, offering both clerical and professional positions. They also hire volunteers for positions related to college major.

Remarks

None.

Application Procedures

Direct inquiries to:

Department of Health and Human Services
Family Support Administration
Division of Personnel Operations
Room 1035, Cohen Building
330 Independence Avenue, S.W.
Washington, DC 20201

(202) 401-5623

HEALTH CARE FINANCING ADMINISTRATION (HCFA)

Nature of Work: Aged/children, funds/funding, health/health care, insurance, low-income people
Number of Employees: 4,000
Headquarters: Baltimore, MD and Washington, DC
Regional Locations: Atlanta, GA; Boston, MA; Chicago, IL; Dallas, TX; Denver, CO; Kansas City, MO; New York, NY; Philadelphia, PA; San Francisco, CA; Seattle, WA
Typical Majors of New Hires: Accounting, business, economics, social sciences

Mission

HCFA provides operational direction and policy guidance for the nationwide administration of the Medicare and Medicaid programs. HCFA administers its program through relationships with state and local governments, the insurance industry, virtually all of the nation's hospitals and nursing homes, home health agencies, and renal disease facilities.

Job Descriptions

ACCOUNTANT: Works on the operating budget of HCFA and monitors the work of contractors and other health-care providers. Classifies and evaluates financial data, records transactions, and analyzes financial reports. Accountants work in HQ and regional offices.

ACTUARY: Uses statistical and mathematical skills to provide analysis and cost estimates concerning the financing of the Medicare and Medicaid programs and related legislative and regulatory modifications to these programs. Actuaries work in HQ offices.

ECONOMIST: Conducts research and interprets economic data related to HCFA programs. Prepares reports on the design, implementation, and evaluation of the

Medicare and Medicaid programs based on economic data and techniques. Economists work in HQ offices.

MEDICAID PROGRAM SPECIALIST: Monitors and evaluates state Medicaid programs to ensure adherence to regulations. Medicaid Program Specialists work in regional offices.

MEDICARE CONTRACTOR OPERATIONS REPRESENTATIVE: Monitors and evaluates Medicare contractor operations to ensure adherence to the provisions of the contract, as well as the intent of the law and regulations. MCOR's work in regional offices.

NURSE CONSULTANT: Serves as a specialist in the review, analysis, and evaluation of Medicare contractors; state survey agencies; and the effectiveness and quality of services delivered by Medicare and Medicaid providers/suppliers. Nurse Consultants work in regional offices.

POLICY SPECIALIST: Provides advice and consultation regarding regulations and policy for complex or controversial issues such as eligibility or noninstitutional reimbursement for the Medicare and Medicaid programs. Policy Specialists work in regional offices.

PROGRAM ANALYST: Analyzes and evaluates programs and develops proposals for improvement. Studies the private health insurance industry, analyzes Medicare and Medicaid policies, and participates in inspection and evaluation activities. Program Analysts work in HQ and regional offices.

SOCIAL SCIENCE RESEARCH ANALYST: Performs research and analysis and tests new policies and processes that are designed to improve Medicaid and Medicare program operation. SSRA's work in HQ offices.

SURVEY AND CERTIFICATION PROGRAM OPERATIONS SPECIALIST: Monitors, evaluates, and provides technical assistance to state certification agencies involving Medicare and Medicaid activities which affect the delivery of health care. Reviews and assesses the quality of health care delivered by Medicare and Medicaid providers or suppliers. This specialty may include, but is not limited to, various health professionals such as nurses, medical technologists, dieticians, and pharmacists. Work in regional offices.

Note: HCFA also hires many entry-level Budget Analysts, Management Analysts, and Computer Specialists. See Chapter 6 on common government positions for job descriptions.

Major Activities and Divisions

HCFA is organized around functions which include:

Operations: Responsible for Medicare/Medicaid program operations and quality control.

Program Development: Responsible for the development and review of Medicare and Medicaid policies and regulations.

Communications: Responsible for liaison with health practitioners and directing public affairs activities.

Alternative Employment Programs

HCFA hires approximately 1–10 co-op students annually to fill professional positions. The program is flexible, allowing students to work summers only, year-round part-time, or full-time. Undergraduate co-ops begin at the GS-4 level, and graduate students begin at the GS-7 or -9 level. Students are usually hired at the junior, senior, master's, or PhD levels. Students may contact HCFA at (301) 966-5514 for more information.

HCFA also participates in the PMI program (301-966-5568), and hires Stay-in-School students for clerical support positions.

Remarks

The Health Care Financing Administration recruits on college campuses throughout the country. HCFA has been granted Delegated Examining Authority and ACWA Schedule B Authority to fill GS-5 and -7 level professional positions. For more information about these hiring programs, refer to Chapter 3.

Application Procedures

Direct inquiries to:

Health Care Financing Administration
Staffing Branch
Room G-55, East High Rise Building
6325 Security Boulevard
Baltimore, Maryland 21207

(301) 966-5505

OFFICE OF HUMAN DEVELOPMENT SERVICES

Nature of Work: Aged/children, funds/funding, handicapped, Native Americans
Number of Employees: 1,046
Headquarters: Washington, DC
Regional Locations: None
Typical Majors of New Hires: Psychology, public administration, social sciences, social work/sociology

Mission

The programs administered by the Office of Human Development Services are broad and varied, serving millions of children, youth, families in need, Native Americans, the aged, and people with disabilities.

Job Descriptions

PROGRAM ANALYST: Conducts analyses of program issues, and prepares reports concerning program outcomes and projections. Provides guidance and information related to the specific program area (Native Americans; children, youth, and families; or the developmentally disabled).

PROGRAM SPECIALIST: Develops objectives for national programs to aid runaway and homeless youth, abused and neglected children, the elderly, disabled persons, Native Americans, and others. Interprets discretionary and service grant solicitations, and conducts on-site reviews of the operations of related programs.

Major Activities and Divisions

Administration on Aging: Advises other federal departments and agencies on the characteristics and needs of older people and develops programs to promote their welfare.

Administration for Children, Youth, and Families: Advises other federal agencies on matters relating to the development of children, youth and families.

Administration for Native Americans: Represents the concerns of American Indians, Alaska Natives, and Native Hawaiians.

Administration on Developmental Disabilities: Increases the provision of quality services to persons with developmental disabilities.

Alternative Employment Programs

The Office of Human Development Services provides temporary positions which may last one year or less. Contact the Office of the Secretary Personnel; W.J. Cohen Building, Room 1035; 330 Independence Ave., SW; Washington, DC, 20201

Remarks

None.

Application Procedures

Direct inquiries to:

DPO Operations Group C
Room 1037, Cohen Building
330 Independence Avenue, S.W.
Washington, DC 20201

(202) 245-6216

SOCIAL SECURITY ADMINISTRATION (SSA)

Nature of Work: Aged/children, insurance, handicapped, health/health care
Number of Employees: Over 60,000
Headquarters: Baltimore, MD
Regional Locations: Atlanta, GA; Boston, MA; Chicago, IL; Dallas, TX; Denver, CO; Kansas City, MO; New York, NY; Philadelphia, PA; San Francisco, CA; Seattle, WA
Typical Majors of New Hires: Business, liberal arts, mathematics, social sciences

Mission

The Social Security Administration conducts a national program of contributory social insurance whereby employees, employers, and the self-employed pay contributions that are pooled in special trust funds. When earnings stop or are reduced because the worker retires, dies, or becomes disabled, monthly cash benefits are paid to replace part of the earnings the family has lost.

Job Descriptions

ACTUARY: Makes actuarial appraisals of existing and proposed social insurance programs and analyzes actuarial data for benefit evaluations. Estimates future claims and program costs, evaluates demographic characteristics, and analyzes trust fund operations.

BENEFIT AUTHORIZERS: Authorizes new types of entitlement for previously entitled beneficiaries, and makes determinations to resume, reinstate, suspend, or terminate benefits. Makes determinations of benefit rates considering such factors of entitlement as type of benefit, age, family maximum, and changes in family composition.

ECONOMIST: Collects, analyzes and reports economic data relating to the retirement, survivors, disability, and supplemental security income programs. Measures the effects of Social Security benefit provisions on the individual, the family, and the economy. Conducts research in the area of general welfare and labor economics.

FOREIGN CLAIMS ADJUDICATORS: Examines Social Security benefits claims for claimants in foreign countries. Adjudicates all claims for retirement, survivors, and disability benefits.

HEARINGS AND APPEALS ANALYST: Reviews disability, retirement, survivors, or health insurance cases that are before the Appeals Council for review or have been appealed to the U.S. district courts. Prepares an analysis of the case with a recommendation to the Appeals Council as to what action should be taken. Conducts post-review of hearing examiner decisions in order to identify problem areas or trends. Responds to inquiries from members of Congress, the legal or medical profession, and individual claimants.

MATHEMATICAL STATISTICIAN: Designs and adapts statistical methodology in the measurement of the impact of Social Security programs. Conducts statistical investigations in regard to the characteristics of beneficiaries, the demographic aspects of Social Security programs, and the economic effects of policy and programs.

SERVICE REPRESENTATIVE: Interviews beneficiaries or inquirers to determine the nature of their problem or interest, and resolve problems with payments or eligibility. Investigates case situations and questionable or incomplete reports and reconciles discrepancies. Provides beneficiaries with information or instruction. Identifies need for social services of people interviewed and refers them to appropriate organizations.

SOCIAL INSURANCE CLAIMS EXAMINER: Determines the validity of Social Security benefit claims and the correctness of the benefit amount. Reviews and evaluates all evidence previously developed, and approves, modifies or reverses the prior adjudication when necessary. Typically works in one of the six payment centers across the USA.

SOCIAL INSURANCE CLAIMS REPRESENTATIVE: Takes and authorizes claims for Social Security benefits. Conducts personal and telephone interviews with claimants, employers, and others in order to obtain evidence for the development of claims and to obtain evidence for the resolution of cases involving discrepancies. Reviews files for completeness of information, and assists claimants in obtaining evidence and in completing necessary forms. Typically works in the district offices across the USA.

SOCIAL INSURANCE PROGRAM ANALYST: Evaluates the effectiveness of the Social Security program. Formulates program objectives, and makes recommendations concerning legislative proposals.

SOCIAL SCIENCE RESEARCH ANALYST: Conducts research on the impact of Social Security programs on beneficiaries and the evaluation of alternative programs. Measures overall Social Security needs and program effectiveness. Conducts economic and social surveys to obtain information on the characteristics of beneficiaries or other population groups.

STATISTICIAN: Develops improved methods for obtaining data and plans forms and procedures for collecting and tabulating data. Uses statistical techniques to measure relationships pertaining to social insurance programs.

Major Activities and Divisions

Principal SSA programs include the Old Age Survivors and Disability Insurance Program, which provides monthly benefits to retired and disabled workers, and the Supplemental Security Income (SSI) program for the aged, blind, and disabled. The responsibility for the administration of the Medicare Program was recently transferred to the Health Care Financing Administration.

Alternative Employment Programs

Paid co-op positions are available for college students with appropriate majors. SSA typically hires 40 or more co-op students per year. These are usually GS-7 level positions for college juniors. Typical job titles are Computer Programmer, Claims Examiner, and Management Analyst. Contact the school placement office, or call the SSA Co-op Director at (301) 965-4414. Unpaid internships are available for any major. Other student hiring programs at SSA include the Stay-in-School program for support positions.

Remarks

None.

Application Procedures

Direct inquiries to the office in which you are interested in working:

Headquarters:

Social Security Administration
Attn: Recruitment and Placement Branch
6401 Security Boulevard
Room G-120, West High Rise Building
Baltimore, MD 21235

(301) 965-4506

Or, address to:

Department of Health and Human Services
Regional Personnel Office

Suite 1601
101 Marietta Tower
Atlanta, GA 30323
(404) 331-2205

Room 1503
J.F. Kennedy Federal Building
Boston, MA 02203
(617) 565-1395

105 W. Adams
Chicago, IL 60603
(312) 353-5175

Suite 930
1200 Main Tower Building
Dallas, TX 75202
(214) 767-4930 (recording)

Federal Office Building
Room 1185
1961 Stout Street
Denver, CO 80294-3538
(303) 844-6391

Room 545-S
601 E. 12 Street
P.O. Box 15186
Kansas City, MO 64106
(816) 426-3630

Room 39-120
26 Federal Plaza
New York, NY 10278
(mail inquiries only)

Room 9400
3535 Market Street
Philadelphia, PA 19101
(215) 596-0108

Operations Branch A
50 United Nations Plaza
San Francisco, CA 94102
(415) 556-1088 (recording)

Mailstop RX05
2201 6th Avenue
Seattle, WA 98121
(206) 442-4365 (recording)

Public Health Service (PHS)

The U.S. Public Health Service is one of the largest federal health agencies in the nation, with 44,586 employees. PHS's goal is to promote the protection and advancement of the nation's physical and mental health. This is accomplished by coordinating with the states to set and implement national health policy, conducting medical and biomedical research, and enforcing laws to assure the safety and efficacy of drugs, foods, and medical devices.

Because its scope is so broad and its divisions so pronounced, the Public Health Service agencies have been treated in this book as separate entries, rather than allowing them to be limited by the brevity that would have been necessary in grouping them together.

The major components of the Public Health Service are:

The Alcohol, Drug Abuse, and Mental Health Administration
The Food and Drug Administration
The Health Resources Administration
The Centers for Disease Control
The National Institutes of Health
The Indian Health Service

These agencies are described in detail on the following pages.

ALCOHOL, DRUG ABUSE, AND MENTAL HEALTH ADMINISTRATION (ADAMHA)

Nature of Work: Drugs/abuse, health/health care, scientific research
Number of Employees: 1,826
Headquarters: Rockville, MD
Regional Locations: Washington, DC
Typical Majors of New Hires: biology, chemistry, medical sciences (pharmacology), psychology, social work/sociology

Mission

ADAMHA provides national leadership in scientific research on drug and alcohol abuse, mental illness, and the related problems of AIDS and the homeless, among others. Strategies are developed to cope with health problems and issues that arise with the use and abuse of alcohol and drugs, and with mental illness and mental health.

Job Descriptions

BIOLOGIST: Performs scientific research in the field of biology, examining the physical and biological effects of drugs and toxic substances on the user, and the biological aspects of mental health and illness.

CHEMIST: Investigates and interprets the composition and properties of drugs and related substances, the transformations which they undergo, and their physiological effects on the user.

MEDICAL OFFICER: Performs professional health-care work and research related to drug abuse and mental health disorders.

NURSE: Provides care to patients in hospitals and clinics. Promotes better health practices in the areas of drug and alcohol abuse.

PHARMACOLOGIST: Conducts research into the uses, qualities, and effects of drugs.

PSYCHOLOGIST: Provides psychological consultation to patients and families, especially in regard to drug and alcohol abuse and its effects. Systematically observes the relationship between behavior and physiological changes brought on by drugs or alcohol.

PUBLIC HEALTH ADVISOR: Provides technical advice to state and local governments, and to various public, private, and nonprofit organizations on matters related to obtaining financial support for projects on drug and alcohol abuse, alcohol patterns, and prevention and control activities. Assists organizations with the evaluation and improvement of their public health activities.

SOCIAL WORKER: Provides direct services to individuals and families which are experiencing problems with drug and alcohol abuse. Provides consultation to members of related professions and community organizations on topics related to drug and alcohol abuse and other social work questions.

SOCIOLOGIST: Conducts studies on behavioral patterns, social interaction, and social situations as they relate to drug or alcohol abuse populations, treatment outcome, or drug dependency. May examine residential areas in relationship to the incidence or prevalence of mental health disorders.

Major Activities and Divisions

National Institute on Alcohol Abuse and Alcoholism: Provides a focus for the federal effort to deal with issues associated with alcohol abuse and alcoholism.

National Institute on Drug Abuse: Provides a focus for the federal effort to deal with issues associated with drug abuse.

National Institute of Mental Health: Provides a focus for the federal effort to deal with mental health issues.

Office for Substance Abuse Prevention: Works to eliminate alcohol and other substance abuse among high-risk youth and other target populations.

Office for Treatment Improvement: Works to enhance programs dealing with the treatment of drug users as well as associated problems of alcoholism and mental illness.

Alternative Employment Programs

The Commissioned Officer Student Training and Extern Program (COSTEP): Assigns students in health professions to work with one of the seven Public Health Service (PHS) agencies. Opportunities provide students various responsibilities and duties that range from research to clinical services. Students are commissioned as Ensigns in the PHS and serve from 31–120 days per assignment. Salary is approximately $1700 per month and other benefits are provided. Contact the Commissioned Corp Director at (301) 443-9272.

ADAMHA also hires several co-op students per year for administrative, technical, and scientific positions. Typically, these students are undergraduates, and begin at the GS-3 level. Contact the Co-op Program Director at (301) 443-5407 for more information.

ADAMHA also hires Master's and PhD students for internship positions, usually beginning at the GS-7 level. For information on the Internship Programs, call the Intern Program Director at (301) 443-5407.

Other ADAMHA student hiring programs include: the PMI program, a volunteer program, the Stay-in-School program for clerks and biological lab technicians, and a Staff Fellowship Program for PhD students.

Remarks

None.

Application Procedures

Direct inquiries to:

Division of Personnel Management
Alcohol, Drug Abuse, and Mental Health Administration
Parklawn Building, Room 15C 12
5600 Fishers Lane
Rockville, MD 20857

(301) 443-5407

JOB HOTLINE NUMBER: (301) 443-2282

U.S. FOOD AND DRUG ADMINISTRATION (FDA)

Nature of Work: Consumer protection, health/health care, scientific research
Number of Employees: 7,698
Headquarters: Rockville, MD
Regional Locations: Atlanta, GA; Baltimore, MD; Boston, MA; Buffalo, NY; Chicago, IL; Cincinnati, OH; Dallas, TX; Denver, CO; Detroit, MI; Houston, TX; Kansas City, MO; Los Angeles, CA; Minneapolis, MN; Nashville, TN; New Orleans, LA; New York, NY; Orlando, FL; Philadelphia, PA; St. Louis, MO; San Francisco, CA; San Juan, PR; Seattle, WA; West Orange, NJ
Typical Majors of New Hires: Biology, biological sciences (entomology), chemistry, food sciences (nutrition), medical sciences (toxicology, pharmacology), physical sciences

Mission

The FDA could be considered the principal consumer protection agency in the federal government. It is responsible for regulating products ranging from lipstick to X-rays, from animal feed to paints, from canned peaches to penicillin. The FDA's goal is to see that all products are safe and effective.

Job Descriptions

BIOLOGIST/MICROBIOLOGIST: Studies the distribution of microorganisms in natural and manmade environments, their reaction to physical and chemical factors, and their role as pathogenic and immunizing agents.

CHEMIST: Investigates, analyzes, and interprets the composition, molecular structure, and properties of substances and how they are affected by their environment. Analyzes the safety factors involved in the presence of certain chemicals.

CONSUMER SAFETY OFFICER: Enforces the laws and regulations protecting consumers from foods, drugs, cosmetics, fabrics, toys, and household products that are impure, improperly labeled, ineffective, or dangerous. Identifies substances and sources of adulteration and contamination, and evaluates manufacturing practices. Requires a knowledge of various scientific fields such as chemistry, biology, pharmacology, and food technology.

PHARMACOLOGIST: Assesses the action, absorption, distribution, metabolism, excretion, and use of drugs, toxic substances, and related chemicals. Analyzes effects in terms of safety and efficacy.

ENTOMOLOGIST: Conducts research into the role of insects as carriers of human disease. Inspects sanitary conditions of food, drug, and cosmetic establishments.

DIETICIAN: Conducts research into the use of diet in the cause and treatment of disease.

FOOD TECHNOLOGIST: Studies problems related to the development, improvement, and evaluation of food products; their production, use, processing, and preservation; and the utilization or disposal of by-products.

PUBLIC HEALTH ADVISOR/ANALYST: Provides assistance to states and nongovernmental agencies in matters relating to the development, execution, and maintenance of public health programs. Conducts studies to identify current and future public health problems.

Major Activities and Divisions

The FDA has 18 field locations, some with laboratories. It is also divided into several Centers, each with a particular research focus.

The Center for Drug Research develops FDA policy with regard to the safety, effectiveness, and labeling of all drug products for human use.

The Center for Biologics Research administers regulation of biological products. It conducts AIDS-related research, inspects manufacturers' facilities for compliance with standards, and tests products submitted for release.

The Center for Food Safety and Applied Nutrition conducts research and develops standards on the composition, quality, nutrition, and safety of food and food additives, colors, and cosmetics.

The Center for Veterinary Medicine develops and conducts programs with respect to the safety and efficacy of veterinary devices, and evaluates proposed use of veterinary preparations for animal safety.

The Center for Devices and Radiological Health carries out a national program designed to control unnecessary exposure of humans to potentially hazardous ionizing and nonionizing radiation.

The National Center for Toxicological Research conducts research programs to study biological effects of potentially toxic chemical substances found in the environment.

Alternative Employment Programs

FDA offers an extensive Summer Hire Program, targeting graduate students to fill positions such as Engineering Aid, Lab Aid, or Computer Aid. Interested students must submit an SF-171 before March 15 to the headquarters address. For more information, call 301-443-HIRE or 301-443-1970.

Remarks

The most numerous entry-level positions at FDA are biologists, chemists, and consumer safety officers.

Application Procedures

Direct inquiries to the regional personnel office which hires for the location in which you would like to work:

Headquarters:

FDA Personnel
5600 Fishers Lane
Room 4B-41
Rockville, MD 20857
(301) 443-1544 (information)
(301) 443-3634 (personnel)
or: (301) 443-HIRE

REGION I
JFK Federal Building, Room 1503
Government Center
Boston, MA 02203
(617) 279-1478

REGION II
Federal Building
26 Federal Plaza
New York, New York 10278

REGION III
P.O. Box 13716
Philadelphia, PA 19101
(215) 597-3691

REGION IV
101 Marietta Tower
Atlanta, GA 30323
(404) 257-3188

REGION V
300 South Wacker Drive
Chicago, IL 60606
(312) 353-9402

REGION VI
1200 Main Tower
Dallas, TX 75202
(214) 767-5428

REGION VII
Federal Office Building, Room 468
601 East 12th Street
Kansas City, MO 64106
(816) 374-6376

REGION VIII
Federal Office Building
19th and Stout Streets
Denver, CO 80294
(303) 236-3051

REGION IX
Federal Office Building
50 United Nations Plaza
San Francisco, CA 94102
(415) 556-4727

REGION X
The Third and Broad Building
2901 3rd Avenue
Seattle, WA 98121
(206) 483-4876

HEALTH RESOURCES AND SERVICES ADMINISTRATION (HRSA)

Nature of Work: Health/health care
Number of Employees: 1,901
Headquarters: Rockville, MD
Regional Locations: None
Typical Majors of New Hires: Health sciences, medical sciences, public health

Mission

HRSA is responsible for health service issues dealing with health-care access, equity, quality, and cost. HRSA assists the states in providing health care to underserved areas through local community health centers and encoraging health maintenance organizations and education for health-care personnel.

Job Descriptions

PUBLIC HEALTH PROGRAM ADMINISTRATOR: Provides assistance to state, local, voluntary, public, and private entities, in matters relating to the planning and maintenance of health-related programs. Conducts studies to identify current and future public health problems, and evaluates the effectiveness of public health programs and methods. May be involved in monitoring issues relating to rural health, acquired immune deficiency syndrome (AIDS), organ procurement, transplant, and donation, and other health-care issues.

Major Activities and Divisions

Bureau of Health Care Delivery and Assistance: Works to ensure the broad availability of health-care services.

Bureau of Health Professions: Coordinates, evaluates, and supports the development of the nation's health personnel.

Bureau of Maternal and Child Health and Resources Development: Develops federal policy and programs pertaining to health-care promotion of mothers and children.

Alternative Employment Programs

HRSA participates in the Stay-in-School and Summer Hire programs, targeting both high school and college students.

Remarks

None.

Application Procedures

Direct inquiries to:

Office of Personnel, HRSA
5600 Fishers Lane, Room 14A-46
Rockville, MD 20857

(301) 443-5460

THE CENTERS FOR DISEASE CONTROL AND AGENCY FOR TOXIC SUBSTANCES AND DISEASE REGISTRY (CDC AND ATSDR)*

Nature of Work: Education, food/nutrition, health/health care, safety, scientific research, statistics
Number of Employees: 5,000
Headquarters: Atlanta, GA
Regional Locations: Anchorage, AK; Cincinnati, OH; Fort Collins, CO; Hyattsville, MD; Morgantown, WV; Research Triangle Park, NC; Rockville, MD; San Juan, PR; Washington, DC
Typical Majors of New Hires: Biology, chemistry, education (health), environmental science, health sciences, medical sciences, psychology, sociology, statistics

Mission

The Centers for Disease Control conducts a wide range of health-related activities both domestically and internationally. CDC's mission includes chronic and environmentally-related diseases, injuries and disabilities, healthy lifestyles, occupational safety, laboratory science, health training and education, health statistics, epidemiology and surveillance, and general prevention services.

Job Descriptions

BEHAVIORAL HEALTH SCIENTIST: Conducts behavioral research and community interventions to promote health, control chronic diseases, infant and maternal mortality, and develop health education techniques.

CHEMIST: Conducts scientific research into the composition, molecular structure, and properties of certain substances. Relates findings to medical uses and purposes.

ENVIRONMENTAL HEALTH SPECIALIST: Investigates, evaluates, and provides information on sanitation practices, techniques, and methods for the purpose of identifying, preventing, and eliminating environmental health hazards. May assist local public health officials at the scene of natural or manmade disasters. Reviews environmental impact statements to assure that major federally supported development projects are reasonably safe. Conducts research to prevent harm from toxic chemicals and natural and manmade radiation.

EPIDEMIOLOGIST: Conducts investigations into the causes of prevalent and rapidly spreading or contagious diseases. Works to control newly discovered infectious diseases such as AIDS, toxic shock syndrome, and legionnaires' disease, as well as old diseases which are resistant to drugs. Control programs can include public edu-

---

* See "Remarks" on page 172.

cation and vaccination. May involve travel or extended assignments in foreign countries.

MEDICAL OFFICER: Performs or advises on professional or scientific work in one or more fields of medicine. Requires a current license to practice medicine and a degree of Doctor of Medicine or Doctor of Osteopathy.

MICROBIOLOGIST: Applies a medical application to the study of microorganisms, especially in the fields of immunology, medical parasitology, physiology, serology, and genetics. Studies the role of microorganisms as pathogenic and immunizing agents through isolation, cultivation, identification, and systematic classification.

PUBLIC HEALTH ASSOCIATE/ADVISOR: Performs disease intervention and prevention activities typically in the areas of sexually transmitted diseases. Interviews patients to obtain information regarding the source and possible spread of the disease, and conducts follow-up activities to prevent further spread. Involves routine contact with health professionals. After 1–2 years as a Public Health Associate, an individual then converts to a Public Health Advisor, taking on more managerial responsibilities.

PUBLIC HEALTH EDUCATOR: Plans health education programs designed to meet the needs of particular individuals, groups, or communities. Selects specialized education methods, and prepares educational materials. Consults with state and local health departments, and with national and local voluntary agencies. Studies health problems and methods of disease prevention, and assists in coordinating mass health programs.

STATISTICIAN: Collects and analyzes vital and health statistics in the U.S. Makes data available to health professionals and the public in published reports. Quantifies such information as the nature and economic impact of illness and disability in the U.S., the availability of hospital and nursing home care, and births, deaths, marriages, and divorces.

TOXICOLOGIST: Conducts scientific research into toxic substances. Determines their chemical and physical properties, examines their effects on the body, and explores possible antidotes and detoxifying agents.

Major Activities and Divisions

Center for Chronic Disease Prevention and Health Promotion: Uses surveillance, epidemiologic and laboratory studies, behavioral research, and community interventions to promote health and control chronic diseases.

Center for Environmental Health and Injury Control: Assists local public health officials at the scene of disasters. Supports research aimed at understanding how to prevent common injuries.

National Institute for Occupational Safety and Health: works closely with employers, labor unions, and other government agencies to evaluate current conditions in the workplace.

Center for Infectious Diseases: investigates outbreaks of infectious disease within the U.S. and internationally, and develops programs to prevent their spread.

Center for Prevention Services: provides financial and technical assistance to control and prevent AIDS, diabetes, sexually transmitted diseases, and tuberculosis.

National Center for Health Statistics: collects the full spectrum of the nation's vital and health statistics.

Epidemiology Program Office: investigates outbreaks of illness throughout the world.

International Health Program Office: works with the Departments of Health in other nations and international organizations to train health workers.

Public Health Practice Program Office: trains the nation's force of public health workers in the latest disease prevention techniques.

Alternative Employment Programs

CDC/ADSTR hires 10-20 co-op students annually to fill positions related to computer, biological, and physical sciences, and statistics. These typically begin at GS-3 or 4, and target the college sophomore. CDC/ADSTR also hires 20-40 interns annually to fill volunteer laboratory positions. Other hiring programs include a summer employment program, and the PMI, Stay-in-School, and volunteer programs.

Remarks

* Hiring for the Agency for Toxic Substances and Disease Registry (ATSDR), a separate and smaller agency of the Public Health Service, is done through the CDC employment office. Job descriptions and qualifications are the same for each agency.

Application Procedures

Direct inquiries to:

Personnel Management Office
1600 Clifton Road, N.E.
Attn: Recruitment and Placement Branch (DOI)
Centers for Disease Control/ATSDR
Atlanta, GA 30333

(404) 639-3616

JOB HOTLINE: (404) 332-4577

NATIONAL INSTITUTES OF HEALTH (NIH)

Nature of Work: Health/health care, libraries, scientific research
Number of Employees: 14,219
Headquarters: Bethesda, MD
Regional Locations: None
Typical Majors of New Hires: Biology, chemistry, library science, medical sciences, psychology

Mission

The mission of NIH is to improve the health of the American people. To carry out this mission, NIH conducts and supports biomedical research into the causes, prevention, and cure of diseases, and communicates biomedical information to the public.

Job Descriptions

BIOLOGIST: Conducts research into the biological aspects and causes of certain diseases, depending upon the specialty of the Institute.

CHEMIST: Applies a professional knowledge of chemistry to conduct research into the composition, molecular structure, and properties of substances that may be linked to certain diseases.

LIBRARIAN: Provides medical library services and on-line bibliographic searching capabilities to private agencies and to the public. Acquires and makes available for distribution audiovisual instructional material for the health education community.

MEDICAL OFFICER: Conducts research and research training on the causes, characteristics, prevention, control, and treatment of a wide variety of diseases.

MEDICAL TECHNOLOGIST: Performs chemical, bacteriologic, hematologic, cytologic, and other tests and examinations of samples of fluids, tissues, and other substances.

MICROBIOLOGIST: Conducts research on the characteristics and life processes of microorganisms, involving the medical applications of work with protozoa, bacteria, viruses, rickettsiae, and other microscopic forms.

NURSE: Performs research in one or more phases of the field of nursing. Promotes better health practices, and advises nurses who provide direct care to patients.

PSYCHOLOGIST: Conducts behavioral research into the process and associated physical, psychological, and social factors of aging, human development, family structure, mental retardation, and the reproductive process.

PUBLIC INFORMATION SPECIALIST: Disseminates biomedical information through informational media and public information techniques. Evaluates the public information potential of written material, illustrations, exhibits, and other materials.

TECHNICAL INFORMATION SPECIALIST: Processes and transmits scientific biomedical information. Must posses a broad knowledge of biomedical scientific disciplines.

Major Activities and Divisions

National Cancer Institute: Conducts a National Cancer Program designed to expand existing scientific knowledge on cancer cause and prevention.

National Heart, Lung, and Blood Institute: Provides leadership for a national program in diseases of the heart, blood vessels, blood, and lungs.

National Library of Medicine: Serves as the nation's chief medical information source.

National Institute of Diabetes and Digestive and Kidney Diseases: Conducts and supports research into the causes, and treatment of metabolic and digestive diseases.

National Institute of Allergy and Infectious Diseases: Conducts and supports research on the causes and treatment of diseases believed to be attributable to infectious agents.

National Institute of Child Health and Human Development: Conducts and supports biomedical research on child health and maternal health.

National Institute on Dental Research: Conducts research directed toward the eradication of tooth decay.

National Institute of Environmental Health Sciences: Conducts research to measure the effects of chemical, biological, and physical factors in the environment on the health of man.

National Institute of General Medical Sciences: Conducts and supports research in basic biomedical science.

National Institute of Neurological and Communicative Disorders and Stroke: Conducts research on human neurological and communicative disorders such as epilepsy and muscular dystrophy.

National Eye Institute: Conducts and supports studies on the eye and visual system.

National Institute on Aging: Conducts research to increase the knowledge of the aging process and associated factors.

National Institute of Arthritis and Musculoskeletal and Skin Diseases: Conducts research in the major disease categories of arthritis and musculoskeletal and skin diseases.

Clinical Center: Brings scientists working in the Center's laboratories into close proximity with clinicians caring for patients.

Fogarty International Center: Promotes research on the development of science internationally as it relates to health.

National Center for Nursing Research: Conducts and supports research related to nursing and patient care.

Alternative Employment Programs

NIH hires approximately 20–40 co-op students annually. They typically begin at GS levels 3 and 4, and begin in their first three years of undergraduate school. Positions filled with co-op students include those relating to accounting, business, biology, computer science, engineering, and physical science. Contact the school placement office for more information.

The COSTEP program is also a part of NIH, in which assignments in the area of public health practice, research, or medical and hospital services are matched with the career plans and educational level of the student. In this program, students work during free periods of the academic year. More information about the COSTEP program is available by calling (301) 443-6324.

NIH also participates in the PMI program, a volunteer program, and Stay-in-School programs for Clerk-Typists, Bio Aids, Lab Aids, Mail Clerks, and Computer Clerks.

There are several other science, medical, and research oriented programs available to students at all levels, from high school to postbaccalaureate. These are referred to as Research and Research Related Manpower Development Programs, and have specific application procedures and qualifying criteria depending upon the program. Information on most programs can be obtained by calling (301) 496-2403. Ask for the NIH Research and Research Related Manpower Development Programs information booklets which are printed by NIH. These booklets also provide details on programs dedicated to minority students.

Remarks

None.

Application Procedures

Direct inquiries to:

National Institutes of Health
Division of Personnel Management
9000 Rockville Pike
Building 31, Room B3C15
Bethesda, MD 20892

(301) 496-2403

JOB HOTLINE NUMBERS:

496-9541 (professional positions)
496-9452 (clerical/technical positions)

INDIAN HEALTH SERVICE (IHS)

Nature of Work: Health/health care, Native Americans
Number of Employees: 12,551
Headquarters: Rockville, MD; Albuquerque, NM (West HQ); Tuscon, AZ (HQ: Office of Health Program Development)
Regional Locations: Aberdeen, SD; Albuquerque, NM; Anchorage, AK; Bemidji, MN; Billings, MT; Nashville, TN; Oklahoma City, OK; Phoenix, AZ; Portland, OR; Sacramento, CA; Tuscon, AZ; Window Rock, AZ
Typical Majors of New Hires: Engineering (biomedical, civil, electrical, environmental, mechanical), health sciences, medical sciences (dentistry, nursing, optometry, ophthalmology), psychology, social work/sociology

Mission

The Indian Health Service provides a comprehensive health services delivery system for American Indians and Alaska Natives with opportunity for maximum tribal involvement in developing and managing programs to meet their health needs. The goal of IHS is to raise the health level of the Indian and Alaska Native people to the highest possible level.

Job Descriptions

COMMUNITY HEALTH NURSE: Plans and coordinates community health programs and services. Assesses health status and determines nursing needs for the individual, the family, and the community. Implements and evaluates health planning and practices, and provides primary health care. Works with expectant Indian mothers and their infants by promoting early care in pregnancy through home visits. Provides counseling and guidance in health promotion and family living to teenagers, and immunizes infants and children against infectious diseases.

COMMUNITY INJURY CONTROL COORDINATOR: Works with the Indian people on issues such as occupational safety and injury control programs. Identifies and recommends remedies for the causes of injury among the Indian people. Performs community and individual premise evaluations to determine and eliminate environmental health or safety deficiencies.

DENTIST: Dental services are carried out in 243 locations, including IHS hospitals and health centers, as well as 167 field offices and 26 mobile dental sites. In some locations, particularly in Alaska, itinerant IHS dental teams with portable equipment visit isolated villages—often by aircraft or boat. The dental program places priority on providing preventative and corrective dental care. Effective caries preventive measures, such as water fluoridation, that provide benefits at the community level are emphasized. Dental health staff often work in coordination with environmental health workers, public health nurses, nutritionists, and pharmacists, in carrying out the objectives of the dental health program.

DIETICIAN/PUBLIC HEALTH NUTRITIONIST: Promotes nutritional health of Indians and Alaska Natives, especially infants, preschool children, adolescents, pregnant women, and the elderly. The dietician provides direct patient care nutrition services, operates the dietetic department in an IHS hospital, and participates in training and career development for Indians in food service and community nutrition programs. The Public Health Nutritionist coordinates health promotion and community development activities with tribal and other federal programs.

ENVIRONMENTAL ENGINEER: Works with the Indian people to improve the home, community, and workplace environments. Sees that the availability and quality of water is adequate for domestic purposes, and provides for safe and sanitary solid and liquid waste disposal facilities. Works with the Indian people in environmental planning; air, water, and solid waste pollution control; and institutional environmental health in reservation areas. Assists tribes in the development and adoption of sanitary ordinances.

GENERAL ENGINEER: Provides for the construction, renovation, and plant operation of hospitals, health centers, personnel quarters, and other health-care facilities serving Indians and Alaskan Natives. Involved in site selection and development, facility planning, design and design review, construction and equipment installation, management and operation of health-care facilities, etc. Opportunities are for disciplines in mechanical, biomedical, civil, and electrical engineering.

HEALTH EDUCATOR: Assists Indians and Alaska Natives to assume individual, family, and community responsibility by increasing the understanding of how diseases can be reduced. Encourages the use of health services, and addresses specific health and safety hazards faced by Indians and Alaska Natives.

MEDICAL SOCIAL WORKER: Working closely with physicians and nurses, professional social workers and paraprofessional associates deal with patient-related problems such as fear of treatment procedures, adjusting to limitations imposed by medical conditions, and worry about child care or loss of income while being hospitalized. If problems are identified in the medical setting which require outside assistance, medical social workers use community contacts to get supplemental services to patients and their families.

PHARMACIST: Works within a multidisciplinary health team. Acts as the primary source of drug information in all services. For ambulatory care, pharmacists are commonly involved in primary care programs for evaluating, treating, and monitoring patients. For inpatient services, pharmacists actively participate in selection, dosing, and monitoring of drug therapy. May also become involved in the broader aspects of health-care management.

PSYCHOLOGIST: Provides counseling and guidance in the Indian and Native Alaskan communities. Focuses on helping the Indian person overcome cultural and linguistic barriers, and to achieve self-sufficiency and maintain a cultural identity.

PHYSICIAN: The IHS health program is a system of inpatient and ambulatory care facilities which the IHS operates on Indian reservations and in Indian and Alaska Native communities. Physicians may work in one of 50 hospitals, 72 health centers, 12 school health centers, or 250 health stations or satellite field health clinics. Provides a full range of preventive, primary medical, community health, and rehabilitative services, as well as alcoholism programs to Indians and Alaska Natives. IHS physicians may also engage in research through the Office of Health Program Development.

OPTOMETRIST/OPHTHALMOLOGIST: Acts as part of a multidisciplinary health team. Examines eyes and related structures to diagnose the presence of vision problems, ocular diseases and other abnormalities. Prescribes corrective lenses and medication to treat identified conditions. Conducts vision screening and vision safety programs for school age children. Optometrists are located at health centers and hospitals. Ophthalmologists are employed in larger medical centers with optometrists.

Major Activities and Divisions

IHS Health Programs: Health programs in IHS are designed specifically to meet the needs of the Indian and Alaska Native people. The programs are carried out in cooperation with Indian organizations at the national, regional, and local levels.

Research and Training: The Office of Health Program Development (OHPD) is responsible for developing new and improved methods of delivery of health services.

Alternative Employment Programs

Extern (Student) Employment Program (COSTEP): The IHS hires individuals enrolled in a school of medicine, osteopathy, dentistry, veterinary medicine, optometry, podiatry, pharmacy, public health, nursing, or allied health professions through the COSTEP program of the Public Health Service. The term of employment is during any nonacademic period of the year, not to exceed one hundred and twenty days. In some cases, the student receives both a salary and payment of the school's tuition and fees.

IHS Scholarship Programs: Provides financial support *for Indian students only* to enroll in courses that will prepare them for acceptance into health professions schools, or to enroll in courses leading to a baccalaureate degree in specific pre-professional areas such as premedicine or predentistry. The scholarship recipient must intend to serve Indian People as a health-care provider upon completion of professional health-care education. A second scholarship program requires recipients to incur a one-year service obligation to the Indian Health Service for each year of scholarship support. Scholarship coordinator addresses and phone numbers are listed below. Approximately 50 students per year receive IHS scholarships.

Other IHS Programs: The Indian Health Service participates in a co-op program for high school and college students, typically beginning at the GS-3 level. These are usually support positions. IHS also participates in the Stay-in-School program. Contact IHS for more information.

Remarks

IHS hires mostly American Indians through its Indian Preference hiring procedures. Applicants of other ethnic backgrounds are encouraged to apply, but American Indian applicants will be given first preference. More than 50% of the IHS staff is of Indian or Alaska Native descent.

Application Procedures

Direct inquiries to:

Headquarters:
Indian Health Service
Twinbrook Metro Plaza, Suite 100
12300 Twinbrook Parkway
Rockville, MD 20852
(301) 443-4242
(800) 962-2817

Headquarters West:
Indian Health Service
2401 12th Street NW Room 316
Albuquerque, NM 87102
(505) 766-5557

Office of Health Program Development
Indian Health Service
7900 South J. Stock Road
Tuscon, AZ 85746-9352
(602) 670-6600

Area Offices:

Aberdeen Area IHS
Federal Building
115 4th Avenue SE
Aberdeen, SD 57401
(605) 226-7521

Scholarship Coordinator:
(605) 226-7553

Alaska Area Native Health Services
250 Gambell Street
Anchorage, AK 99501
(907) 267-1153

Scholarship Coordinator:
(907) 257-1408

Albuquerque Area IHS
505 Marquette, NW, Suite 1502
Albuquerque, NM 87102-0097
(505) 766-2151

Scholarship Coordinator:
(505) 766-1627

Bemidji Area IHS
203 Federal Building
Bemidji, MN 56601
(218) 751-7701

Scholarship Coordinator:
(218) 751-7701

Billings Area IHS
PO Box 2143
Billings, MT 59103
(406) 657-6403

Scholarship Coordinator:
(406) 657 6909

California Area IHS
2999 Fulton Avenue
Sacramento, CA 95821
(916) 978-4202

Scholarship Coordinator:
(916) 978-4191

Navajo Area IHS
PO Box G
Window Rock, AZ 86515
(602) 871-4811

Scholarship Coordinator
at same number

Oklahoma City Area IHS
215 Dean A. McGee Street, NW
Oklahoma City, OK 73102-3477
(405) 231-4796

Scholarship Coordinator:
(405) 231-4448

Phoenix Area IHS
3738 N. 16th Street, Suite A
Phoenix, AZ 85016-5981
(602) 241-2052

Scholarship Coordinator:
(602) 241-2066

Portland Area IHS
Federal Building, Room 476
1220 SW 3rd Avenue
Portland, OR 97204
(503) 326-2020

Scholarship Coordinator:
(503) 221-2019

Nashville Area IHS
3310 Perimeter Hill Drive
Nashville, TN 37217
(615) 736-5104

Scholarship Coordinator
at the same number

HOUSING AND URBAN DEVELOPMENT DEPARTMENT

The Department of Housing and Urban Development (HUD) is one of the newer cabinet agencies, created in 1965. It administers a wide variety of programs that assist the public in its housing needs. These include mortgage insurance programs that help families own their own homes and stimulate the construction and rehabilitation of rental properties; assistance programs that help needy families reside in housing; community development programs that upgrade and preserve neighborhoods; and fair housing laws that combat housing discrimination.

HUD also promotes a strong private-sector housing industry and stimulates public/private joint ventures.

THE DEPARTMENT OF HOUSING AND URBAN DEVELOPMENT (HUD)

Nature of Work: Housing, low-income people
Number of Employees: 13,447
Headquarters: Washington, DC
Regional Locations: Atlanta, GA; Boston, MA; Chicago, IL; Denver, CO; Fort Worth, TX; Kansas City, MO; New York City, NY; Philadelphia, PA; San Francisco, CA; Seattle, WA. These 10 regional offices oversee the 70 field offices that implement HUD's programs.
Typical Majors of New Hires: Accounting, business, computer science, economics, finance/banking, public administration, urban studies

Mission

Administers programs that help families become homeowners and facilitates the construction and rehabilitation of rental units. HUD also offers rental assistance to low-income families, ensures an adequate supply of mortgage credit, and combats housing discrimination.

Job Descriptions

APPRAISER: Determines the market value of residential properties.

ATTORNEY: Ensures HUD programs comply with legal, statutory, and regulatory requirements and represents the Department in court when criminal and administrative cases are involved.

COMMUNITY DEVELOPMENT REPRESENTATIVE: Administers forms of assistance that preserve and revitalize neighborhoods.

ECONOMIST: Assesses the impact of HUD policies and studies national labor, capital, mortgage, and housing markets.

MANAGEMENT ANALYST: Improves the effectiveness of work methods, organizations, personnel utilization, information and documentation systems.

REALTY SPECIALIST: Appraises, acquires, manages, and disposes of real estate in connection with HUD's various programs; services mortgages; and evaluates housing sites.

URBAN PLANNER: Promotes the economic and social welfare of urban areas by analyzing economic trends, social problems, development costs, public finances, intergovernmental relationships, and urban design objectives.

Major Activities and Divisions

Community Planning and Development Program: Administers Community Development Block Grants that provide decent housing and economic opportunities to low- and middle-income citizens.

Fair Housing and Equal Opportunity Program: Develops and implements housing and equal opportunity policies protecting people from discrimination.

Housing Program: Supervises programs supporting the production, financing, and management of new and rehabilitated housing.

Public and Indian Housing Program: Assists local public housing agencies in managing programs for low-income families, Native-American and Alaska Native communities.

Policy Development and Research Program: Determines the extent to which programs are achieving their intended goals.

Government National Mortgage Association: Provides secondary market financing for most FHA and VA home loans.

Alternative Employment Programs

HUD maintains a co-op program for professional, administrative, and technical occupations. The agency also runs a Volunteer Intern Program for college students. Most volunteer internships are in headquarters; however, openings are occasionally available at HUD field offices.

Remarks

HUD's Incentive Awards Program offers bonuses to employees for outstanding job performance, and for superior ideas.

Child-care services and a fitness facility are available for a fee at HUD's headquarters.

Application Procedures

Direct inquiries to:

Chief, Staffing and Classification Branch
Office of Personnel and Training
Department of Housing and Urban Development
451 7th Street, S.W., Room 2260
Washington, D.C. 20410-3100

(202) 708-0408/9
(202) 708-3203 (vacancies)

THE DEPARTMENT OF THE INTERIOR

As the nation's principal conservation agency, the Department of the Interior has responsibility for most of the country's public lands and natural resources. This includes fostering the wisest use of land and water resources, protecting fish and wildlife, preserving the environmental and cultural values of national parks and historical places, and providing for the enjoyment of life through outdoor recreation. The Department assesses the national energy and mineral resources and works to assure that their development is in the best interest of all citizens, communities, and territories of the U.S.

The jurisdiction of the Department of the Interior includes the administration of over 500 million acres of federal land; the conservation and development of mineral and water resources; the conservation, development, and use of fish and wildlife resources; the coordination of federal and state recreation programs; the preservation and administration of the nation's scenic and historic areas; the reclamation of arid lands in the West through irrigation; and the management of hydroelectric power systems.

Agencies within the Department of the Interior include:

The Bureau of Indian Affairs
The Bureau of Land Management
The Bureau of Mines
The Bureau of Reclamation
The Fish and Wildlife Service
The Geological Survey
The Minerals Management Service
The National Park Service
The Office of Surface Mining

BUREAU OF INDIAN AFFAIRS (BIA)

Nature of Work: Education, Native Americans
Number of Employees: 14,575
Headquarters: Washington, DC
Regional Locations: Aberdeen, SD; Albuquerque, NM; Anchorage, AK; Billings, MT; Juneau, AK; Minneapolis, MN; Muskogee, OK; Phoenix, AZ; Portland, OR; Sacramento, CA
Typical Majors of New Hires: Education, minority studies (Native American studies), engineering, biology, forestry, land use planning, social work/sociology, soil science

Mission

The Bureau of Indian Affairs works with American Indian and Alaska natives in the management of their affairs under a trust relationship with the federal government, and facilitates the development of their human and natural resource potential.

Job Descriptions

ELEMENTARY/SECONDARY TEACHER: Teaches Native Americans and Alaska natives in classroom settings, both on- and off-reservation. Includes elementary, secondary, and postsecondary schools, boarding schools, contract schools, and adult education. Assists in the creation and management of educational systems for the benefit of the Native American and Alaska Native people.

ENGINEER: Provides technical expertise in environmental engineering, mining, transportation systems, communication systems, and other fields.

FORESTER: Assists in managing forest resources, including wildlife, timber, and minerals, and recommends techniques which ensure the conservation of these resources.

RANGE CONSERVATIONIST: Assists Native Americans and Alaska Natives in overcoming difficulties such as shortages of water supplies, pastures overgrazed by livestock, or dense brush interfering with forage growth. Plans grazing systems, offers advice on water management, and recommends conservation techniques.

REALTY SPECIALIST: Offers real estate expertise on contractual documents, and the buying, selling, or management of property.

SOCIAL WORKER: Provides assistance and services relating to medical care referrals, vocational guidance, and counseling for individual and family cases. Obtains information on problems through interviews and home visits.

SOIL CONSERVATIONIST: Suggests conservation tactics, pollution control methods, and offers technical help in the construction of ponds, terraces, and contour strip-cropping systems. Often works directly in the field.

Major Activities and Divisions

Tribal Government Services Division: Provides needed social and community development programs.

Education Division: Assists in the creation and management of educational systems.

Trust Services Division: Acts as trustee for the lands and moneys of Native Americans and Alaska Natives.

Alternative Employment Programs

BIA offers summer jobs at the field installations, and gives strong preference to Indian applicants to fill these positions. It does not currently have a co-op or internship program.

Remarks

The BIA gives preference to American Indian applicants, but it does not exclusively hire American Indians. Some recruitment is conducted at colleges and universities with large Native American populations.

Application Procedures

Direct inquiries to the office which handles the hiring for the area in which you would like to work:

Headquarters Address:

Bureau of Indian Affairs
Branch of Personnel Services
1951 Constitution Avenue, N.W.
Code 675, MS331, SIB
Washington, DC 20245
(202) 208-7581

Regional Offices:

115 4th Avenue, S.E.
Aberdeen, SD 57401
(605) 226-7291

PO Box 26567
615 N. 1st Street
Albuquerque, NM 87125-6567
(505) 766-3170

PO Box 368
Anadarko, OK 73005
(405) 247-6673

316 N. 26th Street
Billings, MT 59101
(406) 657-6315

Box 3-8000
Juneau, AK 99802
(907) 586-7177

15 S. 5th Street
Minneapolis, MN 55402
(612) 373-1010

5th and W. Okmulgee
Muskogee, OK 74401
(918) 687-2296

PO Box 10
1 N. 1st Street
Phoenix, AZ 85011
(602) 379-6600

PO Box 3785
1425 NE Irving Street
Portland, OR 97208
(503) 231-6702

2800 Cottage Way
Sacramento, CA 95825
(916) 978-4691

Navajo Area Office
PO Box M
Window Rock, AZ 86515
(602) 871-5151

BUREAU OF LAND MANAGEMENT (BLM)

Nature of Work: Energy, environmental protection, forestry/wildlife, mining, recreation, waterways
Number of Employees: 8,546
Headquarters: Washington, DC
Regional Locations: Anchorage, AK; Alexandria, VA; Billings, MT; Boise, ID; Cheyenne, WY; Denver, CO; Lakewood, CO; Phoenix, AZ; Portland, OR; Reno, NV; Sacramento, CA; Salt Lake City, UT; Santa Fe, NM
Typical Majors of New Hires: Archaeology, biology, cartography, engineering, earth sciences (surveying, hydrology), forestry, geology, land use planning, law, physical sciences, recreation

Mission

The Bureau of Land Management oversees 270 million acres of public lands primarily located in the Far West and Alaska. Resources managed by the Bureau include timber, solid minerals, oil and gas, geothermal energy, wildlife habitat, endangered plant and animal species, rangeland vegetation, and rivers.

Job Descriptions

ARCHAEOLOGIST: Conducts scientific studies into the anthropological and archaeological history of public land areas. Involves field research at dig sites. Makes recommendations as to the use and development of historical properties.

CARTOGRAPHER: Graphically represents geographic information through the use of cartographic methods. Evaluates conflicting evidence concerning the character or physical features of the earth. Constructs maps and charts through mathematical, geodetic, and geographic methods.

ENGINEER: Provides technical expertise in efficient natural resource management, including the building of bridges and waste treatment systems, the use of mechanical equipment for fire control or brush cutting, and communications systems such as remote telephone and microwave systems. BLM hires civil, electrical, communications, and mining engineers.

ENVIRONMENTAL PROTECTION SPECIALIST: Monitors management practices and techniques to ensure that environmental impact is considered in land usage.

FORESTER: Develops and conserves natural forest resources, such as timber, forage, watersheds, land, and wildlife. Conducts research in the development of scientific instruments used in forest management.

GEOLOGIST: Conducts field research on rock types, rock structure, geologic history, and groundwater conditions. May use aerial photos and seismic and electrical resistivity geophysical methods. Solves problems and makes recommendations regarding road construction, timber harvesting, soil stability, and other issues.

HYDROLOGIST: Determines and analyzes watershed conditions and climatic variables in terms of land management potentials and hazards. Studies the influence of grazing, timber harvest, minerals management, recreation use, and other management activities on water resources.

LAND LAW EXAMINER: Researches laws, contracts, and regulations governing the acquisition, management, usage, and leasing of public lands. Makes recommendations regarding resource extraction, the issuance of rights-of-way, payment programs, and other realty and land use issues.

OUTDOOR RECREATION PLANNER: Communicates knowledge of natural resources and wildlife management through the design and implementation of interpretive and educational programs.

PHYSICAL SCIENTIST: Positions involve work in either an advanced specialized area of the physical sciences, or a blend of many physical science areas such as geology, hydrology, and cartography.

RANGE CONSERVATIONIST: Analyzes range resources, fitting the number of livestock and game animals to the available forage supply. Measures how forage plants respond to use by animals, and examines how to convert forage to animal products more efficiently.

SOIL SCIENTIST: Determines the significance of basic differences of soil capability to resource management. Conducts soil inventories, maps soil area boundaries, and makes recommendations regarding soil conservation tactics.

WILDLIFE BIOLOGIST: Coordinates wildlife needs with other land management activities, such as timber harvest, livestock grazing, public use, or road construction. Plans habitat adjustments and suggests courses of action to decrease the detrimental effects on wildlife habitats.

Major Activities and Divisions

The BLM is highly decentralized. It operates with 12 state offices, 55 district offices, and 155 Resource Area Offices throughout the country, though most are in the western states. Local advisory councils, state and local governments, and private citizens participate in the plans and decision-making processes of the BLM.

Alternative Employment Programs

The BLM has a co-op program which targets engineering and physical science majors at the bachelor's and master's levels.

Remarks

None.

Application Procedures

Direct inquiries to the field office which covers the area in which you would like to work:

Headquarters Address:

Bureau of Land Management
Department of the Interior
Washington, DC 20240
(202) 343-7645

Field Office Addresses:

Bureau of Land Management
Division of Personnel

Box 13, 107 C Street
Anchorage, AK 99513
(907) 271-5076

PO Box 16563
Phoenix, AZ 85011
(602) 241-5501

Rm. E-2841 2800 Cottage Way
Sacramento, CA 95825-1889
(916) 978-4743

2850 Youngfield Street
Lakewood, CO 80215
(303) 236-1721

350 S. Pickett Street
Alexandria, VA 22304
(703) 274-0180

3380 Americana Terrace
Boise, ID 83706
(208) 334-1401

PO Box 12000
850 Harvard Way
Reno, NV 89520
(702) 784-5451

PO Box 36800
222 N. 32d Street
Billings, MT 59107
(406) 657-6461

PO Box 1449
S. Federal Place
Santa Fe, NM 87504-1449
(505) 988-6030

PO Box 2965
825 NE. Multnomah Street
Portland, OR 97208
(503) 231-6251

Coordinated Financial Center
324 S. State Street
Salt Lake City, UT 84111-2303
(801) 524-5311

PO Box 1828
2515 Warren Avenue
Cheyenne, WY 82003
(307) 772-2326

BUREAU OF MINES

Nature of Work: Mining, environmental protection, safety, scientific research
Number of Employees: 2,400
Headquarters: Washington, DC
Regional Locations: Alany, OR; Reno, NV; Rolla, MO
Typical Majors of New Hires: Engineering (metallurgics), chemistry, geology, physical science

Mission

The Bureau of Mines has responsibility for conducting research and collecting information on mineral reserves throughout the world. It identifies problems relative to the nation's minerals requirements, including national security needs. It seeks to advance technology to improve efficiency and recovery from mineral deposits, and promotes conservation and environmental safety.

Job Descriptions

CHEMIST: Analyzes and tests substances to determine composition, quality, purity, and other characteristics. Chemists may conduct an applied research and development program, or work on a nonapplied project.

ENGINEER (MINING/CHEMICAL): Conducts technological research into the recovery and processing of mineral deposits.

GEOLOGIST: Maps geological surface deposits, bedrock, and mineral deposits. Makes and records geological field observations, and collects samples for laboratory analyses. Devises field and laboratory techniques and methods.

METALLURGIST: Extracts metals from ores, refines them, and studies their properties and behavior. Performs research to investigate essential metal properties and structures; develops improved alloys; and develops extracting and processing procedures.

PHYSICAL SCIENTIST: Conducts research, analysis, and testing relating to several physical science fields. Some work may involve specialized studies in one scientific discipline.

Major Activities and Divisions

Information and Analysis: Collects and publishes statistical and economic information on all phases of nonfuel mineral resource development, including exploration, production, stocks, prices, imports, and exports.

Research: Provides the technology for the extraction, processing, use, and recycling of the nation's nonfuel mineral resources at a reasonable cost without harm to the environment.

Alternative Employment Programs

The Bureau maintains a Summer Hire program which offers full time employment to students from May-August. The application deadline is in March. A small number of students are also hired through the co-op and Stay-in-School programs.

Remarks

None.

Application Procedures

Direct inquiries to:

US Dept of the Interior
2401 E Street, N.W.
Washington, DC 20241
Mail Stop (MS) 2130 Room 567
Attn: Recruitment Coordinator

(202) 634-1004 (main number)
(202) 634-4719 (employment)

BUREAU OF RECLAMATION

Nature of Work: Agriculture, energy, environmental protection, forestry/wildlife, recreation, waterways
Number of Employees: 7,368
Headquarters: Denver, CO
Regional Locations: Amarillo, TX; Billings, MT; Boise, ID; Boulder City, NV; Denver, CO; Sacramento, CA; Salt Lake City, UT; Washington, DC
Typical Majors of New Hires: Agriculture, agronomy, biology, engineering, agriculture, biology, earth sciences (hydrology), economics, environmental science, geology, land use planning, meteorology, soil science

Mission

The Bureau of Reclamation is responsible for the development and conservation of the nation's water resources in the western U.S. It provides municipal and industrial water supplies, hydroelectric power generation, irrigation water for agriculture, flood control, river navigation, river regulation and control, water quality regulation, fish and wildlife enhancement, and outdoor recreation.

Job Descriptions

AGRONOMIST: Conducts research into such issues as water-weed control and the identification of crop problems.

BIOLOGIST: Studies and assesses the biological impact of Bureau projects, and prepares environmental statements for proposed federal water resource projects.

CIVIL ENGINEER: Plans, constructs, and operates multiple purpose water development projects involving structures such as storage dams, hydroelectric powerplants and pumping plants, canals, tunnels, and pipelines. Specialization is possible in structures, hydraulics, hydrology, geotechnical, construction management, research, project development, or sanitary work.

ELECTRICAL ENGINEER: Designs, installs, operates, and maintains electrical equipment in dams, hydroelectric power plants, pumping plants, and switchyards. Specialization is possible in the applications of computers, microprocessors, electrical equipment, analysis of power systems, power and water control systems, and design of high-voltage transmission systems.

ENVIRONMENTAL ENGINEER: Evaluates the effects of reclamation projects on the environment. Manages air, land, and water resources by developing controls to minimize environmental consequences and to protect and enhance ecosystems. Specialization is possible in water and wastewater treatment, environmental modeling, environmental health, water resources, and hazardous water disposal.

GEOLOGIST: Collects and studies samples of minerals, sediments, rocks, and natural liquids and gases. Investigates the influence of climate, topography, plants and animals, and water bodies on specific geological processes.

HYDROLOGIST: Participates in water-related projects such as salinity control; groundwater recharge; and the development of plans for the conservation of water resources.

MECHANICAL ENGINEER: Designs, installs, operates, and maintains mechanical equipment associated with powerplants, pumping plants, and irrigation systems. Specialization is possible in low-head hydrosolar applications and energy conservation systems, water measurement controls and automation, structural analysis, fabrication and welding, nondestructive testing, and desalinization.

METEOROLOGIST: Conducts research into such weather-related projects as weather modification and cloud seeding.

REALTY SPECIALIST: Makes recommendations as to the protection, orderly development, and use of public lands. Involved in the buying, selling, and leasing of federal lands and maintains public land records.

SOIL SCIENTIST: Studies soil capabilities in regard to effective output and resource management. Conducts soil inventories, maps soil area boundaries, and recommends strategies for soil conservation and efficient usage.

Major Activities and Divisions

The projects of the Bureau of Reclamation are numerous and diverse. At present, Reclamation project facilities in operation include 355 storage reservoirs, 254 diversion dams, 15,855 miles of canals, 1,380 miles of pipeline, 276 miles of tunnels, 17,000 miles of project drains, and 50 hydroelectric power plants.

Alternative Employment Programs

The Bureau's Engineering and Research Center appoints co-op students with majors in civil, electrical, and mechanical engineering, as well as computer science, geology and geophysics. Co-op students are also hired to work in the Bureau's regional locations. Contact the Personnel Management Branch in Denver for more information.

Remarks

None.

Application Procedures

All hiring for the Bureau of Reclamation is done through the Denver office.

Direct inquiries to:

Personnel Management Branch, D-540
Bureau of Reclamation
Engineering and Research Center
P.O. Box 25007
Denver, CO 80225-0007

(303) 234-2039

U.S. FISH AND WILDLIFE SERVICE (FWS)

Nature of Work: Environmental protection, forestry/wildlife, law enforcement, recreation
Number of Employees: 7,100
Headquarters: Washington, DC
Regional Locations: Anchorage, AK; Albuquerque, NM; Atlanta, GA; Denver, CO; Minneapolis, MN; Newton Corner, MA; Portland, OR
Typical Majors of New Hires: Biological sciences (zoology), environmental sciences (natural resource management), natural sciences, recreation

Mission

FWS conserves, protects, and enhances fish and wildlife and their habitats for the continuing benefit of the American people. The Service promulgates an environmental stewardship ethic based on ecological principles, scientific knowledge of wildlife, and a sense of moral responsibility.

Job Descriptions

FISHERY BIOLOGIST: Studies the life history, habitats, classification, and economic relations of aquatic organisms. Manages fish hatcheries and fishery resources. Gathers scientific data on fish species and the effects of natural and human changes in the environment on the survival and growth of fish. Monitors fish hatchery operations and regulates fishing practices.

GENERAL BIOLOGIST: Conducts wildlife management field studies and collects samples for assessment. Designs subject field surveys to ensure that results are scientifically valid, and conducts independent literature surveys in support of field studies.

OUTDOOR RECREATION PLANNER: Designs and conducts a variety of interpretive and educational programs which integrate wildlife areas and programs with public usage. Communicates knowledge of fish and wildlife management. May involve some use of graphic arts, interpretive display techniques, or media production.

REFUGE MANAGER: Manages national wildlife refuges to protect and preserve migratory and native bird species, mammals, endangered species, and other wildlife. Devises wildlife management programs and public use policies at the refuge.

SPECIAL AGENT: Investigates violations of federal laws for the protection and conservation of wildlife. Performs surveillance, raids, contraband seizures, and makes arrests. May also pilot aircraft in connection with enforcement duties.

WILDLIFE BIOLOGIST: Studies the distribution, abundance, habitats, mortality factors, and economic values of mammals, birds, and other wildlife. Plans wildlife management programs, restores or develops wildlife habitats, regulates wildlife populations, and controls wildlife diseases.

Major Activities and Divisions

Wildlife and Fishery Resource Programs: Includes work with migratory birds, mammals and nonmigratory birds, cooperative fish and wildlife research, coastal andronomous fish, Great Lakes fisheries, and other inland fisheries.

Endangered Species Programs: Includes development of the Endangered Species and Threatened Species List, research on propagation methods, operation of wildlife refuges, law enforcement, and consultation with foreign countries.

Resource Management Programs: Includes the protection and improvement of land and water environments through biological monitoring, surveillance of pesticides, heavy metals, and thermal pollution, and environmental impact assessment.

Public Information Programs: Involves preparation of news releases, leaflets, and brochures; operation of environmental study areas; operation of visitor centers and nature trails, and providing activities such as hunting, fishing, and wildlife photography.

FEDERAL AID PROGRAMS: Apportions funds to the states and territories for projects designed to conserve, develop, and enhance the nation's fish and wildlife resources.

Remarks

The above list of regional locations does not include the many National Wildlife Refuges, fish and wildlife laboratories and centers, cooperative research units, and National Fish Hatcheries in which many employees of the Service work across the United States. The Service maintains 442 National Wildlife Refuges, 150 Waterfowl Production Areas, 25 major fish and wildlife laboratories and centers, 36 cooperative research units at universities across the country, and 70 National Fish Hatcheries.

Alternative Employment Programs

The U.S. Fish and Wildlife Service has annual summer positions available at grades 1 through 4. Inquire at a Fish and Wildlife Service Personnel Office for more information about summer, internship, and co-op positions.

Application Procedures

The Fish and Wildlife Service is divided into eight geographic regions, each of which conduct their own hiring processes. Direct inquiries to the regional office which handles hiring at the location in which you would like to work. Address to Personnel Officer, U. S. Fish and Wildlife Service, U.S. Department of the Interior:

18th and C Streets, N.W.
Room 3425
Washington, DC 20240
(202) 343-5634

1011 East Tudor Road
Anchorage, AK 99503
(907) 786-3542

P.O. Box 25486
Denver Federal Center
Denver, CO 80225
(303) 236-7920

Richard B. Russell Building
Suite 1376
75 Spring Street, S.W.
Atlanta, GA 30303
(404) 331-3588

One Gateway Center
Suite 612
Newton Corner, MA 02158
(617) 965-5100

Federal Building, Fort Snelling
Twin Cities, MN 55111
(612) 725-3563

P.O. Box 1306
500 Gold Avenue, S.W.
Albuquerque, NM 87103
(505) 766-2321

Lloyd 500 Building, Suite 1692
500 N.E. Multnomah Street
Portland, OR 97232
(503) 231-6118

U.S. GEOLOGICAL SURVEY (USGS)

Nature of Work: Energy, environmental protection
Number of Employees: 10,900
Headquarters: Reston, VA
Regional Locations: Major regional research centers are in Denver, CO; Menlo Park, CA; and Reston, VA. More than 200 field offices exist throughout the U.S. (see Programs and Divisions below)
Typical Majors of New Hires: Cartography, earth sciences (hydrology, geophysics), environmental sciences, geology

Mission

The USGS is an earth science research agency. Its objectives are to perform surveys and research in cartography, hydrology, and geology, and to assess the water and land resources of the U.S. Examples of current programs include assessing the adverse impact of natural hazards such as floods, volcanoes, and earthquakes; investigating the resource potential of the ocean floor; and identifying geologic criteria for the selection of hazardous waste disposal sites.

Job Descriptions

CARTOGRAPHER: Works in various aspects of cartographic production, including both manual cartography and digital cartographic production. Some positions require security clearances and drug testing. Second- or third-shift work may be involved.

CHEMIST: Analyzes and tests various geologic substances to determine their composition, quality, purity, and other characteristics.

GEOLOGIST: Maps geological surface deposits, bedrock, subsurface phenomena, and mineral deposits. Makes and records geological field observations and collects samples for laboratory analysis.

GEOPHYSICIST: Conducts research concerning the electric, magnetic, and gravitational field of the earth, the motion and constitution of the earth, and cosmic physics in its relation to the earth and its atmosphere.

HYDROLOGIST: Studies the interactions within the hydrologic cycle with relation to precipitation, streamflow, and subsurface water. Investigates the transport of sediment and dissolved materials in natural waters and assesses the biological changes that result.

PHYSICAL SCIENTIST: Conducts research, analysis, and testing which relate to a combination of several physical science fields, with no one science predominant.

Major Activities and Divisions

There are three program divisions within the USGS. Each division is responsible for conducting research in its scientific issue area, and has research centers or offices throughout the U.S.

Water Resources Division Offices are located in Albany, NY; Boston, MA; Champaign, IL; Columbus, OH; Austin, TX; Albuquerque, NM; Cheyenne, WY; Carson City, NV; Bismarck, ND; Boise, ID; Baton Rouge, LA; Atlanta, GA; Columbia, SC; Charleston, WV; Indianapolis, IN; Iowa City, IA; Lawrence, KS; Lincoln, NB; Helena, MT; Little Rock, AR; Jackson, MS; Harrisburg, PA; Louisville, KY; Huron, SD; Madison, WI; Lansing, MI; Oklahoma City, OK; Nashville, TN; Sacramento, CA; St. Paul, MN; Raleigh, NC; Tallahassee, FL; Rolla, MO; Towson, MD; Trenton, NJ; Tuscaloosa, AL; Salt Lake City, UT; Tucson, AZ; Honolulu, HA; San Juan, PR; Portland, OR; Tacoma, WA; Richmond, VA; Hartford, CT; and Augusta, ME.

Geologic Division Field Offices are located in Flagstaff, AZ; Spokane, WA; Vancouver, WA; Woods Hole, MA; and at the Hawaiian Volcano Observatory in Hawaii.

National Mapping Centers are located in Rolla, MO; Reston, VA; Lakewood, CO; and Menlo Park, CA.

Alternative Employment Programs

USGS has a strong internship and co-op program for college students. Positions are available nation-wide. Contact the headquarters or regional personnel offices for more information.

Remarks

The USGS provides technical assistance and participates in cooperative scientific studies in 30 countries. Many upper-level positions involve overseas travel.

Application Procedures

There are five regional USGS personnel offices that are responsible for all entry-level hiring. Direct inquiries to the personnel office which hires for the location in which you would like to work. (See regions, Appendix)

HEADQUARTERS
PERSONNEL OFFICE
Chief, Recruitment and Placement
12202 Sunrise Valley Drive, MS-215
Reston, VA 22092
(703) 648-7788/6131
TAPE RECORDING: (703) 648-7676

SOUTHEASTERN REGIONAL
PERSONNEL OFFICE
Personnel Office, Room 218
75 Spring Street, S.W.
Atlanta, GA 30303
(404) 331-0670
TAPE RECORDING: (404) 331-2310

MID-CONTINENT STATES PERSONNEL OFFICE
Personnel Office
1400 Independence Avenue, MS-100
Rolla, MO 65401
(314) 341-0810
TAPE RECORDING: (314) 341-0909

CENTRAL REGION PERSONNEL OFFICE
Personnel Office
Building 25, Denver Federal Center, MS-203
Box 25406
Denver, CO 80225
(303) 236-5900
TAPE RECORDING: (303) 236-5846

WESTERN REGION PERSONNEL OFFICE
Staffing Chief
345 Middlefield Road, MS-212
Menlo Park, CA 94025
(415) 329-4104
TAPE RECORDING: (415) 329-4122

MINERALS MANAGEMENT SERVICE (MMS)

Nature of Work: Energy, environmental protection, mining, taxes/revenues, scientific research
Number of Employees: 2,118
Headquarters: Washington, DC
Regional Locations: Anchorage, AK; Lakewood, CO; Los Angeles, CA; New Orleans, LA; Vienna, VA
Typical Majors of New Hires: Accounting, biology, chemistry, engineering, environmental sciences, geology, mathematics, meteorology, oceanography, physics

Mission

The Minerals Management Service conducts all leasing and resource management functions for the nation's Outer Continental Shelf, which has the potential to supply a significant portion of this nation's future oil and gas needs. The MMS leases offshore areas for exploration and production and monitors drilling and production activities to protect the coastal environments and ensure proper royalty collection.

Job Descriptions

ENVIRONMENTAL PROTECTION SPECIALIST: Assists state and local governments on matters relating to environmental protection programs and proposals. Writes environmental impact statements in regard to OCS projects.

GEOLOGIST: Maps surficial deposits, bedrock, subsurface phenomena, and mineral deposits. Makes and records geological field observations and collects samples for laboratory analyses.

GEOPHYSICIST: Conducts scientific research in exploration geophysics, including gravimetric, magnetic, electrical, and seismic methods; and laboratory and field studies of the physical properties of rocks and minerals. Prepares reports for reference or publication.

OCEANOGRAPHER: Researches ocean phenomena such as tides, sea ice, currents, waves, and sediments in their relation to temperatures, densities, circulation, etc., including their effect on animal and plant life.

PETROLEUM ENGINEER: Performs engineering studies of oil fields. Works on improving primary and secondary recovery methods, including radioactive tracer experiments in water flooding. Conducts research on subjects such as porous reservoir rock, "bottom hole" samples, and underground storage of natural gas. Also supervises development of departmental oil and gas leases.

PHYSICAL SCIENTIST: Performs work in the field of physical sciences which includes a combination of disciplines and fields. May specialize in one discipline, or conduct work involving several areas of physical science.

Major Activities and Divisions

The MMS is divided into the Royalty Management Program and four Outer Continental Shelf (OCS) regional offices.

Royalty Management Program: Responsible for the collection and distribution of all royalty payments, rentals, fines, and other revenues due the federal government and Indian lessors from the extraction of mineral resources.

OCS *Regional Offices:* Responsible for resource evaluation and classification, environmental review, leasing activities, and inspection and enforcement programs for Outer Continental Shelf lands.

Alternative Employment Programs

MMS hires college students through a paid co-op program. These positions are available in the headquarters and regional offices.

Remarks

Campus recruiting at MMS is typically limited. The personnel office recommends federal college fairs as an effective way to explore employment with MMS.

Application Procedures

Direct inquiries to the office which hires for your region of interest:

Headquarters Address:

Department of the Interior
Minerals Management Service
Staffing and Classifications Branch
MS 634
Atrium Building
381 Eden Street
Herndon, VA 22070
(703) 787-1413
(703) 787-1402 (vacancies)

OCS Regional Offices:

ATLANTIC REGION
Suite 610
1951 Kidwell Drive
Vienna, VA 22180
(703) 285-2165

ALASKA REGION
Rm 110
949 E. 36th Avenue
Anchorage, AK 99508-4302
(907) 261-4010

GULF OF MEXICO REGION
1202 Elmwood Park Boulevard
New Orleans, LA 70123-2394
(504) 736-0557

PACIFIC REGION
1340 W. 6th Street
Los Angeles, CA 90017
(213) 894-2049

ROYALTY MANAGEMENT PROGRAM
PO Box 25165
Lakewood, CO 80225
(303) 231-3386

NATIONAL PARK SERVICE (FNP)

Nature of Work: Environmental protection, forestry/wildlife, historic preservation, law enforcement, recreation
Number of Employees: 7,500 permanent full-time; 21,500 including seasonal employees
Headquarters: Washington, DC
Regional Locations: Alaska; Atlanta, GA; Boston, MA; Denver, CO; Omaha, NE; Philadelphia, PA; San Francisco, CA; Santa Fe, NM; Seattle, WA. Interpretive Design Centers: Denver, CO; Harpers Ferry, WV
Typical Majors of New Hires: Anthropology, archaeology, engineering, English, geography, history, hotel/restaurant management, landscape architecture, land use planning, natural sciences, recreation

Mission

The National Park Service has been preserving, protecting, and managing the natural, cultural, historical, and recreational areas of the National Park System since its creation in 1916. Its mission is to conserve natural and cultural resources, and to provide the public with recreational and educational experiences.

Job Descriptions

ARCHEOLOGIST, HISTORIAN, ANTHROPOLOGIST, GEOGRAPHER: Concerned with the Park System's cultural resources. Most of these staff positions are located in the Denver Service Center or the Regional Offices.

CONCESSIONS SPECIALIST: Evaluates and monitors restaurants and other concessions operated by private contractors in the National Park Service.

ENGINEERS, ARCHITECTS, LANDSCAPE ARCHITECTS, RECREATIONAL PLANNERS: Mostly work in the Planning and Design Facility in Denver, CO. Work on the design of National Park Service sites in terms of environmental impact, educational and inspirational quality, and accessibility.

GEOLOGIST, BIOLOGIST, PHYSICAL SCIENTIST: Research-oriented positions, limited in number and usually requiring advanced degrees or specialized experience.

MUSEUM SPECIALIST: Designs exhibits, manages museum collections and participates in museum education. Most design work is conducted at Harpers Ferry Center. Other curatorial positions are located in parks, involving management of the site collections or technical conservation work.

PARK POLICE: Preserves the peace, investigates and prevents accidents and crimes, arrests violators, and provides crowd control. Includes horse-mounted, motorcycle, helicopter, and canine units. Usually work in a large urban area such as Washington, DC, New York City, or San Francisco.

PARK RANGER: Performs work in the conservation of resources and fire control. Disseminates scientific, natural or historical information, enforces laws, and performs search and rescue missions. Manages wildlife, forests, lakeshores, historic properties, and recreation areas.

WRITER-EDITOR/PUBLIC INFORMATION SPECIALIST: Develops Park Service publications and informational programs. Mostly work in Washington, DC, or the regional offices.

Major Activities and Divisions

Although the Park System is not divided into specific program areas, it has a vast array of sites and services. The System comprises 321 units and 77 million acres of land in 49 states, Puerto Rico, Guam, and the Virgin Islands. It contains national preserves, parks, historic sites, battlefields, parkways, and national monuments.

Alternative Employment Programs

The National Park Service hires employees on a seasonal basis, or as volunteers through the Volunteers in Parks (VIP) program. For more information, contact any regional office, or the Seasonal Employment Unit in Washington.

Remarks

The Park Service provides neither training nor financial aid to prospective employees.

Application Procedures

Direct inquiries to the regional office which handles the hiring for the location in which you would like to work:

Washington Office
National Park Service
Interior Building, Room 2328
P.O. Box 37127
Washington, DC 20012-7127
(202) 619-7256
(202) 619-7111 (vacancies)

North Atlantic Region
15 State Street
Boston, MA 02109
(617) 223-3774

Mid-Atlantic Region
143 South Third Street
Philadelphia, PA 19106
(215) 597-7074

National Capital Region
1100 Ohio Drive, S.W.
Washington, DC 20242
(202) 485-9790

Southeast Region
75 Spring Street, S.W.
Atlanta, GA 30303
(404) 331-5714

Midwest Region
1709 Jackson Street
Omaha, NE 68102
(402) 221-3456

Rocky Mountain Region
12795 West Almeda Parkway
P.O. Box 25287
Denver, CO 80225-0287
(303) 969-2727

Southwest Region
P.O. Box 728
Santa Fe, NM 87501
(505) 988-6427

Western Region
450 Golden Gate Avenue
Box 36063
San Francisco, CA 94102
(415) 556-7230

Pacific Northwest Region
83 South King Street, Suite 212
Seattle, WA 98104
(206) 442-4409

Alaska Region
2525 Gambell Street, Room 107
Anchorage, AK 99503
(907) 257-2575

Harpers Ferry Center
National Park Service
Harpers Ferry, WV 25425
(304) 535-6371

OFFICE OF SURFACE MINING (OSM)

Nature of Work: Environmental protection, funds/funding, mining, safety
Number of Employees: 1,086
Headquarters: Washington, DC
Regional Locations: Albuquerque, NM; Big Stone Gap, VA; Birmingham, AL; Casper, WY; Charleston, WV; Columbus, OH; Denver, CO; Harrisburg, PA; Indianapolis, IN; Kansas City, MO; Knoxville, TN; Lexington, KY; Pittsburgh, PA; Springfield, IL; Tulsa, OK; Wilkes-Barre, PA
Typical Majors of New Hires: Accounting, engineering (mining), environmental science, physical science

Mission

As both a regulatory and funding agency, the OSM works with and through the states to see that the production of coal meets the nation's energy needs and that land and water are restored for future productive use. Now that most coal mining states have assumed prime responsibility for regulating coal mining reclamation activities within their borders, the OSM's main objectives are to oversee mining and reclamation.

Job Descriptions

ENGINEER (CIVIL/GENERAL/MINING): Helps establish technical standards for OSM reclamation and enforcement efforts. Interprets and implements the Surface Mining Control and Reclamation Act, studying performance standards and technical requirements. Technical recommendations may include measures necessary to stabilize landslides, correct erosion and sedimentation problems, abate or treat acid mine drainage, control mine subsidence, and extinguish mine fires. Involves on-site research and investigation. Positions are located in Eastern and Western Field Operations Offices in Pittsburgh, Denver, Wilkes-Barre, and Knoxville.

ENVIRONMENTAL SCIENTIST: Assesses the environmental impact of surface mining techniques in terms of habitat destruction, soil erosion, effect on the hydrologic cycle, and other factors.

FEE COMPLIANCE SPECIALIST (ACCOUNTANT/AUDITOR): Collects civil penalties and abandoned mine land fee payments. Assists in auditing mine land fee payments.

GEOLOGIST: Reviews technical programs designed to meet Surface Mining Control and Reclamation Act (SMCRA) requirements, and provides technical support to federal and state inspectors. Positions are usually located in Denver, Pittsburgh, Wilkes-Barre (PA), and Knoxville, TN.

HYDROLOGIST: Studies and evaluates the effects of surface mining on the quantity, rates of movement, and quality of water in the various phases of the hydrologic cycle. Reviews technical programs designed to meet Surface Mining Control and Reclamation Act (SMCRA) requirements. Positions are usually located in Denver, Pittsburgh, Wilkes-Barre (PA), and Knoxville.

REALTY SPECIALIST: Makes recommendations as to the protection, orderly development, and use of public lands. Conducts sensitive negotiations with landowners, corporate representatives, state and federal officials, and representatives of other political subdivisions. Works with businesses and Indian tribes involving complex special-client relationships. Prepares various realty instruments associated with voluntary consent to enter, use of police power, or acquisition of realty interests. Positions are located in Washington, DC, Denver, Pittsburgh, and Wilkes-Barre.

SURFACE MINING RECLAMATION SPECIALIST: Conducts and oversees survey, reclamation, and enforcement work to ensure that surface mining operations are conducted to protect the environment and that affected lands are returned to a stable condition compatible with the value and uses of surrounding lands. Plans and conducts entire survey process, investigates mining operations for violations of federal and state plans, and conducts surveys of public complaints of damage from blasting and of possible pollution from mine sites. Positions are located in all Field Offices. These positions usually require some travel.

WILDLIFE BIOLOGIST: Studies the effects of surface mining on the habitats of various wildlife species, and proposes reclamation strategies to restore those habitats.

Major Activities and Divisions

Major activities of the Office of Surface Mining are carried out through the Office of the Director, assisted by two Deputy Directors and six Assistant Directors.

Alternative Employment Programs

OSM maintains a co-op program for students at the bachelor's or master's level working toward a degree in the physical sciences. Co-op students usually work as Reclamation Specialists or Engineers. Typically 1–10 co-ops are hired per year. Contact the co-op director at (202) 208-2953. OSM also typically hires 1–4 PMI students annually, and participates in the Stay-in-School program for clerical positions.

Remarks

The Office of Surface Mining actively recruits on college campuses. Check with your campus placement office for interview dates.

Application Procedures

Direct inquiries to the regional office which handles hiring for the location in which you would like to work:

WASHINGTON HEADQUARTERS:

Office of Surface Mining
Personnel Division
1951 Constitution Avenue, S.W., Rm 44
Washington, DC 20240
(202) 208-2953 (employment)
(202) 208-2773 (personnel)

WESTERN FIELD OPERATIONS:

DENVER REGIONAL OFFICE

Office of Surface Mining
1020 15th Street
2nd Floor
Brooks Towers
Denver, CO 80202
(303) 844-2451/2592

EASTERN FIELD OPERATIONS:

PITTSBURGH REGIONAL OFFICE

Office of Surface Mining
10 Parkway Center
Pittsburgh, PA 15220
(412) 937-2828 (Eastern support center)
(412) 937-9212 (personnel)

JUSTICE DEPARTMENT

Often referred to as the nation's largest law firm, the Justice Department represents the public interest. Most of the Department's litigation is handled through its Departmental Offices. They include the Civil Rights Division, Criminal Division, Tax Division, etc. The rest of the Department is comprised of investigatory and enforcement agencies such as the Federal Bureau of Investigation and Immigration and Naturalization Service.

BUREAU OF PRISONS

Nature of Work: Law enforcement
Number of Employees: 15,276
Headquarters: Washington, DC
Regional Locations: Atlanta, GA; Belmont, CA; Dallas, TX; Kansas City, MO; Laurel, MD; Philadelphia, PA
Typical Majors of New Hires: Business, criminal justice, law, medicine, social sciences

Mission

Operates the federal penal system's prisons and community treatment centers.

Job Descriptions

ATTORNEY: Represents the Bureau in matters such as tort claims, conditions-of-confinement, mental competency, personal liability, contract protests, and injunctive actions.

CHAPLAIN: Provides for the spiritual and religious welfare of inmates.

CORRECTIONAL OFFICER: Enforces the rules and regulations governing penal institutions, supervises inmate work assignments, and counsels inmates.

CORRECTIONAL TREATMENT SPECIALIST: Recommends educational, work, vocational training and counseling programs to prisoners. Works with inmates, their families, probation officers, social agencies and others in developing release plans for prisoners.

FINANCIAL MANAGEMENT SPECIALIST: Provides accounting, budget, and financial planning services.

FOOD SERVICE SPECIALIST: Supervises the operations of food supply services at federal prisons including storerooms, kitchen, dining rooms, meat shops, and bakeries.

HUMAN RESOURCES SPECIALIST: Supports the organization in recruiting, labor relations, compensation, benefits, employee relating and security.

MEDICAL OFFICER: Provides medical and dental care to prisoners, and oversees health-care programs at prisons.

NURSE: Provides care to sick or injured prisoners, and promotes better health practices.

PHARMACIST: Compounds prescriptions and dispenses and preserves drugs, medicines, and chemicals.

PSYCHOLOGIST: Provides consultative services to prisoners helping them adjust to prison life and post-release.

RECREATION SPECIALIST: Evaluates, plans, and organizes recreational programs for inmates.

Major Activities and Divisions

The Central Office: Located in Washington, DC, this office issues standards and policy guidelines, and coordinates all Bureau activities on a nationwide basis.

The Correctional Programs Division: Oversees correctional services, drug abuse treatment, and chaplaincy service.

The Administration Division: Performs long-range construction and program planning, and handles the Bureau's budget, fiscal, and business matters.

The Health Services Division: Provides medical, psychiatric, and dental support services, and promotes health and safety at each institution.

Federal Prison Industries, Inc.: A wholly owned, self-supporting government corporation that maintains 75 industrial operations in 40 institutions, and sells goods and services to federal agencies.

Alternative Employment Programs

The Bureau typically hires 40 or more college juniors as co-ops who work as GS-3 Case Managers/Counselors, or as Human Resource Specialists. PMI, internships, and Stay-in-School positions are also available. Call (202) 514-5241 for more information.

Remarks

All employees assigned to an institution must successfully complete the Law Enforcement Officer training program at the Federal Law Enforcement Training Center in Glynco, Georgia.

Application Procedures

Direct inquiries to:

Chief of Recruiting
Federal Bureau of Prisons
Room 446 HOLC
320 First Street, N.W.
Washington, DC 20534

(202) 307-3204
(202) 514-6388 (vacancies)

DEPARTMENT OF JUSTICE—OFFICE OF ATTORNEY PERSONNEL MANAGEMENT

Nature of Work: Law enforcement
Number of Employees: 14,485
Headquarters: Washington, DC
Regional Locations: Atlanta, GA; Chicago, IL; Cleveland, OH; Dallas, TX; New York, NY; Philadelphia, PA; San Francisco, CA
Typical Majors of New Hires: Law

Mission

Provides legal advice to the President and represents the executive branch of government in court.

Job Descriptions

ATTORNEY: Enforces consumer, drug, immigration, naturalization, and criminal laws through investigations and litigation; represents federal agencies involved in law suits; and comments on proposed legislation and regulations.

Major Activities and Divisions

Antitrust Division: Maintains a competitive marketplace by prosecuting criminal bid-rigging and price fixing cases, and by reviewing mergers and acquisitions.

Civil Division: Represents federal agencies and employees in matters involving claims for and against the government; the constitutionality or legality of federal programs; torts; the deportation and detention of aliens; and consumer protection.

Civil Rights Division: Enforces federal laws and executive orders banning unlawful discrimination.

Criminal Division: Prosecutes cases involving public corruption, white collar crime, organized crime, illegal drugs, and internal security.

Land and Natural Resources Division: Litigates matters involving the environment, wildlife, and energy development.

Tax Division: Collects federal revenues using civil actions at the request of the Internal Revenue Service.

Alternative Employment Programs

Each year the Justice Department's Summer Law Intern Program hires at the GS-7 level about 100 students who have finished their second year of law school. Applications are available in law school placement offices at the end of August, with employment beginning the following summer.

The Department also maintains three other law student programs. Paid, part-time positions not exceeding 20 hours per week are available during the school year. These positions are filled at the GS-5 or GS-7 level depending on how much schooling the student has completed. A Work-Study intern program for course credit but no compensation is available when permitted by the student's law school. A Volunteer Program is also available. Although the work schedule is negotiated, it may not exceed 20 hours per week for full-time students. Applications for the Part-Time, Work-Study Intern, and Volunteer Programs may be submitted at any time.

Remarks

A number of organizations within the Justice Department require a three-year employment commitment (with the exception of the Tax Division, which requires a four-year commitment).

All persons accepting an employment offer with the Department may be required to submit to urinalysis to screen for illegal drug use. Some Department employees may also be subject to random drug testing.

Application Procedures

Applicants can apply for attorney positions under two programs—the Experienced Attorney Program, and the Honor Program. To be eligible for the Experienced Attorney Program, applicants must have had their J.D. degree for at least one year and be an active member of the Bar in good standing. Resumes or applications from experienced attorneys are accepted at any time of the year.

The Honor Program is the Justice Department's recruitment program for outstanding third-year law students; graduate law students (applying in the fall of the last year of their graduate law study); and Judicial Law Clerks.

For all attorney positions, apply to:

The U.S. Department of Justice
Office of Attorney Personnel Management
Room 4311, Main Building
Pennsylvania Avenue at 10th Street, N.W.
Washington, DC 20530

(202) 633-3396

DRUG ENFORCEMENT ADMINISTRATION (DEA)

Nature of Work: Drugs/abuse, law enforcement
Number of Employees: 5,916
Headquarters: Washington, DC
Regional Locations: Atlanta, GA; Boston, MA; Chicago, IL; Dallas, TX; Denver, CO; Detroit, MI; Houston, TX; Los Angeles, CA; Miami, FL; Newark, NJ; New Orleans, LA; New York, NY; Philadelphia, PA; Phoenix, AZ; San Diego, CA; San Francisco, CA; Seattle, WA; St. Louis, MO. DEA also has offices in 43 foreign countries.
Typical Majors of New Hires: Chemistry, criminal justice

Mission

Enforces drug laws and regulations by suppressing major trafficking organizations, apprehending their leaders, and seizing their assets. DEA also enforces regulations concerning the legal manufacture and distribution of controlled substances.

Job Descriptions

COMPLIANCE INVESTIGATOR: Audits companies legally producing controlled substances ensuring compliance with applicable laws.

SPECIAL AGENT: Investigates the criminal production and distribution of drugs, gathers evidence, testifies in criminal court proceedings, and gives public presentations on DEA's responsibilities.

Major Activities and Divisions

DEA combats drug abuse by apprehending drug traffickers, managing a national narcotics intelligence system, and training federal, state, and local law enforcement officials.

Alternative Employment Programs

Co-op programs are available depending on funding availability.

Remarks

Compliance Investigators must complete a 7-week training program at the Federal Law Enforcement Training Center at Glynco, Georgia. This consists of written and physical tests in such areas as investigative techniques, drug pharmacology, and drug education. Special Agents must complete a 15-week course which includes, in addition to the material taught to Compliance Investigators, self-defense, firearms proficiency, and drug laws.

Application Procedures

Direct inquiries to:

The Drug Enforcement Administration
Personnel Office
1405 I Street, N.W.
Washington, DC 20537

(202) 307-4055

FEDERAL BUREAU OF INVESTIGATION (FBI)

Nature of Work: Intelligence, law enforcement
Number of Employees: 22,329
Headquarters: Washington, DC
Regional Locations: 59 field offices nationwide
Typical Majors of New Hires: Accounting, engineering, language, law, liberal arts

Mission

Investigates violations of most federal laws. Emphasis is placed on fighting organized crime, drugs, terrorism, white-collar crime, and foreign counterintelligence.

Job Descriptions

SPECIAL AGENT: Investigates violations of over 200 federal statutes; gathers and reports facts, locates witnesses, compiles evidence in cases involving federal jurisdiction; testifies in court.

Major Activities and Divisions

Criminal Investigation: Counters various types of criminal activity including terrorism, violent crime, organized crime, discrimination, and white collar crime.

Identification Division: Operates the Bureau's automated fingerprint service.

Intelligence Division: Gathers and analyzes data on the composition and movement of terrorist, subversive, and organized criminal organizations.

Laboratory Division: Conducts the FBI's forensic research.

Alternative Employment Programs

The FBI maintains a co-op program for certain scientific occupations.

Remarks

Special Agents must successfully complete a 16-week training program at the FBI Academy in Quantico, Virginia. The program includes academic study, physical fitness training, and instruction in firearms and self-defense.

Application Procedures

Direct inquiries to:

Federal Bureau of Investigation
National Recruitment Program
Ninth Street and Pennsylvania Avenue, N.W.
Washington, DC 20535

(202) 324-3000

or contact the Applicant Coordinator at the nearest FBI offfice.

U.S. MARSHALS SERVICE

Nature of Work: Law enforcement
Number of Employees: 3,248
Headquarters: Washington, DC
Regional Locations: 94 locations across the country
Typical Majors of New Hires: Criminal justice

Mission

Protects federal courts, judges, attorneys, and jurors; apprehends most federal fugitives; operates the witness security program; transports federal prisoners; executes court orders and arrest warrants; administers the National Asset Seizure and Forfeiture Program; and prevents civil disturbances.

Job Descriptions

DEPUTY U.S. MARSHAL: Apprehends fugitives who have escaped prison, violated parole, or failed to appear before courts as ordered. Protects federal courts, judges, attorneys, and witnesses. Serves processes and warrants, guards endangered witnesses, transports prisoners, and seizes and manages assets acquired from criminal activities.

Major Activities and Divisions

Office of the Associate Director for Operations: Administers the Service's enforcement, court security, witness protection, prisoner transportation, and asset seizure and forfeiture programs.

Special Operations Group: Quells mob violence in situations requiring federal intervention.

Office of the Assistant Director for Inspections: Investigates and evaluates alleged violations of misconduct by employees of the U.S. Marshals Service.

Alternative Employment Programs

The U.S. Marshals Service maintains a co-op program for students from various disciplines.

Remarks

Deputy U.S. Marshals must successfully complete a 13-week training program at the U.S. Marshals Service Training Academy. The program includes academic study, physical fitness training, and instruction in firearms and self-defense.

Application Procedures

Direct inquiries to:

U.S. Marshals Service
600 Army Navy Drive
Arlington, VA 22202

(202) 307-9629

IMMIGRATION AND NATURALIZATION SERVICE (INS)

Nature of Work: Immigration, law enforcement
Number of Employees: 17,112
Headquarters: Washington, DC
Regional Locations: Burlington, VT; Dallas, TX; Laguna Niguel, CA; Twin Cities, MN. INS also maintains district offices in 34 cities nationwide, and overseas offices in Bangkok, Thailand; Mexico City, Mexico; and Rome, Italy.
Typical Majors of New Hires: Criminal justice

Mission

Controls the entry of aliens into the U.S. by denying admission to unqualified aliens; maintains information on alien status; deports aliens not legally entitled to reside in the U.S.; and facilitates the certification and citizenship process.

Job Descriptions

BORDER PATROL AGENT: Prevents the illegal entry of aliens into the U.S. by patrolling border crossings.

DEPORTATION OFFICER: Tracks the deportation proceedings of illegal aliens, and facilitates their removal by working with foreign embassies to arrange travel documents and transportation.

IMMIGRATION EXAMINER: Reviews applications to become a U.S. citizen, import foreign workers, and other requests.

IMMIGRATION INSPECTOR: Inspects the immigration status of persons arriving at all U.S. ports of entry.

SPECIAL AGENT: Investigates violations of the Immigration and Naturalization Act and other statutes.

Major Activities and Divisions

INS facilitates the entry of foreign visitors and immigrants into the U.S.; provides assistance to individuals seeking permanent resident status or citizenship; prevents unqualified aliens from receiving government benefits or gaining employment; and removes aliens who enter or remain in the country illegally.

Alternative Employment Programs

INS maintains a co-op program for various occupations depending on the availability of funding.

Remarks

Border Patrol Agents must successfully complete a 17-week training program at the Border Patrol Academy at the Federal Law Enforcement Training Center at Glynco, Georgia. Special Agents must complete 14 weeks of training. Both programs consist of instruction in immigration and naturalization laws, Spanish, court procedure, firearms proficiency, and physical training. Immigration Examiners, Immigration Inspectors, and Deportation Officers must complete shorter programs.

Application Procedures

Direct inquiries to the Immigration and Naturalization Service Personnel Division at the regional office where you seek employment.

Headquarters:
1425 I Street, N.W.
Room 6032
Washington, DC 20536
(202) 514-2690
(202) 514-4301 (vacancies)

Eastern Region:
Federal Building
Elmwood Avenue
Burlington, VT 05401
(802) 951-6255

Southern Region:
Skyline Center
Building C
311 N. Stemmons Freeway
Dallas, TX 75207
(214) 767-6070

Northern Region:
Federal Building
Fort Snelling
Twin Cities, MN 55111
(612) 725-3496

Western Region:
Terminal Island
San Pedro, CA 90731
(213) 514-6520

THE DEPARTMENT OF LABOR (DOL)

The purpose of the Department of Labor is to promote the welfare of the wage earners of the nation by fostering opportunities for employment and ensuring safe and healthful working conditions. This mission is carried out through a variety of laws which protect workers' rights, including the rights of special groups such as youths, the handicapped, women, and minorities. The Department also administers laws regarding workers' compensation and unemployment insurance, and sets a minimum hourly wage and overtime pay scale.

The agencies within the Department of Labor are:

Bureau of Labor Statistics
Employment and Training Administration
Employment Standards Administration
Mine Safety and Health Administration
Occupational Safety and Health Administration
Office of Labor Management Standards
Pension Benefit Guaranty Corporation
Pension and Welfare Benefits Administration
Veterans Employment and Training Service

The Department of Labor has a central employment office for all of its agencies. Contact:

Office of Personnel
200 Constitution Ave NW Rm. C5516
Washington, DC 20210

202-523-6646 (personnel)
202-523-6769 (telephone device for the deaf)

BUREAU OF LABOR STATISTICS (BLS)

Nature of Work: Economic policy, statistics
Number of Employees: 2,522
Headquarters: Washington, DC
Regional Locations: Atlanta, GA; Boston, MA; Chicago, IL; Dallas, TX; Kansas City, KS; New York, NY; Philadelphia, PA; San Francisco, CA
Typical Majors of New Hires: Economics, mathematics, statistics, computer science

Mission

The BLS gathers and publishes information about the U.S. economy that is relevant to current issues. This impartial and sometimes sensitive statistical data has become the basis for setting national economic policy affecting employment, unemployment, prices, wages, productivity, industrial relations, and occupational safety and health. The Bureau publishes such statistical collections as *Monthly Labor Review*, *Employment and Earnings*, and *Occupational Outlook Quarterly* as well as surveys such as the *Consumer Price Index* and the *Producer Price Index*.

Job Descriptions

COMPUTER SPECIALIST: Designs and implements data processing systems to support the Bureau's statistical surveys. In all stages of planning, designing, and implementation of computer systems, programmers work as a team with economists and statisticians. The standard programming language at the Bureau is PL/1, although COBOL is used for some applications. The data base management system standard for the Bureau is TOTAL.

ECONOMIST: Gathers economic data by planning and conducting surveys and other techniques. Prepares statistical tables and charts which present economic data, and prepares reports for BLS publications.

MATHEMATICAL STATISTICIAN: Gathers statistical data, and applies statistical methods to draw inferences from these data as to magnitudes, differences, and relationships. Assists in the development of statistical techniques and surveys, and prepares charts, tables, and reports for BLS publications.

Major Activities and Divisions

The BLS divides its statistical databases into six economic areas: Employment and Unemployment Statistics; Prices and Living Conditions; Wages and Industrial Relations; Productivity and Technology; Occupational Safety and Health Statistics; and Economic Growth and Employment Projections.

Alternative Employment Programs

BLS offers a co-op program for college students.

Remarks

None.

Application Procedures

Direct inquiries to the Regional Inspection and Compliance Office in which you would like to work:

College Recruitment/Special Programs	441 G Street, N.W., Room 2827
Bureau of Labor Statistics	Washington, DC 20212
	(202) 523-1591

1371 Peachtree Street, N.E.
Atlanta, GA 30309
(404) 347-4416

1603-B Federal Building
Boston, MA 02203
(617) 565-2327

230 S. Dearborn Street
Chicago, IL 60604
(312) 353-1880

555 Griffin Square Building
Dallas, TX 75202
(214) 767-6970

911 Walnut Street
Kansas City, MO 64106
(816) 426-2481

1515 Broadway
New York, NY 10036
(212) 337-2400

3535 Market Street
Philadelphia, PA 19101
(215) 596-1154

450 Golden Gate Avenue
San Francisco, CA 94102
(415) 744-6600

EMPLOYMENT AND TRAINING ADMINISTRATION (ETA)

Nature of Work: Employment; low-income people
Number of Employees: 1,815
Headquarters: Washington, DC
Regional Locations: Atlanta, GA; Boston, MA; Chicago, IL; Dallas, TX; Denver, CO; Kansas City, MO; New York, NY; Philadelphia, PA; San Francisco, CA; Seattle, WA
Typical Majors of New Hires: Economics, industrial relations, social sciences, psychology

Mission

The ETA administers programs to provide work experience and training for groups having difficulty entering or returning to the workforce, and monitors state employment offices and employment insurance programs.

Job Descriptions

MANPOWER DEVELOPMENT SPECIALIST: Designs and administers programs regarding employment resources, job requirements, employee development, and utilization of the labor force.

UNEMPLOYMENT INSURANCE PROGRAM SPECIALIST: Develops and evaluates federal and state unemployment insurance programs. Sets minimum standards and relays new information regarding state employment security agencies and the administration of their social insurance programs.

Major Activities and Divisions

The Office of Employment Security: Manages programs operated by the state employment agencies.

The Office of Job Training: Develops and issues federal policies pertaining to the operation of the Job Training Partnership Act. The goal of the act is to train or retrain and place eligible (usually economically disadvantaged) individuals in permanent, unsubsidized employment.

Alternative Employment Programs

ETA offers summer internships which are related to a student's major. It also offers co-op and Stay-in-School positions.

Remarks

None.

Application Procedures

Direct inquiries to:

Employment and Training Administration
200 Constitution Avenue, N.W.
Room S5214
Washington, DC 20210

(202) 535-8744

EMPLOYMENT STANDARDS ADMINISTRATION

Nature of Work: Employment, wages/prices/rates
Number of Employees: 4,359
Headquarters: Washington, DC
Regional Locations: Atlanta, GA; Boston, MA; Chicago, IL; Dallas, TX; Denver, CO; Kansas City, MO; New York, NY; Philadelphia, PA; San Francisco, CA; Seattle, WA
Typical Majors of New Hires: Economics, law, liberal arts, social sciences

Mission

The Employment Standards Administration oversees programs dealing with minimum wage and overtime standards; registration of farm labor contractors; determining prevailing wage rates to be paid on government contracts; nondiscrimination on government contracts; and workers' compensation programs.

Job Descriptions

EQUAL OPPORTUNITY SPECIALIST: Evaluates and investigates compliance programs and problems. Participates in research projects which identify patterns of minority and female underutilization or discrimination. Analyzes employment data from compliance reports to determine employment patterns affecting minority group persons in the workforce.

SALARY AND WAGE SPECIALIST: Collects information from selected occupational samples regarding current pay rates and wage benefits. Analyzes pay data and constructs or verifies pay schedules or rates.

WAGE AND HOUR COMPLIANCE SPECIALIST: Investigates commercial, industrial, and agricultural organizations to determine compliance with labor laws. Conducts negotiations to correct violations and to secure future compliance. Makes recommendations concerning compliance, advises state employment staff on the rights of employees, and supplies information regarding federal labor laws.

WORKERS' COMPENSATION CLAIMS EXAMINER: Performs quasi-legal work in developing, adjusting, or authorizing the settlement of claims that pertain to unemployment, disability, and death compensation.

Major Activities and Divisions

Wage and Hour Division: Administers programs designed to protect low-wage income workers.

Federal Contract Compliance Program: Establishes policies to ensure nondiscrimination in employment by government contractors.

Office of Workers' Compensation Programs: Administers the three basic federal workers' compensation laws.

Alternative Employment Programs

The Employment Standards Administration hires co-op students to fill entry-level professional positions and offers a limited summer hiring program.

Remarks

None.

Application Procedures

Direct inquiries to:

Employment Standards Administration
200 Constitution Avenue, N.W.
Room S3316
Washington, DC 20210

(202) 523-7545

MINE SAFETY AND HEALTH ADMINISTRATION (MSHA)

Nature of Work: Mining, safety
Number of Employees: 2,824
Headquarters: Arlington, VA
Regional Locations: There are 16 district offices, 23 subdistrict offices, and 109 field offices throughout the U.S.
Typical Majors of New Hires: Engineering, health sciences

Mission

MSHA develops safety and health programs and standards aimed at preventing and reducing mine accidents and occupational diseases in the mining industry.

Job Descriptions

MINE SAFETY AND HEALTH INSPECTOR/SPECIALIST: Works to prevent conditions that are potentially hazardous to the safety and health of mine workers. Reviews and cites violations in underground and/or surface mines. Usually involves travel.

MINING ENGINEER: Relates the search for, efficient removal of, and transportation of ore to the health and safety of mine workers. Requires general knowledge of construction and excavation methods, materials handling, and the processes involved in preparing mined materials for use.

Major Activities and Divisions

MSHA gets involved in mine safety issues by developing standards and ensuring compliance, working with state mine health and safety programs, developing training programs in cooperation with the states, and conducting research into mine safety in cooperation with the Department of Health and Human Services and the Department of the Interior.

Alternative Employment Programs

MSHA offers a limited co-op program and hires a small number of students to work during the summer.

Remarks

None.

Application Procedures

Direct inquiries to:

Mine Safety and Health Administration
Ballston Towers #3
4015 Wilson Boulevard, Room 500
Arlington, VA 22203
(703) 235-1352

OCCUPATIONAL SAFETY AND HEALTH ADMINISTRATION (OSHA)

Nature of Work: Safety
Number of Employees: 2,548
Headquarters: Washington, DC
Regional Locations: Atlanta, GA; Boston, MA; Chicago, IL; Dallas, TX; Denver, CO; Kansas City, MO; New York, NY; Philadelphia, PA; San Francisco, CA; Seattle, WA
Typical Majors of New Hires: Biology, engineering, physical sciences, psychology, public health, social sciences

Mission

OSHA develops occupational safety and health standards and issues safety regulations. It conducts investigations and inspections to determine the status of compliance with safety and health standards, and issues citations for noncompliance.

Job Descriptions

INDUSTRIAL HYGIENIST: Studies occupational health hazards affecting employees. Develops and enforces federal safety and health standards and provides technical assistance in the development of industrial hygiene programs in both the public and private sector. Usually involves field travel.

SAFETY ENGINEER: Develops safety standards designed to prevent occupational accidents by reducing potential hazards. Evaluates proposed designs to ensure conformance with engineering standards.

SAFETY AND OCCUPATIONAL HEALTH SPECIALIST: Identifies occupational hazards and assesses potential accident risk. Conducts on-site investigations into occupational accidents, and prescribes accident preventive techniques. Requires a knowledge of engineering and scientific principles.

Major Activities and Divisions

OSHA enforces federal safety and health standards for both the private and public sector. It conducts on-site accident investigations, safety research and development, and conducts preventive occupational health and safety training programs.

Alternative Employment Programs

OSHA hires approximately 1–10 co-op students annually to fill positions as Computer Specialists, Engineers, and Industrial Hygienists. These typically begin at the GS-4 level, and are filled by college students in their sophomore and junior years. Contact the co-op director at (202) 523-8013 for more information.

OSHA also participates in the PMI program and the Stay-in-School program for clerical positions.

Remarks

None.

Application Procedures

Direct inquiries to:

Occupational Safety and Health Administration
200 Constitution Avenue, N.W.
Room N3308
Washington, DC 20210

(202) 523-8013

OFFICE OF LABOR MANAGEMENT STANDARDS (OLMS)

Nature of Work: Labor/management relations
Number of Employees: 427
Headquarters: Washington, DC
Regional Locations: Atlanta, GA; Boston, MA; Chicago, IL; Cleveland, OH; Dallas, TX; Detroit, MI; Kansas City, MO; Los Angeles, CA; New York, NY; Philadelphia, PA; Pittsburgh, PA; San Francisco, CA
Typical Majors of New Hires: Business, law, liberal arts, social science

Mission

OLMS regulates internal union procedures and protects the rights of members of approximately 48,000 unions. It seeks to obtain voluntary compliance with the requirements of the law by labor organizations and employers.

Job Descriptions

INVESTIGATOR (LABOR): Investigates complaints of violations against labor laws and negotiates compliance with legislation. Develops violations cases for referral to the Department of Justice, and conducts hearings. Supervises union elections to ensure fair practice.

Major Activities and Divisions

OLMS monitors the handling of union funds, regulates the reporting and disclosure of financial transactions and administrative practices, and oversees the election of union officers.

Alternative Employment Programs

OLMS may offer both co-op and Stay-in-School positions, depending upon budget constraints.

Remarks

None.

Application Procedures

Direct inquiries to:

National Capital Service Center
Office of Labor-Management Standards
200 Constitution Avenue, N.W.
Room C5516
Washington, DC 20210

(202) 523-6677
Direct to OLMS: (202) 523-8595

PENSION BENEFIT GUARANTY CORPORATION (PBGC)

Nature of Work: Business, insurance/benefits
Number of Employees: 586
Headquarters: Washington, DC
Regional Locations: None
Typical Majors of New Hires: Accounting, business, mathematics

Mission

PBGC is a young federal agency which insures more than 100,000 defined benefit pension plans in the private sector. It is a self-financing, wholly owned government corporation governed by a Board of Directors consisting of the Secretaries of Labor, Commerce, and Treasury.

Job Descriptions

ACCOUNTANT: Performs a variety of functions, including overseeing premium collections, transferring assets into the trust fund, collecting employer liability, administering the revolving fund, developing manual and automated systems, and administering revolving funds used in the Corporation's daily operations.

ACTUARY: Analyzes terminated plans in order to determine how plan provisions and ERISA guarantees interact to affect the participant benefits. Develops instructions for benefit determinations, and calculates the present value of guaranteed benefits.

AUDITOR: Serves as a "Case Officer" responsible for coordinating the actions necessary to process distress terminations of plans, including audits of net worth, controlled group, plan assets, and participant data.

BENEFITS EXAMINER: Reviews participant and plan information and makes determinations for current retirees, individuals entitled to lump sum payments, and vested participants applying for benefits.

FINANCIAL ANALYST: Works in several parts of the Corporation, projecting long-range trends, overseeing investments, developing contingency plans, valuing assets, and assisting the legal and executive staffs in conducting settlement negotiations.

INSURANCE EXAMINER: Advises plan administrators and other inquirers on the coverage and classification of defined benefit pension plans, standard termination procedures, and related Corporation rules and processes.

Major Activities and Divisions

Besides its internal administrative offices, PBGC is broken down into three program-related departments: the Insurance Operations Department; the Financial Operations Department; and the Participant and Employer Appeals Department.

Alternative Employment Programs

PBGC hosts an intern program for students typically in their freshman and sophomore years in college. Common positions include Legal Intern and International Foundation Intern. PBGC also participates in the PMI program, typically hiring 1–4 PMI students annually. Contact the Chief, Training Branch at (202) 778-8808 for more information.

PBGC also participates in the federal Stay-in-School program for economically disadvantaged students, including students in both high school and college.

Remarks

PBGC does not engage in campus recruitment.

Application Procedures

Direct inquiries to:

Pension Benefit Guaranty Corporation
Attn: Personnel Department/Human Resources Division
2020 K Street, N.W., Room 3700
Washington, DC 20006

(202) 778-8808

PENSION AND WELFARE BENEFITS ADMINISTRATION (PWBA)

Nature of Work: Insurance/benefits
Number of Employees: 507
Headquarters: Washington, DC
Regional Locations: Atlanta, GA; Boston, MA; Chicago, IL; Dallas, TX; Fort Wright, KY; Kansas City, MO; Los Angeles, CA; New York, NY; Philadelphia, PA; San Francisco, CA
Typical Majors of New Hires: Accounting, business, economics, finance/banking, law

Mission

PWBA enforces the standards designed to protect more than $1 trillion in pension and other benefits.

Job Descriptions

EMPLOYEE BENEFIT PLAN SPECIALIST: Works to protect the interests of employees who participate in private pension and welfare plans and the beneficiaries of those employees.

INVESTIGATOR (PENSION): Conducts investigations into complaints of violations of labor legislation relating to pension administration. Develops violations cases for referral to the Department of Justice and negotiates compliance. Provides technical assistance on pension laws and legislation.

Major Activities and Divisions

PWBA enforces regulations on private pension and welfare plan administrators. This includes requiring administrators to provide plan participants with easily understandable plan summaries; to file those summaries with PWBA; and to report annually on the financial operation of the plans and bonding of persons charged with handling plan funds and assets.

Alternative Employment Programs

PWBA may offer both co-op and Stay-in-School positions, depending upon budget constraints.

Remarks

None.

Application Procedures

Direct inquiries to:

National Capital Service Center
Pension and Welfare Benefits Admin. 200
Constitution Avenue, N.W.
Room C5516
Washington, DC 20210

(202) 523-6677 (service center)
(202) 523-8233 (PWBA direct)

VETERANS EMPLOYMENT AND TRAINING SERVICE (VETS)

Nature of Work: Employment, veterans' programs
Number of Employees: 288
Headquarters: Washington, DC
Regional Locations: There are VETS offices in every Department of Labor region as well as in every state. The regions are: Atlanta, GA; Boston, MA; Chicago, IL; Dallas, TX; Denver, CO; Kansas City, MO; New York, NY; Philadelphia, PA; San Francisco, CA; and Seattle, WA
Typical Majors of New Hires: Business, psychology, public administration, social sciences

Mission

VETS works closely with and provides grants and technical assistance to state employment services to ensure that veterans are provided the priority employment and training services required by law, and administers Job Training Partnership Act grants for the training of eligible veterans.

Job Descriptions

VETERANS' EMPLOYMENT SPECIALIST: Works with State Employment Security Agencies and Job Training Partnership Act recipients to see that veterans are given preferential employment and training services. Coordinates with employers, labor unions, veterans' service organizations, and community organizations through public information and outreach activities. Provides federal contractors with management assistance in complying with their veterans' affirmative action and reporting obligations.

VETERANS' PROGRAM SPECIALIST: Administers the veterans' reemployment rights program. Provides assistance to help restore job, seniority, and pension rights to veterans following absences from work for active military service. Protects employment and retention rights of members of the Reserve or National Guard.

Major Activities and Divisions

VETS directs the Department of Labor's veterans' employment and training programs through a nationwide network that includes regional administrators, directors (in each state), and assistant directors (one for each 250,000 veterans in each state).

Alternative Employment Programs

None.

Remarks

The Veterans' Employment and Training Service, due to its small size, has minimal recruitment activity, and does not have its own personnel office.

Application Procedures

Direct inquiries to:

National Capital Service Center—Personnel
U.S. Department of Labor
200 Constitution Avenue, N.W.
Washington, DC 20210

(202) 523-6437

Or contact any personnel office of the Department of Labor's ten regional offices. They are listed in telephone books under U.S. Department of Labor.

NAVY DEPARTMENT

The U.S. Navy was established in 1775. Since that time, the Navy's mission has remained the same: To protect the United States by engaging enemy forces at sea and supporting the operations of the U.S. armed forces.

COMPTROLLER OF THE NAVY
Nature of Work: Accounting/auditing, military affairs **Number of Employees:** 16,000 **Headquarters:** Washington, DC **Regional Locations:** Nationwide **Typical Majors of New Hires:** Accounting, business, social sciences

Mission

Oversees financial management of the Navy, including budgeting, accounting, progress and statistical reporting, and administrative organization.

Job Descriptions

ACCOUNTANT: Develops and installs accounting systems, interprets financial statements, and provides fiscal advice.

AUDITOR: Evaluates the effectiveness and efficiency of management policies, systems, procedures, and controls. Ensures financial integrity and effective use of resources by the Navy and Marine Corps.

BUDGET ANALYST: Determines financial needs, outlines spending programs, drafts and defends budget documents.

Major Activities and Divisions

The Comptroller of the Navy manages the Navy's budget process, sophisticated accounting systems, and produces statistical and financial reports.

Alternative Employment Programs

The Comptroller of the Navy maintains a co-op and intern program. Its Centralized Financial Management Trainee Program is a two-year program consisting of on-the-job training, formal classroom studies, and rotational assignments.

Remarks

Application deadlines are February 1 of each year.

Application Procedures

Direct inquiries to:

Comptroller of the Navy
Office of Career Management
Code NAFC-312
Crystal Mall 3, Room 119
Washington, DC 20376-5001

(202) 695-3587

NAVAL AIR DEVELOPMENT CENTER (NADC)

Nature of Work: Aviation/space programs, military affairs, scientific research
Number of Employees: 2,400
Headquarters: Warminster, PA
Regional Locations: None
Typical Majors of New Hires: Engineering, mathematics, physics

Mission

As part of the Navy's Space and Naval Warfare Systems Command, NADC develops and tests all Naval aircraft systems.

Job Descriptions

AEROSPACE ENGINEER: Works on airframes and structures, automatic control and stabilization, flight control, high- and low-speed aerodynamics, and flight simulators.

ELECTRICAL AND ELECTRONIC ENGINEER: Develops and evaluates electrical systems and subsystems including antisubmarine avionics; electronic countermeasures; early warning systems; navigation instruments; and digital computers.

MECHANICAL ENGINEER: Designs sonobuoys, helicopter hoists, cooling systems, release mechanisms, and weapon delivery systems.

PHYSICIST: Conducts research in such fields as high-altitude tactical photography, inertial navigation, thin films, solid state mechanics, cryogenics, underwater acoustics, optics, magnetics, and signal processing.

Major Activities and Divisions

Antenna Test Range: Investigates aircraft radar transmissions and signatures.

Dynamic Flight Simulator: Simulates the maneuvers of high-performance Naval aircraft.

Inertial Navigation Laboratory: Develops and tests new instruments allowing for greater navigational precision.

Naval Air Facility: Determines the flight characteristics of prototypes.

Sonar Development Facility: Tests sonobuoys and other types of submarine detection equipment.

Alternative Employment Programs

NADC maintains a co-op program that annually hires about 20 sophomore engineering students at the GS-7 level. Graduate co-op, Stay-in-School, and summer positions are also available.

Remarks

NADC is authorized to pay relocation expenses for new employees and their families.

Application Procedures

Direct inquiries to:

Manager
College Recruiting/Relations
Code 033 FCD

Naval Air Development Center
Warminster, PA 18974-5000

1-800-443-NADC

NAVAL AIR SYSTEMS COMMAND (NAVAIR)
Nature of Work: Aviation/space programs, military affairs, scientific research, weapons **Number of Employees:** 45,128 **Headquarters:** Crystal City, VA **Regional Locations:** Nationwide **Typical Majors of New Hires:** Computer science, engineering

Mission

Develops advanced aircraft, combat systems, avionics, and related equipment for the Navy and Marines.

Job Descriptions

AEROSPACE ENGINEER: Improves the performance of aircraft and missiles by obtaining aerodynamic data from windtunnels.

ELECTRICAL/ELECTRONICS ENGINEER: Develops advanced avionics and control systems, sensors, navigation equipment, integrated computer systems, radars, and fire control systems.

MECHANICAL ENGINEER: Plans the construction of experimental models and test techniques for engines, armaments, and other equipment and components. Develops and modifies mechanical drive systems for helicopters, and works on various components of reciprocating and turbine engines.

METALLURGICAL ENGINEER: Develops special purpose alloys for aircraft, missiles, engines, guns, and armor.

Major Activities and Divisions

Research and Technology: Conducts research leading to improved combat systems, aircraft, weapons, surveillance systems, and avionics.

Electronic Warfare and Mission Support Programs: Administers programs designed to improve logistics, airborne strategic communications, air traffic control equipment, and jet training programs.

Antisubmarine Warfare and Assault Programs: Oversees research, development, and modifications of airborne antisubmarine warfare.

Cruise Missile Projects: Manages programs related to remotely piloted vehicles and cruise missile.

Weapon Programs: Administers research and logistics for the Harpoon missile and other weapon systems.

Systems and Engineering: Responsible for flight systems, crew systems, propulsion and power, reconnaissance and imaging systems.

Tactical Aircraft Programs: Designs and modifies tactical aircraft and crew ejection systems.

Alternative Employment Programs

Summer employment is available for engineering students with 2 or more years of education. Co-op opportunities are available for engineering students as well.

Remarks

None.

Application Procedures

Direct inquiries to:

Naval Air Systems Command
Engineering and Scientist Development Coordinator
Code Air 5003C
Washington, DC 20361-0001

(202) 692-2260

NAVAL INTELLIGENCE COMMAND (NIC)

Nature of Work: Defense/national security, intelligence, international affairs, maritime activities, military affairs, weapons
Number of Employees: Classified
Headquarters: Washington, DC
Regional Locations: Worldwide
Typical Majors of New Hires: Computer science, engineering

Mission

Monitors the operations of foreign navies, and assesses their capabilities and intentions.

Job Descriptions

COMPUTER SCIENTIST: Designs software that assists analysts in interpreting intelligence data.

ENGINEER (ALL TYPES): Assesses the capabilities of ships, submarines, aircraft, and related weapon systems, and determines their impact on national security.

RESEARCH ANALYST: Monitors foreign naval operations, and produces threat assessments by examining strategies, doctrines, tactics, and readiness.

Major Activities and Divisions

Task Force 168: Gathers intelligence information on foreign naval deployment using satellites, aerial and maritime surveillance, foreign networks, and contacts with U.S. and allied intelligence organizations.

Naval Technical Intelligence Center: Determines the capabilities of foreign naval forces and their weapons systems.

Navy Operational Intelligence Center: Identifies potential threats posed by foreign navies by examining their tactics, deployments, and readiness.

Naval Intelligence Automation Center: Processes and distributes intelligence information to the Navy's fleet and shore installations, the White House, and other U.S. intelligence agencies.

Alternative Employment Programs

Co-op opportunities are available for computer science and engineering students.

Remarks

Because of intensive pre-employment security screenings, interested candidates should apply several months prior to graduation.

Application Procedures

Direct inquiries to:

Recruiter
Naval Technical Intelligence Center
4301 Suitland Road
Washington, DC 20390-5140

(301) 763-3694

NAVAL FACILITIES ENGINEERING COMMAND (NAVFAC)

Nature of Work: Environmental protection, military affairs
Number of Employees: 21,000
Headquarters: Alexandria, VA
Regional Locations: Charleston, SC; Norfolk, VA; Philadelphia, PA; San Bruno, CA; San Diego, CA; and other locations worldwide
Typical Majors of New Hires: Architecture, engineering

Mission

Designs, builds, maintains, and repairs all Navy and Marine Corps shore facilities. It also manages energy supply and usage, and provides technical support for environmental protection.

Job Descriptions

ARCHITECT: Designs naval shore installations such as housing, schools, hospitals, and aviation facilities.

CIVIL ENGINEER: Designs military housing, roads, drainage systems, waste treatment plants, floating structures, cargo handling systems, and other Naval structures.

ELECTRICAL ENGINEER: Designs, installs, and maintains large shore-based electrical generating and distribution systems.

ENVIRONMENTAL ENGINEER: Develops methods for controlling and eliminating pollutants.

FIRE PROTECTION ENGINEER: Develops procedures, equipment, and systems for preventing and extinguishing fires.

INDUSTRIAL ENGINEER: Prepares broad engineering programs for plant layouts, buildings, and facilities.

MECHANICAL ENGINEER: Designs or modifies building structures, utilities, and support systems.

STRUCTURAL ENGINEER: Assists in the construction of housing, river channels, missile sites, airbases, and other Naval facilities.

Major Activities and Divisions

Specific NAVFAC programs include contracting, acquisition, military and ocean facility construction, test and evaluation, and environmental safety and health.

Alternative Employment Programs

Summer employment opportunities are available for students with 1 year of college or more. Co-op positions are available for sophomore engineering students. Between 10 and 20 are annually hired at the GS-3 level. PMI, Stay-in-School, and student volunteer programs are also available.

Remarks

Two-year overseas assignments are available to employees with between one and five years of experience.

Application Procedures

Direct inquiries to the installation where you would like to work:

Naval Facilities Engineering Command
Director, Professional Development Center
200 Stovall Street
Alexandria, VA 22332
(703) 325-8522

Naval Facilities Engineering Command
Atlantic Division
Personnel Management Specialist
Building N-21
Norfolk Naval Base
Norfolk, VA 23511-6287
(804) 444-9715

Naval Facilities Engineering Command
Northern Division
Naval Base
Philadelphia, PA 19112
(215) 897-6485

Naval Facilities Engineering Command
Western Division
Professional Staffing Specialist
1000 Commodore Drive
San Bruno, CA 94066
(415) 244-2223

NAVAL MEDICAL COMMAND (NMC)

Nature of Work: Health/health care, scientific research
Number of Employees: 22,012
Headquarters: Washington, DC
Regional Locations: Nationwide
Typical Majors of New Hires: Biology, biological sciences, engineering, health sciences, physical sciences

Mission

Provides medical and dental services to Navy and Marine Corps personnel and performs health-related research.

Job Descriptions

BIOLOGIST: Conducts research in such fields as bacteriology, genetics, and serology.

CHEMIST: Investigates the chemical properties of disease-causing organisms.

DENTIST: Performs all types of dental services including restorative dentistry, periodontics, and endodontics.

INDUSTRIAL HYGIENIST: Works with physicians, engineers, shop supervisors, and managers to protect employees from industrial health hazards.

MEDICAL TECHNOLOGIST: Performs laboratory tests on samples of body fluids and tissues, works with physicians and scientists to identify the causes of diseases, and monitors treatment protocols.

MICROBIOLOGIST: Studies the characteristics and effectiveness of chemotherapeutic treatments, vaccines, disinfectants, and antibiotics.

NURSE: Clinical nurses care for patients in hospitals, or are employed in clinical, educational or administrative positions. Occupational Health Nurses provide health services to employees at Naval installations. The Navy also hires Operating Room nurses and Nurse Anesthetists.

PHARMACIST: Develops unit dose dispensing programs, and performs bulk compounding and stock preparations. Also consults with medical staff on drugs, their side effects, interactions, and dosages.

PHYSICIAN: Performs professional or scientific work in the following fields: clinical, preventive, research disability evaluation, training, and administration.

Major Activities and Divisions

The Naval Medical Command's programs and activities are carried out by the following installations: National Naval Medical Center; National Naval Dental Center; Naval Medical Research and Development Command/Naval Medical Research Institute; Naval Medical Data Services Center; Naval Health Sciences Education and Training Command/Naval School of Health Science.

Alternative Employment Programs

Summer employment and co-op positions are available for science and health-care students.

Remarks

A security clearance is required for certain positions.

Application Procedures

Direct inquiries to:

Civilian Personnel Office
Building 10, Room 1020
National Naval Medical Center
8901 Wisconsin Avenue
Bethesda, MD 20814-5001

(301) 295-6800

NAVAL ORDNANCE STATION

Nature of Work: Military affairs, scientific research, weapons
Number of Employees: 2,230
Headquarters: Indian Head, MD
Regional Locations: None
Typical Majors of New Hires: Engineering

Mission

Conducts research and development on guns, rockets, energetic chemicals, missile propulsion systems, and ordnance.

Job Descriptions

AEROSPACE ENGINEER: Solves problems relating to liquid, solid, turbojet, and ramjet propulsion systems, and provides analytical and technical support in the development of rocket motor, gas generator, and propellant systems.

CHEMICAL ENGINEER: Formulates chemicals used in solid propellants, explosives, and other energetic materials. Also develops manufacturing techniques for casting powder, extruded grains, composite propellants, and explosives.

CIVIL ENGINEER: Oversees the Station's physical plant including heating, water supply, sewage treatment, and industrial waste systems; as well as roads and railroads.

ELECTRICAL ENGINEER: Designs power generation and distribution systems, fire detection systems, lightning protection equipment, and electrical plans for building renovation and construction.

ELECTRONICS ENGINEER: Develops and integrates firmware/hardware, and provides cost-effective life-cycle support. Specific technologies include VMEbus/VXIbus structures, higher order language programming, embedded training, expert systems, and weapon simulations.

INDUSTRIAL ENGINEER: Studies management problems such as organizational structure, position management, and manpower planning.

MECHANICAL ENGINEER: Improves the reliability of missiles, gun propulsion, warheads, explosives, underwater weapons, energetic chemicals, aircrew escape propulsion systems, simulators, and special weapons.

Major Activities and Divisions

Guns, Rockets, and Missile Propulsion: Conducts research on castable or extrudable high-density propellants and composite materials, and assesses other technologies such as laser-initiated arms/firing devices.

Energetic Chemicals: Develops continuous processing and cast plastic bonded explosives for warheads as well as missile and gun propellants.

Ordnance Devices: Researches and tests laser and direct shock pyrotechnic initiation, electronic sequencing for multiplace aircraft, canopy fragilization, and helicopter emergency flotation systems.

Simulators and Training Shapes: Develops complex electromechanical systems to provide more realistic training.

Explosives Process Development Engineering: Conducts research in conventional explosives and warheads, and provides technical support to explosive loading plants.

Alternative Employment Programs

The Naval Ordnance Station maintains a co-op program for engineering students.

Remarks

To provide a more comprehensive view of the organization, each new engineer is rotated in the first year through different functional areas. Engineers are then able to select where they best like to work.

Application Procedures

Direct inquiries to:

Professional Recruiting Officer
Code 0632
Civilian Personnel Department
Naval Ordnance Station
Indian Head, MD 20640

(301) 743-4501
1-800-842-6547

NAVAL RESEARCH LABORATORY (NRL)

Nature of Work: Military affairs, scientific research, weapons
Number of Employees: 3,738
Headquarters: Washington, DC
Regional Locations: 12 research sites and a Flight Support Detachment are located in Virginia, Maryland and Florida.
Typical Majors of New Hires: Chemistry, computer science, engineering, mathematics, physics

Mission

Researches and develops new and improved materials, equipment, techniques, systems, and related operational procedures for the Navy and the nation as a whole.

Job Descriptions

COMPUTER SCIENTIST: Develops technologies involving artificial intelligence, information processing, electronic countermeasures, signal processing, fiber optics, and expert systems.

ELECTRONICS ENGINEER: Designs communications and strategic data systems, shipboard and airborne navigation systems, electronic countermeasures, fire control radars, and surveillance equipment.

MATERIALS SCIENTIST: Conducts research into ceramics, fiber optics, fracture mechanics, and microstructure characterization.

MECHANICAL ENGINEER: Designs spacecraft, remote sensing, propulsion, and other systems; studies alloys, combustion, and nondestructive testing methods.

RESEARCH CHEMIST: Concentrates in such fields as combustion, bio/molecular engineering, fiber optics, and laser physics.

RESEARCH PHYSICIST: Works in such areas as radio wave propagation, gamma ray technology, electronic countermeasures, and communications technologies.

Major Activities and Divisions

Computer Science and Artificial Intelligence: Develops computer hardware, operating systems and realtime support software.

Device Technology: Studies integrated optics, radiation-hardened electronics, and microelectronics.

Directed Energy Technology: Investigates the applications of chemical lasers and charged-particle devices.

Electronic Warfare: Designs electronic countermeasures to hide Naval vessels from hostile tracking systems.

Enhanced Maintainability, Reliability, and Survivability Technology: Formulates new and improved coatings, lubricants, and greases for mechanical equipment. Also investigates ways of increasing the survivability of satellites from attacks by lasers and other weapons.

Environmental Effects on Naval Systems: Researches the meteorological effects on the performance of electro-optics systems, and studies air quality in confined spaces, electromagnetic background in space, solar activity, and ionospheric behavior.

Materials: Investigates advanced alloy systems, rapid solidification technology, and other types of materials.

Surveillance and Sensor Technology: Develops imaging radars, target classification and identification systems, towed acoustic arrays, electromagnetic sensors, and magnetic field detectors.

Undersea Technology: Designs autonomous vehicles, formulates anechoic coatings, and investigates bathymetric technologies.

Space Systems and Technology: Works on advanced space systems, space sensing applications, satellite communications, and spacecraft design.

Alternative Employment Programs

NRL maintains a co-op program for GS-4 engineering, computer science, and physical science positions. More than 40 are hired annually. It also has a summer intern program for students in these same disciplines who have completed 1 year or more of college. Call (202) 404-7955 for more information on the co-op positions and (202) 767-3030 for the internships. NRL also has a volunteer program for high school and undergraduate students. Other programs include a 1040 HR program that allows full-time high school, undergraduate, or graduate students to assist scientific/professional personnel. NRL also has a gifted and talented program and junior fellowships for qualified high school students. For information on these programs, contact the personnel office below.

Remarks

NRL's research equipment consists of a large electromagnetic anechoic chamber, the Cray X-MP/12 supercomputer, a digital-image processing laboratory, a high-energy excimer laser, electron microprobe SEM and STEM systems, and a voice processing and analysis facility.

Application Procedures

Direct inquiries to:
Naval Research Laboratory
General Recruitment
Code 1813.1 RL
Washington, DC 20375-5000

(202) 767-3030

NAVAL SEA SYSTEMS COMMAND (NAVSEA)

Nature of Work: Maritime activities, military affairs, scientific research, weapons
Number of Employees: 112,000
Headquarters: Crystal City, VA
Regional Locations: Naval shipyards are located in Bremerton, WA; Charleston, SC; Long Beach, CA; Pearl Harbor, HI; Philadelphia, PA; Portsmouth, NH; Portsmouth, VA; Vallejo, CA. There are also 57 shore installations nationwide, and 79 worldwide detachments.
Typical Majors of New Hires: Engineering

Mission

Designs, develops, modernizes, and repairs the Navy's ships and shipborne weapons and combat systems.

Job Descriptions

CIVIL ENGINEER: Designs ship structural systems.

COMPUTER ENGINEER: Develops computer programs for integrating diverse combat systems, and uses computer-aided design to determine optimum systems for new ships.

ELECTRICAL/ELECTRONICS ENGINEER: Develops advanced radar and sonar concepts and provides life-time engineering management for internal communications, guidance systems, electro-optic fire control systems, and weapons.

MECHANICAL ENGINEER: Designs mechanical systems for shipboard propulsion, auxiliary, and material handling systems.

NAVAL ARCHITECT: Conceptualizes new ship designs, analyzes ship area and space allocations, and conducts research in such fields as ship structures, habitability, weight, stability, and manning.

NUCLEAR ENGINEER: Works in all aspects of nuclear propulsion including reactor core design, instrumentation, and physics.

Major Activities and Divisions

Ship Design and Integration: Conceives, develops, and integrates Naval ships and shipboard systems.

Ship Systems: Oversees the design and installation of all ship hull, mechanical, propulsion, auxiliary, and electrical systems and equipment.

Combat Systems: Provides engineering services for all ship combat systems and related conventional and nuclear ordnance.

Alternative Employment Programs

NAVSEA maintains a summer employment program for students with more than 1 year of college, and a co-op program for engineering and computer science students. Call (703) 602-1882 for more information.

Civilian engineers can earn additional money by accepting a direct commission as a Naval Reserve Engineering Duty Officer *without* an obligation for active Naval service. The only requirement is to attend two days of weekend drills per month (four days' pay for two days' drill) and two weeks of active duty training yearly. Employees participating in this program are paid both their civil service salary plus military pay for those two weeks. Call NAVSEA's Reserve Program Office—(202) 692-5926 (collect)—for more information.

Remarks

Entry-level engineers are placed in a two-year Engineers-in-Training (EIT) program. During this period, EITs rotate through various offices to gain a broader understanding of the Command.

Application Procedures

Direct inquiries to:

Engineering Recruitment Coordinator
Consolidated Civilian Personnel Office
Crystal City (CCPO-30C)
Naval Sea Systems Command
Washington, DC 20376
(800) 368-3338
In Virginia, call (202) 692-1591

NAVAL SURFACE WARFARE CENTER (NAVSWC)

Nature of Work: Maritime activities, military affairs, scientific research, weapons
Number of Employees: 5,230
Headquarters: Dahlgren, VA
Regional Locations: Fort Lauderdale, FL; Fort Monroe, VA; Silver Spring, MD
Typical Majors of New Hires: Computer science, engineering, mathematics, physics

Mission

Designs, tests, and evaluates surface weapons systems, ordnance, and mines.

Job Descriptions

AEROSPACE ENGINEER: Solves problems related to aerothermodynamics and aeroballistics, and applies that knowledge toward developing surface-to-air missiles and reentry vehicles.

COMPUTER SCIENTIST: Designs hardware and software for operating weapons systems; develops artificial intelligence systems; and constructs computer networks and protocols.

ELECTRICAL/ELECTRONICS ENGINEER: Designs, and installs navigation systems, electronic countermeasures, fire control and phased array radars, and equipment for real-time digital signal and image processing.

MATHEMATICIAN: Develops mathematical models for simulating different combat and aeronautical conditions; designs and evaluates computer software, and artificial intelligence systems.

MECHANICAL ENGINEER: Analyzes stress in shipboard structures such as radar and gun mounts, and missile launchers, and develops structures and weapons components able to survive harsh environments.

PHYSICIST: Develops efficient rocket motors and uses advanced techniques for creating new materials.

Major Activities and Divisions

NAVSWC's laboratories, wind tunnels, and test ranges allow advanced research in ordnance, rocket propulsion, and combat systems; life-support, surveillance, and navigation equipment.

Alternative Employment Programs

NAVSWC maintains a co-op program for engineering and computer science students. Typically, between 20 and 39 sophomores are hired each summer at the GS-3 level to fill various engineering, mathematics, and computer science positions. A Science and Engineering Apprentice Program (SEAP) for high school students is provided in cooperation with the George Washington University. For more information about these positions, call (703) 663-8701.

Remarks

NAVSWC develops its engineers by placing them in various rotational assignments. These assignments expose new employees to different areas of NAVSWC, and are tailored to the individual's personal development goals.

Application Procedures

Direct inquiries to the facility where you seek employment:

Naval Surface Warfare Center
College Recruitment Coordinator
Staffing and Classification
Programs Division (P60)
Dahlgren, VA 22448-5000
(703) 663-8701

Naval Surface Warfare Center
College Recruitment Coordinator
Staffing and Classification
Programs Division (P60)
Silver Spring, MD 20910-5000
(301) 394-2506

NAVAL UNDERSEA WARFARE ENGINEERING STATION (NUWES)

Nature of Work: Maritime activities, military affairs, scientific research, weapons
Number of Employees: 3,250
Headquarters: Keyport, WA
Regional Locations: Lualualei, HI; San Diego, CA
Typical Majors of New Hires: Engineering

Mission

Tests and evaluates underwater weapons and components. Supports antisubmarine warfare (ASW) exercises by operating acoustic and tracking ranges.

Job Descriptions

COMPUTER ENGINEER: Designs software that simulates weapons tests, as well as system performance and life cycles.

ELECTRONICS ENGINEER: Designs electronic assemblies used in torpedoes, target, fire control, and sonar systems, as well as the instrumentation used for tracking and acoustic measurement.

MECHANICAL ENGINEER: Designs recovery and test equipment and evaluates torpedoes and mines.

Major Activities and Divisions

Data Processing Department: Develops information systems and communications networks, and conducts testing in such fields as artificial intelligence, robotics, voice recognition/response, and other software technologies.

Weapons Department: Repairs torpedoes, target, fire control, and sonar systems.

Weapons Quality Engineering Center: Evaluates the functional, physical, chemical, and metallurgical characteristics of weapons systems.

Proof, Test, and Evaluation Department: Develops tests that assess the performance of the hardware under different conditions.

Southern California Detachment: Operates an underwater tracking range consisting of underwater and airborne tracking platforms and mobile targets.

Research and Engineering Department: Develops underwater tracking ranges by focussing on signal processing systems, oceanographic systems, ship launch and recovery systems, and various acoustic and telemetry systems.

In-Service Engineering Department: Ensures that surface ships and submarines, torpedoes, targets, countermeasures, fire control and other systems meet requirements at the lowest life-cycle costs.

Hawaii Detachment: Operates underwater tracking instrumentation, ASW test ranges, mobile targets, and training vehicles.

Alternative Employment Programs

Summer employment and co-op positions are usually available for students majoring in computer, electrical/electronics, and mechanical engineering.

Remarks

Various continuing education opportunities are available including an on-site Advanced Technology Training Center with robotics, fiber-optics, computer, and microprocessor laboratories. Master's degrees are available on-site through video coursework sponsored by major universities.

Application Procedures

Direct inquiries to:

Naval Undersea Warfare Engineering Station
Civilian Personnel Office
Code 0614R
Keyport, WA 98345-0580

(206) 396-2020

NAVAL UNDERWATER SYSTEMS CENTER (NUSC)
Nature of Work: Maritime activities, military affairs, scientific research, weapons **Number of Employees:** 3,300 **Headquarters:** Newport, RI; New London, CT **Regional Locations:** Field detachments are located along the east coast of the U.S., the Bahamas, and other locations around the world. **Typical Majors of New Hires:** Computer science, engineering

Mission

As part of the Navy's Space and Naval Warfare Systems Command, NUSC concentrates on antisubmarine warfare technology.

Job Descriptions

COMPUTER ENGINEER: Develops systems for tracking targets and firing weapons, as well as computers that detect and track submarines and simulate combat situations.

ELECTRONICS ENGINEER: Conducts research in such fields as sonar systems using transducers and array geometry, signal processing, reconnaissance systems, and communications.

MECHANICAL ENGINEER: Designs systems for storing, handling, loading, and launching weapons

Major Activities and Divisions

Combat Control Systems: Designs sensors that identify submarine positions, determines which are hostile, and selects the type of weapons to counter them.

Communications Systems: Works on projects linking submarines with surface vessels, shore installations, and aircraft.

Fire Control Systems: Develops systems that track targets and guide torpedoes.

Periscopes: Applies fiber optics, laser emission, and other technologies toward improving periscopes.

Sonar Systems: Designs sonars that incorporate transducer, array geometry, and other technologies.

Torpedoes: Develops more accurate, faster, and quieter torpedoes.

Alternative Employment Programs

None.

Remarks

NUSC's proximity to a large number of major universities provides opportunities for postgraduate studies. Educational plans are available for professional development including tuition and salary grants.

Application Procedures

Direct inquiries to:

Naval Underwater Systems Center
Personnel Staffing Division (PG)
Newport, RI 02841-5047

(401) 841-3585

NAVAL WEAPONS CENTER (NWC)

Nature of Work: Military affairs, scientific research, weapons
Number of Employees: 5,000
Headquarters: China Lake, CA
Regional Locations: None
Typical Majors of New Hires: Computer science, engineering, mathematics, physics

Mission

As part of the Navy's Space and Naval Warfare Systems Command, the Naval Weapons Center develops and evaluates missile systems for air warfare, and operates a test range for parachutes.

Job Descriptions

AERONAUTICAL ENGINEER: Studies the aerodynamic heating of missiles; designs rocket and ramjet motors; and performs stability analyses.

COMPUTER SCIENTIST: Writes and documents microprocessor applications and systems software; develops simulation and integration software for avionics systems.

ELECTRICAL/ELECTRONICS ENGINEER: Designs guidance system hardware and software; performs analog and digital simulations; develops radar and antenna systems; designs and integrates receivers of logic processing circuits; creates microprocessors for fuzes; and develops inertial systems and sensors.

MATHEMATICIAN: Analyzes aircraft/weapon performance; performs feasibility and target vulnerability studies.

MECHANICAL ENGINEER: Designs and tests airframes, rocket motor nozzles, valves and control system actuators, and conducts stress analyses of structural components of rocket propellant grains.

PHYSICIST: Applies electro-optic and laser technologies to guidance systems; conducts research and development involving low-power laser systems, pattern recognition technologies, and holographic computer design codes.

SOFTWARE ENGINEER: Designs, tests, evaluates, and documents software for real time, highly constrained embedded computer systems.

Major Activities and Divisions

NWC engineers work on more than 1,500 programs. The areas of major involvement include air-to-air and air-to-surface weapons; antiradiation weapons; parachute systems; avionics hardware and software for the A-6, A-7, AV-8B, F/A-18, and AH-1 aircraft; tactical electronic warfare and countermeasures systems; and propulsion, explosives, warhead, guidance, and fuze technology.

Alternative Employment Programs

The Naval Weapons Center maintains a summer employment program for students with more than 1 year of college, and a co-op program for engineering and computer science students.

Remarks

All employees with bachelor's and master's degrees are assigned to the Junior Professional Development Program during their first year of employment. The program allows new employees to explore career options through mentored rotations lasting two to three months.

Graduate-level courses in a variety of disciplines are taught on-site. Off-site graduate and undergraduate programs are taught by California State University faculty.

Application Procedures

Direct inquiries to:

Naval Weapons Center
Professional Recruitment—CRS
Code 22502
China Lake, CA 93555-6001

(619) 939-3371

SPACE AND NAVAL WARFARE SYSTEMS COMMAND (SPAWAR)

Nature of Work: Aviation/space programs, maritime activities, military affairs, scientific research, weapons
Number of Employees: 28,253
Headquarters: Washington, DC
Regional Locations: See "Remarks," below
Typical Majors of New Hires: Engineering (electronics)

Mission

Develops, purchases, repairs, and modifies Naval warfare systems such as space systems. SPAWAR also coordinates all advanced antisubmarine warfare development programs, and manages seven research and development centers and eight engineering centers.

Job Descriptions

ELECTRONICS ENGINEER: Develops diverse Naval warfare systems including satellite communications, space and ocean surveillance platforms, navigation aids, electronic warfare devices, and communications equipment.

Major Activities and Divisions

Command and Control: Develops electronic data processing and display systems that allow commanders at sea or on shore to see in real time both his forces and the enemy's.

Marine Corps Systems: Develops communications systems, surveillance radars, and air traffic control systems.

Shipboard Communications: Conducts research in such fields as fiber optics, electromagnetic wave theory, high-speed circuit switching, and integrated voice/data transmission.

Submarine Communications: Develops systems allowing submarines to transmit, receive, and process communication signals using extremely-low and extremely-high frequencies.

Shore Communications: Develops shore-based communications systems allowing shore installations to transmit and receive command and control information to and from ships and submarines.

Antisubmarine Warfare: Designs advanced electronic and computer-based signal processing systems to detect and track enemy submarines.

Space Systems: Works with satellites, space systems, and their instrumentation for the purposes of oceanography and meteorology; microwave imagery; navigation; cryptology; surveillance; and directed energy weapons.

Systems Effectiveness: Ensures that equipment continues to operate in severe environments such as temperature, humidity, vibration, shock, and electromagnetic fields.

Alternative Employment Programs

SPAWAR maintains a summer employment program for students with more than 1 year of college, and a co-op program for engineering students.

Remarks

SPAWAR manages the research, development and engineering activities at the following facilities: Applied Physics Lab, Laurel, MD and Seattle, WA; Naval Underwater Systems Center, Newport, RI and New London, CT*; Naval Air Development Center, Warminster, PA*; David Taylor Research Laboratories, Bethesda and Annapolis, MD; Naval Surface Warfare Center, Dahlgren, VA and Silver Spring, MD*; Naval Electronic Systems Engineering Center, Charleston, SC, Portsmouth, VA, Vallejo, CA, and San Diego, CA; Applied Research Laboratory, State College, PA, and Austin, TX; Naval Electronic Systems Security Engineering Center, Washington, DC; Naval Electronic Systems Engineering Activity, St. Inigoes, MD; Navy Management Systems Support Office, Norfolk, VA; Naval Coastal Systems Center, Panama City, FL; Naval Weapons Center, China Lake, CA*; Navy Space Systems Activity, Los Angeles, CA; Naval Ocean Systems Center, San Diego, CA.

Application Procedures

Direct inquiries to:

Space and Naval Warfare Systems Command
Consolidated Civilian Personnel Office
SPAWAR Recruiting Coordinator
c/o CCPO-42
Washington, DC 20376

(202) 692-7104

STATE DEPARTMENT

Established in 1789, the State Department is the senior executive department of the U.S. government. Over the years, as the country's foreign responsibilities have grown, so too have the duties of the Department become more detailed and complex.

The Department's professional workforce is composed of two types of employees: Foreign Service and Civil Service. Foreign Service employees work in U.S. diplomatic missions around the world and carry out U.S. foreign pol-

* See separate entry for this agency.

icy. Civil Service employees are responsible for the internal operations of the Department itself.

STATE DEPARTMENT

Nature of Work: International affairs, immigration
Number of Employees: 26,028
Headquarters: Washington, DC
Regional Locations: Over 230 embassies and consulates in more than 140 countries.
Typical Majors of New Hires: Economics, history, international affairs, languages, law, political science

Mission

Advises the President on foreign policy by monitoring events in foreign countries. The Department also represents the U.S. government overseas, negotiates treaties with other nations, and protects U.S. citizens and their property abroad.

Job Descriptions

Civil Service positions:

ATTORNEY: Prepares cases for trial or quasi-judicial hearings, interprets and drafts regulations and procedures, and examines contracts and other legal documents.

COMPUTER SPECIALIST: Designs software and implements systems that meet the State Department's automated data processing requirements.

PASSPORT EXAMINER: Processes applications for U.S. passports and related services.

PUBLIC INFORMATION SPECIALIST: Disseminates information concerning the State Department's activities through such media as newspapers, magazines, radio and television.

TECHNICAL INFORMATION SPECIALIST: Analyzes and transmits scientific, technological, and other specialized information.

VISA EXAMINER: Determines whether an applicant who has applied for a U.S. visa is suitable for entry into the U.S.

Foreign Service positions:

FOREIGN SERVICE OFFICER—ADMINISTRATIVE AFFAIRS: Supports the operations of U.S. embassies and consulates overseas such as identifying budget priorities, operating telecommunications and pouch/mail facilities, procuring supplies and arranging leases, managing personnel, maintaining the security of embassies and consulates.

FOREIGN SERVICE OFFICER—CONSULATE AFFAIRS: Issues visas, and assists Americans overseas involved in serious accidents or emergencies.

FOREIGN SERVICE OFFICER—ECONOMIC AFFAIRS: Analyzes and reports on key economic indicators affecting U.S. interests.

FOREIGN SERVICE OFFICER—POLITICAL AFFAIRS: Monitors and interprets political matters affecting U.S. interests.

Major Activities and Divisions

Regional Bureaus: The State Department's five geographic bureaus (the Bureaus of African Affairs, European and Canadian Affairs, East Asian and Pacific Affairs, Inter-American Affairs, and Near Eastern and South Asian Affairs), conduct U.S. foreign policy throughout the world.

Functional Bureaus:

The Bureau of Economic and Business Affairs formulates policies relating to food, energy, trade, finance, development, and aviation and maritime issues.

The Bureau of Intelligence and Research produces intelligence studies and coordinates intelligence and research programs with other federal agencies.

The Bureau of International Organization Affairs develops policies relating to U.S. participation in international organizations such as the United Nations.

The Bureau of Public Affairs provides news organizations and the general public with information on foreign policy.

The Bureau of Consular Affairs administers and enforces immigration and nationality laws.

The Bureau of Politico-Military Affairs provides policy guidance on military assistance, nuclear issues, and arms control.

The Bureau of Oceans and International Environmental Affairs oversees foreign policy as it relates to oceans, fisheries, environment, population, nuclear technology, energy, outerspace, and technology transfer.

The Bureau of Human Rights and Humanitarian Affairs formulates policy relating to human rights practices.

The Bureau for Refugee Programs assists refugees through repatriation, or by selecting, processing, and training them for admission to the U.S.

The Office of the Chief of Protocol advises the President, Vice President, and the Secretary of State on diplomatic procedures and international customs.

The Legal Adviser counsels the Secretary of State on matters of international law arising from the conduct of U.S. foreign relations.

Alternative Employment Programs

The State Department offers paid summer internships and year-round unpaid work-study internships. Most positions are located in Washington, D.C.; however, a limited number of openings are overseas. Since most intern positions require a security clearance (a 6-month process), the application deadline is usually November 1 of the preceding year. Students interested in spring or fall internships should apply at least 6 months prior to that date. Direct inquiries to:

Recruitment Division
U.S. Department of State
Box 9317
Rosslyn Station
Arlington, VA 22209

(202) 647-7152

Remarks

See the section on Foreign Service for more information on Foreign Service careers and the Foreign Service exam.

Application Procedures

For information on civil service careers, direct inquiries to:

Staffing Services Division
Office of Civil Service Personnel
(PER/CSP)
Department of State
Room 2429
Washington, DC 20520
(202) 647-7152
(202) 647-7284 (24 hour Civil Service vacancy hotline)

Recruitment Division
U.S. Department of State
Box 9317
Rosslyn Station
Arlington, VA 22209
(703) 875-7247
(703) 875-7109 (24 hour Foreign Service vacancy hotline)

THE DEPARTMENT OF TRANSPORTATION (DOT)

The Department of Transportation's mission covers all aspects of transportation in the nation, from urban mass transit to aviation. It sets safety standards for the operation of vehicles ranging from automobiles to railroads, and conducts research for the development of motor vehicle fuel economy and highway safety program standards.

The Department of Transportation consists of eight administrations which focus on highway planning, construction, and safety; urban mass transit; railroads; aviation; and the safety of waterways, ports, and pipelines.

They are:

Federal Aviation Administration
Federal Highway Administration
Federal Railroad Administration
Maritime Administration
National Highway Traffic Safety Administration
Research and Special Programs Administration
United States Coast Guard
Urban Mass Transportation Administration

The Department of Transportation has a central employment office which can be reached at:

Department of Transportation
Central Employment Info M-18.1
400 7th Street SW Room 9113
Washington, DC 20590

202-366-9391

FEDERAL AVIATION ADMINISTRATION (FAA)

Nature of Work: Aviation/space programs, defense and national security, safety, scientific research, transportation
Number of Employees: 49,210
Headquarters: Washington, DC
Regional Locations: Anchorage, AK; Atlanta, GA; Atlantic City, NJ; Burlington, MA; Des Plaines, IL; Fort Worth, TX; Jamaica, NY; Kansas City, MO; Los Angeles, CA; Oklahoma City, OK; Seattle, WA
Typical Majors of New Hires: Computer science, engineering (aerospace, civil, electrical, electronics, mechanical)

Mission

The Federal Aviation Administration regulates air commerce in ways that best promote its development and safety, and fulfill the requirements of national defense. It controls the use of navigable airspace of the U.S. and regulates both civil and military operations. The FAA oversees the air traffic control and navigation systems for civil and military aircraft, and works to control aircraft noise, sonic boom, and other environmental effects of aviation.

Job Descriptions

AIR TRAFFIC CONTROL SPECIALIST (EN ROUTE CENTERS): Gives aircraft instructions, air traffic clearances, and advice regarding flight conditions during the en route portions of the flight. Provides separations between aircraft flying along the federal airways or operating into or out of airports not served by a terminal facility. Uses radar and manual procedures to keep track of the progress of all instrument flights within the center's airspace. Transfers control of aircraft to other controllers when the aircraft enters another facility's airspace. Over 8,000 controllers work in en route centers. The controller staff can range from 300 to 700, with more than 150 on duty during peak periods. The typical center has responsibility for more than 100,000 square miles of airspace extending over several states.

AIR TRAFFIC CONTROL SPECIALIST (FLIGHT SERVICE STATIONS): Relays air traffic control instructions, assists pilots in emergency situations, provides airport advisory services, and initiates and participates in searches for missing or overdue aircraft. Provides information on the station's particular area, including terrain, weather peculiarities, preflight and inflight weather information, suggested routes, icing, and any other information important to the safety of a flight. Often meets pilots face to face. Approximately 4,000 controllers work in the 275 flight service stations across the U.S. The number of employees in a facility ranges from 10 to 70.

AIR TRAFFIC CONTROL SPECIALIST (TOWERS): Directs air traffic so it flows smoothly and efficiently. Gives pilots taxiing and takeoff instructions, air traffic clearances, and advice based on their own observations and information received from the National Weather Service. Provides separation between landing and departing aircraft, transfers control of aircraft on instrument flights to the en route controllers when the aircraft leaves their airspace, and receives control of aircraft coming into their airspace from controllers at adjacent facilities. Over 9,000 controllers work in the 328 operating towers. The number of controllers in a facility vary from 10 to 150. Some controllers work in the glass-walled room at the top of the tower, and some work in the radar room below it.

AVIATION SAFETY INSPECTOR (AVIONICS): Conducts surveillance of the avionics portion of air carrier and air taxi programs. Evaluates avionics technicians and repair facilities, and inspects aircraft for airworthiness. Investigates and reports on accidents and violations. Requires related work experience.

AVIATION SAFETY INSPECTOR (MAINTENANCE): Evaluates mechanics and repair facilities for initial and continuing certification. Inspects aircraft and related equipment for airworthiness, and evaluates the overall maintenance programs of air carriers and similar commercial operators. Investigates and reports on accidents and violations. Requires related work experience.

AVIATION SAFETY INSPECTOR (MANUFACTURING): Inspects prototype or modified aircraft, aircraft parts, and avionics equipment for conformity with design specifications and safety standards. Assumes FAA certificate responsibility for assigned manufacturing facilities and makes original airworthiness determinations. Requires related work experience.

AVIATION SAFETY INSPECTOR (OPERATIONS): Examines airmen for initial and continuing certification and qualification. Evaluates the operations of air carriers and similar commercial aviation operations for adequacy of facilities, equipment, procedures, and overall management to ensure safe operation of the aircraft. Investigates and reports on accidents and violations. Requires related work experience and an airline transport pilot certificate or commercial pilot certificate with instrument airplane rating.

Major Activities and Divisions

Safety Regulation: The FAA issues and enforces regulations and minimum standards for the manufacture, operation, and maintenance of aircraft, as well as the rating and certification of airmen.

Airspace and Air Traffic Management: The FAA ensures the safe and efficient utilization of the navigable airspace.

Air Navigation Facilities: The FAA is responsible for the electronic aids to air navigation, such as voice/data communications equipment and radar facilities.

Research, Engineering, and Development: The FAA conducts research activities directed toward providing the devices, procedures, and facilities needed for a safe and efficient system of air navigation and air traffic control.

Test and Evaluation: The FAA conducts tests and evaluations of aviation systems, equipment, and procedures.

Airport Programs: The agency conducts programs related to airport requirements, noise, and other issues.

Registration and Recordation: The FAA provides a system for the registration of aircraft and recording of documents.

Civil Aviation Abroad: The FAA promotes aviation safety and civil aviation abroad by exchanging aeronautical information with foreign aviation authorities.

Alternative Employment Programs

The FAA offers co-op positions for students enrolled in an accredited secondary or postsecondary institution. Students may be trained in the fields of air traffic control, computer science, electronic technology, personnel administration, management analysis, electronics engineering, mechanical engineering, civil engineering, aerospace engineering, electrical engineering, mathematics, accounting, engineering technology, maintenance mechanics, aviation safety inspection, and secretarial support. Interested students may contact the Cooperative Education Program Coordinator at the locations indicated below.

Remarks

Aviation Safety Inspectors begin at grades 9, 11, or 12, depending upon experience. Applicants for these positions must submit FAA Form 3330-47 or GS-1825 along with the SF-171. Those interested in Air Traffic Control Specialist positions must successfully complete the written ATCS examination, and must submit OPM form 1203-M along with the SF-171.

Application Procedures

Positions are located in the contiguous United States, Alaska, Hawaii, and the Caribbean. Applicants are given the opportunity to choose up to two regions as geographic preferences. For more information, direct inquiries to the appropriate FAA regional office:

Headquarters
Federal Aviation Administration
(AHR-150)
800 Independence Avenue, S.W.
Washington, DC 20591
(202) 267-3870
(202) 267-3902 (vacancies)

Alaskan Region
Federal Aviation Administration
(AAL-14)
222 West 7th Avenue, #14
Anchorage, AK 99513
(907) 271-5747

Eastern Region
Federal Aviation Administration
(AEA-14)
JFK International Airport
Jamaica, NY 11430
(718) 917-1060

Central Region
Federal Aviation Administration
(ACE-14)
601 East 12th Street
Kansas City, MO 64106
(816) 426-3304

Great Lakes Region
Federal Aviation Administration
(AGL-14)
2300 East Devon Avenue
Des Plaines, IL 60018
(312) 694-7731

New England Region
Federal Aviation Administration
(ANE-14)
12 New England Executive Park,
Box 510
Burlington, MA 01803
(617) 273-7345

Northwest Mountain Region
Federal Aviation Administration
(ANM-14)
17900 Pacific Highway South (C-68966)
Seattle, WA 98168
(206) 431-2014

Southern Region
Federal Aviation Administration
(ASO-12)
PO Box 20636
Atlanta, GA 30320
(404) 763-7812

Southwest Region
Federal Aviation Administration
(ASW-14)
Fort Worth, TX 76193
(817) 624-5014

Western-Pacific Region
Federal Aviation Administration
(AWP-14)
PO Box 92007
Worldway Postal Center
Los Angeles, CA 90009
(213) 297-1819

Technical Center (ACM-170)
Federal Aviation Administration
Atlantic City, NJ 08405
(609) 484-6623

Mike Monroney Aeronautical Center (AAC-14)
Federal Aviation Administration
PO Box 25082
Oklahoma City, OK 73125
(405) 686-4506

FEDERAL HIGHWAY ADMINISTRATION (FHWA)

Nature of Work: Highways/roads, safety, transportation
Number of Employees: 3,745
Headquarters: Washington, DC
Regional Locations: Albany, NY; Atlanta, GA; Baltimore, MD; Fort Worth, TX; Homewood, IL; Kansas City, MO; Lakewood, CO; Portland, OR; San Francisco, CA. There are also 52 Division Offices, generally in the capital of each state.
Typical Majors of New Hires: Economics, business, urban studies, marketing, mathematics, engineering (civil)

Mission

The FHWA encompasses highway transportation in its broadest scope, seeking to coordinate highways with other modes of transportation to achieve the most effective balance of transportation systems.

Job Descriptions

CIVIL ENGINEER: Develops policy and standards for testing in the quality control of construction material. Evaluates highway project proposals and environmental impact statements. Participates in the planning, design, construction and maintenance aspects of highways. Coordinates the design and preparation of the state highway plans, including preliminary specifications and estimates for construction contracts.

COMMUNITY PLANNER: Provides policy direction and technical assistance to other elements of the FHA, state highway agencies, and local planning agencies in establishing highway planning programs that are consistent with state and national goals. Conducts or assists in technical reviews, evaluations, and coordination of statewide and urban transportation planning programs.

CONTRACT SPECIALIST: Procures supplies, construction, research, and other services related to highway projects using formal advertising and negotiating methods. Evaluates contract price/cost proposals.

ECONOMIST: Forecasts future highway travel demand, analyzes future highway system requirements, and projects future highway funding options. Involves the development and application of statistical and economic analysis packages.

MOTOR CARRIER SAFETY SPECIALIST: Conducts on-site safety and hazardous materials compliance reviews and enforcement investigations of motor carriers. Performs periodic roadside vehicle inspections and on-site compliance reviews of carriers' business records and operating practices for evidence of safety violations. Often requires experience in the safety field.

OPERATIONS RESEARCH ANALYST: Develops transportation policy analysis models and highway-related data bases. Prepares travel forecasts and studies of cost allocation issues.

REALTY SPECIALIST: Participates in the development and implementation of policies and procedures relating to right-of-way appraising, acquisition, relocation assistance payments and service on federal and federal-aid projects. Communicates with State Highway Department officials concerning federal policy and procedures.

Major Activities and Divisions

The Federal-Aid Highway Program: Provides financial assistance for the construction and preservation of the approximately 42,500-mile National System of Interstate and Defense Highways. The Program also involves improving access for the handicapped, providing relocation assistance to those displaced by highway construction, and preserving the natural beauty of areas surrounding highways.

Highway Safety Programs: Administers highway-related safety guidelines providing for the identification and surveillance of accident locations; highway design, construction, and maintenance; traffic engineering services, and highway-related aspects of pedestrian safety. Provides funding assistance to states which establish specific highway safety programs in accordance with national guidelines.

Motor Carrier Programs: Maintains a National Network for trucks, reviews state truck size and weight enforcement programs, and assists in obtaining uniformity among the states in the area of commercial motor carrier registration and taxation reporting.

Federal Lands Highway Program: Funds more than 80,000 miles of federally owned roads that are open to the public and serve federal lands, such as forest highways, park roads, and Indian reservation roads.

Research, Development and Technology Transfer Program: Searches for ways to improve the quality and durability of highways and streets, reduce construction costs, and reduce the negative impacts of highway transportation.

Alternative Employment Programs

FHWA maintains a co-op program, typically for students in the engineering field. Most positions begin at GS-4, and are filled by sophomore and junior level college students. For more information, contact the training division at (202) 366-1168.

FHWA also participates in the Junior Fellowship Program, the Stay-in-School Program, and it conducts a volunteer program for students.

Remarks

None.

Application Procedures

Direct inquiries to the office which hires for your region of interest. Address to:

Federal Highway Administration

400 7th Street, N.W., Room 4334
Washington, DC 20590
ATTN: Chief, Classification and Staffing Branch
(202) 366-0541

Rm. 719
Leo W. O'Brien Federal Building
Albany, NY 12207
(518) 472-6476

Rm. 1633
31 Hopkins Plaza
Baltimore, MD 21201
(301) 962-0093

18209 Dixie Highway
Homewood, IL 60430
(312) 799-6300

819 Taylor Street
Fort Worth, TX 76102
(817) 334-3908

6301 Rockhill Road
Kansas City, MO 64141
(816) 926-7563

Rm. 1100
211 Main Street
San Francisco, CA 94105
(415) 974-9890

Rm. 312
708 S.W. 3rd Avenue
Portland, OR 97204
(503) 221-2053

Suite 200
1720 Peachtree Road, N.W.
Atlanta, GA 30367
(404) 347-4078

Rm. 400
555 Zang Street
Lakewood, CO 80228
(303) 236-3300

FEDERAL RAILROAD ADMINISTRATION (FRA)

Nature of Work: Railroads, safety, transportation
Number of Employees: 593
Headquarters: Washington, DC
Regional Locations: Pueblo, CO
Typical Majors of New Hires: Accounting, business, computer science, economics, engineering, physical science

Mission

The FRA's mission is to enforce rail safety regulations, to administer railroad financial assistance programs, to conduct research in railroad safety, and to set national rail policy.

Job Descriptions

ACCOUNTANT: Assists in the administration of financial assistance to shortline and regional railroads. Audits Amtrak's financial performance, and monitors the financial trends of the railroad industry.

ECONOMIST: Tracks the economic health of the railroad industry, assesses the economic impact of nonsafety regulations, identifies economic trends, and monitors labor issues. Conducts economic modeling to monitor industry conditions and to establish an analytical base from which the agency formulates its positions on mergers and acquisitions.

ENGINEER: Conducts research and development related to improving railroad safety, and enhancing intercity ground transportation through advances in railroad technology.

RAILROAD SAFETY INSPECTOR: Inspects for compliance with federal laws, regulations, and standards. Conducts and reports on accident investigations, ensuring the maintenance of safe operating conditions throughout the nation's network of rail lines. Often requires experience in rail safety practices.

Major Activities and Divisions

The Office of Safety: Oversees the 54 nationwide field offices. Ensures that U.S. safety standards are met in regard to all aspects of railroad industry. Mostly consists of Safety Inspectors and Engineers.

The Office of Policy: Establishes policy on rail issues such as rail mergers, regulation and deregulation, carrier issues, and rail-line shutdowns.

The Office of Chief Counsel: Investigates noncompliance reports. Mostly consists of lawyers and other legal personnel.

The Office of Research and Development: Conducts research on rail tracks, newly manufactured cars, and equipment. Mostly consists of Engineers.

The Office of Passenger and Freight Services: Issues grants and loans within the railroad industry.

The Transportation Test Center: A 50-square-mile facility in Pueblo, CO, which provides testing for advanced and conventional rail systems and techniques designed to improve ground transportation.

Alternative Employment Programs

The FRA hires some engineers at the graduate level for co-op positions. Currently no paid internship program exists.

Remarks

The FRA does not currently conduct college recruitment. In the future, engineers may join the FRA through a specialized training program.

Application Procedures

All hiring for the FRA is centralized through the headquarters office in Washington. Direct inquiries to:

Department of Transportation
Federal Railroad Administration
Office of Personnel
400 7th Street, S.W.
Washington, DC 20590

(202) 366-0881

MARITIME ADMINISTRATION (MARAD)

Nature of Work: Emergency preparedness, maritime activities, trade, transportation, waterways
Number of Employees: 1,071
Headquarters: Washington, DC
Regional Locations: Des Plaines, IL; Kings Point, NY (Merchant Marine Academy); New Orleans, LA; New York, NY; Norfolk, VA; San Francisco, CA
Typical Majors of New Hires: Architecture, engineering, transportation

Mission

MARAD administers programs to aid in the development and operation of the U.S. Merchant Marine. It supervises the construction of merchant type ships for the government, and directs emergency merchant ship operations.

Job Descriptions

ENGINEER: Works with Naval Architects in designing and maintaining merchant marine ships, and in examining and evaluating National Defense Reserve Fleet (NDRF) vessels. Applies a professional knowledge of engineering technology including strength and strain analysis, elastic limits, maximum unit stresses, co-efficients of expansion, and resistance to corrosion.

NAVAL ARCHITECT: Performs engineering and architectural work concerning the form, strength, performance, and operational characteristics of ships. Makes stability and buoyancy calculations, and develops data for launching, loading, operations, and drydocking of ships in an efficient manner. Examines NDRF vessels for seaworthiness.

SHIP OPERATIONS ANALYST: Conducts analyses on water transportation systems and service, including commercial trade systems, shipbuilding or acquisition vessel plans, and domestic waterborne shipping systems.

SUBSIDY RATE ANALYST: Analyzes the differential in foreign and domestic vessel operating costs. Determines a direct subsidy amount to be paid to U.S. shipping companies to offset the higher cost of operating vessels in foreign trade under the American flag, compared to operating costs under foreign flags.

TRADE SPECIALIST: Examines domestic fleet and U.S. flag vessel services in terms of trade markets, commodities moves, and modal competition.

TRANSPORTATION INDUSTRY ANALYST: Conducts research and makes recommendations as to current maritime development and future trends in trade, markets, intermodal transportation, emerging technologies, economic developments, fuels and materials, and national defense requirements.

TRANSPORTATION SPECIALIST: Compiles information on domestic fleet and U.S. flag vessel services as they relate to industry regulatory controls, customs and competitive practices of vessels, and industry operations and services.

Major Activities and Divisions

Policy and International Affairs: Works to achieve equitable access to foreign markets for U.S. shipping firms.

Marketing: Conducts marketing programs to increase U.S. flag participation in the nation's oceanborne foreign commerce.

Shipbuilding and Ship Operations: Supervises the construction of merchant type ships for the government.

Maritime Aids: Offers financial support to help ship operators narrow the cost advantages of foreign shipping lines.

Reserve Fleet: MARAD maintains an inactive reserve of over 300 ships in the National Defense Reserve Fleet.

Alternative Employment Programs

None.

Remarks

MARAD operates the U.S. Merchant Marine Academy at Kings Point, NY, which trains men and women to be officers in the American Merchant Marine. Applicants to the Academy must be nominated by a member of Congress. All academy graduates receive U.S. Coast Guard licenses and Bachelor of Science degrees.

Application Procedures

All hiring for the Maritime Administration is handled through the Washington headquarters, except for the Western Region, which handles its own hiring. Direct inquiries to:

Maritime Administration
U.S. Department of Transportation
400 Seventh Street, S.W., Room 7219
Washington, DC 20590
(202) 366-4141

Maritime Administration
Western Region Director
211 Main Street, Room 1112
San Francisco, CA 94105
(415) 974-7893

NATIONAL HIGHWAY TRAFFIC SAFETY ADMINISTRATION (NHTSA)

Nature of Work: Highways/roads, safety, transportation, scientific research
Number of Employees: 701
Headquarters: Washington, DC
Regional Locations: Atlanta, GA; Cambridge, MA; Denver, CO; East Liberty, OH (test facility); Fort Worth, TX; Homewood Heights, IL; Kansas City, MO; Linthicum, MD; San Francisco, CA; Seattle, WA; White Plains, NY
Typical Majors of New Hires: Engineering, mathematics, psychology, public relations

Mission

NHTSA was established to carry out a congressional mandate to reduce the mounting number of deaths, injuries, and economic losses resulting from traffic accidents on the nation's highways. The administration also establishes safeguards to protect purchasers of motor vehicles and to prescribe safety features and levels of safety-related performance for vehicles.

Job Descriptions

ENGINEER (ELECTRICAL): Studies the design of motor vehicles from an electrical safety standpoint. Examines vehicles for defects, and ensures that detected problems are properly handled by the manufacturer of the vehicle. Provides guidance and leadership in the regulation and planning aspect of the automobile industry. Some engineers work in the Vehicle Research and Testing facility in East Liberty, OH. Most are stationed at headquarters in Washington.

ENGINEER (MECHANICAL): Studies vehicle safety issues such as seat-belt and air bag effectiveness, defects investigation, and crash-worthiness. Provides guidance and leadership in the regulation and planning aspect of the automobile industry. Some engineers work in the Vehicle Research and Testing facility. Most are stationed at headquarters in Washington.

ENGINEERING RESEARCH PSYCHOLOGIST: Conducts research in the interdisciplinary areas of driver behavior and driver-vehicle interaction. Studies human and vehicle factors in accident avoidance, pedestrian safety, standards enforcement, and occupant protection. Must have a BA with at least 24 semester hours in psychology.

HIGHWAY SAFETY SPECIALIST: Provides technical and administrative leadership to state and local governments in the development of highway safety programs. Works with private organizations and community groups in promoting NHTSA programs in such areas as bicycle safety, seat belt usage, school bus safety, and drunk driving awareness.

MATHEMATICAL STATISTICIAN: Works with analysts and engineers to compile statistics based on NHTSA research. Prepares statistical information for use in enforcement, safety, and public education programs.

OPERATIONS RESEARCH ANALYST: Conducts scientific and technical analyses to develop a system to evaluate the effectiveness of NHTSA programs and standards. Requires a technical background in a math- or research-related major.

Major Activities and Divisions

Motor Vehicle Safety Programs: Works to reduce the occurrence of highway crashes and to decrease the severity of injuries in motor vehicle accidents.

Traffic Safety Programs: Provides federal matching funds to assist states with their driver, pedestrian, and motor vehicle safety programs.

Research and Development: NHTSA administers a broad program of research, development, testing, demonstration, and evaluation of motor vehicles, operator and pedestrian safety, and accident data collection and analysis.

Alternative Employment Programs

NHTSA participates in a national co-op program for college students. The agency also hires Student Aid, Stay-in-School, and volunteer students.

Remarks

None.

Application Procedures

Direct inquiries to:

Director of Personnel
U.S. Department of Transportation
National Highway Traffic Safety Administration
400 Seventh Street, S.W., Room 5306
Washington, DC 20590

(202) 366-1784

RESEARCH AND SPECIAL PROGRAMS ADMINISTRATION (RSPA)

Nature of Work: Emergency preparedness, hazardous materials, safety, scientific research, transportation
Number of Employees: 795
Headquarters Location: Washington, DC
Regional Locations: Atlanta, GA; Cambridge, MA; Denver, CO; Houston, TX; Kansas City, MO; Oklahoma City, OK
Typical Majors of New Hires: Computer science, engineering (materials, mechanical, petroleum, structural), transportation

Mission

RSPA is responsible for a number of transmodal programs involving safety regulation, emergency preparedness, and research and development. Emphasis is given to hazardous material transportation and pipeline safety, transportation emergency preparedness, safety training, technology sharing, multimodal transportation research activities, and the collection and dissemination of air carrier economic data.

Job Descriptions

GENERAL ENGINEER/PETROLEUM ENGINEER: Serves as part of a nationwide team which applies engineering and enforcement techniques to investigate gas operators and liquid carriers for compliance with federal pipeline safety standards. Investigates pipeline accidents by examining pipeline components involved, assessing the impact of the accident on the area, interviewing witnesses, and evaluating other data to determine if there are violations of regulations. All types of pipeline facilities are inspected for construction, design, operation, and maintenance. Pipelines may be located offshore or in deepwater ports, and may involve the transport of hazardous liquids, natural gas, or liquified natural gas. Travel is regional within an approximate ten-state area, and is typically 50 percent.

TRANSPORTATION SPECIALIST: Conducts research activities involving one or more specialized transportation functions. Reviews and interprets safety regulations, and collects data on issues of safety, hazardous materials transportation, economy, environmental impact, and operation.

Major Activities and Divisions

Office of Hazardous Materials Transportation: Enforces regulations for the safe transportation of hazardous materials.

Office of Pipeline Safety: Enforces safety standards for the transportation of gas and hazardous liquids by pipeline.

Transportation Systems Center: Focuses on air and marine transportation systems; the social, economic, and environmental effects of transportation; and the maintenance of national transportation statistics.

Office of Emergency Transportation: Develops plans for maintaining a high state of federal transportation emergency preparedness, including national defense and emergencies caused by natural disasters.

Office of Aviation Information Management: Develops and issues regulations for the submission of uniform aviation economic information by the air transportation industry.

Office of Research and Technology: Coordinates the Department's research and development program.

Alternative Employment Programs

RSPA maintains a co-op program, typically filling engineer positions at the GS-3, -4, and -5 levels. The agency also hires several interns each year to fill varied positions. Each program typically fills 1–10 positions annually. Contact (202) 366-5608 for more information.

RSPA also participates in the Stay-in-School program for clerical support positions, and sponsors a volunteer internship program.

Remarks

Little college recruitment is conducted by RSPA. Most positions are currently filled at the GS-13 level and above, and require professional experience.

Application Procedures

Direct inquiries to:

Research and Special Programs Administration
Office of Personnel
400 Seventh Street, S.W., Room 8401
Washington, DC 20590

(202) 366-5608

JOB HOTLINE: (202) 366-9397

U.S. COAST GUARD

Nature of Work: Defense and national security, disaster assistance, law enforcement, maritime activities, military affairs, transportation, waterways
Number of Employees: 5,443
Headquarters: Washington, DC
Regional Locations: Alameda, CA; Baltimore, MD; New York, NY; Portsmouth, VA
Typical Majors of New Hires: Communications, engineering, environmental science

Mission

The Coast Guard is a branch of the Armed Forces of the United States at all times and is a service within the Department of Transportation except when operating as part of the Navy in time of war or when the president directs. The Coast Guard's responsibilities are diverse, and include maritime law enforcement, search and rescue, and waterways management.

Job Descriptions

ENGINEER (AEROSPACE): Performs maintenance engineering and design engineering on aircraft being modified or procured for use in U.S. Coast Guard air interdiction operations. Investigates and resolves technical problems concerning the modification of structures, discrepancies, and malfunctions.

ENGINEER (CHEMICAL): Recommends, monitors, and evaluates research and development projects related to materials safety in the transportation and containment of bulk liquids, liquified gases, and other transported elements.

ENGINEER (CIVIL): Evaluates civil engineering projects in terms of their effect on Coast Guard missions, compliance with applicable laws, and engineering adequacy.

ENGINEER (ELECTRICAL): Develops regulations related to commercial vessel electrical systems. Evaluates proposals submitted by shipbuilders and others.

ENGINEER (ELECTRONICS): Plans, acquires, installs, and maintains Coast Guard Loran-C equipment, racons, radio beacons, and Vessel Traffic Service (VTS) systems, among other Coast Guard electronic devices.

ENGINEER (ENVIRONMENTAL): Ensures that compliance and restoration projects meet the requirements of federal environmental regulations.

ENGINEER (FIRE PREVENTION): Ensures that specifications are met for the design, construction, and general fire safety features of vessels.

ENGINEER (MECHANICAL): Designs, evaluates, and produces various Coast Guard Aids to Navigation (AtoN), and other marine equipment.

ENGINEER (STRUCTURAL): Applies a knowledge of engineering and construction practices to bridge structures and construction specifications and procedures.

ENVIRONMENTAL PROTECTION SPECIALIST: Assesses the environmental impact of projects pending Coast Guard approval. Identifies, evaluates, and documents environmental impact prior to final Coast Guard decision on the project.

MERCHANT MARINE LICENSING SPECIALIST: Evaluates merchant marine license applications. Prepares authoritative replies to correspondence concerning the regulatory, policy, and interpretive aspects of licensing.

MARINE INFORMATION SPECIALIST: Evaluates incoming navigational data and prepares usable information for Notice to Mariners, Light Lists, and miscellaneous chart and publication corrective information. Consults with personnel from each Coast Guard district, the Defense Mapping Agency, and the National Ocean Service to exchange information and resolve conflicting data.

MARINE INSURANCE EXAMINER: Examines applications for Certificates of Financial Responsibility submitted by all types of vessel owners and operators including shipyards, scrappers, and politically sensitive vessel owners.

MARINE SAFETY SPECIALIST: Reviews marine casualty boards and casualty investigations of vessel collisions to determine the extent of violation of Rules of the Road. Assesses Coast Guard programs for Navigation Safety and considers the need for revision.

MARINE TRANSPORTATION SPECIALIST: Develops written merchant marine engineering examinations and associated publications.

MARINE VESSEL OPERATIONS SPECIALIST: Develops merchant marine deck officer and operator examinations and associated publications.

NAVAL ARCHITECT: Develops policy for the regulation of merchant vessels in the areas of vessel maneuverability, dynamically supported craft, and naval vessel design.

VESSEL TRAFFIC SPECIALIST: Provides technical marine traffic management expertise in planning the establishment of vessel traffic services.

Major Activities and Divisions

Defense Readiness: The Coast Guard works in coordination with all the U.S. Armed Forces in all phases of operations on land, sea, or air in the U.S. Maritime Defense Zones. It also safeguards the nation's ports and waterways.

Maritime Safety: The Coast Guard conducts search and rescue efforts, maintains Aids to Navigation, and acts to minimize damage caused by pollutants released in coastal waters.

Maritime Law Enforcement: The Coast Guard enforces all applicable federal laws on the high seas and waters subject to U.S. jurisdiction, including the interdiction of illegal drugs and migrants.

Alternative Employment Programs

The Coast Guard hires a small number of co-op students each year for engineering and administrative positions. These typically begin at the GS-3 and -4 levels. Contact your school placement office to learn more. The Coast Guard also participates in the PMI program, the Stay-in-School program, and a student volunteer program.

Remarks

Some recruitment is conducted for students with a marine/environmental-related engineering degree.

Application Procedures

For civilian positions, direct inquiries to the appropriate office:

U.S. Coast Guard Headquarters
G-CAS-5, Room 3416
2100 Second Street, S.W.
Washington, DC 20593-0001
(202) 267-2331

U.S. Coast Guard Yard
Civilian Personnel Office
Curtis Bay
Baltimore, MD 21226-1797
(301) 789-1600

Commander (pc)
U.S. Coast Guard MLC-PAC
Coast Guard Island
Alameda, CA 94501-5100
(415) 437-3930

Commander (pc)
U.S. Coast Guard MLC-ATL
Governors Island
New York, NY 10004-5098
(202) 668-7085

Commander (pc)
U.S. Coast Guard
MLC-ATL-Portsmouth
Federal Building
431 Crawford Street
Portsmouth, VA 23704-5004
(804) 398-6452

JOB HOTLINE: (202) 366-9397

URBAN MASS TRANSPORTATION ADMINISTRATION (UMTA)

Nature of Work: Funds/funding, transportation, safety
Number of Employees: 451
Headquarters: Washington, DC
Regional Locations: Atlanta, GA; Cambridge, MA; Chicago, IL; Denver, CO; Fort Worth, TX; Kansas City, MO; New York, NY; Philadelphia, PA; San Francisco, CA; Seattle, WA
Typical Majors of New Hires: Accounting, engineering, public administration, urban studies

Mission

UMTA assists in the funding, planning, and development of urban mass transportation systems with the cooperation of public and private mass transportation companies.

Job Descriptions

TRANSPORTATION PROGRAM SPECIALIST: Acts as liaison between UMTA and transit authorities. Plans and establishes improved mass transportation facilities, equipment, and techniques. Typically employed in a regional office.

GRANTS MANAGEMENT SPECIALIST: Administers grants and loans which assist communities in acquiring or improving equipment and facilities needed for urban mass transit systems.

COMMUNITY PLANNER: Provides policy direction and technical assistance to other elements of UMTA and to local planning agencies in establishing mass transit systems that are consistent with area and national goals.

Major Activities and Divisions

Grant Programs: UMTA has several grant programs, divided according to recipient and purpose.

Technical Assistance: UMTA conducts a program of research in the areas of urban and suburban mobility, human resources management, rail modernization, safety, and security.

Safety: The UMTA Safety Program supports state and local agencies in ensuring the safety of urban mass transit facilities and services.

Alternative Employment Programs

UMTA participates in the following student-hire programs: Co-op, Federal Junior Fellowship, Student Volunteer, Stay-in-School, and Summer Youth Employment. Most students are hired through the Stay-in-School program.

Remarks

Applications for entry-level careers should only be sent to UMTA in response to specific vacancy announcements.

Application Procedures

All hiring for UMTA is centralized, and is coordinated through the Washington office.

Washington Address:

Office of Personnel
Urban Mass Transportation Administration
Department of Transportation
400 Seventh Street S.W.
Washington, DC 20590

(202) 366-2513

TREASURY DEPARTMENT

Since it was founded in 1789, the Treasury Department's mission has grown so that today it formulates economic, financial, tax, and fiscal policies, enforces various laws, serves as the financial agent for the U.S. government, and manufactures coins and currency.

BUREAU OF ALCOHOL, TOBACCO, AND FIREARMS (BATF)

Nature of Work: Drugs/abuse, law enforcement, taxes/revenue
Number of Employees: 3,882
Headquarters: Washington, DC
Regional Locations: Compliance Operations are located in Atlanta, GA; Chicago, IL; Dallas, TX; New York City, NY; and San Francisco, CA. Law Enforcement District Offices are located in Atlanta, GA; Birmingham, AL; Boston, MA; Charlotte, NC; Chicago, IL; Cleveland, OH; Dallas, TX; Detroit, MI; Houston, TX; Kansas City, MO; Los Angeles, CA; Louisville, KY; Miami, FL; Nashville, TN; New Orleans, LA; New York City, NY; Philadelphia, PA; San Francisco, CA; Seattle, WA; St. Louis, MO; St. Paul, MN; Washington, DC
Typical Majors of New Hires: Accounting, business, criminal justice, law

Mission

Regulates the alcohol, tobacco, firearms, and explosives industry, and enforces federal firearms and explosives laws.

Job Descriptions

INSPECTOR/SPECIAL AGENT: Investigates violations of federal laws involving explosives, arson, firearms, illicit liquor, and tobacco.

AUDITOR: Ensures collection of all excise taxes through site visits to businesses selling alcoholic beverages, tobacco products, firearms, and explosives.

Major Activities and Divisions

Law Enforcement Operations: Eliminates the illegal sale, possession, and use of firearms and explosives; detects arson-for-profit schemes; prevents illegal sales of distilled spirits; and suppresses interstate traffic in contraband cigarettes.

Compliance Operations: Collects federal taxes on alcohol products and tobacco; helps federal, state, and local agencies resolve revenue protection problems; issues permits; regulates the storage facilities for explosives; and serves as the central agency for all firearms tracing.

Alternative Employment Programs

BATF maintains a co-op program for two occupations: Alcohol, Tobacco and Firearms Inspector; and Alcohol, Tobacco and Firearms Special Agent.

Remarks

Inspectors and Special Agents must undergo 14 weeks of specialized instruction at the Federal Law Enforcement Training Center at Glynco, Georgia. This consists of written and physical tests, as well as graded practical exercises and a firearms proficiency test.

Application Procedures

Direct inquiries to:

Personnel Staffing Specialist
Personnel Division
Room 1215
Bureau of Alcohol, Tobacco, and Firearms
1200 Pennsylvania Avenue, N.W.
Washington, DC 20226

(202) 566-7321

U.S. SAVINGS BONDS DIVISION

Nature of Work: Bonds/commodities, marketing
Number of Employees: 266
Headquarters: Washington, DC
Regional Locations: Atlanta, GA; Boston, MA; Chicago, IL; Cleveland, OH; Dallas, TX; Detroit, MI; Greensboro, NC; Los Angeles, CA; New York City, NY; Minneapolis, MN; Newark, NJ; Pittsburgh, PA; San Francisco, CA; Seattle, WA; St. Louis, MO. These district offices supervise 52 field offices.
Typical Majors of New Hires: Business, economics, finance/banking

Mission

Promotes the sale and retention of U.S. Savings Bonds.

Job Descriptions

BOND SALES PROMOTION REPRESENTATIVE: Maintains personal contact with financial institutions, business, labor, farm, school, the media, and community leaders to increase their awareness of the savings bond program.

Major Activities and Divisions

A continuing effort is made to enlist volunteer support to further the sales of savings bonds.

Alternative Employment Programs

No co-op or intern programs. However, the agency participates in the Stay-in-School program.

Remarks

None.

Application Procedures

Direct inquiries to:

U.S. Savings Bonds Division
Vanguard Building, Room 225
1111 20th Street, N.W.
Washington, DC 20226

(202) 634-5368

INTERNAL REVENUE SERVICE (IRS)

Nature of Work: Accounting/auditing, law enforcement, taxes/revenue
Number of Employees: 137,373
Headquarters: Washington, DC
Regional Locations: Atlanta, GA; Chicago, IL; Cincinnati, OH; Dallas, TX; New York, NY; Philadelphia, PA; San Francisco, CA. There is also a Data Center in Detroit, MI; at least one District Office in each state; and 10 Tax Service Centers.
Typical Majors of New Hires: Accounting, business, computer science, criminal justice, economics, finance/banking, law, liberal arts, political science

Mission

Collects the revenue that finances the federal government, and investigates instances of tax abuse and fraud.

Job Descriptions

COMPUTER SPECIALIST: Designs and operates automated data processing systems that maintain and update individual and business tax accounts. Also produces data used for refund checks, bills, and notices.

INTERNAL AUDITOR: Audits and evaluates all levels of the Service's internal operations.

INTERNAL SECURITY INSPECTOR: Investigates prospective employees to ensure they meet integrity standards, and, when warranted, investigates criminal allegations against current employees.

REVENUE AGENT: Reviews individual and business tax returns to determine correct tax liability, and determines the tax treatment of employee benefit plans and exempt organizations.

REVENUE OFFICER: Collects delinquent taxes and returns.

SPECIAL AGENT: Investigates instances of tax evasion and tax fraud.

TAX AUDITOR: Reviews the returns of small businesses and individuals and determines tax liability.

TAXPAYER SERVICE SPECIALIST: Assists taxpayers in resolving problems or complaints arising from their federal tax returns.

Major Activities and Divisions

National Office: Formulates national policies and programs for the administration of tax laws and regulations.

Regional Offices: Implements national tax policies and programs, and directs operations of the District Offices and Service Centers within the Regions.

District Offices: Audits federal tax returns, reviews tax cases and decides tax liability, assists taxpayers, collects delinquent taxes, and investigates tax law violations.

Service Centers: Processes tax returns and related documents. Also evaluates techniques to improve the processing of tax returns to provide better service to the public.

National Computer Center: Maintains and updates individual and business tax accounts. Also produces data used for refund checks, bills, and notices. Assists in law enforcement by conducting delinquency checks, detecting fraudulent refund claims, and classifying returns for audits.

Alternative Employment Programs

IRS maintains a co-op program for the following occupations: Internal revenue agent; internal auditor; tax auditor; internal security inspector; tax law specialist; revenue officer; computer specialist; and special agent (criminal investigation).

IRS also has an Administrative Intern Program for employees demonstrating potential for rapid advancement. They receive intensive classroom and on-the-job instruction in personnel, facilities management, fiscal management, and related fields. Upon successful completion of the program, interns are permanently assigned to administrative positions with the IRS.

Remarks

IRS is a highly decentralized organization. The highest concentration of professional employees is at the district level.

Application Procedures

Direct inquiries to:

Personnel Office
Internal Revenue Service
111 Constitution Avenue, N.W.
Washington, DC 20024

(202) 566-6151
(202) 535-5384 (vacancies)

OFFICE OF THRIFT SUPERVISION (OTC)

Nature of Work: Banks
Number of Employees: 3,500
Headquarters: Washington, DC
Regional Locations: Boston, MA; New York, NY; Philadelphia, PA; Cleveland, OH; Richmond, VA; Atlanta, GA; Chicago, IL; St. Louis, MO; Minneapolis, MN; Kansas City, KS; Dallas, TX; and San Francisco, CA
Typical Majors of New Hires: Accounting, business administration, computer science, economics, finance, law

Mission

Guards against the failure of thrift institutions by ensuring that they operate in accordance with laws and regulations.

Job Descriptions

ACCOUNTANT: Designs accounting policies and procedures.

ATTORNEY: Represents the Office in litigation and administrative proceedings.

COMPUTER SYSTEMS ANALYST: Conducts management and feasibility studies, and develops and maintains current application systems.

ECONOMIST: Models savings and mortgage markets and the operations of thrift institutions.

SAVINGS AND LOAN EXAMINER: Assesses the financial condition, management practices, and accounting procedures at thrift institutions, and determines whether they are operated in accordance with applicable laws and regulations.

Major Activities and Divisions

Regulates thrift institutions ensuring they are financially stable and are operated using sound management and accounting procedures.

Alternative Employment Programs

OTC has several co-op positions available depending on funding.

Remarks

None.

Application Procedures

Direct inquiries to:

Human Resources Division
Office of Thrift Supervision
Second Floor
1700 G Street, N.W.
Washington, DC 20552

(202) 906-6060

U.S. SECRET SERVICE

Nature of Work: Law enforcement
Number of Employees: 4,411
Headquarters: Washington, DC
Regional Locations: Sixty-three district offices in the United States; overseas offices in London, Paris, and Rome
Typical Majors of New Hires: Business, criminal justice, liberal arts, social sciences

Mission

Protects the President, Vice President, and their families, presidential candidates, and foreign leaders visiting the United States. The Secret Service also investigates violations of counterfeiting laws, and fraud or forgery involving government securities, credit cards, computers, and electronic fund transfers.

Job Descriptions

UNIFORMED DIVISION OFFICER: Guards the White House and the official residence of the Vice President. Also protects foreign diplomatic missions in the United States.

SPECIAL AGENT: Provides personal security to the President, Vice President, and their families, as well as candidates to those offices. Protects foreign leaders visiting the United States, and enforces counterfeiting and forgery laws.

Major Activities and Divisions

Investigations: Uses various investigative techniques including forensics to solve crimes.

Protective Research: Uses intelligence and technical security in order to enhance protective services.

Protective Operations: Oversees the activities of the uniformed and special agents.

Alternative Employment Programs

No regular programs. Inquire with the personnel office.

Remarks

Division Officers and Special Agents must undergo 14 weeks of instruction at the Federal Law Enforcement Training Center at Glynco, Georgia. This consists of written and physical tests, as well as graded practical exercises, and a firearms proficiency test.

Application Procedures

Direct inquiries to:

Chief of Staffing
U.S. Secret Service
1800 G Street, N.W.
Room 912
Washington, DC 20223

(202) 535-5800

OFFICE OF THE COMPTROLLER OF THE CURRENCY (OCC)

Nature of Work: Banks
Number of Employees: 3,294
Headquarters: Washington, DC
Regional Locations: Atlanta, GA; Chicago, IL; Dallas, TX; Kansas City, MO; New York, NY; San Francisco, CA. These regional offices oversee numerous field offices nationwide.
Typical Majors of New Hires: Accounting, business, economics, finance/banking

Mission

Supervises the operations of national banks, including their overseas operations.

Job Descriptions

BANK EXAMINER: Working as part of a team, bank examiners supervise domestic and international activities of national banks. This is accomplished by off- and on-site analyses of loan and investment portfolios, capital, earnings, liquidity, funds management, and internal controls.

Major Activities and Divisions

Examines banks for financial soundness, and takes legal action against banks violating federal laws and regulations. Bank Examiners at OCC's field offices supply most of the information upon which the Washington headquarters bases its actions.

Alternative Employment Programs

OCC maintains a co-op program for bank examiners.

Remarks

OCC's continuing education program exposes bank examiners to all phases of the financial services industry. It consists of technical classes, electives, specialized programs that teach expertise in specific banking areas, and a management education program for developing leadership skills.

Since many examinations are conducted on-site, substantial travel may be required.

Application Procedures

Direct inquiries to the District Personnel Officer, Office of the Comptroller of the Currency, in the geographical area where you want to work:

Midwestern District
2345 Grand Avenue
Suite 700
Kansas City, MO 64108
(816) 556-1800

Southwestern District
1600 Lincoln Plaza
500 North Akard
Dallas, TX 75201-3394
(214) 720-0656

Western District
50 Fremont Street
Suite 3900
San Francisco, CA
94105
(415) 545-5900

Northeastern District
1114 Avenue of the Americas
Suite 3900
New York, NY 10036
(212) 819-9860

Southeastern District
Marquis One Tower
Suite 600
245 Peachtree Center Avenue, N.E.
Atlanta, GA 30303
(404) 659-8855

Central District
One Financial Place
Suite 2700
440 South LaSalle Street
Chicago, IL 60605
(312) 663-8130

UNITED STATES MINT

Nature of Work: Arts, marketing
Number of Employees: 2,098
Headquarters: Washington, DC
Regional Locations: Denver, CO; Fort Knox, KY; Philadelphia, PA; San Francisco, CA; West Point, NY
Typical Majors of New Hires: Business, engineering, marketing, finance/banking

Mission

Produces bullion, domestic and foreign coins, and manufactures and sells national commemorative medals.

Job Descriptions

MARKETING SPECIALIST: Promotes the sale of commemorative coins such as the American Eagle Gold Coin as well as other types of uncirculated coin sets.

MECHANICAL ENGINEER: Designs and integrates fabrication machinery into the Mint's production processes.

METALLURGIST: Develops new techniques for fabricating numismatic items out of bullion.

Major Activities and Divisions

Marketing: Advertises and sells bullion coins and other numismatic products.

Operations: Oversees the production of coins and other products, conducts research and development, and ensures final products conform to specified quality standards.

Alternative Employment Programs

The Mint maintains a co-op program for Marketing Specialists, Mechanical Engineers, and Metallurgists.

Remarks

None.

Application Procedures

Direct inquiries to:

Chief of Staffing
U.S. Mint
633 3rd Street, N.W., Suite 655
Washington, DC 20220

(202) 634-2133

BUREAU OF ENGRAVING AND PRINTING

Nature of Work: Arts, scientific research
Number of Employees: 2,309
Headquarters: Washington, DC
Regional Locations: Fort Worth, TX
Typical Majors of New Hires: Chemistry, engineering, graphic arts (printing sciences), physical sciences, statistics

Mission

Designs and prints currency, postage stamps, Treasury obligations, and customs and revenue stamps.

Job Descriptions

CHEMIST: Formulates inks and papers resulting in durable documents that resist counterfeiting.

ELECTRICAL ENGINEER: Designs, installs, and maintains electrical networks.

INDUSTRIAL ENGINEER: Evaluates the interplay of employees and machines to improve productivity.

MECHANICAL ENGINEER: Designs and integrates electromechanical printing processes and equipment.

PRINTING MANAGEMENT SPECIALIST: Establishes printing standards and determines production runs.

STATISTICIAN: Applies statistical techniques that improve quality.

Major Activities and Divisions

Office of Applied Research and Technical Services: Solves various printing problems such as counterfeit-resistant currency and securities.

Office of Engineering: Oversees the installation and operation of the Bureau's presses and other equipment.

Office of Quality Assurance: Ensures that printed documents are produced according to standards of acceptable quality.

Alternative Employment Programs

Co-op opportunities are available for Printing Management Specialists and certain other occupations depending on funding.

Remarks

The Bureau prints over 40 billion security documents each year.

Application Procedures

Direct inquiries to:

Bureau of Engraving and Printing
Office of Industrial Relations
Room 202-A
14th and C Streets, S.W.
Washington, DC 20228

(202) 447-9840

FINANCIAL MANAGEMENT SERVICE (FMS)

Nature of Work: Taxes/revenue
Number of Employees: 2,375
Headquarters: Washington, DC
Regional Locations: Austin, TX; Birmingham, AL; Chicago, IL; Kansas City, MO; Philadelphia, PA; San Francisco, CA
Typical Majors of New Hires: Accounting, business, computer science, finance/banking

Mission

Receives tax collections, duties, and other public monies; manages the government's central accounting and financial system; settles claims for lost or forged government checks and mutilated currency; and invests Social Security and other trust funds.

Job Descriptions

ACCOUNTANT: Reviews agency financial data, develops and installs new accounting systems, and prepares and analyzes financial statements and reports.

COMPUTER SPECIALIST: Designs and operates automated accounting and other types of information systems.

FINANCIAL MANAGEMENT SPECIALIST: Coordinates budget, accounting, and managerial financial reporting; evaluates and reports on program accomplishments.

MANAGEMENT ANALYST: Determines whether management controls are consistent with desirable business methods, and creates organizations capable of achieving diverse objectives.

PROGRAM ANALYST: Determines whether a program is successfully accomplishing its objectives and recommends improvements.

Major Activities and Divisions

Working Capital Management: Oversees programs for improving governmentwide cash management, credit management, debt collection, and financial management systems.

Payments: Pays all Treasury checks issued for federal salaries, goods and services, and income tax refunds; pays recipients of federal aid programs such as social security.

Collections: Supervises the collection of government receipts.

Central Accounting and Reporting: Maintains the central system that accounts for the monetary assets and liabilities of the Treasury.

Alternative Employment Programs

FMS maintains co-op positions depending on funding.

Remarks

None.

Application Procedures

Direct inquiries to:

Recruitment Coordinator
Personnel Operations Branch
Financial Management Service
401 14th Street, S.W., First Floor
Washington, DC 20027

(202) 287-0834

U.S. CUSTOMS SERVICE

Nature of Work: Drugs/abuse, import/export, international affairs, law enforcement, taxes/revenue

Number of Employees: 18,790

Headquarters: Washington, DC

Regional Locations: Boston, MA; Chicago, IL; Houston, TX; Los Angeles, CA; Miami, FL; New Orleans, LA; New York, NY. These regional offices oversee operations at 44 sublocations and about 240 ports of entry. Foreign offices are in Mexico City, Mexico; London, England; Ottawa, Canada; Paris, France; Bonn, Germany; Bangkok, Thailand; Brasilia, Brazil; Brussels, Belgium; Karachi, Pakistan; Panama City, Panama; Riyadh, Saudi Arabia; The Hague, Holland; Seoul, South Korea; St. Cloud-INTERPOL; Vienna, Austria; Rome, Italy; Hong Kong; and Tokyo, Japan. The Customs Service also operates a Canine Enforcement Training Center at Front Royal, VA.

Typical Majors of New Hires: Business, criminal justice

Mission

Assesses and collects duties on imported items; regulates the import and export of merchandise; combats narcotics and pornography smuggling; processes persons, carriers, cargo and mail into and out of the United States; enforces export control laws; administers certain navigation laws; and detects and apprehends violators of copyright, trademark, and patent provisions on imported merchandise.

Job Descriptions

CANINE ENFORCEMENT OFFICER: Trains and uses dogs to prevent drug smuggling.

CUSTOMS INSPECTOR: Prevents smuggling, fraud, and other criminal acts by inspecting baggage, cargo, and mail arriving in the U.S. Assesses and collects duties, excise taxes, fees and penalties levied on imported merchandise.

CUSTOMS INVESTIGATOR: Prevents smuggling and other crimes by apprehending suspects at U.S. ports of entry. Evidence is gathered by interviewing witnesses, conducting searches, speaking to informants, and undercover surveillance.

CUSTOMS SPECIAL AGENT: Investigates violations of U.S. Customs laws such as the illegal shipment of arms and high-technology goods to foreign countries and conspiracies to defraud the U.S. government of revenue.

IMPORT SPECIALIST: Assesses duties and taxes on commercial cargo arriving at international airports, border crossings, and other locations. Enforces fair trade laws, copyright and trademark laws, health and safety laws, as well as quota and visa restrictions.

Major Activities and Divisions

In addition to enforcing Customs statutes, the Customs Service intercepts illegal high-technology exports to Soviet-bloc countries, enforces reporting requirements of the Bank Secrecy Act, and collects international trade statistics. The Customs Service also ensures that products entering the country comply with U.S. laws such as auto safety and emission control standards.

Alternative Employment Programs

The Customs Service maintains a co-op program for Customs Inspectors, Import Specialists, Intelligence Aids, Special Agent/Criminal Investigator, Auditor, and Physical Science Technician.

Remarks

Canine Enforcement Officers must successfully complete 14 weeks of enforcement and dog handler training at the U.S. Customs Service Canine Enforcement Training Center at Front Royal, Virginia. Training consists of written and physical tests, graded practical exercises, and a firearms proficiency test.

Customs Special Agents and Investigators must undergo 14 weeks of training at the Federal Law Enforcement Training Center at Glynco, Georgia. Customs Inspectors must complete 9 weeks of training.

Import Specialists must successfully complete 5 weeks of technical training at the Federal Law Enforcement Training Center.

Customs Investigators, Special Agents, Inspectors, and Canine Enforcement Officers must be willing to work overtime, shift work, and under strenuous and sometimes stressful conditions. Investigators and Special Agents must be available for temporary and permanent assignments at a variety of geographic areas.

Application Procedures

Direct inquiries to:

Servicewide Special Emphasis Program Coordinator
Office of Human Resources
U.S. Customs Service
2120 L Street, Room 7402
Washington, DC 20229

(202) 634-5270

BUREAU OF THE PUBLIC DEBT

Nature of Work: Accounting/auditing
Number of Employees: 1,954
Headquarters: Washington, DC
Regional Locations: Parkersburg, WV
Typical Majors of New Hires: Accounting, business, computer science

Mission

Borrows money needed to operate the federal government. Accounts for the resulting public debt by selling government securities.

Job Descriptions

ACCOUNTANT: Classifies and evaluates financial data, records transactions in financial records, develops and installs new accounting systems, prepares and analyzes financial statements.

COMPUTER PROGRAMMER: Supports the Bureau's data processing capabilities and programs computers to publish data.

MANAGEMENT ANALYST: Determines the most effective organizational structure to accomplish objectives and improves work methods and procedures.

PROGRAM ANALYST: Reviews the Bureau's operations to see whether they are conducted efficiently.

Major Activities and Divisions

The Bureau maintains extensive financial and accounting records that track debt, transactions, and costs.

Alternative Employment Programs

The Bureau maintains a co-op program for accountants, budget analysts, management analysts, program analysts, and computer programmers.

Remarks

None.

Application Procedures

Direct inquiries to:

Bureau of the Public Debt
300 13th Street, S.W., Room 446
Washington, DC 20239-1400

(202) 447-9798

DEPARTMENT OF VETERANS AFFAIRS (VA)

The Department of Veterans Affairs operates the nation's largest health-care system, and nearly one-half of all physicians have received all or part of their training in the VA system. Over one-third of the entire U.S. population is potentially eligible for VA benefits and services.

The VA sends out more than $15 billion annually in compensation, pension, and education benefits, oversees a multi-billion dollar insurance program, guarantees home loans, and operates the 112 cemeteries in the National Cemetery System. The Department of Veterans Affairs, a Cabinet-level Department, replaced the Veterans Administration in March, 1989.

DEPARTMENT OF VETERANS AFFAIRS (VA)

Nature of Work: Employment, handicapped, health/health care, insurance/benefits, veterans programs
Number of Employees: Over 245,000
Headquarters: Washington, DC
Regional Locations: VA has 58 regional offices across the U.S., as well as hundreds of medical centers and facilities.
Typical Majors of New Hires: Dental sciences, medical sciences, pharmacy, psychology, recreation, religious studies, social work, therapy sciences

Mission

The Department of Veterans Affairs operates diverse programs to benefit veterans and their families. These benefits include compensation payments for disabilities or death related to military service; pensions; education and rehabilitation; home loan guaranty; burial; and a medical care program.

Job Descriptions

CEMETERY ADMINISTRATOR: Manages the operations of cemeteries. Requires ability to meet and deal with diverse people and to budget, schedule, and supervise.

CHAPLAIN: Performs professional work involved in a program of spiritual welfare and religious guidance for patients in the VA health-care system.

CORRECTIVE THERAPIST: Applies practices of physical education and rehabilitation therapy, using physical exercise to maintain the health or to achieve physical or mental rehabilitation of patients.

DENTAL OFFICER: Performs professional work in the prevention, diagnosis, and treatment of diseases, injuries, and deformities of the teeth, jaws, organs of the mouth, and other structures associated with the oral cavity.

DIETITIAN: Plans and directs the preparation and service of regular and modified diets to patients. Instructs patients in the requirements of prescribed diets.

EDUCATIONAL THERAPIST: Evaluates the learning ability or educational level of patients by use of educational tests and measurements. Some work to rehabilitate the blind, or to diminish emotional stress and channel energies into acceptable forms of behavior.

HEALTH SYSTEM ADMINISTRATOR: Coordinates resources and programs to achieve the critical balance between the administrative and clinical functions in the VA health-care system. May manage a health-care delivery system involving several institutions, or may be responsible for the administrative management of a division of an individual health-care system.

HOSPITAL HOUSEKEEPING MANAGER: Supervises hospital housekeeping programs, ensuring sanitation with acceptable levels of bacteriological cleanliness.

MANUAL ARTS THERAPIST: Evaluates vocational potential of patients, and devises projects and equipment to maintain or improve skills of patients.

MEDICAL OFFICER: Performs professional work in one or more fields of medicine. Requires a Doctor of Medicine or Doctor of Osteopathy degree and a license to practice medicine.

MEDICAL RADIOLOGIST: Applies the use of radiant energy equipment and instruments for radiographic, observational or therapeutic purposes.

MEDICAL TECHNICIAN: Performs or directs chemical, bacteriologic, hematologic, cytologic and other tests of samples of fluids, tissues, and other substances.

NURSE: Provides care to patients in the VA health-care system. Promotes better health practices.

OCCUPATIONAL THERAPIST: Treats patients using remedial activities such as handicrafts to promote recovery or achieve rehabilitation of patients. Performs disability evaluations, such as manual dexterity, attention span, and work tolerance.

OPTOMETRIST: Examines the eye for diseases and defects and prescribes correctional lenses or exercises. Requires a license to practice optometry.

PATHOLOGIST: Makes the final diagnostic examinations of specimens of human tissues and/or cell preparations. Conducts work in histopathology and cytology.

PHARMACIST: Prepares, selects, compounds, and dispenses drugs, medicines, and chemicals. Conducts research in developing special variations of standard formulas to meet the needs of individual patients.

PHYSICAL THERAPIST: Treats patients using therapeutic exercise, massage, and physical agents such as air, water, electricity, sound, and radiant energy.

PROSTHETIC REPRESENTATIVE: Renders prosthetic and sensory aids services to disabled patients. Serves as an advisor to physicians with regard to selection, prescriptions, and acquisition of prosthetic devices.

PSYCHOLOGIST: Performs professional work in human behavior, applying knowledge of psychological principles, theories, and methods to practical situations and problems.

RECREATION/CREATIVE ARTS THERAPY: Evaluates the history, interests, aptitudes, and skills of patients by interviews and tests. Devises therapy activities involving dance, art, music, and/or psychodrama.

RECREATION SPECIALIST: Evaluates the recreation needs of patients. Administers recreation activities and programs which promote the physical, creative, and social development of patients.

SOCIAL SERVICES REPRESENTATIVE: Provides assistance to individuals and families served by social welfare programs. Obtains background information through interviews and home visits, establishes eligibility to make use of agency resources, and explains and encourages the use of agency and community resources.

SOCIAL WORKER: Provides direct services to individuals and families in need of social resources or support.

SPEECH PATHOLOGIST/AUDIOLOGIST: Studies and provides therapeutic treatment for communications disorders, as reflected in impaired hearing, voice, language, or speech.

VETERANS CLAIMS EXAMINER: Performs quasi-legal work involved in examining the settlement of claims filed by veterans and their dependents or beneficiaries.

VOCATIONAL REHABILITATION SPECIALIST: Works on the vocational rehabilitation problems of the physically or mentally disabled. Plans training programs for those whose employability is impaired, and places them in gainful employment. Counsels, supervises, and motivates during the adjustment to training or the work situation.

Major Activities and Divisions

Veterans Health Services and Research Administration: Provides hospital, nursing home, and domiciliary care to eligible veterans. It operates 172 medical centers, 16 domiciliaries, 228 clinics, and 116 nursing home care units in the U.S.

Veterans Benefits Administration: Administers vocational rehabilitation and education programs to eligible veterans. Provides credit assistance to satisfy the housing credit needs of eligible veterans. Provides VA life insurance for the benefit of service members, veterans, and their beneficiaries.

National Cemetery System: Provides cemeterial services to veterans and other eligibles.

Alternative Employment Programs

The VA has an extensive co-op program, hiring more than 40 students per year to fill administrative and semi-professional positions. Co-ops typically begin at the GS-4 or -5 levels, and are usually in their junior year in college. Contact your school placement office for more information.

The VA also participates in the PMI program, the Stay-in-School program, and conducts a volunteer program for students to fill administrative positions.

Remarks

Many of the positions requiring medical expertise are under VA's excepted merit system and therefore do not require typical civil service application procedures.

Application Procedures

Hiring decisions are made locally. Direct inquiries to the personnel officer at the VA facility in which you wish to work. For more information, you may contact the VA headquarters:

Office of Personnel and Labor Relations (054E)
Department of Veterans Affairs
810 Vermont Avenue, N.W.
Washington, DC 20410

(202) 233-3771 or 1-800-368-5629
TDD line: (202) 233-3225

Legislative and Judicial Agencies

ADMINISTRATIVE OFFICE OF THE UNITED STATES COURTS

Nature of Work: Law/justice
Number of Employees: 861
Headquarters: Washington, DC
Regional Locations: None
Typical Majors of New Hires: Business, computer science, criminal justice, law, mathematics, social sciences

Mission

Manages the administrative affairs of the U.S. Court System such as maintaining transcripts, files, and records.

Job Descriptions

ATTORNEY: Advises judges and other court officials on administrative matters such as case management, court governance, and local rules of court.

COMPUTER PROGRAMMER: Programs computer systems using C Language with UNIX Shell programming, Sequential Query Language, and report writing.

COMPUTER PROGRAMMER ANALYST: Works closely with user groups to develop programming specifications.

COMPUTER SYSTEMS ANALYST: Defines user requirements and prepares feasibility studies.

MANAGEMENT ANALYST: Reviews and evaluates the management and operations of the federal courts.

PROBATION PROGRAMS SPECIALIST: Develops policies on probation and pretrial work in such areas as drug and alcohol treatment, witness protection, and sentencing.

Major Activities and Divisions

Bankruptcy Division: Determines the duty stations and staff needs of bankruptcy judges and clerks.

Court Administration: Examines the accounts of court officers; allocates money for court operations; prepares statistical reports; and oversees court travel.

Magistrates Division: Administers the offices of U.S. magistrates and prepares legal and administrative manuals.

Probation Division: Manages the financial accounts and procedures of the federal probation offices.

Statistical Analysis Division: Compiles and analyzes data on financial and programmatic operations.

Alternative Employment Programs

None.

Remarks

None.

Application Procedures

Direct inquiries to:

Administrative Office of the United States Courts
Division of Personnel
Room 701
Washington, DC 20544

(202) 633-6116
(202) 633-6061 (Recorded job information)

CONGRESSIONAL BUDGET OFFICE (CBO)

Nature of Work: Economic policy
Number of Employees: 250
Headquarters: Washington, DC
Regional Locations: None
Typical Majors of New Hires: Economics, public administration

Mission

Provides the Congress with nonpartisan information relating to the U.S. economy, the federal budget, and federal programs.

Job Descriptions

PROGRAM ANALYST: Examines specific issues affecting the federal budget by analyzing current policies, developing alternative approaches, and projecting their impacts.

RESEARCH ASSISTANT: Supports the work of Program Analysts by tracking legislation, drafting testimony, collecting and manipulating data, and conducting policy research.

Major Activities and Divisions

Office of Intergovernmental Relations: Studies budgetary issues involving the organization and management of the federal government.

Budget Analysis Division: Develops cost estimates of specific pieces of legislation, studies budget reform proposals, and develops automated budgetary information systems.

Tax Analysis Division: Estimates tax revenue and analyzes expenditures.

Natural Resources and Commerce Division: Analyzes policies relating to agriculture, energy, the environment, industry, public works, and technology.

Human Resources and Community Development Division: Studies the costs and effectiveness of policies dealing with income assistance, Social Security, health education, employment and training, social services, housing, and community development.

National Security Division: Analyzes budgetary issues relating to manpower and strategic and conventional forces.

Alternative Employment Programs

CBO maintains a summer- and semester-intern program. Details can be obtained from the personnel office.

Remarks

Because of its nonpolitical mandate, CBO makes no policy recommendations, but instead presents options and alternatives for Congress to consider.

Application Procedures

Direct inquiries to:

Congressional Budget Office
Ford House Office Building
Room 493
Washington, DC 20515

(202) 226-2628

CONGRESSIONAL RESEARCH SERVICE (CRS)

Nature of Work: Scholarly research
Number of Employees: 860
Headquarters: Washington, DC
Regional Locations: None
Typical Majors of New Hires: Economics, engineering, international affairs, law, political science, statistics

Mission

Provides nonpartisan analytical research and reference assistance to Congress including policy analyses, legal information, and legislative histories.

Job Descriptions

AUDIO-VISUAL SPECIALIST: Produces audio-visual representations of CRS research products.

BILL DIGESTER: Indexes and digests bills introduced in Congress.

ISSUE BRIEF EDITOR: Edits and manages the publication of Issue Briefs which summarize public policy issues.

LEGISLATIVE ATTORNEY: Analyzes the legal implications of legislation and public policy.

LIBRARIAN: Provides reference and bibliographic support.

PARALEGAL ASSISTANT: Provides research and reference assistance to attorneys as well as members and committees of Congress.

POLICY ANALYST: Conducts policy research in the social sciences, economics, foreign affairs, biology, general engineering, physical sciences, and operations research.

PUBLIC AFFAIRS SPECIALIST: Arranges and coordinates seminars, conferences, orientations and briefings for members of Congress and their staff.

RESEARCH ASSISTANT: Supports policy analysts by providing research and reference assistance.

TRANSLATOR: Translates documents and technical materials into and from a variety of foreign languages.

Major Activities and Divisions

American Law Division: Conducts research in all areas of U.S. public law.

Economics Division: Performs policy research in business and labor, industry and transportation, international economics, housing, and taxation and government finance.

Education and Public Welfare Division: Conducts research in the following fields: Education, health, income maintenance, social services, and social science methodology.

Environment and Natural Resources Policy Division: Analyzes policies relating to environmental protection, food and agriculture, fuels and minerals, and natural resources.

Foreign Affairs and National Defense Division: Conducts policy research pertaining to international affairs, defense and arms control, international organizations, international development, and armed forces manpower.

Government Division: Prepares reports on the federal budget process, Congressional organization, civil rights, and political institutions.

Science Policy Research Division: Analyzes policies relating to advanced technology, biomedicine, geosciences, energy, transportation, and technology.

Alternative Employment Programs

The CRS Graduate Recruit Program is for students enrolled in master's or PhD programs and majoring in political science, economics, international relations, biological/physical sciences, law, library science, business, administration, or other related fields.

The Foreign and Defense Policy Research Associate Program hires 5 temporary analysts for 3-month appointments, year-round. Candidates must be nominated by the dean of a graduate program related to foreign or defense policy, or the director of an organization that performs such research.

Remarks

CRS operates a computerized system called ALERT through which it mails copies of vacancy announcements. To obtain an application form, call (202) 707-8803.

Application Procedures

Direct inquiries to:

Congressional Research Service
Administration Office
Library of Congress
Washington, DC 20540

(202) 707-8803

GENERAL ACCOUNTING OFFICE (GAO)

Nature of Work: Accounting/auditing
Number of Employees: 5,100
Headquarters: Washington, DC
Regional Locations: Atlanta, GA; Boston, MA; Chicago, IL; Cincinnati, OH; Dallas, TX; Denver, CO; Detroit, MI; Honolulu, HI; Kansas City, MO; Los Angeles, CA; New York, NY; Norfolk, VA; Philadelphia, PA; San Francisco, CA; Seattle, WA. An overseas office is located in Frankfurt, Germany.
Typical Majors of New Hires: Accounting, business, computer science, public administration

Mission

Investigates whether government programs comply with applicable laws and regulations and determines whether they are achieving desired results.

Job Descriptions

ACCOUNTANT: Audits agency financial statements and accounting systems; develops and interprets accounting and auditing policy.

COMPUTER SCIENTIST: Reviews the government's acquisition and use of computer and telecommunications systems.

EVALUATOR: Designs and implements reviews of federal programs and policies using a variety of analytical techniques.

Major Activities and Divisions

Accounting and Financial Management Division: Reviews agency accounting and internal control techniques and assesses ways of improving federal financial management.

Resources, Community, and Economic Development Division: Evaluates domestic federal programs such as food and agriculture, energy, environment, transportation, housing, and natural resources.

National Security and International Affairs Division: Audits weapons programs, foreign military and economic assistance, and international relations and trade.

General Government Division: Examines issues pertaining to civilian personnel, law enforcement, tax administration and policy, and federal oversight of financial institutions.

Human Resources Division: Reviews social programs that address employment, education, health-care financing, and income security.

Information Management and Technology Division: Evaluates the acquisition, development, and use of automated data processing, telecommunications, and other information systems in federal agencies.

Program Evaluation and Methodology Division: Conducts program evaluations in all issue areas and develops sound evaluation methodologies.

Alternative Employment Programs

GAO maintains a co-op program for graduate and undergraduate students majoring in public administration, accounting, computer science, and related programs.

Paid summer internships are available for public administration graduate students and undergraduate accounting and computer science students.

Volunteer student internship positions are available throughout the year.

Remarks

GAO's Training Institute offers classes in computers, statistics, and management. The agency's headquarters has modern fitness and daycare facilities.

Application Procedures

Direct inquiries to:

U.S. General Accounting Office
Office of Recruitment
441 G Street, N.W.
Washington, DC 20548

(202) 275-6092
(202) 275-6017

LIBRARY OF CONGRESS

Nature of Work: Libraries, scholarly research
Number of Employees: 4,805
Headquarters: Washington, DC
Regional Locations: None
Typical Majors of New Hires: Computer science, languages, library science

Mission

As the national library of the U.S., the Library of Congress possesses books and pamphlets on every subject in a variety of languages; the world's largest collection of aeronautical literature; the personal papers of presidents; maps; movies; photographs; recordings; government documents; and newspapers and periodicals from around the world.

Job Descriptions

COMPUTER SPECIALIST: Operates the Library of Congress' data base which contains bibliographic and cataloging information on the Library's vast holdings. Also designs software and networks that facilitate distribution of these data to users across the country.

LIBRARIAN: Selects, catalogs, and classifies publications, other printed works, and audiovisual material, and provides reference services.

RESEARCH ANALYST: Assists in classifying and cataloging the Library's holdings.

Major Activities and Divisions

Copyright Office: Reviews and grants copyrights to literary works, musical compositions, and other types of intellectual property.

Law Library: Maintains the Library's collection of legal material which is comprised of the following divisions: American-British Law; European Law; Far Eastern Law; Hispanic Law; and Near Eastern and African Law.

National Programs: Operates the Library's various extension services such as the American Folklore Center, Children's Literature Center, and Education Liaison Office.

Area Studies: Maintains the Library's African, Middle Eastern, Asian, European, and Hispanic literature.

General Reference: Provides reference services relating to federal research, and science and technology.

Special Collections: Acquires and preserves the Library's holdings of maps, manuscripts, motion pictures, music, prints, photographs, and rare books.

Alternative Employment Programs

The Library of Congress has a co-op program for graduate students enrolled in programs related to the following occupations: Librarian, Social Analyst, Economist, Foreign Afffairs Analyst, Legislative Attorney, Administative Officer, and Computer Science Analyst.

Its Foreign Area Associates program gives students experience in fields related to foreign area studies and foreign language.

Remarks

The Library of Congress has its own personnel system and is not under the competitive service.

Application Procedures

Direct inquiries to:

Recruitment and Placement Office
Department E
The Library of Congress
101 Independence Avenue, S.E.
LM 107
Washington, DC 20540

(202) 707-5620
(202) 707-6295 (for 24-hour job vacancy information)

OFFICE OF TECHNOLOGY ASSESSMENT (OTA)

Nature of Work: Scholarly research, scientific research
Number of Employees: 200
Headquarters: Washington, DC
Regional Locations: None
Typical Majors of New Hires: Liberal arts, health sciences, physical sciences

Mission

OTA serves the U.S. Congress by providing objective analyses of major public policy issues related to scientific and technological change.

Job Descriptions

RESEARCH ASSISTANT: Explores complex issues involving science and technology, helping Congress resolve uncertainties and conflicting claims, and providing foresight into developments that could have important implications for future federal policy. Assessment projects may take 1–2 years to complete. Research Assistants may conduct briefings, testimony, and special reports before Congress.

Major Activities and Divisions

OTA has three divisions, each with a specific scientific and technological emphasis. They are Energy Materials and International Security; Health and Life Sciences; and Science Information and Natural Resources.

Alternative Employment Programs

OTA offers paid internships for students typically in their junior or senior year in college. The typical position title is Research Assistant. Interns usually begin work in the summer, and enter at the GS-4 level.

Remarks

None.

Application Procedures

Send a resume or SF-171 to:

Office of Technology Assessment
Attn: Personnel
U.S. Congress
Washington, DC 20510

(202) 224-8713

THE SUPREME COURT OF THE UNITED STATES

Nature of Work: Law/justice, libraries
Number of Employees: 325
Headquarters: Washington, DC
Regional Locations: None
Typical Majors of New Hires: Criminal justice, law (JD), library science (academic backgrounds vary widely)

Mission

The Supreme Court comprises the Chief Justice of the United States and eight Associate Justices. Power to nominate the Justices is vested in the President of the United States, and appointments are made with the advice of the Senate. The officers of the Supreme Court are the Clerk, the Reporter of Decisions, the Librarian, and the Marshal. The term of the court begins, by law, the first Monday in October of each year and continues as long as the business before the Court requires, usually until about the end of June. Approximately 5,000 cases are passed upon in the course of a term.

Job Descriptions

LAW CLERK: Assists justices in background research of cases. Assigned one-year appointments. Hired by individual justices. Should be in the top 5 percent of graduating class of law school. These positions begin at the GS-12 equivalent level. Interested students must either write or telephone an individual justice for consideration.

ASSISTANT LIBRARIAN: Selects, catalogues, and classifies materials in the Supreme Court library, which is open to members of the bar of the Court, attorneys for the various federal departments and agencies, and members of Congress. May involve searching services and/or the development of information retrieval systems. Some positions require a broad knowledge of law.

POLICE OFFICER: Polices the courts, and ensures the safety of court personnel and litigants. Police Officers are paid on the Capitol Hill police scale (approximately a GS-7 level entry equivalent).

Major Activities and Divisions

Lower Courts: Known as constitutional courts, the lower courts share in the exercise of judicial power. These courts have judges who hold office during good behavior, with no power in Congress to provide otherwise. They include the U.S. Court of Appeals, the U.S. Court of Appeals for the Federal Circuit, the United States District Courts, the Territorial Courts, and the Judicial Panel on Multidistrict Litigation.

Special Courts: Known as legislative courts, the special courts are created by Congress, and their judges hold office for such term as Congress prescribes, whether it be for a fixed period of years or during good behavior. These include the United States Claims Court, the United States Court of International Trade, the United States Court of Military Appeals, the United States Tax Court, and the Temporary Emergency Court of Appeals.

Alternative Employment Programs

Although the Supreme Court does not offer co-op or internship positions, it does hire high school or college graduates to be Messengers. These are temporary positions (90-day appointments) with the possibility of permanent placement.

Remarks

None.

Application Procedures

The Supreme Court is considered an excepted service agency and therefore does not require the ACWA test. SF-171's are required—resumes are not accepted.

Direct inquiries to:

Supreme Court of the United States
1 First Street, N.E.
Personnel Office, Room 3
Washington, DC 20543

(202) 479-3404

UNITED STATES GOVERNMENT PRINTING OFFICE (GPO)

Nature of Work: Communications/media
Number of Employees: 5,100
Headquarters: Washington, DC (the Central Office)
Regional Locations: Atlanta, GA; Boston, MA; Chicago, IL; Columbus, OH; Dallas, TX; Denver, CO; Hampton, VA; Los Angeles, CA; New York, NY; Philadelphia, PA; St. Louis, MO; San Francisco, CA; Seattle, WA (Regional printing procurement offices)
Typical Majors of New Hires: Graphic arts (printing sciences, printing management or printing technology)

Mission

Created primarily to satisfy the printing needs of Congress, GPO is today the focal point for printing, binding, and information dissemination for the federal community. Approximately 35 customer agencies and departments, in addition to the Congress, rely on the printing and procurement services of GPO. Probably the best-known ongoing effort of GPO is production of the Congressional Record, the printed compilation of each daily session of Congress. The office also distributes and sells millions of books, pamphlets, and other publications each year.

Job Descriptions

PRINTING SPECIALIST (CUSTOMER SERVICE DEPARTMENT): Coordinates printing and binding requests from Congress and federal agencies. Acts as liaison with agencies, determines whether work should be produced in-house or procured, schedules work, prepares estimates, and maintains an inventory of paper products.

PRINTING SPECIALIST (OFFICE OF FINANCIAL MANAGEMENT): Analyzes production charges on the jacket cost summaries, develops set rates for Congressional work, computes complicated billing of rider requisitions, and resolves disputes relating to customer billings. Examines and certifies vouchers, processes contractual and tort claims, and contacts contractors relative to disputes.

PRINTING SPECIALIST (PRINTING PROCUREMENT DEPARTMENT): Develops contracts for printing and binding services with printing plants in the private sector. Prepares pre-award surveys, develops and writes specifications for advertised contracts, monitors contract compliance of commercial contractors, prepares bid lists, issues invitations for bids, recommends awards for contracts, and administers contracts. Works in the Central Office or at one of 20 field establishments.

PRINTING SPECIALIST (PRODUCTION DEPARTMENT): Coordinates and controls printing functions within five major production areas: Electronic Systems Development; Graphic Systems Development; Electronic Photocomposition; Press; and Binding Divisions. Studies and makes recommendations on printing operations, procedures, equipment, and work-flow. Involved in the development and use of automated micro-computer-based composition systems.

Major Activities and Divisions

GPO has five field printing offices, 14 regional procurement offices with several satellite facilities, a major distribution facility, and 24 bookstores. More than 2,000 orders are processed daily either for internal production or commercial procurement.

Alternative Employment Programs

GPO hires a small number of printing science or computer science majors for co-op positions in its central office. The co-op program typically targets juniors in an undergraduate program, to begin at the GS-4 level. Students should contact their school placement office for more information, or may call the agency directly at (202) 275-1137.

GPO also offers an internship program, typically filling Printing Assistant, Accountant, Computer Scientist, and other professional positions. These are usually filled by undergraduate-level students.

The agency also offers a Volunteer Program for students interested in clerical positions. It does not participate in the PMI or Stay-in-School programs.

Remarks

GPO has a nationwide recruitment program which targets college campuses with strong printing sciences or graphic arts programs. Printing Specialist positions are continuously open, and GPO has direct hire authority.

PRINTING SPECIALISTS enter into a two-year training program. Trainees will be provided rotational assignments within their department, and will take part in special classroom courses and technical on-the-job training.

Application Procedures

Applicants possessing a baccalaureate degree with a major in printing management or printing technology may submit an SF-171, Application for Federal Employment, to:

Personnel Director
U.S. Government Printing Office
Employment Branch (Stop: PSE)
North Capitol and H Streets, N.W.
Washington, DC 20401
(202) 275-1137

For information on other positions within GPO, such as Librarian, Investigator, Lawyer, or Chemist, contact the Personnel Department for vacancy announcements at (202) 275-1137.

Independent Agencies

The following entries make up the federal government's independent agencies, that is, those that do not fall within a certain cabinet level department. Agencies that are independent typically are more at liberty to make individual employment decisions without using the Office of Personnel Management hiring system as described in Chapter 3. Thus, the hiring procedures may be quicker and more direct.

The authors have chosen for inclusion in this section all independent agencies that employ 200 people or more, or have missions that may be of particular interest to certain individuals so as to warrant inclusion.

Only a handful of agencies have been excluded because of their small numbers, notably:

Administrative Conference of the United States	23 employees
Advisory Committee on Intergovernmental Relations	37 employees
Appalachian Regional Commission	8 employees
Board for International Broadcasting	23 employees
Commission of Fine Arts	7 employees
Delaware River Basin Commission	2 employees
Federal Mine Safety and Health Review Commission	50 employees
InterAmerican Foundation	72 employees
National Capital Planning Commission	50 employees
National Mediation Board	57 employees
Occupational Safety and Health Review Commission	86 employees
Office of the Special Counsel	65 employees
Overseas Private Investment Corporation	145 employees
Pennsylvania Avenue Development Corporation	31 employees
Susquehanna River Basin Commission	2 employees
U.S. Commission on Civil Rights	101 employees

For information on these agencies, refer to the U.S. Government Manual, printed annually by the Government Printing Office. It can be found at most public libraries.

ACTION

Nature of Work: Aged/children, regional development, low-income people, volunteers
Number of Employees: 440
Headquarters: Washington, DC
Regional Locations: Atlanta, GA; Boston, MA; Chicago, IL; Dallas, TX; Denver, CO; New York, NY; Philadelphia, PA; San Francisco, CA; Seattle, WA
Typical Majors of New Hires: Education, psychology, social sciences

Mission

ACTION's mission is to promote the spirit and practice of voluntarism. This is carried out by more than 400,000 local volunteers in communities around the country. Whether the goal is to help adults learn to read, to help young people stay drug-free, or to provide companionship and services to the home-bound elderly, ACTION programs and volunteers join citizens together to address the needs of a community and its people.

Job Descriptions

STATE PROGRAM SPECIALIST: Develops, monitors, and evaluates a variety of community-based ACTION social service programs. Makes on-site visits to inspect and review conduct of assigned projects and programs. Provides technical assistance to project/program sponsors, and maintains liaison with government and local officials. Assists in training events, workshops, and conferences.

Major Activities and Divisions

ACTION works to better America through several programs: The Foster Grandparent Program, the Retired Senior Volunteer Program, the Senior Companion Program, Volunteers in Service to America (VISTA), and the Student Community Service Program.

Alternative Employment Programs

ACTION does not have a co-op or intern program. It does offer the Stay-in-School program and a volunteer program for support staff, technical, and general clerical positions.

Remarks

None.

Application Procedures

Direct inquiries to the Personnel Management Division in the regional office in which you wish to work:

HEADQUARTERS:

ACTION
Personnel Office
1100 Vermont Avenue, N.W.
Washington, DC 20525
(202) 634-9263
(202) 634-1000 (vacancies)

Region I
10 Causeway Street, Room 473
Boston, MA 02222-1039
(617) 565-7000

Region II
6 World Trade Center Building
Room 758
New York, NY 10048
(212) 466-3481

Region III
U.S. Customs House
Room 108
2nd and Chestnut Streets
Philadelphia, PA 19106-2912
(215) 597-9972

Region IV
101 Marietta Street, N.W.
Suite 1003
Atlanta, GA 30323-2301
(404) 841-2859

Region V
10 West Jackson Boulevard
6th Floor
Chicago, IL 60604-3964
(312) 353-5107

Region VI
1100 Commerce Street
Room 6B11
Dallas, TX 75242-0696
(214) 767-9494

Region VIII
Executive Tower Building
Suite 2930
1405 Curtis Street
Denver, CO 80202-2349
(303) 844-2671

Region IX
211 Main Street
Room 530
San Francisco, CA 94105-1914
(415) 744-3046

Region X
Federal Office Building
909 First Avenue
Seattle, WA 98174-1103
(206) 442-4520

AGENCY FOR INTERNATIONAL DEVELOPMENT (AID)

Nature of Work: Agriculture, developing countries, health/health care, international affairs, low-income people

Number of Employees: 4,862

Headquarters: Washington, DC

Regional Locations: AID has field missions in approximately 70 developing countries in Africa, Asia, Latin America and the Caribbean, and the Near East

Typical Majors of New Hires: Accounting, agriculture, anthropology, business, communications, education, economics, finance, food sciences (nutrition), international relations, marketing, political science, public health, social sciences, urban studies

Mission

AID's purpose is to help people in the Third World acquire the knowledge and resources to build the economic, political, and social institutions needed for a more prosperous life. This assistance covers many diverse areas including agriculture, rural development, nutrition, family planning, health, education, energy, and technology.

Job Descriptions

**NOTE:* A graduate degree is required for some positions as noted below. The others require a bachelor's degree in an appropriate field. All positions require two years of experience beyond education.

ACCOUNTANT: Maintains a comprehensive accounting system and provides financial and statistical data; develops systems of internal control for the disbursement and collection of funds; and provides advice on financial implications of existing grant loan agreements with host countries. Requires a CPA or MBA.

ADMINISTRATIVE MANAGEMENT OFFICER: Oversees a range of management and administrative support functions including personnel, contracting, and procurement. Plans for future support requirements at the assigned duty station.

AGRICULTURE/RURAL DEVELOPMENT/NATURAL RESOURCES OFFICER: Advises senior AID and host government officials on agriculture, rural development, or natural resources-related project studies. Identifies problems and proposes solutions, and participates in project development and program management. Duties include coordinating the flow of resources for agricultural projects, analyzing the effects on agriculture of proposed policies, and monitoring natural resources and environmental concerns. Requires a graduate degree in an agricultural, social, or environmental science.

CONTRACT/COMMODITY MANAGEMENT OFFICER: Negotiates, awards, and administers contracts, grants and other agreements with individuals, firms, and institutions to carry out AID-financed projects. Advises host country importers in the development of commodity procurement plans.

EDUCATION/HUMAN RESOURCES DEVELOPMENT OFFICER: Assists with the development of host country educational systems. Strategies are designed to improve existing educational programs as well as to promote organizational competencies related to institutional development. Participates in agency policy formulation, program design, and evaluation of activities. Requires a graduate degree in education, psychology, sociology, anthropology, or communications.

HEALTH/POPULATION/NUTRITION OFFICER: Assists host country leaders in designing and managing health delivery systems, population and family planning projects, and nutrition and feeding programs. Works in conjunction with U.S. government personnel, contractors, grantees, and international agencies. Requires a Master of Public Health or Master of Science of Public Health degree.

HOUSING/URBAN DEVELOPMENT OFFICER: Assists, through the Office of Housing and Urban Programs, in planning, implementing, and monitoring AID's shelter programs for below-median income families in developing countries, and with AID's broader urban programs.

PROGRAM ECONOMIST: Conducts analyses of both the macroeconomic conditions of host countries and the microeconomic feasibility of individual projects. Examines balance of payments, government budgets, growth prospects, and income distribution. Conducts cost-benefit analysis at the micro level. Requires a graduate degree in Economics.

PRIVATE ENTERPRISE OFFICER: Designs and manages the overall private sector strategy. Develops policies and mechanisms for financing the establishment, improvement, and expansion of productive private enterprise in a foreign country. Expands local, indigenous private sector activities, and involves the U.S. private sector in the development process.

PROGRAM OFFICER: Advises the Mission Director and technical staff on AID program policy. Ensures that proposed projects are feasible. Assists in designing AID's country development strategy and in preparing AID's budget.

PROJECT DEVELOPMENT OFFICER: Assists in the planning and implementation of AID projects. Provides assistance to host government authorities and to private and public entities on non-technical and financial aspects of projects. Ensures that proposed projects are feasible, and monitors projects to assure compliance with the provisions of project agreements.

Major Activities and Divisions

Private Sector: AID strives to stimulate the growth of market economies in developing countries and to interest U.S. companies in investing in those countries.

Policy Dialogue: AID emphasizes the importance of government policy reform in the development process.

Institution Building: AID helps build schools and other institutions vital to the growth of developing countries.

Research and Technology Transfer: AID promotes the transfer of appropriate technology to developing countries.

Humanitarian Relief: AID conducts relief activities for victims of natural calamities.

Alternative Employment Programs

AID conducts the International Development Intern (IDI) Program. This entry-level program trains qualified persons to become career Foreign Service Officers who will assume positions of increasing responsibility in managing AID's foreign economic assistance programs. Training for the program begins in Washington, DC and consists of orientation to the agency and subjects related to the foreign economic assistance program. Each intern then begins individual on-the-job training in

Washington, which usually lasts about one year and includes language training. Interns also spend some time learning overseas.

Remarks

Foreign language proficiency is required for tenure in the Foreign Service, but is not a requirement for hiring. Foreign Service Officers will spend the majority of their careers overseas and must be willing to accept assignment anywhere in the world.

Application Procedures

Direct inquiries to:

International Development Intern Program
Recruitment Staff—PM/RS
Agency for International Development
Washington, DC 20523-0114

(202) 663-1291

CENTRAL INTELLIGENCE AGENCY (CIA)

Nature of Work: Defense/national security, intelligence, international affairs
Number of Employees: Classified
Headquarters: Langley, Virginia
Regional Locations: Worldwide—exact locations are classified
Typical Majors of New Hires: Accounting, business, computer science, engineering, finance/banking, liberal arts, physics, physical sciences, public administration

Mission

Gathers and analyzes information on foreign adversaries; conducts counterintelligence operations abroad to frustrate foreign espionage; and undertakes covert action overseas at the President's direction.

Job Descriptions

Careers are available in many scientific and technical fields; management; business; accounting; finance; liberal arts; languages; and the social sciences.

Major Activities and Divisions

Directorate of Operations: Conducts the agency's clandestine assignments which include foreign intelligence collection, and, in some instances, covert action.

Directorate of Science and Technology: Develops and applies advanced systems to collect, interpret, and disseminate information. Projects include video and image enhancement; chemical imagery; advanced antenna design; electro-optics; large systems modeling and simulation; and laser, analog, digital, and satellite communications. It also collects and processes intelligence information from broadcast and print media, telecommunications, and overhead photography.

Directorate of Intelligence: Evaluates and interprets information obtained from the Directorates of Operations and Science and Technology, assesses its implications, and passes the findings to government leaders.

Directorate of Administration: Provides services such as personnel and financial management, communications, computer programming, medicine, security, logistics, and training.

Alternative Employment Programs

Co-op programs and summer internships are available for undergraduate and graduate students. Address inquiries to :

Coordinator for Student Programs
Department S, 4N20J
P.O. Box 1925
Washington, DC 20013

Remarks

CIA personnel serving overseas receive special pay, as well as allowances for housing, education for dependents, medical care, and other considerations.

Applicants must submit to strict background and medical evaluations, as well as a polygraph test. Because the entire application process may take six or more months to complete, applicants should begin this process long before they are available for employment.

Application Procedures

Direct inquiries to:

Personnel Representative (FCD)
Central Intelligence Agency
PO Box 1925
Department S, Room 4N20
Washington, DC 20013

(703) 874-4400
(703) 351-2028 (vacancies)

COMMODITY FUTURES TRADING COMMISSION (CFTC)

Nature of Work: Bonds/commodities, economic policy, law enforcement
Number of Employees: 569
Headquarters: Washington, DC
Regional Locations: Chicago, IL; Kansas, City, MO; Los Angeles, CA; Minneapolis, MN; New York, NY
Typical Majors of New Hires: Accounting, business, computer science, economics, law

Mission

Regulates trading on 11 U.S. futures exchanges; monitors the activities of commodity exchange members, public brokerage houses, CFTC-registered futures industry salespeople, commodity pool operators, and commodity trading advisers.

Job Descriptions

ATTORNEY: Advises the Commission on the legality of policies and regulations; works with U.S. attorneys in pursuing criminal violations of commodities regulations.

AUDITOR: Reviews transactions and activities of commodity exchange members ensuring compliance with Commission rules.

COMPUTER SPECIALIST: Develops, operates, and supports market surveillance and other automated systems.

ECONOMIST: Studies the economic impact of Commission actions on manufacturers, farmers, exporters, wholesalers, and consumers; and uses econometric modeling to forecast economic and market trends.

FUTURES TRADING SPECIALIST/INVESTIGATOR: Investigates illegal trading activity such as market manipulations, fraud, and trade abuses; assists state or federal law enforcement agencies conducting commodity violations.

Major Activities and Divisions

Division of Enforcement: Investigates and prosecutes Commodity Exchange Act violations.

Division of Trading and Markets: Drafts, implements, and enforces exchange regulations that prevent fraud, protect customer investments, and ensure the stability of commodity trading firms.

Office of the General Counsel: Provides legal advice to the Commission's operating divisions.

Division of Economic Analysis: Supervises daily futures market transactions, reviews new futures and options contract proposals, and conducts economic studies.

Alternative Employment Programs

CFTC maintains a co-op program for college students. Summer intern employment is also available.

Remarks

None.

Application Procedures

Direct inquiries to:

Director of Personnel
Commodity Futures Trading Commission
2033 K Street, N.W., Room 202
Washington, DC 20581

(202) 254-3275

THE ENVIRONMENTAL PROTECTION AGENCY (EPA)

Nature of Work: Environmental protection, law enforcement, scientific research
Number of Employees: 15,246
Headquarters: Washington, DC
Regional Locations: Atlanta, GA; Boston, MA; Chicago, IL; Dallas, TX; Denver, CO; Kansas City, MO; New York, NY; Philadelphia, PA; San Francisco, CA; Seattle, WA. Research and development laboratories are located in Research Triangle Park, NC; Cincinnati, OH; and Las Vegas, NV. EPA's National Enforcement Investigation Center is located in Denver, CO. Its Mobile Source Air Pollution Control facility is in Ann Arbor, MI.
Typical Majors of New Hires: Biology, chemistry, computer science, criminal justice, engineering, geology, law, physical sciences, public administration, veterinary medicine

Mission

Prevents air, land, and water pollution by regulating the manufacture, use, and disposal of toxic substances. EPA also oversees the cleanup of polluted sites and supports research and antipollution activities.

Job Descriptions

ATTORNEY: Drafts legislation and regulations; represents the agency in litigation; helps prosecute criminal violators of environmental regulations.

BIOLOGIST: Identifies biological hazards in the environment and develops remedies to stabilize or remove them.

CHEMICAL ENGINEER: Studies methods of removing pollutants by chemical and biological means; designs, evaluates, and sets standards for waste treatment plants.

CRIMINAL INVESTIGATOR: Investigates alleged violations of environmental laws.

ENVIRONMENTAL ENGINEER: Studies the impact of pollutants on the environment, develops remedial technologies, and evaluates pollution control techniques.

ENVIRONMENTAL PROTECTION SPECIALIST: Develops environmental protection plans and programs, and works on related grant proposals.

ENVIRONMENTAL SCIENTIST: Reviews, analyzes and evaluates air and water quality and assesses pollution control regulations.

GENETICIST: Evaluates the environmental hazards of bio-engineered organisms.

GEOLOGIST: Examines geological formations and determines their capacity for containing toxic wastes.

HYDROLOGIST: Studies and predicts hydrologic phenomena such as precipitation, evaporation, and streamflow.

MECHANICAL ENGINEER: Creates and evaluates pollution control technologies and monitoring systems.

METEOROLOGIST: Compiles data on local and national weather patterns to help in the study and regulation of airborne pollutants.

PATHOLOGIST: Examines various pollution hazards and their relationship to the growth and transmission of diseases.

PHARMACOLOGIST: Reviews and evaluates pharmacological and toxicological data to determine whether a chemical meets approved standards for safety and labeling.

RADIATION ENGINEER: Assesses and controls airborne radioactive emissions and measures radiation levels in the environment.

TOXICOLOGIST: Evaluates residue chemistry and toxicology data to ensure that levels of pesticides and other chemicals found in the environment will not harm public health.

VETERINARY OFFICER (VETERINARIAN): Researches the toxicological and pathological effects of chemicals used in the control of livestock and plant pests.

Major Activities and Divisions

Research and Development: Investigates the impact of pollutants on the environment and human health, and studies the transport and control of pollutants.

Air and Radiation: Regulates and monitors six principal air pollutants, as well as exceptionally hazardous substances such as beryllium and mercury. Also sets standards for the manufacture and sale of fuels or fuel additives, and regulates airborne radioactive emissions.

Solid Waste and Emergency Response: Issues permits for hazardous waste management facilities, and removes or stabilizes hazardous waste sites.

Water: Reduces water pollution by regulating municipalities and industries and by assisting states in developing effective control methods.

Pesticides and Toxic Substances: Registers new products; reviews hazards from existing products; and enforces pesticide use rules.

Enforcement and Compliance. Enforces environmental laws, investigates the illegal discharge of toxic wastes into waterways and landfills, and the deliberate destruction or falsification of environmental reports.

Alternative Employment Programs

EPA maintains a co-op program for engineering students. Its Stay-in-School Program provides employment to highly qualified students who need financial assistance in order to continue their education.

EPA also has a 2-year Management Intern Program that allows participants to complete a number of rotational assignments within EPA, other federal agencies, or Congress. The deadline for applications is usually in mid-January of each year. For more information, contact the recruitment center below.

Remarks

None.

Application Procedures

Direct inquiries to:

Recruitment Center
(PM-224)
Environmental Protection Agency
401 M Street, S.W.
Washington, DC 20460

(202) 382-3305 (personnel)
(202) 755-5055 (vacancies)
1-800-338-1350 (toll-free)

EXPORT-IMPORT BANK OF THE UNITED STATES (EXIMBANK)

Nature of Work: Banks, international affairs, marketing, trade, import/export
Number of Employees: 329
Headquarters: Washington, DC
Regional Locations: None
Typical Majors of New Hires: Accounting, business, economics, finance/banking, law

Mission

Enables U.S. exporters to compete in overseas markets by providing them with loans, guarantees, and insurance. Helps U.S. companies market new products abroad, assists new exporters in breaking into foreign markets, and aids established exporters in maintaining their foreign markets.

Job Descriptions

ACCOUNTANT: Records financial transactions resulting from loan repayments, service fees, and claims payments.

ATTORNEY: Ensures loans comply with federal export laws, banking statutes, and other regulations.

ECONOMIST: Monitors and evaluates economic trends in foreign countries, determines economic impact of particular transactions, and assesses the viabililty of loans.

FINANCIAL ANALYST: Analyzes financing proposals and determines whether there is reasonable assurance of loan repayment.

LOAN SPECIALIST: Analyzes financial and credit risk factors and develops policies and procedures governing loan programs.

Major Activities and Divisions

Export Finance Group: Administers Eximbank's loan, guarantee, and insurance programs.

Working Capital Guarantee Program: Provides eligible exporters with access to working capital loans from commercial lenders.

Engineering Division: Evaluates the technical feasibility of proposed projects and monitors projects in progress.

Claims and Recoveries Division: Processes claims filed under Eximbank's guarantee and insurance programs, and makes collections and recoveries.

Alternative Employment Programs

Eximbank has a volunteer internship program for students interested in working for a summer or a semester. Co-op positions are available when there is available funding.

Remarks

None.

Application Procedures

Direct inquiries to:

Personnel Director
Export-Import Bank of the United States
811 Vermont Avenue, N.W.
Washington, DC 20571

(202) 566-8834

FEDERAL COMMUNICATIONS COMMISSION (FCC)

Nature of Work: Communications/media
Number of Employees: 1,770
Headquarters: Washington, DC
Regional Locations: Atlanta, GA; Bellevue, WA; Kansas City, MO; Park Ridge, IL; Quincy, MA; San Francisco, CA. FCC also has 36 field offices that do investigative and enforcement work.
Typical Majors of New Hires: Engineering (electronic), law

Mission

Regulates interstate and international communications by radio, television, wire, satellite, and cable. It assigns frequencies, power and call signs; authorizes communications circuits; modifies and reviews licenses; inspects transmitting equipment; and controls interference.

Job Descriptions

ATTORNEY: Reviews applications for radio licenses and represents the FCC before administrative law judges in formal adjudicatory hearings. Attorneys also perform appellate litigation and enforcement proceedings in the federal courts, and review tariffs of telephone and telegraph companies.

ELECTRONIC ENGINEER: Investigates illegal or clandestine radio stations; inspects radio equipment on ships and land-based broadcast stations; determines the feasibility of directional antenna proposals; calculates horizontal and vertical plane radiation patterns for antenna systems; and develops methods of increasing spectrum usage.

Major Activities and Divisions

Mass Media Bureau: Licenses commercial and noncommercial radio and television stations, directs broadcast satellites, and other electronic mass media.

Common Carrier Bureau: Regulates communications common carriers' charges, rates of return, mergers, classifications, accounting methods, and depreciation rates.

Private Radio Bureau: Regulates aviation, marine, amateur, industrial, and public safety radio useage.

Field Operations Bureau: Monitors, inspects, and investigates radio and wire facilities for technical compliance with federal statutes, Commission rules and international treaties.

Office of the General Counsel: Advises the Commission and its various bureaus and offices on legal matters.

Office of Engineering and Technology: Advises the Commission and its subunits on scientific and engineering matters. Sets technical standards for electronic devices and allocates the electromagnetic spectrum.

Alternative Employment Programs

The FCC has a Summer Law Intern Program where students can acquire first-hand knowledge of the Commission. Applications must be received by November 1 of each year.

The FCC also has a Work-Study program for law students. Although they are not compensated, students may obtain course credit.

Co-op opportunities are available for engineering students. Direct inquiries to:

Associate Managing Director
Human Resources Management
Federal Communications Commission
1919 M Street, N.W., Room 212
Washington, DC 20554

(202) 632-7106

Remarks

None.

Application Procedures

Direct inquiries to:

Chief, Personnel Operation Branch
Federal Communications Commission
Washington, DC 20554

(202) 632-7106

FEDERAL DEPOSIT INSURANCE CORPORATION (FDIC)

Nature of Work: Accounting/auditing, banks/banking, consumer protection, insurance/benefits
Number of Employees: 8,060
Headquarters: Washington, DC
Regional Locations: Atlanta, GA; Boston, MA; Chicago, IL; Dallas, TX; Kansas City, MO; Memphis, TN; New York, NY; San Francisco, CA
Typical Majors of New Hires: Accounting, business, economics, finance/banking

Mission

The Federal Deposit Insurance Corporation was established to promote and preserve public confidence in banks and to protect the money supply through provision of insurance coverage for bank deposits and periodic examinations of insured banks that are not members of the Federal Reserve System.

Job Descriptions

BANK EXAMINER TRAINEE: Performs an audit function at financial institutions to determine their safety and soundness, and to ensure compliance with regulations. Assesses the adequacy of internal procedures, management functions, and financial conditions. Bank Examiners conduct on-site audits as a team effort. Travel takes place within an assigned region and can be as high as 90%. When not traveling, Bank Examiners work in an FDIC regional or HQ office.

BANK LIQUIDATION SPECIALIST (TRAINEE): Liquidates accounts such as installment loans, charged-off-assets, or small commercial loans. Advertises properties to be sold, checks current status of payments made by debtors, inspects collateral, and meets with debtors concerning repayment schedules.

Major Activities and Divisions

Division of Bank Supervision: Monitors banking practices at federally insured institutions to protect depositors and reduce risks.

Division of Liquidation: Approves or disapproves a proposal to reduce or retire the capital of a bank. Terminates the insured status of a bank that engages in unsound practices.

Alternative Employment Programs

FDIC offers internship positions. The agency does not participate in the co-op program.

Remarks

FDIC has a continuing college recruitment program. Approximately 500–700 graduating college students per year are hired for the Bank Examiner position. Bank Examiners make up approximately 60% of FDIC's staff.

Application Procedures

FDIC hires Bank Examiners and Bank Liquidation Specialist Trainees on an open season basis. Specially designed application forms have been developed which are available for distribution only during the open period of the announcement, and must be received from the applicant during the open period as well. The announcement number for the Bank Examiner Trainee position is FDIC-100.

You may direct inquiries to the office in which you are interested:

Federal Deposit Insurance Corporation
Office of Personnel Management:

Recruitment and Placement Branch
550 Seventeenth Street, N.W.
Washington, DC 20429-9990
(202) 898-8890

245 Peachtree Center Avenue, N.E.
Atlanta, GA 30303
(404) 880-3000

160 Gould Street
Needham, MA 02194

30 S. Wacker Drive
Chicago, IL 60606
(312) 207-0200

1910 Pacific Avenue
Dallas, TX 75201
(214) 754-0098

2345 Grand Avenue
Kansas City, MO 64108

5100 Poplar Avenue
Memphis, TN 38137

21st Floor
452 5th Avenue
New York, NY 10018
(212) 704-1200

25 Ecker Street
San Francisco, CA 94105
(416) 546-1801

FEDERAL ELECTION COMMISSION (FEC)

Nature of Work: Funds/funding
Number of Employees: 242
Headquarters: Washington, DC
Regional Locations: None
Typical Majors of New Hires: Accounting, law, political science

Mission

Enforces the Federal Election Campaign Act of 1971 which provides for the public funding of presidential elections, requires public disclosure of the financial activities of political committees, and regulates contributions made to influence federal elections.

Job Descriptions

ATTORNEY: Analyzes complaints alleging violations of the Campaign Act, and researches questions regarding FEC regulations and federal laws.

AUDITOR: Audits recipients of federal campaign funds and determines whether they comply with laws and regulations.

PUBLIC AFFAIRS SPECIALIST: Provides candidates, political committees, special interest groups, and the general public with information on the Campaign Act and FEC regulations.

Major Activities and Divisions

Audit Division: Certifies federal payments to primary candidates, general election nominees, and national nominating conventions.

Disclosure Division: Reveals the sources and expenditures of campaign funds from political committees supporting federal candidates.

Office of the General Counsel: Enforces campaign finance laws through reconciliation and court action.

Alternative Employment Programs

FEC maintains a summer intern program for law students. Interns perform legal research on specific topics, and support FEC's litigation, enforcement, and regulatory functions.

Remarks

None.

Application Procedures

Direct inquiries to:

Federal Election Commission
Personnel Division
Room 812
999 E Street
Washington, DC 20463

(202) 376-5290
800-424-9530 (toll free)

THE FEDERAL EMERGENCY MANAGEMENT AGENCY (FEMA)

Nature of Work: Disaster assistance, emergency preparedness, hazardous materials
Number of Employees: 2,451
Headquarters: Washington, DC
Regional Locations: Atlanta, GA; Boston, MA; Bothell, WA; Chicago, IL; Denton, TX; Denver, CO; Kansas City, MO; New York, NY; Philadelphia, PA; San Francisco, CA
Typical Majors of New Hires: Business, engineering, public administration

Mission

FEMA was created to provide a single point of accountability for all federal emergency preparedness, mitigation, and response activities. The agency's goal is to enhance the use of emergency preparedness and response resources in preparing for and responding to the full range of emergencies, including natural, technological, and attack-related emergencies.

Job Descriptions

EMERGENCY MANAGEMENT SPECIALIST INTERN: Conducts research, supervises, and manages programs related to manmade, natural, and nuclear crises, including civil disaster response, recovery, and mitigation. Supports state and local governments in disaster preparedness, coordinates federal aid for presidentially declared disasters, and plans civil emergency preparedness for peacetime nuclear or hazardous materials accidents. Interns begin at the GS-5 or -7 level, and after one year in the internship program, may be promoted to the next highest level. See Remarks.

Major Activities and Divisions

The National Preparedness Directorate: Develops national policy relating to national security emergencies.

The State and Local Programs Support Directorate: Administers support programs to state and local governments, and develops plans for the federal response to catastrophic natural and technological occurrences.

The Federal Insurance Administration: Administers the National Flood Insurance Program, and works to reduce future flood damage through floodplain management.

The Unites States Fire Administration: Coordinates the federal government's response to the nation's fire problem.

Alternative Employment Programs

FEMA hires high school and college students through the Federal Summer Employment Program, mostly at the GS-1-4 levels.

Remarks

Emergency Management Specialist Interns enter the agency as a class, usually beginning in June. Selectees MUST relocate to Washington, DC to begin the program, which lasts two years. During this time, interns may be sent on rotational assignments at one or more of FEMA's regional offices for a period of up to six months. Upon graduation from the two-year program, interns are placed into permanent Emergency Management Specialist positions at any of the headquarters or field locations.

Application Procedures

Applicants must submit a full application package no later than March 31 of the year in which they plan to enter the program. Mail to:

Federal Emergency Management Agency
Office of Personnel and Equal Opportunity
EMS Intern Desk—Room 816
500 C Street, S.W.
Washington, DC 20472

(202) 432-4088
(202) 646-4041 (vacancies)

FEDERAL LABOR RELATIONS AUTHORITY (FLRA)

Nature of Work: Labor/management relations, law/justice
Number of Employees: 246
Headquarters: Washington, DC
Regional Locations: Atlanta, GA; Boston, MA; Chicago, IL; Dallas, TX; Denver, CO; Los Angeles, CA; New York, NY; San Francisco, CA; Washington, DC
Typical Majors of New Hires: Industrial relations, law, political science, psychology, public administration

Mission

The FLRA oversees the federal service labor management relations program. It administers the law that protects the rights of employees of the federal government to organize, bargain collectively, and participate through labor organizations in decisions affecting them.

Job Descriptions

ATTORNEY/LAW CLERK TRAINEE: Analyzes assigned cases, including charges of unfair labor practices and representation petitions. Interviews witnesses and takes affidavits. Makes preliminary evaluation as to merits of the case and appropriate course of action. Under direction of the Regional Attorney, prepares for trial, including preparing notice of hearing, pleading, trial briefs, pretrial motions and opposition to pretrial motions of other parties, and other formal documents. Serves as hearing officer in representation proceedings, and conducts representation elections. Makes investigation of challenged ballots and/or objections to elections. This position often requires frequent travel. All applicants must have graduated from an accredited law school. Applicants for Law Clerk Trainee do not have to be members of the Bar. Applicants for Attorney must be admitted to a Bar.

LABOR RELATIONS SPECIALIST: Conducts investigations into allegations of unfair labor practices raised by employees, agencies, or labor unions. Makes preliminary evaluation of the case's merits, recommends withdrawal of petition or charge when appropriate, and negotiates for informal/formal settlement agreement when litigation is not warranted. Serves as hearing officer in representation proceedings and prepares hearing officer's report, and makes investigation of challenged ballots or objections to elections or the conduct of elections. Provides advice to labor and management on interpretation and application of the law and participates in programs to make the public more aware of the federal labor relations program. This position often requires frequent travel.

Major Activities and Divisions

The General Counsel of the Authority: Investigates alleged unfair labor practices, and files and prosecutes unfair labor practice complaints before the Authority.

The Federal Service Impasses Panel: Provides assistance in resolving negotiation impasses between agencies and unions.

The Foreign Service Labor Relations Board and the *Foreign Service Impasses Disputes Panel:* Administers a labor-management relations program for Foreign Service employees of the U.S. government.

Alternative Employment Programs

The FLRA has a limited co-op/intern program.

Remarks

All hiring is coordinated through the headquarters office in Washington, DC.

Application Procedures

Direct inquiries to:

Federal Labor Relations Authority
Office of Personnel
Equal Employment Opportunity and Security
500 C Street, S.W., Room 225
Washington, DC 20424

(202) 382-0740

FEDERAL MARITIME COMMISSION (FMC)

Nature of Work: Maritime activities, trade, wages/prices/rates, waterways
Number of Employees: 230
Headquarters: Washington, DC
Regional Locations: Hato Rey, PR; Houston, TX; Los Angeles, CA; Miami, FL; New Orleans, LA; New York, NY; San Francisco, CA
Typical Majors of New Hires: Economics, law

Mission

Regulates U.S. and foreign-flag ocean carriers calling at American ports, and freight forwarders and ocean terminal operators who participate in ocean commerce.

Job Descriptions

ATTORNEY: Approves or denies tariff and license filings, drafts regulations, and participates in formal investigations and administrative hearings.

ECONOMIST: Studies competition in various trade areas, future commodity trends, and the economic impact of rates and tariffs.

INVESTIGATOR: Ensures that common carriers, terminal operators, freight forwarders, and others involved in waterborne commerce comply with shipping statutes.

TRANSPORTATION SPECIALIST: Analyzes rates, tariffs, and subsidies for the purposes of improving water-borne commerce.

Major Activities and Divisions

Agreements: Reviews agreements between common carriers, terminal operators, and other parties subject to shipping statutes.

Tariffs: Accepts or denies tariff filings and regulates carrier rates.

Licenses: Grants or denies licenses to persons, partnerships, corporations, or associations wishing to engage in ocean freight forwarding.

Passenger Indemnity: Issues certificates of financial responsibility of shipowners and operators, requiring them to pay judgments for personal injury or death, or to refund fares in cases of nonperformance of voyages.

Informal Complaints: Investigates and resolves alleged violations of shipping statutes.

Formal Adjudicatory Procedure: Conducts formal investigations and hearings and adjudicates complaints.

Investigation, Audit, and Financial and Economic Analyses: Ensures compliance with shipping statutes through data collection, field investigations, and audits of activities and practices of common carriers.

International Affairs: Works with the Department of State to eliminate practices on the part of foreign governments that discriminate against U.S. shipping.

Alternative Employment Programs

FMC maintains a co-op program depending on the availability of funding.

Remarks

None.

Application Procedures

Direct inquiries to:

Director of Personnel
Federal Maritime Commission
1100 L Street, N.W.
Room 10103
Washington, DC 20573-0001

(202) 523-5773

THE FEDERAL MEDIATION AND CONCILIATION SERVICE (FMCS)

Nature of Work: Labor/management relations
Number of Employees: 316
Headquarters: Washington, DC
Regional Locations: More than 70 offices in 38 states
Typical Majors of New Hires: Industrial relations

Mission

The primary duty of FMCS is to promote labor-management peace. This responsibility is carried out by providing mediation assistance to labor and management in preventing and settling collective bargaining disputes. FMCS services are offered without charge to both private and public sector parties.

Job Descriptions

FEDERAL MEDIATOR TRAINEE: Applies knowledge of collective bargaining and labor-management problems in influencing bargainers to adjust their differences. Conducts meetings impartially, and leads discussions to promote frank dialogue and alleviate tension. Confers with representatives of labor and management, analyzes the issues in dispute, and measures their susceptibility to compromise. Formulates concrete suggestions for alternative solutions, and suggests imaginative and practical arrangements to minimize crisis negotiations. Most Federal Mediators begin at the GS-12 level, and must have a minimum of seven years experience in collective bargaining negotiations. Well-qualified applicants who do not meet the experience requirement may be considered for a small number of Mediator Trainee positions at a lower-entry salary level.

Major Activities and Divisions

FMCS is involved in mediation services which include dispute resolution, consultation and liaison activities, arbitration services, and preventive mediation. It also provides grant funds for labor-management committees who explore labor relations topics, and offers training programs in such subjects as leadership, labor history, and the handling of complaints and grievances.

Alternative Employment Programs

FMCS hires volunteer interns for various positions. No paid student employment programs exist.

Remarks

Applicants for the Federal Mediator position must be willing to accept an assignment in any part of the U.S. The position requires the ability to travel and attend meetings on short notice, without regard to clock or calendar.

Application Procedures

Send completed applications or direct inquiries to:

Personnel Office—Recruitment Manager
Federal Mediation and Conciliation Service
2100 K Street, N.W.
Washington, DC 20427

(202) 653-5260

FEDERAL RESERVE SYSTEM (FRS)

Nature of Work: Banking
Number of Employees: 1,498
Headquarters: Washington, DC
Regional Locations: Federal Reserve Banks are located in Boston, MA; New York, NY; Philadelphia, PA; Cleveland, OH; Richmond, VA; Atlanta, GA; Chicago, IL; St. Louis, MO; Minneapolis, MN; Kansas City, KS; Dallas, TX; and San Francisco, CA. Branch banks are located in 25 other cities.
Typical Majors of New Hires: Business, computer science, economics, finance/banking, law

Mission

Formulates and oversees policies affecting consumer credit and monetary issues. It also regulates banks, maintaining a stable industry.

Job Descriptions

ATTORNEY: Counsels the Federal Reserve Board on matters relating to commercial, corporate, antitrust, administrative, and banking law.

BANK EXAMINER: Audits Federal Reserve and Branch Banks ensuring that operations comply with established standards.

COMPUTER SCIENTIST: Operates mainframe data base systems, artificial intelligence systems, applications generators, local area networks, and distributed processing equipment.

ECONOMIST: Analyzes domestic financial markets and studies the competitive implications of bank mergers.

FINANCIAL ANALYST: Monitors the health of state member banks and bank holding companies by reviewing financial data.

OPERATIONS ANALYST: Reviews the productivity of Reserve Banks by examining data processing, securities processing, auditing, electronic payments, and other operations.

Major Activities and Divisions

The Board of Governors: Determines general monetary, credit, and operating policies for the Federal Reserve System.

Legal Division: Counsels the Board of Governors on matters such as bank mergers, bank holding companies, interest payments by member banks, reserve requirements, and foreign banking operations.

Division of Consumer and Community Affairs: Enforces consumer credit laws such as the Truth in Lending, Equal Credit Opportunity, and Electronic Fund Transfer Acts.

Division of Research and Statistics: Monitors and analyzes the impact of monetary policy on domestic financial markets.

Division of Monetary Affairs: Oversees open market operations, and analyzes developments in money, credit, and Treasury markets.

Division of International Finance: Analyzes economic and financial developments in industrialized and developing countries.

Division of Banking Supervision and Regulations: Regulates the structure and conduct of the banking industry and approves bank mergers.

Division of Federal Reserve Bank Operations: Reviews the budgets of Federal Reserve Banks and oversees their financial transactions.

Alternative Employment Programs

The Federal Reserve Board offers co-op positions depending on funding.

Remarks

Bank Examiners travel virtually 100 percent of the time as audits are conducted on-site. Frequent weekend trips home are paid for by the Federal Reserve. Operations Analysts spend about 30 percent of their time traveling. The Federal Reserve System also has a separate grade and salary structure.

Application Procedures

Direct inquiries to:

Board of Governors of the Federal Reserve System
Division of Human Resources Management
MS 156
20th Street and Constitution Avenue, N.W.
Washington, DC 20551

(202) 452-3880
(202) 452-3038 (24-hour job line)
1-800-448-4894 (toll free)

FEDERAL TRADE COMMISSION (FTC)

Nature of Work: Consumer protection, law enforcement, marketing
Number of Employees: 999
Headquarters: Washington, DC
Regional Locations: Atlanta, GA; Boston, MA; Chicago, IL; Cleveland, OH; Dallas, TX; Denver, CO; Los Angeles, CA; New York, NY; San Francisco, CA; Seattle, WA
Typical Majors of New Hires: Law, economics

Mission

Prevents unfair methods of competition in commerce and administers a wide variety of consumer protection laws.

Job Descriptions

ATTORNEY: Enforces federal consumer protection statutes such as truth-in-lending and fair-credit reporting laws, as well as statutes prohibiting price fixing, and anticompetitive corporate mergers.

CONSUMER PROTECTION SPECIALIST: Investigates alleged violations of consumer protection laws and gathers evidence for use in legal proceedings. Supplies information to consumer groups and mass media to educate consumers on unfair trade practices.

ECONOMIST: Assesses the benefits and costs of potential FTC actions and studies the economic effects of regulations.

Major Activities and Divisions

Bureau of Consumer Protection: Ensures a free marketplace by suppressing unfair, deceptive and fraudulent practices. This is acccomplished through investigations, litigation, rulemaking, and consumer and business education.

Bureau of Competition: Regulates business practices that restrain competition.

Bureau of Economics: Advises on the economic merits of antitrust actions and formulates plans to improve competition.

Alternative Employment Programs

FTC maintains a co-op program for various disciplines, and also has legal and economics internships. An Economic Fellows program that seeks to establish closer ties to the economics community and industry is available as well.

Remarks

None.

Application Procedures

Direct inquiries to the Personnel Office in the regional office where you would like to work:

FTC Headquarters:

6th Street and Pennsylvania
Avenue, N.W.
Room 151
Washington, DC 20580
(202) 326-2020/2022

1718 Peachtree Street, N.W.
Room 1000
Atlanta, GA 30367
(404) 347-4836

10 Causeway Street
Room 1184
Boston, MA 02222-1073
(617) 723-6344

55 East Monroe Street
Suite 1437
Chicago, IL 60603
(312) 353-4423

688 Euclid Avenue
Suite 520-A
Cleveland, OH 44114
(216) 522-4210

100 North Central Expressway
Suite 500
Dallas, TX 75201
(214) 767-5503

1405 Curtis Street
Suite 2900
Denver, CO 80202-2393
(303) 844-2271

11000 Wilshire Boulevard
Suite 13209
Los Angeles, CA 90024
(213) 209-7890

26 Federal Plaza
New York, NY 10278
(212) 264-1207

901 Market Street
Suite 570
San Francisco, CA 94103
(415) 995-5220

2806 Federal Building
915 Second Avenue
Seattle, WA 98174
(206) 442-4656

GENERAL SERVICES ADMINISTRATION (GSA)

Nature of Work: Communications, historic preservation, inventory/supply, safety
Number of Employees: 19,966
Headquarters: Washington, DC
Regional Locations: Atlanta, GA; Chicago, IL; Ft. Worth, TX; Kansas City, KS; New York, NY; Philadelphia, PA; San Francisco, CA
Typical Majors of New Hires: Accounting, architecture, business, communications, engineering (electronic, electrical, civil, mechanical)

Mission

GSA was established in 1949 to assume central responsibility throughout the government for procurement and management of property, supplies, and general services. As its role has evolved, GSA now only provides its services when a centralized approach will bring significant advantages.

Job Descriptions

BUDGET ANALYST: Implements modern, effective, primary accounting systems through the use of off-the-shelf software and cross-servicing arrangements with client agencies. Counsels clients on how to achieve administrative savings.

COMMUNICATIONS MANAGEMENT SPECIALIST: Works to set in place and maintain a modern, cost-effective telecommunications system in the federal community. Works in cooperation with other agencies to reduce the time required to procure automated data processing equipment for federal agencies.

COMMUNICATIONS SPECIALIST: Provides help to other federal agencies in developing, promoting, and distributing information to the public. Cooperates with private sector sponsors to provide the resources and funding needed to bring new consumer information to the public.

COMPUTER SPECIALIST: Provides technical expertise in the computer field. Advocates the modernization of the government's automated data processing operations to achieve the levels of efficiency present in the private sector. Works with client agencies to apply information technology which will improve operating effectiveness.

MANAGEMENT ANALYST: Provides information, assistance, and counseling to business organizations on contracting opportunities with GSA and other federal agencies.

REALTY SPECIALIST: Acquires real estate interests across the country. Disposes of real estate at a fair value for the greatest benefit to the government and the public, and transfers real estate to other federal agencies for continued federal use. Plans and manages real estate to attain its most efficient use. Requires a knowledge of real estate principles, practices, markets, and values.

Major Activities and Divisions

The Public Buildings Service (PBS): Emphasizes improving quality in the workplace and the more efficient use of space. Restores historic structures, and provides art for buildings through its Art-in-Architecture Program.

The Federal Supply Service (FSS): Contracts with private companies to supply the products and services used by the federal government around the world.

The Information Resources Management Service (IRMS): Advises agencies on software development and procurement.

Federal Property Resources Service (FPRS): Releases real estate assets no longer needed by the government.

Alternative Employment Programs

GSA participates in the co-op program, the Federal Summer Intern Program, the Junior Fellowship program, and the PMI program. PMIs are hired through the Central Office; others are hired directly by the regional office. Call (202) 501-2401 (Special Programs) for more information.

Remarks

None.

Application Procedures

Direct inquiries to:

U.S. General Services Administration
Personnel Division (WCP)
7th and D Streets, S.W.
Washington, DC 20405

(202) 708-5300/5361

U.S. General Services Administration
18th and F Streets
Washington, DC 20405
(202) 501-0370

(Central Office)

INTERNATIONAL TRADE COMMISSION (ITC)

Nature of Work: International affairs, import/export, trade
Number of Employees: 493
Headquarters: Washington, DC
Regional Locations: None
Typical Majors of New Hires: Agriculture, business, chemistry, economics, engineering, forestry, law, marketing

Mission

Studies all matters relating to U.S. foreign trade, including anticompetitive practices and their effects on domestic production, employment, consumption, and the global competitiveness of U.S. products.

Job Descriptions

ATTORNEY: Investigates anticompetitive trading practices by foreign countries and executes cease and desist orders, tariff increases, and other ITC sanctions.

INTERNATIONAL ECONOMIST: Studies the effects of unfair trading practices on U.S. firms, assesses the international competitiveness of U.S. industries, and examines how particular trade developments affect domestic industries.

INTERNATIONAL TRADE ANALYST: Collects and analyzes data on the manufacture, distribution cost, and import and export of specific products. Data is obtained through contacts with trade associations, visits to factories, seminars, and conferences.

STATISTICIAN: Tracks U.S. imports and exports, collects and interprets data on specific U.S. industries, and designs procedures for gathering uniform statistical data.

Major Activities and Divisions

Import Relief for Domestic Industries: Determines whether an item is being imported into the U.S. in sufficient quantities to harm domestic industries.

Unfair Practices in Import Trade: Investigates allegations of unfair competition, and when such practices are found, issues orders cease and desist or exclusion orders.

Imports Sold at Less than Fair Value: Assists the Commerce Department in determining whether domestic industries are being injured through imports of subsidized merchandise.

Alternative Employment Programs

ITC maintains a limited number of co-op and summer jobs.

Remarks

Each year, ITC furnishes dozens of studies on the competitive posture of specific U.S. industries to the President and Congressional Committees.

Application Procedures

Employment applications are generallly accepted only during open periods of vacancy announcements. Direct inquiries to:

Office of Personnel
U.S. International Trade Commission
Room 314
500 E Street, S.W.
Washington, DC 20436

(202) 252-1651

INTERSTATE COMMERCE COMMISSION

Nature of Work: Railroads, transportation
Number of Employees: 704
Headquarters: Washington, DC
Regional Locations: Chicago, IL; Philadelphia, PA; San Francisco, CA
Typical Majors of New Hires: Business, economics, mathematics, social sciences, transportation

Mission

The Interstate Commerce Commission regulates surface transportation including trains, trucks, buses, water carriers, freight forwarders, transportation brokers, and a coal slurry pipeline. The Commission assures that the carriers it regulates will provide the public with rates and services that are fair and reasonable.

Job Descriptions

TRANSPORTATION INDUSTRY ANALYST: Analyzes and evaluates the operations and economics of the transportation industry. Works to protect the public interest and ensure equity in industry practices. Applies knowledge of the transportation industry regulatory controls, and the customs and competitive practices of carriers.

Major Activities and Divisions

Transportation Economics Programs: Settles controversies over rates and charges among competing transportation modes.

Transportation Service Programs: Grants transportation companies and brokers the right to operate.

Consumer Protection Programs: The Commission ensures that rates will be fair and service will be reasonable.

Alternative Employment Programs

ICC has no co-op or internship programs, and does not engage in recruitment activities.

Remarks

None.

Application Procedures

Send an SF-171 or direct inquiries to:

Director of Personnel
Interstate Commerce Commission
Washington, DC 20423

(202) 275-7288

MERIT SYSTEMS PROTECTION BOARD (MSPB)

Nature of Work: Labor-management relations
Number of Employees: 308
Headquarters: Washington, DC
Regional Locations: Atlanta, GA; Boston, MA; Chicago, IL; Dallas, TX; Denver, CO; New York, NY; Philadelphia, PA; St. Louis, MO; San Francisco, CA
Typical Majors of New Hires: Law, public administration

Mission

Ensures that federal employees are protected from abuses by agency management and that employment decisions are based on merit. Also conducts special studies on federal employees and federal employment.

Job Descriptions

ATTORNEY: Litigates cases involving prohibited personnel practices, prohibited political activities, and other merit system violations.

RESEARCH ANALYST: Conducts studies of the federal civil service to determine whether it is free of prohibited personnel practices. Also produces research reports on such topics as recruitment and retention practices, labor relations, and the Senior Executive Service.

Major Activities and Divisions

MSPB hears and adjudicates appeals by federal employees concerning adverse personnel actions such as removals, suspensions, and demotions. It also resolves cases concerning pay increase denials, and charges of merit system violations.

Alternative Employment Programs

Co-op positions are sometimes available depending on funding.

Remarks

None.

Application Procedures

Direct inquiries to:

Personnel Division
Merit Systems Protection Board
Room 850
1120 Vermont Avenue, N.W.
Washington, DC 20419

(202) 653-5916

THE NATIONAL AERONAUTICS AND SPACE ADMINISTRATION (NASA)

Nature of Work: Aviation/space programs, defense and national security, energy, scientific research, transportation

Number of Employees: 22,000

Headquarters: Washington, DC

Regional Locations: Cleveland, OH; Edwards, CA; Greenbelt, MD; Hampton, VA; Houston, TX; Huntsville, AL; Kennedy Space Center, FL; Moffett Field, CA; Stennis Space Center, MS

Typical Majors of New Hires: Computer science, engineering, mathematics, physics, physical sciences, space sciences

Mission

NASA was created in 1958 to pursue the peaceful exploration of the solar system. Until this time, space research was conducted by the military, which focused its work on ballistic missiles. NASA's focus is to research the civilian applications of space, such as communication and weather satellites, manned transportation, and astrophysics, but it is also involved in strategic defense systems.

Job Descriptions

ENGINEER (AEROSPACE, ELECTRICAL, MECHANICAL), COMPUTER SCIENTIST, MATHEMATICIAN, SCIENTIST: All entry-level engineers, scientists, and mathematicians engage in the research, development, design, testing, and evaluation of various projects relating to their area of expertise. Entry-level employees can specialize in one of the following areas:

APPLICATIONS SCIENCES: Involves the design and applications of remote sensing systems.

DATA SYSTEMS: Involves the recording and mathematical computation of aerospace data, and the numeric simulation of aerospace problems.

FACILITIES AND OPERATIONS: Involves all phases of the aerospace research and development facilities and equipment including design, operation, and management.

FLIGHT SYSTEMS: Works with aerospace flight systems.

FLUID AND FLIGHT MECHANICS: Involves aerospace vehicle flight dynamics, including environmental interaction research.

LIFE SCIENCES AND SYSTEMS: Examines the biological impact of the space environment, and studies the nature and origin of life.

MATERIALS AND STRUCTURES: Works with aerospace flight vehicle structures and the evaluation of their behavior.

MEASUREMENT AND INSTRUMENTATION SYSTEMS: Works with tracking systems, telemetry, and radio, optical, and mechanical systems to measure aerospace physical phenomena.

PROPULSION SYSTEMS: Works with aerospace propulsion systems for the conversion of energy into power for transportation.

SPACE SCIENCE: Studies the atmospheres of earth and space, celestial mechanics, and astrophysics.

TECHNICAL MANAGEMENT: Involves a management perspective in the aerospace research and development programs.

Major Activities and Divisions

Aeronautics and Space Technology: Develops technological advances in the areas of aeronautics and space for scientific, commercial, and military use.

Space Science and Applications: Conducts research on the origin and evolution of the universe and applies space systems and techniques to solve everyday problems on earth.

Space Flight: Works to improve the efficiency of all phases of the space shuttle system, and to define the shuttle's role in such things as launching and rescuing communications satellites.

Space Tracking and Data Systems: Provides tracking, command, telemetry, and data acquisition support for earth-orbital science and other scientific missions.

Alternative Employment Programs

NASA has a special PIP (Professional Intern Program) program and a nationwide co-op program for students pursuing a bachelor's or master's degree in science, engineering, mathematics, or computer science.

Remarks

NASA has a very active campus recruitment program. Contact your college placement office for details. All centers offer tuition reimbursement programs and many are located on campus-like settings with special amenities on premises.

Application Procedures

Address inquiries directly to the NASA Center in which you are interested. If you are a college student or recent college graduate, add Attn: College Recruitment Program Manager below the Personnel Office line.

Ames Research Center
Personnel Office
Moffett Field, CA 94035
(415) 604-5000

Aeronautical research laboratory. Focuses on aerodynamics, computational fluid dynamics, powered-lift and rotorcraft technology, flight simulation, human factors, and airborne science.

Dryden Flight Research Facility
Ames Research Center NASA
Personnel Office
PO Box 273
Edwards, CA 93525
(805) 258-3311

Connected with the Ames Research Center, although the two facilities conduct their own hiring.

Goddard Space Flight Center
Personnel Office
Greenbelt, MD 20771
(301) 286-2000

Conducts remotely controlled, earth-orbiting and sounding rocket missions. Also works on the development and monitoring of a worldwide tracking and communications network. Acquires data relating to weather and climate research, earth resources, astronomy, and communications. Will also play an active role in the space station program. The Wallops Flight Facility in Wallops Island, VA, is a directorate of the Goddard Space Flight Center.

Jet Propulsion Laboratory
NASA Personnel Office
4800 Oak Grove Dr.
Pasadena, CA 91109
(818) 354-4321

Conducts research into space science issues, especially deep space missions.

John F. Kennedy Space Center
Personnel Office
Kennedy Space Center, FL 32899
(407) 867-7110

The major launch facility for the Space Shuttle and unmanned space missions. Plans and directs preflight preparation of space vehicles and their cargoes.

Langley Research Center
Personnel Office
Hampton, VA 23665
(804) 864-1000

An extensive aeronautical research facility with over 50 wind tunnels. Known for its airfoil research, the creation of spin avoidance and auto control techniques in high-performance military fighters, and the development of integrated software systems for aerospace engineering and design.

Lewis Research Center
Personnel Office
21000 Brookpark Road
Cleveland, OH 44135
(216) 433-4000

Directs the U.S. aerospace propulsion and power programs. Devoted to the development of more efficient engine systems and is engaged in energy conservation research for communications satellites. Houses a supersonic propulsion wind tunnel.

Lyndon B. Johnson Space Center
Personnel Office
Houston, TX 77085
(713) 483-0123

Marshall Space Flight Center
Personnel Office
Huntsville, AL 35812
(205) 544-2121

The primary center for the design and development of the space transportation system, such as the Lunar Roving Vehicle and Skylab. Also principal center for rocket propulsion systems.

Stennis Space Center
Personnel Office
Stennis Space Center, MS 39529
(601) 688-2211

Supports the testing of the Space Shuttle's main engine and main orbiter propulsion systems.

Headquarters Address:

National Aeronautics and Space Administration
Code: NPM
Washington, DC 20546

(202) 453-2607
(202) 755-6299 (vacancies)

NATIONAL ARCHIVES AND RECORDS ADMINISTRATION (NARA)

Nature of Work: Historic preservation, libraries, scholarly research
Number of Employees: 3,000
Headquarters: Washington, DC
Regional Locations: Anchorage, AK; Bayonne, NJ; Boston, MA; Chicago, IL; Dayton, OH (RC only); Denver, CO; East Point, GA; Ft. Worth, TX; Kansas City, MO; Los Angeles, CA; Philadelphia, PA; St. Louis, MO (2) (RC only); San Francisco, CA; Seattle, WA; Suitland, MD
Typical Majors of New Hires: Business, English (journalism), history

Mission

The National Archives and Records Administration is responsible for establishing procedures for managing the records of the U.S. government. The National Archives assists federal agencies in documenting their activities, administering their records management programs, and retiring their noncurrent records to Federal Records Centers. The agency also accessions, arranges, preserves, and makes available to the public the historically valuable records of the government, and manages the Presidential Libraries system.

Job Descriptions

ARCHIVIST: Appraises and arranges public records and historic documents. Provides reference service from record and manuscript depositories. Prepares inventories and guides to facilitate use of records. Conducts scholarly research using archival principles and techniques. Requires a comprehensive knowledge of the history of the U.S. and the institutions and organizations of the federal government. The majority of archivists work in the Office of National Archives, or in the archives' field branches.

WRITER-EDITOR: Applies subject-matter knowledge and writing and editing skills to review written material and/or present pertinent facts in written form. Analyzes data for subject-matter content and determines the type of presentation best suited to the audience being addressed. The majority of Writer-Editors work in the Office of Federal Register; some also work in the Office of Public Programs.

Major Activities and Divisions

Office of National Archives: Located in Washington, DC. Maintains the historically valuable records of the U.S. government.

Office of Federal Register: Prepares and publishes a variety of public documents, including the *Federal Register, United States Statutes at Large,* the *Code of Federal Regulations,* and the *United States Government Manual.*

Office of Records Administration: Manages and categorizes records such as electronic records, military records, etc.

National Historical Publications and Records Commission (NHPRC): Cooperates with nonfederal agencies in gathering and publishing papers important to the study of American history.

Office of Public Programs: Conducts educational programs to introduce NARA to school groups and instructors.

Office of Federal Records Centers: Provides reference services and furnishes information from records.

Office of Presidential Libraries: Preserves and makes available for use the Presidential records and personal papers that document the actions of a particular President's administration.

External Affairs: The External Affairs staff maintains contact with congressional offices.

Alternative Employment Programs

NARA maintains a co-op program for college students with appropriate majors. Contact (314) 263-6953 for information on the program.

Remarks

Archivists begin their employment in a formal training program. The annual hires proceed together as a class, being assigned to various offices on a rotational basis to give a broader view of NARA as a whole. After sucessfully completing two years, they are eligible for the journeyman level (GS-11).

NARA offers several educational opportunities on archival and records management:

The Modern Archives Institute is a 2-week course for archivists that introduces students to the techniques of archival work. It is offered twice a year, in February and June, for a fee. Inquiries should be made to the Office of Public Programs (202) 501-5200.

"Going to the Source" is an annual 4-day course which introduces researchers to research methodology at the National Archives. For further information, contact the Education Branch at (202) 501-5600.

The NHPRC Institute for the Editing of Historical Documents is held for 2 weeks each summer at the University of Wisconsin, Madison. Admission is competitive and applicants should hold a master's degree in American history or American studies. Tuition is $250. For further information, contact NHPRC at (202) 523-5384.

"The Federal Register: What It Is and How To Use It" is a course open to the public which provides instruction on how to research federal regulations. The program is conducted in Washington and in major regional cities. For further information, call (202) 501-5600.

Fellowships: The NHPRC offers three fellowships annually in advanced documentary editing and three fellowships in mid-level archival administration. The fellows receive stipends and fringe benefits for a 9- to 10-month period. For more information, contact NHPRC at (202) 501-5600.

Application Procedures

All external hiring is coordinated through the personnel office in St. Louis. Some campus recruiting occurs for academic scholars.

Direct inquiries to:

National Archives and Records Administration
Personnel Operations Branch
9700 Page Boulevard, Room 2002
St. Louis, MO 63132

1-800-634-4898

Washington address:

National Archives and Records Administration
Personnel Services Division, NAP
7th Street and Pennsylvania Avenue, N.W.
Washington, DC 20408

(202) 501-6102

NATIONAL CREDIT UNION ADMINISTRATION (NCUA)

Nature of Work: Accounting/auditing, insurance/benefits
Number of Employees: 885
Headquarters: Washington, DC
Regional Locations: Albany, NY; Atlanta, GA; Austin, TX; Chicago, IL; San Francisco, CA; Washington, DC
Typical Majors of New Hires: Accounting

Mission

The National Credit Union Administration is responsible for chartering, insuring, supervising, and examining federal credit unions.

Job Descriptions

FINANCIAL INSTITUTION EXAMINER: Maintains contact with the twenty to thirty credit unions in his/her assigned district, which may be approximately 200 square miles. Conducts on-site audits which, depending on the size of the credit union, may take from one day to three weeks. Determines solvency and compliance with regulations, and assists credit unions in management and operations. Occasionally works in a team setting with other examiners at the audit site, but usually works independently. Advises groups interested in chartering federal credit unions. On days when no on-site work is scheduled, the examiner works out of his/her home. Makes own audit and travel schedule. Requires self-motivation and independence.

Major Activities and Divisions

Chartering: The NCUA grants charters to groups sharing a common bond of occupation or association.

Share Insurance: The NCUA provides for a program of share insurance, allowing credit union members' accounts to be insured up to $100,000.

Alternative Employment Programs

NCUA has a small co-op program and offers summer clerical positions.

Remarks

Financial Institution Examiners enter into an accelerated training program upon employment at NCUA. New employees spend four days in Washington, then travel to the different locales as part of the learning process. Time is also spent in one of several credit union training sites, and with a seasoned examiner in several audit settings. After 6 months, the Financial Institution Examiner is given a promotion to the next higher grade level, and handles a district independently.

The Financial Institution Examiner position is currently an open vacancy announcement, indicating that applications for the position are accepted on a continuous basis.

College campus recruiting is conducted nationwide.

Application Procedures

All hiring is coordinated through the headquarters office in Washington, DC. Direct inquiries to:

National Credit Union Administration
Personnel Office (RB)
1776 G Street, N.W., Room 7201
Washington, DC 20456

(202) 682-9720

THE NATIONAL LABOR RELATIONS BOARD (NLRB)

Nature of Work: Business, labor/management relations, law/justice
Number of Employees: 2,400
Headquarters: Washington, DC
Regional Locations: Albany, NY; Albuquerque, NM; Anchorage, AK; Atlanta, GA; Baltimore, MD; Birmingham, AL; Boston, MA; Brooklyn, NY; Buffalo, NY; Chicago, IL; Cincinnati, OH; Cleveland, OH; Coral Gables, FL; Denver, CO; Detroit, MI; El Paso, TX; Ft. Worth, TX; Hato Rey, PR; Honolulu, HI; Houston, TX; Indianapolis, IN; Jacksonville, FL; Kansas City, MO; Las Vegas, NV; Little Rock, AK; Los Angeles, CA (2); Memphis, TN; Milwaukee, WI; Minneapolis, MN; Nashville, TN; Newark, NJ; New Orleans, LA; New York, NY; Oakland, CA; Peoria, IL; Philadelphia, PA; Phoenix, AR; Pittsburgh, PA; Portland, OR; St. Louis, MO; San Antonio, TX; San Diego, CA; San Francisco, CA; Seattle, WA; Tampa, FL; Tulsa, OK; Washington, DC; Winston-Salem, NC
Typical Majors of New Hires: Accounting, business, economics, industrial relations, law, political science

Mission

The NLRB administers the law that governs relations between labor unions and the employers whose operations affect interstate commerce. The NLRB determines, through secret ballot elections, the democratic choice by employees as to whether or not they wish to be represented by a union. The agency also acts to prevent unfair labor practices by either employers or unions.

Job Descriptions

ATTORNEY (BOARD MEMBER OFFICES, WASHINGTON): Reads and becomes familiar with the record and formal documents of the case assigned. Ascertains and discusses the issues, and researches the law. Prepares legal memoranda for the Board's consideration, and after the case has been decided, prepares a draft of the final decision. Functions in much the same way as a law clerk does for a judge. Occasional travel.

ATTORNEY (OFFICE OF THE GENERAL COUNSEL, WASHINGTON): Analyzes, researches, and discusses issues pertaining to assigned cases. Drafts memoranda, briefs, and other documents. May be assigned to the Division of Advice, the Office of Appeals, the Division of Enforcement Litigation, or the Legal Research and Policy Planning Branch. Occasional travel.

FIELD ATTORNEY (REGIONAL OFFICES): Begins by investigating cases, and progresses into other functions. Drafts complaints, prepares cases for trial, and tries cases before Administrative Law Judges. In appropriate cases, field attorneys may seek injunctive relief in the federal district courts. Other duties may include serving as Hearing Officer in a contested representation election case, preparing drafts of decisions for the Regional Director, assisting in conducting representation elections, and advising members of the public. Frequent travel within the region.

FIELD EXAMINER: Conducts investigations into assigned cases. Gathers facts by meeting with employees and their foremen, shop stewards, business agents, personnel officers, and attorneys representing both labor and management. Recommends appropriate action on each case, including possible remedies, or dismissal of the case. Arranges and conducts elections among groups of employees ranging in size from two to several thousand to determine whether or not they wish to be represented by a labor organization. Serves as Hearing Officer in disputed representation cases.

Major Activities and Divisions

The NLRB is organized into two major parts: the five-member Board itself, which has its own staff, and the Office of the General Counsel. Agency authority is divided by law. The Board acts primarily as a quasi-judicial body in deciding cases upon formal records. The General Counsel is responsible for the investigation and processing of cases including their prosecution in the courts. The General Counsel also has general supervision over the agency's field offices.

Alternative Employment Programs

NLRB participates in the federal co-op program and hires students for summer positions as the budget permits. Call (202) 254-9044 for more information.

Remarks

The NLRB has over 750 attorneys. About one-third of them are assigned to the Washington office. 1,600 of the 2,400 total employees of the NLRB are located in the Regional, Subregional, and Resident Offices listed above. Location preferences of prospective applicants are taken into account, and new hires may be given a choice of several office locations in which to begin employment.

Application Procedures

Direct inquiries to:

Personnel Branch
National Labor Relations Board
1717 Pennsylvania Avenue, N.W.
Washington, DC 20570-0001

(202) 254-9106

Completed application forms and transcripts should be submitted to the NLRB Office of interest to you. Please consult the telephone directory in that city for complete address.

NATIONAL SCIENCE FOUNDATION (NSF)

Nature of Work: Education, funds/funding, scientific research
Number of Employees: 1,200
Headquarters: Washington, DC
Regional Locations: None
Typical Majors of New Hires: Accounting, business, computer science, economics, engineering, liberal arts, mathematics, physical sciences, social sciences

Mission

The Foundation is committed to expanding the nation's supply of scientists, engineers, and science educators. It does this by supporting a variety of programs and activities for education in science, mathematics, and engineering. NSF awards grants and contracts to academic research institutions, private research firms, industrial labs, and major research facilities. Experienced researchers and educators from around the country volunteer their time to help Foundation staff assess the merits of some 30,000 proposals a year.

Job Descriptions

SCIENCE ASSISTANT: Provides scientific assistance in all phases of the proposal review process. Participates in volunteer reviewer selection by reading professional journals in the scientific field and doing library research to expand the volunteer reviewer base. Identifies reviewer conflicts-of-interests and makes recommendations regarding the proposal review process. This position can be established for graduate-level students in any science area. NSF divisions typically cover engineering, biological and environmental sciences, social sciences and economics, behavioral and neural sciences, computer science, geosciences, mathematics, physical sciences, and science/engineering education.

GRANTS AND CONTRACTS SPECIALIST: Examines grants and contracts to be awarded to scientific and educational institutions for accuracy, clarity, and compliance with NSF policy and federal regulations.

PUBLIC AFFAIRS SPECIALIST: Communicates the mission and accomplishments of NSF to the public. The format of this communication can be written or visual—portable exhibits, brochures, films, or videos.

Major Activities and Divisions

The National Science Foundation is run by a presidentially appointed Director and Board of 24 scientists and engineers, top university officials, and industry officials. Outside advisory groups from various disciplines also play a key role.

Alternative Employment Programs

NSF is beginning a new co-op program in 1991. Students will work part-time while attending school, and will be eligible for full-time employment upon graduation. Typical co-op positions: Accountant, Grants and Contracts Specialist. Contact the Co-op Director at (202) 357-9682 for more information.

NSF also hires students at the graduate levels for internship positions as Science Assistants. Contact the internship Director at (202) 357-7198 for more information.

Other student programs: NSF participates in the PMI program (typical positions: Science Assistant, Public Affairs Specialist), the Stay-in-School program for clerical positions, and an extensive summer program in which college students are hired for office clerical positions.

Remarks

NSF does not conduct research itself and thus has no in-house laboratories or similar facilities.

Application Procedures

Direct inquiries to:

National Science Foundation
Office of Personnel
1800 G Street, N.W.
Washington, DC 20550

(202) 357-7602
(202) 357-7735 (vacancies)

TDD Number: (202) 357-7492
(Telephone Device for the Deaf)

NATIONAL TRANSPORTATION SAFETY BOARD (NTSB)

Nature of Work: Aviation/space programs, maritime activities, railroads, safety, transportation
Number of Employees: 306
Headquarters: Washington, DC
Regional Locations: Anchorage, AK; Atlanta, GA; Chicago, IL; Denver, CO; Fort Worth, TX; Los Angeles, CA; Miami, FL; Kansas City, MO
Typical Majors of New Hires: Engineering, physics, physical sciences

Mission

Investigates the causes of accidents involving aircraft, railroads, highways, ships, and pipelines.

Job Descriptions

METALLURGIST: Conducts postaccident analyses of wreckage ranging from aircraft parts to railroad tracks to determine whether failures resulted from inadequate design strength, excessive loading, or corrosion.

SAFETY INVESTIGATOR: Performs on-site accident analyses. Assignments vary by expertise and can include specialists in air traffic control, aircraft operations, aircraft maintenance, locomotives and signals, and human factors.

Major Activities and Divisions

Aviation: Investigates accidents involving all air carriers, and general aviation accidents with fatalities. Recommends safety improvements to the Federal Aviation Administration in such areas as pilot training, aircraft maintenance and design, air traffic control procedures, and post-accident survival.

Railroad: Investigates all fatal rail accidents, or any incident where damage exceeds $150,000. Recommends safety improvements to such agencies as the Federal Railroad Administration, the Urban Mass Transportation Administration, Amtrak, state regulatory agencies, rapid transit agencies, trade associations, and common carriers.

Marine: Investigates all major accidents occurring on U.S. navigable waters, as well as major marine accidents in international waters involving U.S. merchant ships, and public and nonpublic vessels. Makes safety recommendations to agencies such as the Coast Guard, U.S. Army Corps of Engineers, shipping firms, and maritime trade organizations.

Highway: Investigates highway accidents with broad safety implications. These include bridge collapses, fatal accidents involving public transportation vehicles, and fatal collisions at grade crossings. Safety recommendations are directed to the U.S. Department of Transportation, state and local agencies, trade associations, and manufacturers.

Hazardous Materials: Investigates selected accidents resulting in the release of hazardous materials. NTSB concentrates on the affects of any materials released upon the public or emergency response teams; the handling of the emergency by local authorities; and the adequacy of federal standards for the transport of hazardous materials.

Pipeline: Investigates all pipeline accidents involving a fatality or where there is substantial property damage. Investigations include accidents on pipelines transporting natural gas, volatile liquids, and other petroleum products.

Alternative Employment Programs

None.

Remarks

NTSB consists of five board members appointed by the President with the advice and consent of the Senate. Each member serves a 5-year term.

Application Procedures

Direct inquiries to:

Personnel and Training Division
National Transportation Safety Board
Washington, DC 20594

(202) 382-6717

NUCLEAR REGULATORY COMMISSION (NRC)

Nature of Work: Environmental protection, nuclear energy/issues, hazardous materials
Number of Employees: 3,287
Headquarters: Rockville, MD
Regional Locations: Arlington, TX; Atlanta, GA; Glen Ellyn, IL; King of Prussia, PA; Walnut Creek, CA
Typical Majors of New Hires: Chemistry, engineering (electrical, environmental, materials, mechanical, nuclear), physics (geophysics, health physics), physical sciences (hydrology)

Mission

The NRC protects the public health and the environment in the civilian uses of nuclear materials in the United States. This is accomplished through the licensing of nuclear facilities and the possession, use, and disposal of nuclear materials; the development and implementation of requirements governing licensed activities; and inspection and enforcement activities to assure compliance with these requirements.

Job Descriptions

EFFLUENTS RADIATION SPECIALIST: Assesses the effectiveness of the various programs of power and fuel reactors and research facilities which deal with the management and control of radioactive waste. Is assigned program review responsibility for a number of facilities and visits each facility several times a year. Interacts with state officials who have overview responsibilities with regard to the radiological programs of NRC facilities.

EMERGENCY PREPAREDNESS SPECIALIST: Assesses the quality and effectiveness of the Emergency Response programs of the facilities that use nuclear materials. Inspects the overall Emergency Response program and evaluates performance in drills. Verifies the operational readiness of the on-site facilities and personnel designated for emergency response.

HEALTH PHYSICIST: Develops policy, procedures, and criteria for regulating the use of radioactive materials. Evaluates environmental impact of facilities, sites, and activities involving uranium, thorium, and special nuclear materials. Performs radiological and environmental assessments using computer codes and technology. Locations: Headquarters only.

MATERIAL HEALTH PHYSICIST: Performs radiological and environmental protection inspections and investigations at various types of licensees facilities which possess, use, and process by-product, source, and special nuclear materials. Verifies public health and safety and determines the status of compliance with NRC license conditions and federal regulations. Regulates activities involving nuclear medicine, isotope manufacturing, industrial uses of radioactive materials, research, and academic applications.

RADIATION SPECIALIST: Conducts specialized radiological inspections, including emergency preparedness, at all types of facilities licensed by the NRC. Inspections are conducted to assure protection of plant and facility workers and the public against any possibility of hazardous exposure to nuclear radiation.

REACTOR ENGINEER: Develops regulations and provides guidance to ensure that licensed operators have the skills necessary to operate nuclear power plants safely. Formulates examiner training programs and reviews and evaluates the operator licensing examination area.

REACTOR INSPECTOR: Serves as a member of the technical staff in the regional offices with responsibility for the inspection of reactors and related investigations. Plans and conducts inspections in both construction and operation, including licensee quality assurance programs. Represents the NRC to the licensee and to state and local officials.

REGIONAL HEALTH PHYSICIST: Conducts on-site inspections of facilities which are regulated and licensed by the NRC to possess and use radioactive materials. Documents inspections and findings, responds to emergencies, reviews license applications for the use of radioactive materials, and provides assessments of licensees' program effectiveness for NRC management.

REGIONAL RADIATION SPECIALIST: Assesses the effectiveness of radiation protection programs of power and research reactors and fuel facilities by conducting on-site evaluation of the radiation safety program. Discusses radiation protection programs with all levels of the plant staff, evaluates the adequacy of procedures and policies, and directly observes personnel performance. Visits several power reactors two to four times a year. Develops periodic summary evaluation reports for the NRC management to use in characterizing the effectiveness of the licensee's program.

RESIDENT INSPECTOR: Serves on-site at nuclear power plants. Plans and conducts inspections at assigned plants during construction, pre-operational testing, startup, and operation to assure that plants are built and operated in accordance with NRC requirements.

Major Activities and Divisions

The Office of Nuclear Reactor Regulation: Evaluates all license applications, issues licenses, and regulates nuclear facilities.

The Office of Nuclear Materials Safety and Safeguards: Ensures public health and safety and protects the national security and environmental values in the licensing and regulation of nuclear materials.

The Office of Nuclear Regulatory Research: Conducts research relating to reactor safety and environmental protection.

Alternative Employment Programs

The NRC maintains both a co-op program and a summer internship program for undergraduate students, primarily for individuals pursuing degrees in engineering and applicable scientific disciplines. Students for both the cooperative and summer programs should have completed at least their sophomore year, be above average academically, and have geographic flexibility. Direct inquiries to the College Recruitment Coordinator.

Remarks

As part of the technical staffing program, the NRC conducts a college recruitment program designed to attract new or recent college graduates at the B.S. and M.S. levels to fill entry-level professional positions. Recruitment is done by the Headquarters Office and by Regional Offices.

Application Procedures

If you are interested in working in the Headquarters Office or in Region V (Alaska, Arizona, California, Hawaii, Nevada, Oregon, and Washington), direct inquiries to:

The U.S. Nuclear Regulatory Commission
Office of Personnel
Mail Stop W-468
Washington, DC 20555

(301) 492-8234 or (301) 492-4601
for a list of vacancies

JOB HOTLINE: (301) 492-9090

If you are interested in working in one of the other four regions, send inquiries or applications directly to that office:

Region I
U.S. NRC
475 Allendale Road
King of Prussia, PA 19406
(215) 337-5000

Region II
U.S. NRC
101 Marietta Street
Suite 2900
Atlanta, GA 30323
(404) 331-4503

Region III
U.S. NRC
799 Roosevelt Road
Glen Ellyn, IL 60137
(312) 790-5500

Region IV
U.S. NRC
611 Ryan Plaza Drive, Suite 1000
Arlington, TX 76011
(817) 860-8100

OFFICE OF PERSONNEL MANAGEMENT (OPM)

Nature of Work: Education, employment, labor/management relations
Number of Employees: 6,632
Headquarters: Washington, DC
Regional Locations: Atlanta, GA; Chicago, IL; Dallas, TX; Philadelphia, PA; San Francisco, CA
Typical Majors of New Hires: Business, education, industrial relations, psychology, social sciences

Mission

OPM's role is to ensure that the federal government provides an array of personnel services to applicants and employees. Through a range of programs designed to develop and encourage the effectiveness of the government employee, OPM supports government program managers in their personnel management responsibilities and provides benefits to retired employees.

Job Descriptions

EMPLOYEE DEVELOPMENT SPECIALIST: Plans and administers programs designed to train and develop employees. Provides guidance to management concerning employee training and its relationship to management problems. Applies a knowledge of the techniques of education and training.

INSURANCE BENEFITS CLAIMS EXAMINER: Determines the validity of insurance benefit claims and the correctness of the amount. Reviews all evidence previously developed, and evaluates evidence for accuracy and validity.

PAY/LEAVE SPECIALIST: Assists federal agencies by providing policy guidance and program implementation on pay- and leave-benefit administration.

PERSONNEL INVESTIGATOR: Determines the suitability of applicants under consideration for appointment in the federal government by checking on applicants for positions requiring national security or professional requirements.

PERSONNEL MANAGEMENT SPECIALIST: Directs or assists in directing a personnel management program. Provides technical assistance for work which involves specialized personnel functions.

PERSONNEL STAFFING SPECIALIST: Performs work in recruitment, examination, selection, or placement of employees to staff government organizations.

Major Activities and Divisions

Recruiting and Examining: OPM is responsible for the nationwide recruiting and examining of applicants for positions in the federal competitive service at grades 1 through 15.

Personnel Investigations: OPM conducts investigations of applicants to support the selection and appointment process.

Affirmative Recruiting and Employment: OPM coordinates governmentwide efforts to employ and advance minorities.

Employee Development and Training: OPM sets standards for governmentwide programs for the development and training of federal employees. Through a nationwide network of d interagency training centers, a European center, Executive Seminar Centers, and the Federal Executive Institute, it offers a wide range of courses.

Performance Awards: OPM provides assistance to federal agencies in the administration of the governmentwide Incentive Awards program.

Alternative Employment Programs

OPM offers volunteer internships in numerous career fields, providing work assignments relevant to studies and career goals. The program is offered year-round, and is generally six to eight weeks full- or part-time. Eligible applicants must be full- or part-time students currently enrolled in a college or university. Contact the program coordinator at (202) 632-7484 or TDD (202) 632-9345; or write to OPM, division of Recruitment and Special Employment Programs, Attn: Student Volunteer Program.

Remarks

None.

Application Procedures

Direct inquiries to:

Office of Personnel Management
Office of Personnel and EEO
1900 E Street, N.W., Room 1447
Washington, DC 20415 (202) 606-1014/2424

OFFICE OF THE UNITED STATES TRADE REPRESENTATIVE

Nature of Work: Commerce, international affairs
Number of Employees: 164
Headquarters: Washington, DC
Regional Locations: None
Typical Majors of New Hires: Law, economics

Mission

Directs all trade negotiations for the U.S. and formulates U.S. international trade policy.

Job Descriptions

ATTORNEY: Advises trade negotiators on the legality of agreements and renders legal opinions on specific policy, trade, and commodity matters.

INTERNATIONAL ECONOMIST: Conducts trade negotiations with other countries and international organizations, and gathers and interprets international trade data used in setting policy.

Major Activities and Divisions

The U.S. Trade Representative represents the U.S. at meetings of General Agreement on Tariffs and Trade and the Organization for Economic Cooperation and Development. It also negotiates through the United Nations Conference on Trade and Development, and acts to eliminate investment barriers.

Alternative Employment Programs

Co-op positions may be available depending on funding. Contact the personnel office for more information.

Remarks

The Office of the United States Trade Representative is a cabinet-level agency. The head of the organization, his or her three deputies, and two other senior officials all hold the rank of Ambassador.

Application Procedures

Direct inquiries to:

Office of the United States Trade Representative
Office of Personnel
600 17th Street, N.W.
Washington, DC 20506

(202) 395-7360

PEACE CORPS

Nature of Work: Agriculture, developing countries/foreign assistance, education, volunteers
Number of Employees: 1,206
Headquarters: Washington, DC
Regional Locations: Chicago, IL; New York, NY; San Francisco, CA
Typical Majors of New Hires: Agriculture, biological sciences, education, engineering, languages, liberal arts, medical sciences

Mission

The activities of the Peace Corps are directed toward helping developing countries meet basic needs, fight disease and hunger, increase food production, and improve education levels, so that eventually they are self-sufficient. Peace Corps volunteers and staff traditionally assist in agriculture, natural resources, health, rural development, education, science, business and skilled trades projects.

Job Descriptions

AREA MEDICAL OFFICER (APCMO): Maintains the medical office at his or her assigned post. Conducts immunization and environmental health programs, provides treatment directly or arranges for other professional practitioners to provide treatment, and handles medical emergencies. Assists in program development for health, home economics, and agriculture projects. Works closely with the Country Director and the Office of Medical Services in Washington, DC. Qualifications: A medical degree and a current U.S. practitioner's license in medicine, osteopathy, or a degree and license in nursing or certification as a physician's assistant.

ASSOCIATE PEACE CORPS DIRECTOR (APCD): Acts as the intermediary between volunteers and local officials, Peace Corps staff in Washington, the host country government, U.S. embassy personnel, and employees from other international agencies. Works with other agencies to generate funding for projects, improve and develop new programs, evaluate volunteer sites, train volunteers, and monitor project progress. Peace Corps selects approximately thirty applicants for APCD positions each year. About half of the APCD positions require fluency in either French or Spanish. Most positions require strong communications and interpersonal skills, management expertise, and practical experience in program development. The following are specializations within the APCD position:

ACPD/(AGRICULTURE): Assists volunteers involved in agricultural and natural resources projects designed to increase food production. These projects include agriculture education, animal husbandry, beekeeping, farm mechanics, soil science, forestry, and fisheries sciences. To qualify, a degree in agriculture, forestry, natural resources or an agriculture-related discipline is often required.

APCD/(RURAL DEVELOPMENT): Creates a physical infrastructure to expand development efforts throughout the country. Works with volunteers on road and bridge construction, irrigation and sanitation systems, urban and rural planning, buildings for education and health, and electrification networks. To qualify, a degree in rural sociology, or a discipline related to rural development such as civil engineering, architecture, construction, public works, or vocational education is often required.

APCD/(HEALTH): Works with volunteers committed to expanding health care to rural areas of developing countries. The projects include disease control, nutrition extension, laboratory technology, nursing, occupational and physical therapy, and sanitation. To qualify, a degree and three to five years experience in public health, medicine, or a related discipline is often required.

APCD/(EDUCATION): Works with volunteers assigned to primary, secondary, and vocational schools, and community education efforts. The subjects taught include math, science, business, English, physical education, library science, and industrial arts. The Peace Corps also has a large international special education program. To qualify, a four-year degree in education or an advanced degree in a related discipline is often required.

APCD/(TRAINING): Directs the training staff, manages the training budget, and is responsible for ensuring that volunteers receive the highest quality language instruction, cross-cultural sensitivity training, and technical preparation. To qualify, a degree in education or behavioral or managerial sciences is often required.

APCD/(PROGRAMMING AND TRAINING): Works closely with other staff members to ensure that programs are consistent with Peace Corps and host country development plans. Organizes and supervises training activities for incoming and current volunteers, and hires training staff. To qualify, a degree in education, management, international affairs, social sciences, or a discipline related to planning is usually required.

APCD/(ADMINISTRATION): Oversees the financial, administrative, and personnel operations. Manages the disbursement of funds, obligations and liquidations; certifies travel and petty cash vouchers; purchases, maintains, and disposes of property and vehicles; maintains files and prepares reports as requested; and coordinates with the American Embassy administrative staff. To qualify, a degree in management, business, or public administration and three to five years experience in a related field are usually required.

Major Activities and Divisions

The Peace Corps overseas staff is divided into paid staff (APCD's and APCMO's) and volunteer staff. Volunteers are needed with degrees and/or experience in agriculture, natural resources, education, liberal arts, fisheries, engineering, business, health professions, home economics, and the trade specialties.

Alternative Employment Programs

There are no co-op or internship programs available in the Peace Corps.

Remarks

APCD's and APCMO's have "Excepted" Foreign Service positions with appointments approximately thirty months long. Training and orientation for new overseas staff lasts approximately thirty days and is offered four times a year, usually in Washington, DC. Salaries for APCDs depend on relevant experience and education, and range from $22,000 to $67,800 per year. APCMO's are paid on a range between $40,000 and $60,000 annually. In most countries, Peace Corps also provides government-leased housing, or in some cases provides a lodging allowance. Employees may receive education allowances for children aged four to twenty-one while enrolled in school.

Application Procedures

APCD's and APCMO's are recruited by the Office of Personnel Policy and Operations, International Operations Divisions. For more information, direct inquiries to:

PEACE CORPS
Office of Personnel Policy and Operations
Division of International Operations
Suite P-307A
806 Connecticut Avenue, N.W.
Washington, DC 20526

(202) 606-3336 (personnel)
(202) 775-2214 (vacancies)
(800) 424-8580 Ext. 2214

POSTAL RATE COMMISSION

Nature of Work: Postal services, wages/prices/rates
Number of Employees: 60
Headquarters: Washington, DC
Regional Locations: None
Typical Majors of New Hires: Accounting, economics, engineering, law, statistics

Mission

The Postal Rate Commission issues decisions to the U.S. Postal Service for postage rates, fees and mail classifications. It also proposes nationwide changes in postal services, initiates studies, and investigates complaints from the mailing public.

Job Descriptions

ACCOUNTANT: Conducts cost analyses and cost accounting research to assess and evaluate postal operating costs.

ATTORNEY: Works in one of two professional groups: the advisory group which supports the efforts of the Commissioners in preparing their decisions, or the litigation group which represents the interests of the general public. Assignments are not rigidly structured; staff members will participate in a full range of projects.

ENGINEER: Applies a knowledge of industrial engineering and market analysis to a full range of projects concerning rate and classification design. Receives general guidance from senior personnel, but a minimum of detailed supervision.

STATISTICIAN: Conducts market research related to postal systems, rates, and operating costs. Quantifies and evaluates gathered data.

Major Activities and Divisions

The Commission is a permanent professional federal agency. It is not part of the U.S. Postal Service. The Commission's staff is divided into technical and legal personnel, both of which participate in postal rate proceedings in order to represent the interests of the general public.

Alternative Employment Programs

None.

Remarks

The Commission offices are in a new office building in the rapidly growing commercial area around 14th Street and Franklin Square.

Application Procedures

The Postal Rate Commission accepts resumes outlining education and/or work experience. Send resume or direct inquiries to:

Postal Rate Commission
Washington, DC 20268
Attn: Administrative Office

(202) 789-6840

RAILROAD RETIREMENT BOARD (RRB)

Nature of Work: Insurance/benefits, railroads
Number of Employees: 1,660
Headquarters: Chicago, IL
Regional Locations: Atlanta, GA; Cleveland, OH; Hackensack, NJ; Kansas City, MO; San Francisco, CA; Washington, DC
Typical Majors of New Hires: Accounting, criminal justice, liberal arts

Mission

The Railroad Retirement Board administers comprehensive retirement-survivor and unemployment-sickness benefit programs for the nation's railroad workers and their families.

Job Descriptions

AUDITOR: Conducts audits at railroad industry sites to ensure that funds are intact and that monies due the Railroad Retirement Board are paid in a timely manner.

CLAIMS EXAMINER (UNEMPLOYMENT): Examines claims for sickness benefits to ensure that eligibility requirements have been met. Also examines unemployment claims for eligibility. Positions located in HQ.

CLAIMS SPECIALIST (HIB): Handles medicare claims from railroad workers. Coordinates with the Social Security Act on welfare coverage issues. Positions located in HQ.

CONTACT REPRESENTATIVE: Takes initial applications for benefits, occasionally setting up itinerate services so as to handle claims in remote locations. Involves approximately 50% public contact and can involve extensive travel throughout the assigned district. No test is required for this position.

CRIMINAL INVESTIGATOR: Examines cases where fraud is suspected.

FIELD OFFICE CLAIMS EXAMINER: Handles unemployment claims that are submitted to a field office location. Examines records and documents for proof of eligibility. No test is required for this position.

RAILROAD CLAIMS EXAMINER (RETIREMENT): Examines claims for retirement annuities. Coordinates with the Social Security Act in the computation, payment, and financing of railroad retirement annuities.

Major Activities and Divisions

The Railroad Retirement Board is divided into several directorates. These include the Bureau of Retirement Claims; the Bureau of Unemployment and Sickness Insurance; and the Bureau of Field Service, which encompasses the regional offices.

Alternative Employment Programs

None.

Remarks

Most Claims Examiner positions require a written test which focuses on reading, writing, and basic math skills.

The Railroad Retirement Board actively recruits on college campuses in the Illinois/Northern Indiana/ Southern Wisconsin region, especially for the Auditor, Claims Examiner, and Criminal Investigator positions.

The headquarters office is located on Chicago's gold coast in the historic Watertower District.

Application Procedures

Direct inquiries to:

Bureau of Personnel
Railroad Retirement Board
844 Rush Street
Chicago, IL 60611

(312) 751-4650

SMALL BUSINESS ADMINISTRATION (SBA)

Nature of Work: Business, minorities/women
Number of Employees: 4,600
Headquarters: Washington, DC
Regional Locations: Atlanta, GA; Boston, MA; Chicago, IL; Dallas, TX; Denver, CO; Kansas City, KS; New York, NY; Philadelphia, PA; San Francisco, CA; Seattle, WA. See below for District Offices.
Typical Majors of New Hires: Accounting, business, economics, finance, marketing, public administration

Mission

The Small Business Administration concerns itself with the health of the nation's economy as seen in the growth of small businesses. It gives advice to new businesses, ensures opportunities for the socially and economically disadvantaged, and services small business loans.

Job Descriptions

BUSINESS DEVELOPMENT SPECIALIST: Provides advice to small businesses through programs such as SCORE. Acts as consultant and conducts management workshops for established as well as prospective businesspersons in overcoming management problems.

BUSINESS OPPORTUNITY SPECIALIST: Works to ensure that small business opportunities are available for the socially or economically disadvantaged. Most work in the Office of Minority Small Business and Capital Ownership Development.

LOAN SPECIALIST: Engages in the servicing of loans and is involved in small business liquidations. Most work in the Office of Finance and Investment or in the Disaster Offices.

Major Activities and Divisions

There are three operational offices in the Small Business Administration: the Office of Minority Small Business and Capital Ownership Development; the Office of Business Development; and the Office of Finance Investment and Procurement. There are 10 regional offices, 68 district offices, and four disaster area offices. The latter offices are in service only when there is a declared disaster. Their mission is to issue loans needed to repair or replace homes, businesses, and farms damaged or destroyed by disasters.

Alternative Employment Programs

The Small Business Administration participates in the following programs for students: Stay-in-School, Student Assistant, Summer Aid, Cooperative Education, College Work-Study, Presidential Management Intern Program, the Summer Employment Program, the Federal Junior Fellowship Program, Legal Internships, and the Student Volunteer Service.

The co-op program focuses mainly on undergraduate college students for positions as Business Development Specialists and Business Opportunity Specialists. Contact your school placement office for more information, or call (202) 653-6567.

The internship program is geared toward legal interns only, and the positions are typically filled by master's-level graduate students. Contact (202) 653-6659 for more information.

Remarks

None.

Application Procedures

Direct inquiries to the personnel office which hires for the area or district office (DO) in which you would like to work:

Central Office
1441 L Street, N.W., Room 300
Washington, DC 20416
(202) 653-6608

Region I
60 Batterymarch Street
10th Floor
Boston, MA 02110
(617) 451-2023

D.O.'s in Boston, MA; Augusta, ME; Concord, NH; Hartford, CT; Montpelier, VT; Providence, RI

Region II
26 Federal Plaza, Room 31-08
New York, NY 10278
(212) 264-2455

D.O.'s in New York, NY; Hato Rey, PR; Newark, NJ; Syracuse, NY

Region III
Allendale Square
475 Allendale Rd.
King of Prussia, PA 19406
(215) 962-3725

D.O.'s in King of Prussia, PA; Baltimore, MD; Clarksburg, WV; Pittsburgh, PA; Richmond, VA; Washington, DC

Region IV
1375 Peachtree Street, N.E.
5th Floor
Atlanta, GA 30367-8102
(404) 347-4943

D.O.'s in Atlanta, GA; Birmingham, AL; Charlotte, NC; Columbia, SC; Jackson, MI; Jacksonville, FL; Louisville, KY; Miami, FL; Nashville, TN

Region V
230 South Dearborn Street, Room 510
Chicago, IL 60604
(312) 353-6614

D.O.'s in Chicago, IL; Cleveland, OH; Columbus, OH; Detroit, MI; Indianapolis, IN; Madison, WI; Minneapolis, MN

Region VI
8625 King George Drive
Building C
Dallas, TX 75235-3391
(214) 767-7628

D.O.'s in Dallas, TX; Albuquerque, NM; Houston, TX; Little Rock, AK; Lubbock, TX; Harlingen, TX; New Orleans, LA; Oklahoma City, OK; San Antonio, TX; El Paso, TX

Region VII
911 Walnut Street, 13th Floor
Kansas City, MO 64106
(816) 374-5288

D.O.'s in Kansas City, MO; Cedar Rapids, IA; Des Moines, IA; Omaha, NE; St. Louis, MO; Witchita, KS

Region VIII
999 18th Street, Suite 701
Denver, CO 80202
(303) 294-7110

D.O.'s in Denver, CO; Casper, WY; Fargo, ND; Helena, MT; Salt Lake City, UT; Sioux Falls, SD

Region IX
450 Golden Gate Avenue
San Francisco, CA 94102
(415) 556-5935

D.O.'s in San Francisco, CA; Las Vegas, NV; Honolulu, HI; Los Angeles, CA; Phoenix, AZ; San Diego, CA

Region X
4th and Vine Building, Room 440
2615 4th Avenue
Seattle, WA 98121
(206) 442-7646

D.O.'s in Seattle, WA; Anchorage, AK; Portland, OR; Spokane, WA

SMITHSONIAN INSTITUTION

Nature of Work: Arts/humanities, education, libraries, scientific research, scholarly research
Number of Employees: 5,000
Headquarters: Washington, DC
Regional Locations: Arizona, Florida, Maryland, Massachusetts, Virginia, and the Republic of Panama
Typical Majors of New Hires: Anthropology, biology, biological sciences (entomology, ornithology, paleobiology, physiology, zoology), botany, history, physical sciences (astrophysics)

Mission

In 1829, James Smithson, son of the Duke of Northumberland, bequeathed a sum of money to the United States to found an "Establishment for the increase and diffusion of knowledge among men." Today, it is the world's largest museum complex and an important center for research. Its thirteen museums and the National Zoo hold more than 70 million objects and specimens. About one percent of the total is on public display, with the rest used for research.

Job Descriptions

CONSERVATOR: Supervises or performs professional work related to research, collections, and exhibits in the various Smithsonian museums.

DESIGNER: Communicates information through visual means. Designs and displays such materials as photographs, illustrations, diagrams, graphs, models, and exhibits.

EDUCATION SPECIALIST: Disseminates information through educational programs and materials relating to exhibits and museum collections. Designs, prepares, and schedules programs that enhance current exhibitions and develops independent activities to serve the needs of the school community.

EXHIBITS SPECIALIST: Plans, constructs, and operates exhibits. Oversees the restoration or preparation of items to be exhibited, or the restoration of historic buildings or properties. Applies artistic abilities and technical skills to the preparation of exhibits projects.

LIBRARIAN: Collects, organizes, and preserves recorded knowledge in printed, written, audiovisual, or other media forms. Catalogues, classifies, and retrieves materials.

MUSEUM SPECIALIST/MUSEUM TECHNICIAN: Performs technical work in connection with the operation of public museums. Manages museum collections, and monitors exhibits projects.

PHOTOGRAPHER: Depending upon the nature of the assignment, this position may include the performance of still, motion picture, television, high-speed, aerial, or other camera work, and/or photographic processing work. May require a knowledge about the subject matter to be photographed.

RESEARCH ASSISTANT: Conducts technical and scholarly research on projects relating to museum collections and associated issues.

STAFF LECTURER: Provides lectures to the general public and special interest groups on topics relating to exhibits and museum collections.

Major Activities and Divisions

Anacostia Museum: Exhibits, researches, and provides educational programs related to the Afro-American experience from the beginning of the slave trade to modern times.

Archives of American Art: Collects and preserves some 2,000 personal and professional papers of American painters, sculptors, critics, dealers, collectors, and records of museums and art societies.

Arthur M. Sackler Gallery: Devoted to the acquisition, study, interpretation, and exhibition of Asian art museums and art societies.

Conservation Analytical Laboratory: Provides a focus within the Smithsonian for conservation of the millions of artifacts in the museum collections.

Cooper-Hewitt Museum of Design and Decorative Arts: The over 300,000 items in this collection include drawings, furniture, glass, woodwork, wallcoverings, and other media. These serve as visual information for the study of design.

Freer Gallery of Art: Houses a collection of oriental art which consists of over 26,800 works.

Hirshhorn Museum and Sculpture Garden (HMSG): Includes paintings by modern European and Latin masters, and works representing 150 years of American and European sculpture.

John F. Kennedy Center for the Performing Arts: The Center presents a year-round program of the finest in music, dance, and drama from the U.S. and abroad.

National Air and Space Museum (NASM): The twenty-three exhibit halls trace the history of flight from the beginnings in balloon craft to the latest shuttle flight. The

Paul E. Garber facility in Silver Hill, Maryland houses the aircraft restoration operations for the museum.

National Gallery of Art: Houses one of the finest art collections in the world, illustrating Western man's achievements in painting, sculpture, and the graphic arts.

National Museum of African Art (NMAA): NMAA is devoted to the acquisition, study, and exhibition of African paintings, sculpture, and graphic arts.

National Museum of American Art: Devoted to American painting, sculpture, and graphic art from the 18th century to the present. Houses a permanent collection of over 25,000 works.

National Museum of American History (NMAH): NMAH is devoted to the exhibition, maintenance, and study of artifacts which reflect the experience of the American people. NMAH also offers the Dibner Library, a collection of rare books relating to the history of science and technology; the Eisenhower Institute for Historical Research, focusing on military history; and *Technology and Culture*, the international quarterly of the Society for the History of Technology.

National Museum of Natural History (NMNH): Through its collection of over 84 million plants, animals, rocks and minerals, and cultural artifacts, NMNH provides a record of the natural and cultural history of the earth. The NMNH also operates the Smithsonian Marine Station at Link Port, Florida.

National Portrait Gallery (NPG): NPG presents American history through the lives of men and women who have contributed significantly to its development, as depicted in a collection of portraiture in all media.

National Zoological Park (NZP): NZP maintains a collection of over 2,500 animals representing about 500 species. There is a conservation and research center for endangered species in Front Royal, VA.

Smithsonian Astrophysical Observatory (SAO): SAO is devoted to research into the basic physical processes which determine the nature and evolution of the universe. Data gathering facilities include the Fred Lawrence Whipple Observatory in Arizona; the Oak Ridge Observatory in Massachusetts; and the George R. Agassiz Station in Texas. Research activities are organized into seven divisions: atomic and molecular physics, high energy astrophysics, optical and molecular physics, high energy astrophysics, planetary sciences, radio and geoastronomy, solar and stellar physics, and theoretical astrophysics. In addition to scientists, the observatory employs over 250 support staff. Generally, an earned doctorate in astronomy, astrophysics, physics, or a related field is required for professional research positions.

Smithsonian Environmental Research Center (SERC): The SERC's research programs emphasize two major areas: regulatory and environmental biology; and projects which include radio-carbon dating, education, and public information.

Smithsonian Tropical Research Institute (STRI): The STRI conducts research on basic biological processes, provides support of advanced training and tropical research by visiting scientists, and works on behalf of conservation in the tropics. Staff and students work throughout tropical regions of the Americas, Asia, and Africa, with headquarters in the Republic of Panama.

Alternative Employment Programs

The Smithsonian Institution conducts an extensive Volunteer Service program. Persons may serve as tour guides or information volunteers, or may participate in an independent program in which their educational and professional backgrounds are matched with curatorial or research requests from within the Smithsonian. Direct inquiries to the Visitor Information and Associates' Reception Center, 1000 Jefferson Drive, S.W., Washington, DC 20560. Call (202) 357-2700 or TDD 381-4448 (for the hearing impaired).

The Kennedy Center runs an independent Volunteer Services program. For information, write to Friends of the Kennedy Center, Washington, DC 20566. Phone, (202) 254-8700.

Remarks

The Smithsonian offers predoctoral and postdoctoral grants through its Office of Fellowships and Grants. It also conducts a graduate program in the material aspects of American civilization for graduate students enrolled in cooperating universities through its Office of American Studies.

Application Procedures

Inquiries regarding employment in the Washington, DC, metropolitan area may be directed to:

The Office of Personnel Administration
Smithsonian Institution
900 Jefferson Drive, S.W.
Washington, DC 20560

(202) 287-3100
(202) 287-3102 (vacancies)

Employment information for the following locations may be obtained by contacting the organizations directly:

Cooper-Hewitt Museum
2 East 91st Street
New York, NY 10028
(212) 860-6868

Smithsonian Astrophysical Observatory
Personnel Department
160 Concord Avenue
Cambridge, MA 02138
(617) 495-7371

National Gallery of Art
Fourth Street and Constitution Avenue, N.W.
Washington, DC 20565
(202) 737-4215

John F. Kennedy Center for the Performing Arts
Washington, DC 20566
(202) 872-0466

TENNESSEE VALLEY AUTHORITY (TVA)

Nature of Work: Agriculture, energy, environmental protection, forestry/wildlife, nuclear energy/issues, recreation, waterways
Number of Employees: 26,404
Headquarters: Knoxville, TN
Regional Locations: Chattanooga, TN; Golden Pond, KY; Muscle Shoals, AL
Typical Majors of New Hires: Biology, chemistry, engineering, physical sciences

Mission

Advances economic development in the Tennessee Valley region by controlling floods, maintaining navigable waterways, generating electricity, creating new fertilizers, improving outdoor recreation, and developing forests and wildlife.

Job Descriptions

CHEMIST: Develops and improves fertilizers and investigates the use of organic materials as fuels.

ELECTRICAL ENGINEER: Designs and maintains electrical generating and distributions systems, and develops electromechanical components and systems.

MECHANICAL ENGINEER: Assists in the planning and construction of generating facilities, oversees the installation of equipment, and supervises modifications.

NUCLEAR ENGINEER: Designs components of nuclear power facilities such as reactor cores and instrumentation. Supervises servicing, modifications, inspections, safety, and radiological control, and prepares technical specifications.

Major Activities and Divisions

Generating Group: Supplies wholesale power to local, municipal, and cooperative electric systems, as well as federal installations and industries with unusually large power requirements.

Customer Group: Provides power transmission, distributor marketing services, rate design, and business operations to customers.

Resources Group: Conducts forestry, fish and game, and watershed protection research. Advises communities on such matters as industrial development, regional waste management, and tourism.

Alternative Employment Programs

TVA maintains a co-op program for engineering and computer science students. Call (615) 632-3822 for more information.

Remarks

None.

Application Procedures

Direct inquiries to:

Employment Services, ET 5P-K
Tennessee Valley Authority
400 West Summit Hill Drive
Knoxville, TN 37902

(615) 632-7746

U.S. ARMS CONTROL AND DISARMAMENT AGENCY (ACDA)
Nature of Work: Defense and national security, international affairs, weapons **Number of Employees:** 295 **Headquarters:** Washington, DC **Regional Locations:** None **Typical Majors of New Hires:** International affairs, political science

Mission

The ACDA conducts studies and provides advice relating to arms control and disarmament policy formation. It prepares for and manages U.S. participation in international negotiations in the arms control and disarmament field, and disseminates and coordinates public information about arms control.

Job Descriptions

FOREIGN AFFAIRS SPECIALIST: Conducts research into international negotiation strategies and arms control. Analyzes selected defense programs for their arms control implications, and makes recommendations regarding arms control and disarmament strategies.

Major Activities and Divisions

The U.S. Arms Control and Disarmament Agency is divided into four program areas: *The Bureau of Multilateral Affairs*; the *Bureau of Nuclear and Weapons Control*; the *Bureau of Strategic Programs*; and the *Bureau of Verification and Intelligence*.

Alternative Employment Programs

The Agency occasionally hires summer interns for Foreign Affairs Specialist positions depending upon budget constraints. It also participates in the Stay-in-School Program for clerical positions.

Remarks

The ACDA publishes such documents as *World Military Expenditures, Documents on Disarmament,* and *Arms Control and Disarmament Agreements.* These publications are available through the Government Printing Office.

Application Procedures

Direct inquiries to:

U.S. Arms Control and Disarmament Agency
320 Twenty-first Street, N.W.
Washington, DC 20451

(202) 647-2034

U.S. EQUAL EMPLOYMENT OPPORTUNITY COMMISSION (EEOC)

Nature of Work: Business, employment, insurance/benefits, minorities/women
Number of Employees: 3,200
Headquarters: Washington, DC
Regional Locations: Atlanta, GA; Baltimore, MD; Birmingham, AL; Charlotte, NC; Chicago, IL; Cleveland, OH; Dallas, TX; Denver, CO; Detroit, MI; Houston, TX; Indianapolis, IN; Los Angeles, CA; Memphis, TN; Miami, FL; Milwaukee, WI; New Orleans, LA; New York, NY; Philadelphia, PA; Phoenix, AZ; St. Louis, MO; San Antonio, TX; San Francisco, CA; Seattle, WA; Washington, DC
Typical Majors of New Hires: Criminal justice, law, liberal arts, psychology

Mission

The EEOC enforces the laws against employment discrimination, including Title VII, the Age Discrimination in Employment Act, and the Equal Pay Act. EEOC coordinates all federal equal employment opportunity regulations and policies, and is the appellate authority for federal sector complaints of employment discrimination.

Job Descriptions

ATTORNEY: Conducts all of the agency's civil litigation except for Title VII cases against state and local governments and Supreme Court cases, which are litigated by the Solicitor General of the U.S. About one-eighth of EEOC's staff are attorneys or law clerks, 60 percent of which are located in field offices outside Washington, D.C. Most work in the Office of General Counsel, the Office of Legal Counsel, or the Office of Review and Appeals.

INVESTIGATOR: Receives and investigates employment discrimination charges. Meets with charging parties, employers, and other witnesses to secure information relative to a charge, analyzes the data, and writes recommendations on the findings. Visits employer facilities to investigate charges and helps resolve them by negotiating settlements between the complainants and employers.

Major Activities and Divisions

The Office of General Counsel: Employs attorneys at EEOC HQ and in 23 district offices. Conducts class, systematic, and individual discrimination lawsuits.

The Office of Legal Counsel: Located in Washington, D.C. only, it is the principal advisor to the Commission on policy and nonenforcement litigation matters, and represents EEOC and staff in defensive litigation and administrative hearings.

The Office of Review and Appeals: Located in Washington, D.C., this office decides or recommends decisions on appeals from federal agency employees on equal opportunity complaints and petitions.

The Office of Program Operations: Manages, directs, and coordinates field office operations.

Alternative Employment Programs

Co-op Investigator positions are available for students at the sophomore level and above. Internships are also available. They are nonpaid, but can be used for course credit. Other more specialized programs:

The Legal Intern Program: For ABA-approved law school students who have completed their first year. Hiring is conducted individually by each EEOC office. GS-5 or 9.

The Summer Legal Intern Program: For law students who have completed their first year or more at an ABA approved law school. Term of employment is between May 13 and Sept. 30, but superior employees may be offered a permanent position effective upon graduation. Candidates must apply by March 15. GS-5 or 9.

The Federal Summer Employment Program: Temporary administrative or professional jobs available from May 13 to September 30, and during other school breaks.

Remarks

EEOC conducts a Law School Recruitment Program which is designed for outstanding third-year law students, graduate law students, and judicial clerks. Interviewing is done on the college campus or at the EEOC office. All JD graduates must pass the bar exam within 14 months for entry on duty. Upon bar membership, the individual may be appointed to a permanent attorney position. GS-9, 11, 12.

Application Procedures

Direct inquiries to the Personnel Management Specialist in the District Office in which you would like to work, or to EEOC headquarters:

EEOC Headquarters
Washington, DC 20507
(202) 634-7002
Washington Field Office

Atlanta District Office
75 Piedmont Avenue, N.E., Suite 1100
Atlanta, GA 30335
(404) 331-6093
Savannah Local Office

Baltimore District Office
109 Market Place, Suite 4000
Baltimore, MD 21202
(301) 962-3932
Norfolk Area Office
Richmond Area Office

Birmingham District Office
2121 8th Avenue, North, Suite 824
Birmingham, AL 35203
(205) 731-0082
Jackson Area Office

Charlotte District Office
5500 Central Avenue
Charlotte, NC 28212
(704) 567-7100
Greensboro Local Office
Greenville Local Office
Raleigh Area Office

Chicago District Office
536 S. Clark Street, Room 930-A
Chicago, IL 60605
(312) 353-2713

Cleveland District Office
1375 Euclid Avenue, Room 600
Cleveland, OH 44115
(216) 522-2001
Cincinnati Area Office

Dallas District Office
8303 Elmbrook Drive, 2nd Floor
Dallas, TX 75247
(214) 767-7015
Oklahoma City Area Office

Denver District Office
1845 Sherman Street, 2nd Floor
Denver, CO 80203
(303) 866-1300

Detroit District Office
477 Michigan Avenue, Room 1540
Detroit, MI 48226
(313) 226-7636

Houston District Office
405 Main Street, 6th Floor
Houston, TX 77002
(713) 653-3320

Indianapolis District Office
26 E. Ohio Street, Room 456
Indianapolis, IN 46204
(317) 269-7212
Louisville Area Office

Los Angeles District Office
3660 Wilshire Boulevard, 5th Floor
Los Angeles, CA 90010
(213) 251-7278
San Diego Local Office

Memphis District Office
1407 Union Avenue, Suite 502
Memphis, TN 38104
(901) 521-2617
Little Rock Area Office
Nashville Area Office

Miami District Office
1 Northeast First Street, 6th Floor
Miami, FL 33132
(305) 536-4491
Tampa Area Office

Milwaukee District Office
310 W. Wisconsin Avenue, Suite 800
Milwaukee, WI 53203
(414) 291-1111
Minneapolis Local Office

New Orleans District Office
701 Loyola Avenue, Suite 600
New Orleans, LA 70110
(504) 589-2329

New York District Office
90 Church Street, Room 1501
New York, NY 10007
(212) 264-7161
Boston Area Office
Buffalo Area Office

Philadelphia District Office
1421 Cherry Street, 10th Floor
Philadelphia, PA 19102
(215) 597-7784
Newark Area Office
Pittsburgh Area Office

Phoenix District Office
4520 N. Central Avenue, Suite 300
Phoenix, AZ 85012-1848
(602) 261-3882
Albuquerque Area Office

St. Louis District Office
625 N. Euclid Street, 5th Floor
St. Louis, MO 63108
(314) 425-6585
Kansas City Area Office

San Antonio District Office
5410 Fredericksburg Road
Suite 200
San Antonio, TX 78229
(512) 229-4810
El Paso Local Office

San Francisco District Office
901 Market Street, Room 500
San Francisco, CA 94103
(415) 995-5049
Fresno Local Office
Honolulu Local Office
Oakland Local Office
San Jose Local Office

Seattle District Office
1321 2nd Avenue, 7th Floor
Seattle, WA 98101
(206) 442-0968

U.S. INFORMATION AGENCY (USIA)

Nature of Work: Communications/media, education, international affairs
Number of Employees: 8,718
Headquarters: Washington, DC
Regional Locations: U.S. embassies around the world
Typical Majors of New Hires: Communications, international affairs, languages, liberal arts, political science

Mission

Strengthens foreign understanding and support for U.S. policies and actions through international radio broadcasts, satellite television, movies, magazines, exhibits, personal contacts, lectures, and exchange programs.

Job Descriptions

FOREIGN SERVICE OFFICER (PUBLIC AFFAIRS): Manages the public diplomacy activities of an embassy, and advises the ambassador on local trends in public opinion and the media.

FOREIGN AFFAIRS OFFICER (INFORMATION): Serves as an embassy's spokesperson by holding press conferences, briefing journalists, and handling public relations.

FOREIGN AFFAIRS OFFICER (CULTURAL AFFAIRS): Administers educational and cultural exchange programs, facilitates lectures and seminars with American speakers, manages American libraries, and organizes exhibits.

Major Activities and Divisions

The Voice of America: Produces radio programs in English and 43 foreign languages for overseas transmission.

Bureau of Programs: Provides bulletins to all USIA posts containing official texts and other material needed to portray events in the U.S.

Bureau of Educational and Cultural Affairs: Promotes international scholarly and educational exchange programs.

Office of Cultural Centers and Resources: Provides policy directions, program support, and materials to USIA libraries and binational centers abroad.

Office of Private Sector Programs: Develops cooperative projects with private firms that offer educational and cultural exchanges between Americans and citizens of other countries.

Office of International Visitors: Plans and implements all international visitor programs.

Office of Academic Programs: Organizes academic exchanges between the U.S. and other countries.

Alternative Employment Programs

When funding is available, USIA offers a limited number of salaried summer internships. The agency also actively recruits for Guides to participate in USIA exhibits in Eastern Europe, the Soviet Union, and world expositions. Applicants must be U.S. citizens, at least 21 years old, and fluent in the language of the country in which the exhibit is held. Guides are hired for periods ranging from 1 to 7 months. For more information, write to:

Employment Branch
United States Information Agency
301 4th Street, S.W.

Washington, D.C. 20547

(202) 619-5618
(202) 619-4539 (vacancies)

The Voice of America (VOA) offers a limited number of 2-year paid broadcast internships that can lead to careers in radio journalism at VOA. Student volunteer internships are available throughout the year which enable participants to earn college credit. For more information, write to:

Office of Personnel
Voice of America
330 Independence Avenue, S.W.
Room 1543
Washington, D.C. 20547

(202) 619-3117
(202) 619-0909 (vacancies)

Most intern positions require a security clearance, which may take as long as 6 months; applicants should therefore apply early in the academic year.

Remarks

Before accepting employment, candidates must agree to be available for worldwide assignment. All Foreign Service Officer candidates receive several weeks of orientation at the State Department's Foreign Service Institute in Washington, D.C. Candidates may receive as much as 7 months of additional training before their first overseas assignment. Most of this consists of language instruction. For more information, see the section on Foreign Service Careers.

Application Procedures

For positions at USIA, direct inquiries to:
Office of Personnel
Special Services Branch
United States Information Agency
301 4th Street, S.W.
Washington, DC 20547

(202) 485-2618

For positions at the Voice of America, direct inquiries to:

Office of Personnel
Voice of America
330 Independence Avenue, S.W.
Room 1543
Washington, D.C. 20547

(202) 485-8063
(202) 472-6909 (24-hour job vacancy line)

U.S. POSTAL SERVICE

Nature of Work: Postal
Number of Employees: 765,000
Headquarters: Washington, DC
Regional Locations: The five Postal regions are headquartered at Chicago, IL; Memphis, TN; North Windsor, CT; Philadelphia, PA; and San Bruno, CA. These regions oversee 73 field division offices and over 40,000 post offices nationwide
Typical Majors of New Hires: Business, computer science, criminal justice, engineering, labor relations (personnel), law, liberal arts, public administration

Mission

A fundamental commitment of the Postal Service is to provide swift and reliable mail delivery. To provide postal services responsive to public needs, the Postal Service operates its own planning, research, engineering, real estate, and procurement programs, and maintains close ties with international postal organizations.

Job Descriptions

ENGINEER: Applies a knowledge of the physical and engineering sciences to develop and test electronic and automation equipment related to mail, mail sorting, address identification, and other postal needs.

POSTAL INSPECTOR: Inspects post offices and related postal units to ensure compliance with postal laws and regulations. Investigates postal laws, and surveys operating problems.

REALTY SPECIALIST: Appraises land and acquires real estate through negotiation of a contract or lease. Plans and manages real estate to attain its most efficient use.

SYSTEMS ANALYST: Designs, develops, and tests automation equipment related to the efficient organization and management of the major post offices and postal services.

Major Activities and Divisions

Customer Cooperation: The Postal Service provides customer cooperation activities including the representation of interests of the individual mail customer through the Consumer Advocate.

Mail Delivery: The Postal Service maintains extensive processing and delivery systems and integrated bulk mail handling systems.

Postal Operations: The Postal Service maintains the postal rate structure and develops mail classification standards.

Law Enforcement: The Postal Inspection Service, the law enforcement arm of the Postal Service, protects the mails, postal funds, and property.

Alternative Employment Programs

There are two major employment programs for individuals wishing to enter a management position with the Postal Service:

1. MANAGEMENT INTERN PROGRAM: The primary purpose of this program is to develop interns to meet future management and executive needs. The program is two to four years in length, and consists of 2- to 9-month rotational assignments at all levels of the organization. All undergraduate degree requirements must be completed before entering the program. Interns are based at headquarters in Washington, DC, although some assignments are located in the regional and field division offices. Starting salaries are approximately $26,000 to $43,000 per year based on education and experience. Management Interns are eligible for bonuses up to 12% of base salary annually.

To apply: Submit completed PS Form 991-MI (Application for Management Intern) and two letters of recommendation from an employer or professor to:

United States Postal Service
Employee Development and Education Division
475 L'Enfant Plaza West, S.W.
Washington, DC 20260-4352
ATTN: Management Intern Program

Applications are accepted only during an approximate 6-week period in early spring (1990 acceptance dates were Feb. 1–March 13). Interviews begin shortly after the closing date, and interns usually begin in mid-June.

2. MANAGEMENT ASSOCIATE PROGRAM: This program's purpose is to develop high-potential individuals to meet future management needs. The program normally runs three years and consists of on-the-job developmental assignments and related training at one of 73 Postal field divisions. The Associate gains a broad understanding of the Postal Service's mission through hands-on experience in various functions within the organization. An advanced degree or a bachelor's degree with two years of supervisory experience is required. Management Associates are based in any of the 73 field divisions. The salary range is approximately $29,000 to $35,000, depending on experience, education, and current salary.

To apply: Submit completed PS Form 991-M (Application for Management Associate Program), and an official transcript from the college from which you obtained the highest degree. Mail to the region where you wish to be considered:

U.S. Postal Service
Regional Director, Human Resources

Eastern Region
Philadelphia, PA 29297-0840

Northeast Region
Windsor, CT 06006-0840

Southern Region

Memphis, TN 38166-0840

Western Region
San Bruno, CA 94044-0840

Remarks

The Postal Service does not follow the GS pay schedule as described in Chapter 4. U.S. Postal Service salaries are competitive with those of other leading corporations. Benefits are similar to those offered in other government organizations, including 13 paid vacation days per year, 13 paid sick days per year, and ten paid holidays.

Application Procedures

Direct inquiries to:

United States Postal Service
Employee Development and Education Division
Training and Development Dept.
475 L'Enfant Plaza, S.W.
Washington, DC 20260-4352
(202) 268-3643
(202) 268-3218 (vacancies)

Information about Inspection Service employment may be obtained from the Chief Postal Inspector. Phone, (202) 268-4267.

Information about jobs such as clerk, letter carrier, etc., including information about programs for veterans, may be obtained by contacting the nearest post office.

U.S. SECURITIES AND EXCHANGE COMMISSION (SEC)

Nature of Work: Business, bonds/commodities
Number of Employees: 2,123
Headquarters: Washington, DC
Regional Locations: Atlanta, GA; Boston, MA; Chicago, IL; Denver, CO; Fort Worth, TX; Los Angeles, CA; New York, NY; Philadelphia, PA; Seattle, WA
Typical Majors of New Hires: Accounting, business economics, finance/banking, law (JD)

Mission

The SEC administers and enforces federal securities laws. The Commission regulates the nation's securities markets, stock brokers, investment companies and investment advisers, and prescribes certain requirements for companies that issue stock or other securities.

Job Descriptions

ACCOUNTANT: Drafts accounting and reporting regulations that apply to corporations whose securities are sold to the public. Examines financial statements filed with registration statements to determine if there is adequate disclosure of financial information. Reviews financial data to ascertain whether there have been violations of law or regulations in connection with the issue, purchase, and sale of securities. The SEC hires accountants at the GS-11, 12, and 13 levels. These positions require an undergraduate degree plus at least three years of professional experience. A CPA is preferred.

ATTORNEY: Investigates violations of federal securities laws. Inspects self-regulatory systems, including the review of existing laws and conducts hearings regarding the introduction of new rules. Examines registration and proxy statements, indentures, and applications.

FINANCIAL ANALYST: Analyzes prospectuses, proxy statements, and reports of corporations to determine that full and fair disclosure has been made. Reviews reports and other data required to supervise and regulate transactions and trading on national securities exchanges and in the over-the-counter market. Reviews filings to ensure compliance with the financial standards of the Public Utility Holding Company Act of 1935. Works with attorneys and investigators in the surveillance of unusual trading activity. Typically works in the Divisions of Corporate Finance, Investment Management, Market Regulation, and Enforcement. Applicants are considered at the GS-9, 11, and 12 levels. A GS-9 requires a masters degree in business, accounting, finance, or economics.

FINANCIAL ECONOMIST: Studies the impact of proposed Commission actions upon the capital markets, securities industries, and the Commission's regulatory program. All positions are located in Washington, and the number of financial economist positions filled annually is small.

INVESTIGATOR: Investigates and analyzes unusual market activity which may indicate possible violations of the law.

SECURITIES COMPLIANCE EXAMINER: Examines the operational and financial practices and records of broker-dealers, investment advisers, mutual funds, and other classes of registrants. Investigates the registrants' procedures for safeguarding funds and securities of customers, and assesses the financial liquidity of a broker-dealer to determine the adequacy of the firm's net capital and its overall financial health. Examines the distribution and selling of securities in over-the-counter and exchange trading. Securities Compliance Examiners generally have financial or accounting training, and are principally employed in regional or branch offices. Applicants are considered at the GS-5 to GS-12 levels.

Major Activities and Divisions

The Division of Corporate Finance oversees public disclosure of financial and business information of companies that issue securities.

The Division of Enforcement is the chief investigative arm of the Commission. Investigations and trials are the day-to-day work of the staff of the Division of Enforcement.

The Division of Investment Management administers federal securities laws as they apply to regulation of and disclosure by investment companies and investment advisers. The Commission staff visits investment companies on a regular basis to review adherence to statutory requirements.

The Division of Market Regulation regulates the nation's securities markets and the activities of transfer agents, broker-dealers, and other market professionals.

The Office of the Chief Accountant is the principal adviser to the Commission on accounting, auditing, and financial reporting matters.

Alternative Employment Programs

Summer Employment Program: Available to law and finance students. Students assist staff members in daily duties or special projects which relate to their course of study.

Co-op Program: Students entering a master's or doctoral program in business, finance, accounting or economics can be chosen for the program. Students are employed at SEC for a minimum of 16 weeks on a full-time basis. Upon graduation, the co-op student can become a permanent member of the SEC staff.

Law Student Observer Program: Third-year law students are eligible to work for 15 to 20 hours a week at the SEC. Participants are not paid for their time, but are given course credit through the law school they attend.

Remarks

The Commission operates a college and law school recruitment program, including on-campus visitations for interview purposes. Direct inquiries to the Director of Personnel, (202) 272-2519.

Application Procedures

Direct inquiries to:

Director of Personnel
Securities and Exchange Commission
450 Fifth Street, N.W.
Washington, DC 20549-0001

(202) 272-2550

Speech or hearing-impaired applicants may call (202) 272-2552.

APPENDIX

Office of Personnel Management Federal Job Information Centers

Contact the Federal Job Information Center which is nearest the location where you would like to work for information on job opportunities in that area and the forms needed to apply.

ALABAMA
Huntsville:
Building 600, Suite 347
3322 Memorial Pkwy., South,
35801-5311
(205) 544-5802

ALASKA
Anchorage:
222 W. 7th Ave., #22, 99513-7572
(907) 271-5821

ARIZONA
Phoenix:
Century Plaza Bldg., Rm. 1415
3225 N. Central Ave., 85012
(602) 640-5800

ARKANSAS
(See Oklahoma Listing)

CALIFORNIA
Los Angeles:
9650 Flair Drive, Suite 100A
El Monte, 91731
(818) 575-6510

Sacramento:
4695 Watts Ave., North Highland
(916) 551-1464
(mail) 1029 J Street 95814

San Diego:
Federal Bldg., Room 4-S-9
880 Front St., 92188
(619) 557-6165

San Francisco:
211 Main St., 2nd Fl., Rm. 235
(mail) P.O. Box 7405, 94120
(415) 744-5627

COLORADO
Denver:
12345 W. Alameda Pkwy., Lakewood
(mail) P.O. Box 25167, 80225
(303) 969-7050
For forms and local supplements, dial (303)969-7055

CONNECTICUT
Hartford:
Federal Bldg., Rm. 613
450 Main St., 06103
(203) 240-3096 or 3263

DELAWARE
(See Philadelphia Listing)

DISTRICT OF COLUMBIA
Metro Area:
1900 E St., N.W., Rm. 1416, 20415
(202) 606-2700

FLORIDA
Orlando:
Commodore Bldg., Suite 125
3444 McCrory Pl., 32803-3701
(407) 648-6148

GEORGIA
Atlanta:
Richard B. Russell Federal Bldg., Room 940A
75 Spring St., S.W., 30303
(404) 331-4315

HAWAII
Honolulu (and other Hawaiian Islands and Overseas):
Federal Bldg., Rm. 5316
300 Ala Moana Blvd., 96850
(808) 541-2791
Overseas Jobs—(808) 541-2784

IDAHO
(See Washington Listing)

ILLINOIS
Chicago:
175 W. Jackson Blvd., Rm. 530, 60604
(312) 353-6192
(For Madison & St. Clair Counties, see St. Louis, MO listing)

INDIANA
Indianapolis:
Minton-Capehart Federal Bldg.
575 N. Pennsylvania St., 46204
(317) 226-7161
(For Clark, Dearborn, & Floyd Counties, see Ohio listing)

IOWA
(See Kansas City, Missouri listing)
(816) 426-7757
(For Scott County, see Illinios listing; for Pottawatamie County, see Kansas listing)

KANSAS
Wichita:
One-Twenty Bldg., Rm. 101
120 S. Market St., 67202
(316) 269-6794
(For Johnson, Leavenworth, and Wyandotte Counties, dial (816) 426-5702

KENTUCKY
(See Ohio listing; for Henderson County, see Indiana listing)

LOUISIANA
New Orleans:
1515 Poydras St., Suite 608, 70112
(504) 589-2764

MAINE
(See New Hampshire Listing)

MARYLAND
Baltimore:
Garmatz Federal Bldg., Rm. 1200
101 W. Lombard Street, 21201
(301) 962-3822

MASSACHUSETTS
Boston:
Thos. P. O'Neill, Jr. Federal Bldg.
10 Causeway St., 02222-1031
(617) 565-5900

MICHIGAN
Detroit:
477 Michigan Ave., Rm. 565, 48226
(313) 226-6950

MINNESOTA
Twin Cities:
Federal Building, Room 501
Ft. Snelling, Twin Cities, 55111
(612) 725-3430

MISSISSIPPI
(See Alabama Listing)

MISSOURI

Kansas City:
Federal Building, Rm. 134
601 E. 12th St., 64106
(816) 426-5702
(For Counties west of and including Mercer, Grundy, Livingston, Carroll, Saline, Pettis, Benton, Hickory, Dallas, Webster, Douglas, and Ozark)

St. Louis:
400 Old Post Office Bldg.
815 Olive St., 63101
(314) 539-2285
(For all other Missouri Counties not listed under Kansas City above)

MONTANA

(303)969-7052)
(See Colorado Listing)

NEBRASKA

(See Kansas Listing)

NEVADA

(See Sacramento, CA Listing)

NEW HAMPSHIRE

Portsmouth:
Thomas J. McIntyre Federal Bldg.
80 Daniel St., Rm. 104, 03801-3879
(603) 431-7115

NEW JERSEY

Newark:
Peter W. Rodino, Jr., Federal Bldg.
970 Broad Street, 07102
(201) 645-3673
In Camden, dial (215) 597-7440

NEW MEXICO

Albuquerque:
Federal Building Room 101
421 Gold Avenue, S.W., 87102
(505) 766-2906

NEW YORK

New York City:
Jacob K. Javits Federal Bldg., Second Floor, Room 120
26 Federal Plaza, 10278
(212) 264-0428

Syracuse:
James M. Hanley Federal Building
100 S. Clinton St., 13260
(315) 423-5660

NORTH CAROLINA

Raleigh:
P.O. Box 25069
4505 Falls of the Neuse Rd.
Suite 445, 27611-5069
(919) 856-4361

NORTH DAKOTA

(See Minnesota Listing)

OHIO

Dayton:
Federal Building, Rm. 506
200 W. 2nd Street, 45402
(513) 225-2720
(For Van Wert, Auglaize, Hardin, Marion, Crawford, Richland, Ashland, Wayne, Stark, Carroll, Columbiana Counties and all Counties north of these see Michigan listing)

OKLAHOMA

Oklahoma City:
(Mail or phone only)
200 N.W. Fifth St., 2nd Floor, 73102
(405) 231-4948
TDD- (405) 231-4614
For Forms, dial (405) 231-5208

OREGON

Portland:
Federal Bldg., Room 376
1220 S.W. Third Ave., 97204
(503) 326-3141

PENNSYLVANIA

Harrisburg:
Federal Bldg., Rm. 168
P.O. Box 761, 17108
(717) 782-4494

Philadelphia:
Wm. J. Green, Jr., Federal Bldg.
600 Arch St., 19106
(215) 597-7440

Pittsburgh:
Federal Building
1000 Liberty Ave., Rm. 119, 15222
(412) 644-2755

PUERTO RICO

San Juan:
Federico Degetau Federal Building
Carlos E. Chardon St.
Hato Rey, P.R. 00918
(809) 766-5242

RHODE ISLAND

Providence:
Pastore Federal Bldg.
Rm. 310, Kennedy Plaza, 02903
(401) 528-5251

SOUTH CAROLINA

(See Raleigh, NC Listing)

SOUTH DAKOTA

(See Minnesota Listing)

TENNESSEE

Memphis:
200 Jefferson Avenue
Suite 1312, 38103-2335
(901) 544-3956

TEXAS

Corpus Christi:
(See San Antonio Listing)
(512) 884-8113

Dallas:
(Mail or phone only)
1100 Commerce St., Rm. 6B10, 75242
(214) 767-8035

Houston:
(See Dallas Listing)
(713) 759-0455

San Antonio:
8610 Broadway, Rm. 305, 78217
(512) 229-6611 or 6600

UTAH

(303) 969-7053
(See Colorado Listing)

VERMONT

(See New Hampshire Listing)

Virgin Islands

(See Puerto Rico Listing)
(809) 774-8790

VIRGINIA

Norfolk:
Federal Building, Room 220
200 Granby St., 23510-1886
(804) 441-3355

WASHINGTON

Seattle:
Federal Building
915 Second Ave., 98174
(206) 553-4365

WEST VIRGINIA

(See Ohio listing)
(513) 225-2866

WISCONSIN

For Dane, Grant, Green, Iowa, Lafayette, Rock, Jefferson, Walworth, Milwaukee, Waukesha, Racine, and Kenosha Counties, see Illinois Listing
(312) 353-6189
(For all other Wisconsin Counties not listed above, see Minnesota listing)

WYOMING

(303) 969-7054
(See Colorado Listing)

Career America College Hotline

1-900-990-9200 (A fee call - 40 cents per minute)

Career Search Index

AGENCY NAME

FEDERAL DEPT.	AGRICULTURE																		AIR FORCE			ARMY													
PAGE #	54	55	58	60	62	64	65	67	69	70	72	73	75	79	81	84	85	86	89	93	91	108	96	106	105	97	98	101	100	103	115	112	114	111	110
COLLEGE MAJOR	AMS	ARS	ASCS	APHIS	ERS	ES	FmHA	FCIC	FGIS	FNS	FSIS	FAS	FOREST	NAL	NASS	OICD	REA	SCS	COMMUNICATIONS	AF SYSTEMS	LOGISTICS	AVSCOM	ARMAMENT	TRADOC	TEC	AUDIT	CECOM	LAB	CORPS	MISSILE	TANK-AUTO	TRAFFIC	NATICK	MRDC	BELVOIR
ACCOUNTING			●				●	●									●			●				●		●									
AEROSPACE SCI.																																			
AGRICULTURE	●	●	●		●	●	●	●	●			●		●		●		●																	
AGRONOMY	●	●	●			●									●			●																	
ANTHROPOLOGY																																			
ARCHAEOLOGY													●																						
ARCHITECTURE																																			
ARTS																																			
BIOLOGICAL SCI.		●		●		●							●					●															●		
BUSINESS	●		●				●	●	●	●					●	●	●			●				●								●			
CHEMISTRY		●																			●				●			●					●		●
COMMUNICATIONS																																			
COMPUTER SCI.																			●	●		●	●	●			●	●							
CRIMINAL JUST.																																			
EARTH SCI.		●	●										●					●		●															
ECONOMICS			●		●				●			●				●																			
EDUCATION						●							●			●								●											
ENGINEERING		●											●				●	●	●	●	●	●	●	●	●		●	●	●	●	●	●	●		●
ENGLISH																																			
ENVIRO. SCI.				●									●					●																	
FINANCE							●										●			●															
FORESTRY													●					●																	
GEOGRAPHY					●													●																	
HEALTH SCI.										●																							●	●	
HISTORY					●																														
HOME ECON.						●				●																									
INTERNATIONAL AFFAIRS																								●											
LABOR RELATIONS																																			
LANGUAGES																								●											
LAW					●																														
LIBERAL ARTS																																			
LIBRARY SCI.														●																					
MANAGEMENT																																			
MARKETING	●		●					●				●																							
MATHEMATICS			●		●										●					●		●	●		●			●							
MEDICAL SCI.																																		●	
METEOROLOGY																				●															
MINORITY STUDIES																																			
OCEANOGRAPHY																																			
PHYSICAL SCI.		●																		●															
PHYSICS																									●			●		●			●		●
POLITICAL SCI.					●																														
PSYCHOLOGY																																			
PUBLIC ADMIN.										●																									
RECREATION																		●																	
RELIGION																																			
SOCIAL SCI.					●																														
STATISTICS			●		●			●							●																				
TRANSPORTATION			●																																
UBRAN STUDIES																																			
VETERINARY MED.		●		●							●																								

AGENCY NAME

COLLEGE MAJOR	CENSUS	BEA	EDA	ITA	NIST	NOAA	NTIS	NTIA	MBDA	PTO	USTTA	US & FCS	DCA	DCAA	DIA	DIS	DLA	DMA	DNA	NSA	EDUCATION	DOE	FERC	FAMILY	HCFA	HDS	SSA	ADAMHA	FDA	HRSA	CDC/ATSDR	NIH	IHS	HUD	BIA
FEDERAL DEPT.	COMMERCE												DEFENSE								EDUCATION	ENERGY		HHS										HUD	INTERIOR
PAGE #	117	118	119	120	123	124	126	127	122	129	131	130	132	134	135	136	137	139	141	142	144	146	152	155	156	158	160	163	166	168	170	173	176	180	183
ACCOUNTING		●												●			●				●	●	●		●									●	
AEROSPACE SCI.																																			
AGRICULTURE																							●												
AGRONOMY																																			
ANTHROPOLOGY																																			
ARCHAEOLOGY																																			
ARCHITECTURE																						●													
ARTS																																			
BIOLOGICAL SCI.						●				●									●			●	●					●	●		●	●			●
BUSINESS			●						●		●	●					●			●		●	●		●		●							●	
CHEMISTRY					●	●				●									●				●					●	●		●	●			
COMMUNICATIONS								●																											
COMPUTER SCI.	●	●			●	●	●	●					●		●		●		●	●														●	
CRIMINAL JUST.																●																			
EARTH SCI.						●												●				●													●
ECONOMICS	●	●	●	●					●						●						●		●		●									●	
EDUCATION																					●										●				●
ENGINEERING			●		●			●		●			●		●		●		●	●		●	●										●		●
ENGLISH																						●													
ENVIRO. SCI.																						●	●								●				
FINANCE			●				●		●													●												●	
FORESTRY																																			●
GEOGRAPHY						●									●			●																	
HEALTH SCI.																														●	●		●		
HISTORY																																			
HOME ECON.																																			
INTERNATIONAL AFFAIRS				●								●			●																				
LABOR RELATIONS																																			
LANGUAGES																				●															
LAW				●						●											●														
LIBERAL ARTS																●											●								
LIBRARY SCI.																																●			
MANAGEMENT																																			
MARKETING							●		●		●	●																							
MATHEMATICS	●				●	●							●		●					●							●								
MEDICAL SCI.																												●	●	●	●	●	●		
METEOROLOGY						●																													
MINORITY STUDIES																																			●
OCEANOGRAPHY						●																													
PHYSICAL SCI.					●															●		●							●						
PHYSICS						●				●			●						●																
POLITICAL SCI.															●																				
PSYCHOLOGY																										●		●			●	●	●		
PUBLIC ADMIN.								●	●												●			●		●								●	
RECREATION																																			
RELIGION																																			
SOCIAL SCI.																						●		●	●	●	●	●			●		●		●
STATISTICS	●	●									●																				●				
TRANSPORTATION																																			
UBRAN STUDIES																																		●	
VETERINARY MED.																																			

AGENCY NAME

COLLEGE MAJOR

FEDERAL DEPT.	INTERIOR								JUSTICE						LABOR										NAVY										
PAGE #	185	188	189	191	194	196	198	200	207	208	210	209	203	205	212	215	214	217	219	218	220	222	223	224	225	227	229	228	231	232	234	236	238	241	239
	BLM	MINES	RECLAMATION	FWS	USGS	MMS	FNP	OSM	DEA	FBI	INS	MARSHAL	PRISONS	JUSTICE	BLS	ESA	ETA	MSHA	OLMS	OSHA	PBGC	PWBA	VETS	COMPTROLLER	NADC	NAVAIR	NAVFAC	NIC	NMC	ORDNANCE	NRL	NAVSEA	NAVSWC	NUSC	NUWES
ACCOUNTING						●		●		●											●	●		●											
AEROSPACE SCI.																																			
AGRICULTURE			●																																
AGRONOMY			●																																
ANTHROPOLOGY							●																												
ARCHAEOLOGY	●						●																												
ARCHITECTURE																											●								
ARTS																																			
BIOLOGICAL SCI.	●		●	●		●														●									●						
BUSINESS													●						●		●	●	●	●							●				
CHEMISTRY		●				●			●																										
COMMUNICATIONS																																			
COMPUTER SCI.															●											●		●			●		●	●	
CRIMINAL JUST.									●		●	●	●																						
EARTH SCI.	●	●	●	●	●	●	●																												
ECONOMICS			●												●	●	●					●													
EDUCATION																																			
ENGINEERING	●	●	●			●	●	●		●								●		●					●	●	●	●	●	●	●	●	●	●	●
ENGLISH							●																												
ENVIRO. SCI.	●		●	●	●	●		●																											
FINANCE																						●													
FORESTRY	●																																		
GEOGRAPHY	●				●		●																												
HEALTH SCI.																		●		●									●						
HISTORY							●																												
HOME ECON.																																			
INTERNATIONAL AFFAIRS																																			
LABOR RELATIONS																	●																		
LANGUAGES										●																									
LAW	●									●			●	●		●			●			●													
LIBERAL ARTS										●						●			●																
LIBRARY SCI.																																			
MANAGEMENT							●																												
MARKETING																																			
MATHEMATICS						●									●						●				●						●		●		
MEDICAL SCI.													●																						
METEOROLOGY			●			●																													
MINORITY STUDIES																																			
OCEANOGRAPHY						●																													
PHYSICAL SCI.	●	●						●												●									●						
PHYSICS						●																			●						●		●		
POLITICAL SCI.																																			
PSYCHOLOGY																	●			●			●												
PUBLIC ADMIN.																							●												
RECREATION	●			●			●																												
RELIGION																																			
SOCIAL SCI.													●			●	●		●	●			●	●											
STATISTICS															●																				
TRANSPORTATION																																			
UBRAN STUDIES																																			
VETERINARY MED.																																			

AGENCY NAME

FEDERAL DEPT.	NAVY		STATE	TRANSPORTATION								TREASURY										VET	INDEPENDENT										
PAGE #	242	244	246	249	253	256	257	259	261	263	266	267	277	281	278	270	272	274	279	276	269	273	282	300	301	304	306	307	310	311	313	314	316	317
COLLEGE MAJOR	NWC	SPAWAR	STATE	FAA	FHWA	FRA	MARAD	NHTSA	RSPA	COAST	UMTA	BATF	PRINT	DEBT	FMS	IRS	OTC	OCC	CUSTOMS	MINT	BONDS	SECERT	VETERANS	ACTION	AID	CIA	CFTC	EPA	EXIMBANK	FCC	FDIC	FEC	FEMA	FLRA
ACCOUNTING						●					●	●		●	●	●	●	●							●	●	●		●		●	●		
AEROSPACE SCI.																																		
AGRICULTURE																									●									
AGRONOMY																																		
ANTHROPOLOGY																									●									
ARCHAEOLOGY																																		
ARCHITECTURE							●																											
ARTS													●																					
BIOLOGICAL SCI.																												●						
BUSINESS					●	●						●		●	●	●	●	●	●	●	●	●			●	●	●		●		●		●	
CHEMISTRY													●															●						
COMMUNICATIONS										●															●									
COMPUTER SCI.	●			●		●			●					●	●	●	●									●	●	●						
CRIMINAL JUST.												●				●			●			●						●						
EARTH SCI.																												●						
ECONOMICS			●		●	●										●	●	●			●				●		●		●		●			
EDUCATION																								●	●									
ENGINEERING	●	●		●	●	●	●	●	●	●	●		●							●						●		●		●			●	
ENGLISH																																		
ENVIRO. SCI.										●																								
FINANCE															●	●	●	●		●	●				●	●			●		●			
FORESTRY																																		
GEOGRAPHY																																		
HEALTH SCI.																							●		●									
HISTORY			●																															
HOME ECON.																																		
INTERNATIONAL AFFAIRS			●																						●									
LABOR RELATIONS																																		●
LANGUAGES			●																															
LAW			●									●				●	●										●	●	●	●		●		●
LIBERAL ARTS																●						●				●								
LIBRARY SCI.																																		
MANAGEMENT																																		
MARKETING					●															●					●									
MATHEMATICS	●				●			●																										
MEDICAL SCI.																							●											
METEOROLOGY																																		
MINORITY STUDIES																																		
OCEANOGRAPHY																																		
PHYSICAL SCI.						●							●													●		●						
PHYSICS	●																									●								
POLITICAL SCI.			●													●									●							●		●
PSYCHOLOGY								●															●	●										●
PUBLIC ADMIN.											●															●		●					●	●
RECREATION																							●											
RELIGION																							●											
SOCIAL SCI.																						●	●	●	●									
STATISTICS													●																					
TRANSPORTATION							●		●																									
UBRAN STUDIES					●						●														●									
VETERINARY MED.																												●						

AGENCY NAME

FEDERAL DEPT.	INDEPENDENT																												LEGISLATIVE & JUDICIAL							
PAGE #	319	320	322	324	325	327	328	330	331	335	337	339	341	342	344	347	349	350	352	354	355	358	362	363	364	367	370	372	286	287	288	290	292	294	295	296
COLLEGE MAJOR	FMC	FMCS	FRS	FTC	GSA	ITC	ICC	MSPB	NASA	NARA	NCUA	NLRB	NSF	NTSB	NRC	OPM	TRADE	PEACE	POST RATE	RRB	SBA	SMITHSONIAN	TVA	ACDA	EEOC	USIA	POSTAL	SEC	COURTS	CBO	CRS	GAO	LIBRARY	OTA	SUPREME	GPO
ACCOUNTING					●						●	●	●						●	●	●							●				●				
AEROSPACE SCI.									●																											
AGRICULTURE						●												●																		
AGRONOMY																																				
ANTHROPOLOGY																						●														
ARCHAEOLOGY																																				
ARCHITECTURE					●																															
ARTS																																				●
BIOLOGICAL SCI.																		●				●	●													
BUSINESS			●		●	●	●			●		●	●			●					●						●	●	●			●				
CHEMISTRY						●									●								●													
COMMUNICATIONS					●																					●										
COMPUTER SCI.			●						●				●														●		●			●	●			
CRIMINAL JUST.																				●					●		●		●						●	
EARTH SCI.																																				
ECONOMICS	●		●	●		●	●					●	●				●		●		●							●		●	●					
EDUCATION																●		●																		
ENGINEERING					●	●			●				●	●	●			●	●				●				●				●					
ENGLISH										●																										
ENVIRO. SCI.																																				
FINANCE			●																		●							●								
FORESTRY						●																														
GEOGRAPHY																																				
HEALTH SCI.																																		●		
HISTORY										●												●														
HOME ECON.																																				
INTERNATIONAL AFFAIRS																								●		●					●					
LABOR RELATIONS		●										●				●											●									
LANGUAGES																		●								●							●			
LAW	●		●	●		●		●				●					●		●						●	●	●	●	●		●				●	
LIBERAL ARTS													●					●		●					●		●							●		
LIBRARY SCI.																																	●		●	
MANAGEMENT																																				
MARKETING						●															●															
MATHEMATICS							●		●				●																●							
MEDICAL SCI.																		●																		
METEOROLOGY																																				
MINORITY STUDIES																																				
OCEANOGRAPHY																																				
PHYSICAL SCI.									●				●	●	●							●	●											●		
PHYSICS									●					●	●																					
POLITICAL SCI.												●												●		●					●					
PSYCHOLOGY																●									●											
PUBLIC ADMIN.								●													●						●			●		●				
RECREATION																																				
RELIGION																																				
SOCIAL SCI.							●						●			●													●							
STATISTICS																			●												●					
TRANSPORTATION							●																													
UBRAN STUDIES																																				
VETERINARY MED.																																				

AGENCY NAME

FEDERAL DEPT.	AGRICULTURE																		AIR FORCE			ARMY													
PAGE #	54	55	58	60	62	64	65	67	69	70	72	73	75	79	81	84	85	86	89	93	91	108	96	106	105	97	98	101	100	103	115	112	114	111	110
AGENCY MISSION	AMS	ARS	ASCS	APHIS	ERS	ES	FmHA	FCIC	FGIS	FNS	FSIS	FAS	FOREST	NAL	NASS	OICD	REA	SCS	COMMUNICATIONS	AF SYSTEMS	LOGISTICS	AVSCOM	ARMAMENT	TRADOC	TEC	AUDIT	CECOM	LAB	CORPS	MISSILE	TANK-AUTO	TRAFFIC	NATICK	MRDC	BELVOIR
AGRICULTURE	●	●	●	●	●	●	●	●	●			●		●	●	●		●																	
ARTS																																			
AUDITING																										●									
AVIATION/SPACE																			●	●	●	●													
BANKING																	●																		
BUSINESS																																			
COMMUNICATION					●														●								●								
CONSUMER PROTECTION	●										●																								
DEFENSE																			●	●	●	●	●	●	●	●	●	●	●	●	●	●	●	●	●
DISASTER ASSIST.			●				●	●																											
DISCRIMINATION																																			
ECONOMIC POLICY					●																														
EDUCATION						●				●														●											
EMPLOYMENT																																			
ENERGY																																			
ENVIRONMENT			●	●									●					●											●						
FOOD/NUTRITION										●	●																						●		
FOREIGN AID																●																			
HEALTH				●						●	●																							●	
HISTORIC PRESER.																																			
IMMIGRATION																																			
INSURANCE								●																											
INTELLIGENCE																																			
INTERNATIONAL AFFAIRS												●				●																			
LAW/JUSTICE																																			
LAW ENFORCEMENT																																			
LIBRARIES														●																					
MARITIME ACTIVITIES																																			
MARKETING	●		●									●																							
MINING																		●																	
NATIVE AMERICANS																																			
NUCLEAR ENERGY																																			
POSTAL SERVICE																																			
RECREATION													●					●																	
SAFETY																																			
SCIENTIFIC RESEARCH	●	●				●										●				●	●	●	●		●		●	●		●	●		●	●	●
SCHOLARLY RESEARCH					●																														
SOCIAL SERVICES										●																									
STATISTICS															●																				
TRADE	●		●	●					●			●																							
TRANSPORTATION																															●	●			
VETERANS																																			
VOLUNTEERS						●																													

AGENCY NAME

FEDERAL DEPT.	COMMERCE												DEFENSE								EDUCATION	ENERGY		HHS										HUD	INTERIOR
PAGE #	117	118	119	120	123	124	126	127	122	129	131	130	132	134	135	136	137	139	141	142	144	146	152	155	156	158	160	163	166	168	170	173	176	180	183
AGENCY MISSION	CENSUS	BEA	EDA	ITA	NIST	NOAA	NTIS	NTIA	MBDA	PTO	USTTA	US & FCS	DCA	DCAA	DIA	DIS	DLA	DMA	DNA	NSA	EDUCATION	DOE	FERC	FAMILY	HCFA	HDS	SSA	ADAMHA	FDA	HRSA	CDC/ATSDR	NIH	IHS	HUD	BIA
AGRICULTURE																																			
ARTS																																			
AUDITING														●																					
AVIATION/SPACE																																			
BANKING																																			
BUSINESS		●							●	●		●																							
COMMUNICATION							●	●					●																						
CONSUMER PROTECTION																													●						
DEFENSE													●	●	●	●	●	●	●	●		●													
DISASTER ASSIST.																						●													
DISCRIMINATION																																			
ECONOMIC POLICY		●	●																																
EDUCATION																					●										●				●
EMPLOYMENT			●																																
ENERGY																						●	●												
ENVIRONMENT						●																●	●												
FOOD/NUTRITION																															●				
FOREIGN AID																																			
HEALTH																									●		●	●	●	●	●	●	●		
HISTORIC PRESER.																																			
IMMIGRATION																																			
INSURANCE																									●		●								
INTELLIGENCE															●					●															
INTERNATIONAL AFFAIRS				●								●								●															
LAW/JUSTICE										●																									
LAW ENFORCEMENT																●																			
LIBRARIES							●																									●			
MARITIME ACTIVITIES																		●																	
MARKETING											●	●																							
MINING																																			
NATIVE AMERICANS																										●							●		●
NUCLEAR ENERGY																			●			●													
POSTAL SERVICE																																			
RECREATION																																			
SAFETY																															●				
SCIENTIFIC RESEARCH					●	●												●	●	●		●						●	●		●	●			
SCHOLARY RESEARCH																																			
SOCIAL SERVICES									●															●	●	●	●	●						●	
STATISTICS	●	●									●																				●				
TRADE				●								●																							
TRANSPORTATION																																			
VETERANS																																			
VOLUNTEERS																																			

AGENCY NAME

FEDERAL DEPT.	INTERIOR								JUSTICE						LABOR									NAVY											
PAGE #	185	188	189	191	194	196	198	200	207	208	210	209	203	205	212	214	215	217	218	219	220	222	223	224	225	227	229	228	231	232	234	236	238	241	239
AGENCY MISSION	BLM	MINES	RECLAMATION	FWS	USGS	MMS	FNP	OSM	DEA	FBI	INS	MARSHAL	PRISONS	JUSTICE	BLS	ETA	ESA	MSHA	OSHA	OLMS	PBGC	PWBA	VETS	COMPTROLLER	NADC	NAVAIR	NAVFAC	NIC	NMC	ORDNANCE	NRL	NAVSEA	NAVSWC	NUSC	NUWES
AGRICULTURE			●																																
ARTS																																			
AUDITING																								●											
AVIATION/SPACE																									●	●									
BANKING																																			
BUSINESS																					●														
COMMUNICATION																																			
CONSUMER PROTECTION																																			
DEFENSE																								●	●	●	●	●		●	●	●	●	●	●
DISASTER ASSIST.																																			
DISCRIMINATION																																			
ECONOMIC POLICY															●																				
EDUCATION																																			
EMPLOYMENT																●	●			●			●												
ENERGY	●		●		●	●																													
ENVIRONMENT	●	●	●	●	●	●	●	●																			●								
FOOD/NUTRITION																																			
FOREIGN AID																																			
HEALTH																													●						
HISTORIC PRESER.							●																												
IMMIGRATION											●																								
INSURANCE																					●	●													
INTELLIGENCE										●																		●							
INTERNATIONAL AFFAIRS																												●							
LAW/JUSTICE																																			
LAW ENFORCEMENT				●			●		●	●	●	●	●	●																					
LIBRARIES																																			
MARITIME ACTIVITIES																												●				●	●	●	●
MARKETING																																			
MINING	●	●				●			●									●																	
NATIVE AMERICANS																																			
NUCLEAR ENERGY																																			
POSTAL SERVICE																																			
RECREATION	●		●	●			●																												
SAFETY		●						●										●	●																
SCIENTIFIC RESEARCH		●				●																			●	●			●	●	●	●	●	●	●
SCHOLARY RESEARCH																																			
SOCIAL SERVICES																●																			
STATISTICS															●																				
TRADE																																			
TRANSPORTATION																																			
VETERANS																							●												
VOLUNTEERS																																			

AGENCY NAME

FEDERAL DEPT.	NAVY		STATE	TRANSPORTATION								TREASURY											VET	INDEPENDENT										
PAGE #	242	244	246	249	253	256	257	259	261	263	266	267	277	281	278	270	272	274	279	276	269	273	282	300	301	304	306	307	310	311	313	314	316	317
AGENCY MISSION	NWC	SPAWAR	STATE	FAA	FHWA	FRA	MARAD	NHTSA	RSPA	COAST	UMTA	BATF	PRINT	DEBT	FMS	IRS	OTC	OCC	CUSTOMS	MINT	BONDS	SECERT	VETERANS	ACTION	AID	CIA	CFTC	EPA	EXIMBANK	FCC	FDIC	FEC	FEMA	FLRA
AGRICULTURE																									●									
ARTS													●							●														
AUDITING														●	●	●															●			
AVIATION/SPACE		●		●																														
BANKING																	●	●											●		●			
BUSINESS																																		
COMMUNICATION																														●				
CONSUMER PROTECTION																															●			
DEFENSE	●	●		●						●																●								
DISASTER ASSIST.							●		●	●																							●	
DISCRIMINATION																																		
ECONOMIC POLICY																											●							
EDUCATION																																		
EMPLOYMENT																							●											●
ENERGY																																		
ENVIRONMENT							●		●	●																		●					●	
FOOD/NUTRITION																																		
FOREIGN AID																									●									
HEALTH																							●		●									
HISTORIC PRESER.																																		
IMMIGRATION			●																															
INSURANCE																							●								●			
INTELLIGENCE																										●								
INTERNATIONAL AFFAIRS			●																●						●	●			●					
LAW/JUSTICE																																		●
LAW ENFORCEMENT										●		●				●			●			●					●	●						
LIBRARIES																																		
MARITIME ACTIVITIES		●					●			●																								
MARKETING																				●	●								●					
MINING																																		
NATIVE AMERICANS																																		
NUCLEAR ENERGY																																		
POSTAL SERVICE																																		
RECREATION																																		
SAFETY				●	●	●		●	●		●																							
SCIENTIFIC RESEARCH	●	●		●				●	●				●															●						
SCHOLARY RESEARCH																																		
SOCIAL SERVICES																							●	●	●									
STATISTICS																																		
TRADE							●												●								●		●					
TRANSPORTATION				●	●	●	●	●	●	●	●																							
VETERANS																							●											
VOLUNTEERS																								●										

AGENCY NAME

FEDERAL DEPT.	INDEPENDENT																												LEGISLATIVE & JUDICIAL							
PAGE #	319	320	322	324	325	327	328	330	331	335	337	339	341	342	344	347	349	350	352	354	355	358	362	363	364	367	370	372	286	287	288	290	292	294	295	296
AGENCY MISSION	FMC	FMCS	FRS	FTC	GSA	ITC	ICC	MSPB	NASA	NARA	NCUA	NLRB	NSF	NTSB	NRC	OPM	TRADE	PEACE	POST RATE	RRB	SBA	SMITHSONIAN	TVA	ACDA	EEOC	USIA	POSTAL	SEC	COURTS	CBO	CRS	GAO	LIBRARY	OTA	SUPREME	GPO
AGRICULTURE																		●					●													
ARTS																						●														
AUDITING											●																					●				
AVIATION/SPACE									●					●																						
BANKING			●																																	
BUSINESS												●									●				●			●								
COMMUNICATION					●																					●										●
CONSUMER PROTECTION				●																																
DEFENSE									●															●												
DISASTER ASSIST.																																				
DISCRIMINATION																					●				●											
ECONOMIC POLICY																														●						
EDUCATION													●			●		●				●				●										
EMPLOYMENT		●						●				●				●									●											
ENERGY									●														●													
ENVIRONMENT	●														●								●													
FOOD/NUTRITION																																				
FOREIGN AID																		●																		
HEALTH																																				
HISTORIC PRESER.					●					●																										
IMMIGRATION																																				
INSURANCE											●									●					●											
INTELLIGENCE																																				
INTERNATIONAL AFFAIRS						●											●							●		●										
LAW/JUSTICE												●																	●	●					●	
LAW ENFORCEMENT				●																																
LIBRARIES										●												●								●			●		●	
MARITIME ACTIVITIES	●													●																						
MARKETING				●																																
MINING																																				
NATIVE AMERICANS																																				
NUCLEAR ENERGY															●								●													
POSTAL SERVICE																			●								●									
RECREATION																							●													
SAFETY					●									●																						
SCIENTIFIC RESEARCH									●				●									●												●		
SCHOLARY RESEARCH										●												●									●		●	●		
SOCIAL SERVICES																																				
STATISTICS																																				
TRADE	●					●											●																			
TRANSPORTATION							●		●					●						●																
VETERANS																																				
VOLUNTEERS																		●																		

AGENCY NAME

FEDERAL DEPT.	AGRICULTURE																		AIR FORCE			ARMY														COMMERCE				
PAGE #	54	55	58	60	62	64	65	67	69	70	72	73	75	79	81	84	85	86	89	93	91	108	96	106	105	97	98	101	100	103	115	112	114	111	110	117	118	119	120	123
LOCATION	AMS	ARS	ASCS	APHIS	ERS	ES	FmHA	FCIC	FGIS	FNS	FSIS	FAS	FOREST	NAL	NASS	OICD	REA	SCS	COMMUNICATIONS	AF SYSTEMS	LOGISTICS	AVSCOM	ARMAMENT	TRADOC	TEC	AUDIT	CECOM	LAB	CORPS	MISSILE	TANK-AUTO	TRAFFIC	NATICK	MRDC	BELVOIR	CENSUS	BEA	EDA	ITA	NIST
Ala.																									●					X				●						
Alaska													●																											
Ariz.																									●		●													
Ark.																									●															
Calif.		●						●		●	●		●							●	●	●				●								●		●				
Colo.		●								●			●																							●		●		●
Conn.																																								
Del.																																								
Fla.																				●																				
Ga.		●						●		●	●		●								●					●												●		
Hawaii																																								●
Idaho																																								
Ill.		●						●		●																										●		●		
Ind.								●																																
Iowa								●			●																													
Kans.								●																			●									●				
Ky.																																								
La.													●																											
Maine																																								
Mass.										●										●								●					X	●		●				
Md.		●												X						X			●		X	●		X						X		X				X
Mich.																															X					●				
Minn.								●			●																													
Miss.		●						●																																
Mo.			●								●											X				●														
Mont.								●					●																											
N.C.								●					●															●								●				
N.Dak.								●																																
Nebr.								●																																
Nev.																																								
N.Y.																				●			●													●				
N.H.																																								
N.J.										●													X				X	●												
N.Mex.													●							●					●			●												
Ohio																				●	X	●																		
Okla.								●											X		●						●													
Oreg.													●																											
Pa.		●						●			●		●													●										●		●		
R.I.																																								
S.C.								●																																
S.Dak.																																								
Tenn.								●												●																				
Texas		●						●		●	●									●	●					●								●		●		●		
Utah			●										●								●				●															
Va.										X												●		X		X	●					X			X					
Vt.																																								
Wash.								●																												●		●		
Wisc.													●																											
W.Va.																																								
Wyo.																																								
P.Rico			●																																					
Overseas				●								●							●							●			●			●								
Nationwide			●				●		●						●			●						●					●			●						●	●	
Wash. D.C	X	X	X	X	X	X	X	X	X		X	X	X	●	X	X	X	X											X					●			X	X	X	

*An "x" indicates the agency's headquarters location

**The Nationwide category indicates that there are regional offices located throughout the U.S., sometimes one per state.

AGENCY NAME

FEDERAL DEPT.	COMMERCE							DEFENSE								EDUCATION	ENERGY		HHS										HUD	INTERIOR					
PAGE #	124	126	127	122	129	131	130	132	134	135	136	137	139	141	142	144	146	152	155	156	158	160	163	166	168	170	173	176	180	183	185	188	189	191	194
LOCATION	NOAA	NTIS	NTIA	MBDA	PTO	USTTA	US & FCS	DCA	DCAA	DIA	DIS	DLA	DMA	DNA	NSA	EDUCATION	DOE	FERC	FAMILY	HCFA	HDS	SSA	ADAMHA	FDA	HRSA	CDC/ATSDR	NIH	IHS	HUD	BIA	BLM	MINES	RECLAMATION	FWS	USGS
Ala.																																			
Alaska																										●		●		●	●			●	
Ariz.																												X		●	●				
Ark.																																			
Calif.				●					●		●	●				●	●	●		●		●		●				●	●	●	●		●		●
Colo.			●													●				●		●		●		●			●		●		X	●	●
Conn.																																			
Del.																																			
Fla.				●		●																		●											
Ga.				●					●		●	●				●	●	●		●		●		●		X			●					●	
Hawaii								●																											
Idaho																	●														●		●		
Ill.				●				●			●	●				●	●	●		●		●		●					●						
Ind.																																			
Iowa																																			
Kans.																●																			
Ky.																																			
La.																								●											
Maine																																			
Mass.			●	●					●		●	●				●				●		●		●					●					●	
Md.	●													●	X					X		X	X	X	X	●	X	X							
Mich.																								●											
Minn.																								●				●		●				●	
Miss.																																			
Mo.												●	●							●		●		●					●			●			
Mont.																												●		●	●		●		
N.C.																										●									
N.Dak.																																			
Nebr.																																			
Nev.																	●														●	●	●		
N.Y.				●								●				●		●		●		●		●					●						
N.H.																																			
N.J.											●													●											
N.Mex.														●			●											X		●	●			●	
Ohio												●												●		●									
Okla.																												●		●					
Oreg.																		●										●		●	●	●		●	
Pa.				●					●			●				●				●		●		●					●						
R.I.																																			
S.C.																																			
S.Dak.																												●		●					
Tenn.																	●							●				●							
Texas				●					●		●	●	●			●				●		●		●					●				●		
Utah																															●		●		
Va.		X			X			X	X		●	X	●	X																	●				X
Vt.																																			
Wash.																●	●			●		●		●					●						
Wisc.																																			
W.Va.																										●									
Wyo.																															●				
P.Rico																								●		●									
Overseas						●	●	●	●	●	●				●																				
Nationwide	●						●		●																										●
Wash. D.C	X		X	X		X	X			X	X		X			X	X	X	X	X	X		●			●			X	X	X	X		X	

AGENCY NAME

FEDERAL DEPT.	INTERIOR			JUSTICE						LABOR									NAVY														STATE	TRANSPORTATION						
PAGE #	196	198	200	207	208	210	209	203	205	212	214	215	217	218	219	220	222	223	224	225	227	229	228	231	232	234	236	238	241	239	242	244	246	249	253	256	257	259	261	263
LOCATION	MMS	FNP	OSM	DEA	FBI	INS	MARSHAL	PRISONS	JUSTICE	BLS	ETA	ESA	MSHA	OSHA	OLMS	PBGC	PWBA	VETS	COMPTROLLER	NADC	NAVAIR	NAVFAC	NIC	NMC	ORDNANCE	NRL	NAVSEA	NAVSWC	NUSC	NUWES	NWC	SPAWAR	STATE	FAA	FHWA	FRA	MARAD	NHTSA	RSPA	COAST
Ala.			●																																					
Alaska	●	●																																●						
Ariz.				●																																				
Ark.																																								
Calif.	●	●		●		●		●	●	●	●	●		●	●		●	●				●					●			●	X	●		●	●		●	●		●
Colo.	●	●	●	●							●	●		●				●																	●	●		●	●	
Conn.																													X			●								
Del.																																								
Fla.				●																						●		●				●								
Ga.		●		●				●	●	●	●	●		●	●		●	●																●	●			●	●	
Hawaii																											●			●										
Idaho																																								
Ill.			●	●					●	●	●	●		●	●		●	●																●	●		●	●		
Ind.			●																																					
Iowa																																								
Kans.										●																														
Ky.			●														●																							
La.	●			●																																	●			
Maine																																								
Mass.		●		●						●	●	●		●	●		●	●																●				●	●	
Md.								●																	X	●		●				●			●			●		●
Mich.				●											●																									
Minn.						●																																		
Miss.																																								
Mo.			●	●				●			●	●		●	●		●	●																●	●			●	●	
Mont.																																								
N.C.																																								
N.Dak.																																								
Nebr.		●																																						
Nev.																																								
N.Y.				●					●	●	●	●		●	●		●	●																●	●		●	●		●
N.H.																											●													
N.J.				●																														●						
N.Mex.		●	●																																					
Ohio			●						●						●																							●		
Okla.			●																															●					●	
Oreg.																																			●					
Pa.		●	●	●				●	●	●	●	●		●	●		●	●		X		●					●					●								
R.I.																													X			●								
S.C.																						●					●					●								
S.Dak.																																								
Tenn.			●																																					
Texas				●		●		●	●	●	●	●		●	●		●	●														●		●	●			●	●	
Utah																																								
Va.	●		●										X								X	X				●	X	X				●					●			●
Vt.						●																																		
Wash.		●		●							●	●		●				●									●			X		●		●				●		
Wisc.																																								
W.Va.		●	●																																					
Wyo.			●																																					
P.Rico																																								
Overseas				●		●																●	●				●		●				●							
Nationwide					●	●	●	●					●					●	●		●			●											●					
Wash. D.C	X	X	X	X	X	X	X	X	X	X	X	X		X	X	X	X	X	X				X	X		X						X	X	X	X	X	X	X	X	X

AGENCY NAME

LOCATION	UMTA	BATF	PRINT	DEBT	FMS	IRS	OTC	OCC	CUSTOMS	MINT	BONDS	SECRET	VETERANS	ACTION	AID	CIA	CFTC	EPA	EXIMBANK	FCC	FDIC	FEC	FEMA	FLRA	FMC	FMCS	FRS	FTC	GSA	ITC	ICC	MSPB	NASA
FEDERAL DEPT.	TRANSP.	TREASURY											VET.	INDEPENDENT																			
PAGE #	266	267	277	281	278	270	272	274	279	276	269	273	282	300	301	304	306	307	310	311	313	314	316	317	319	320	322	324	325	327	328	330	331
Ala.		●			●																												●
Alaska																																	
Ariz.																																	
Ark.																																	
Calif.	●	●			●	●	●	●	●		●			●			●	●		●	●		●	●	●		●	●	●		●	●	●
Colo.	●													●				●					●	●				●				●	
Conn.																																	
Del.																																	
Fla.		●							●																●								●
Ga.	●	●				●	●	●			●			●				●		●	●		●	●			●	●	●			●	
Hawaii																																	
Idaho																																	
Ill.	●	●			●	●	●	●	●		●			●			●	●		●	●		●	●			●	●	●		●	●	
Ind.																																	
Iowa																																	
Kans.							●																				●		●				
Ky.		●																															
La.		●							●																●								
Maine																																	
Mass.	●	●					●		●		●			●				●		●	●		●	●			●	●				●	
Md.																																	●
Mich.						●					●							●															
Minn.		●					●				●						●										●						
Miss.																																	●
Mo.	●	●			●		●	●			●						●	●		●	●		●				●					●	
Mont.																																	
N.C.		●									●							●															
N.Dak.																																	
Nebr.																																	
Nev.																		●															
N.Y.	●	●				●	●	●	●		●			●			●	●			●		●	●	●		●	●	●			●	
N.H.																																	
N.J.											●																						
N.Mex.																																	
Ohio		●				●	●				●							●									●	●					●
Okla.																																	
Oreg.																																	
Pa.	●	●			●	●	●				●			●				●					●				●		●		●	●	
R.I.																																	
S.C.																																	
S.Dak.																																	
Tenn.		●																			●												
Texas	●	●			●	●	●	●	●		●			●				●			●		●	●	●		●	●	●			●	●
Utah																																	
Va.							●		●							X											●						●
Vt.																																	
Wash.	●	●									●			●				●		●			●					●					
Wisc.																																	
W.Va.				●																													
Wyo.																																	
P.Rico																									●								
Overseas									●						●	●																	
Nationwide						●		●	●		●	●	●							●						●	●						
Wash. D.C	X	X	X	X	X	X	X	X	X	X	X	X	X	X	X		X	X	X	X	X	X	X	X	X	X	X	X	X	X	X	X	X

AGENCY NAME

FEDERAL DEPT.	INDEPENDENT																			LEGISLATIVE & JUDICIAL							
PAGE #	335	337	339	341	342	344	347	349	350	352	354	355	358	362	363	364	367	370	372	286	287	288	290	292	294	295	296
LOCATION	NARA	NCUA	NLRB	NSF	NTSB	NRC	OPM	TRADE	PEACE	POST RATE	RRB	SBA	SMITHSONIAN	TVA	ACDA	EEOC	USIA	POSTAL	SEC	COURTS	CBO	CRS	GAO	LIBRARY	OTA	SUPREME	GPO
Ala.			●									●		●		●											
Alaska			●		●																						
Ariz.			●										●			●											
Ark.			●									●															
Calif.	●	●	●		●	●	●		●		●	●				●		●	●				●				●
Colo.	●		●		●							●				●			●				●				●
Conn.												●						●									
Del.																											
Fla.			●		●							●	●			●											
Ga.	●	●	●		●	●	●				●	●				●			●				●				●
Hawaii			●																				●				
Idaho																											
Ill.	●	●	●		●	●	●		●		X	●				●		●	●				●				●
Ind.			●									●				●											
Iowa																											
Kans.												●															
Ky.												●		●													
La.			●									●				●											
Maine												●															
Mass.	●		●									●	●						●				●				●
Md.	●		●			X						●	●			●											
Mich.			●									●				●							●				
Minn.			●									●															
Miss.																											
Mo.	●		●		●						●					●							●				●
Mont.																											
N.C.			●									●				●											
N.Dak.																											
Nebr.																											
Nev.																											
N.Y.		●	●						●			●				●			●				●				●
N.H.												●															
N.J.	●		●								●	●															
N.Mex.			●									●															
Ohio	●		●								●	●				●							●				●
Okla.			●									●															
Oreg.			●																								
Pa.	●		●			●	●					●				●		●	●				●				●
R.I.												●															
S.C.												●															
S.Dak.																											
Tenn.			●									●		X		●		●									
Texas	●	●	●		●	●	●					●				●			●				●				●
Utah																											
Va.												●	●										●				●
Vt.												●															
Wash.	●		●									●				●			●				●				●
Wisc.			●									●				●											
W.Va.												●															
Wyo.																											
P.Rico			●									●															
Overseas													●				●						●				
Nationwide																		●									
Wash. D.C	X	X	X	X	X		X	X	X	X		X	X		X	X	X	X	X	X	X	X	X	X	X	X	X